WHAT TIME OF DAY WAS THAT?

History by the Minute

Dale R. Patterson

Fitzhenry & Whiteside

What Time of Day Was That?

To my mother.

Fitzhenry and Whiteside Limited
195 Allstate Parkway
Markham, Ontario L3R 4T8

In the United States:
121 Harvard Avenue, Suite 2
Allston, Massachusetts 02134

www.fitzhenry.ca   godwit@fitzhenry.ca

Fitzhenry & Whiteside acknowledges with thanks the Canada Council for the Arts, the Government of Canada through its Book Publishing Industry Development Program, and the Ontario Arts Council for their support of our publishing program.

Canadian Cataloguing in Publication Data

Patterson, Dale R., 1952-
  What time of day was that?: history by the minute

Includes bibliographical references.
ISBN 1-55041-123-3

1. Chronology, Historical. I. Title.

D11.5.P37 2001   902'.02   C00-930612-9

Design: Darrell McCalla
Cover image: Tom Mareschal/The Image Bank
Printed and bound in Canada

Contents

Introduction

 There is a certain timelessness to history books.

Pick up your average historical publication, and you will learn the year an event took place, most likely the date and maybe even the day of the week. But what time of day was that?

This book answers that question.

From the important (What time was President Kennedy shot?) to the not so important (What time was the last cigarette commercial aired on U.S. network TV?) to the ridiculous (when was the first Beatle record played in North America?) to the downright scary (when was the first atomic bomb detonated?) to the sporting (what time did Bobby Thomson hit his famous shot heard around the world?), you'll find out just how "time-ly" history can really be.

Knowing what time of day an event occurred puts it in a different perspective. Did the Battle of Bunker Hill begin in the mists of the early morning, or in the heat of the late afternoon? Did Beethoven breathe his last at breakfast, lunch or dinner? Was the first Super Bowl played at night or in the afternoon? Did the Great San Francisco Earthquake wake people up, disturb them at work, or deal its devastating force at bedtime? You'll find out the answers to these questions, and more.

More than 1,000 achievements, disasters, firsts, deaths, sporting successes and other historic events are profiled in this book. Local times only are used for all entries, with the exception of space exploits (eastern time for U.S. achievements; Moscow time for Soviet entries) and events dealing with the exploration of the North and South Poles (Greenwich Mean Time is used here).

In some cases, the time is rounded off. A source might say so-and-so died "around midnight," so we take midnight as the official time. At the other extreme, in a handful of cases I have managed to get the time down to the second, but these are rare indeed.

Certain major events, such as the Kennedy assassination, have many different times associated with them. In these cases, we've used the time most closely associated with the event.

The book is divided into 24 chapters, one for each hour of the day, and entries are arranged in order of time. The first entry in the first chapter is midnight local time; the last entry in the last chapter is 11:58 p.m.

Enjoy! (and take your time)

Acknowledgements

Toronto and the surrounding area has a tremendous library system, the facilities of which were a great help in researching this book. Of specific help to me were the Burlington Central Library, the Central Research Library in Toronto and the McLaughlin Library in Oshawa.

I would also like to thank all of those who offered moral support, including my wife Sherree who also provided much-needed technical assistance and a sharp editing eye. Bravo to Richard Dionne of Fitzhenry and Whiteside for seeing this project through. Thanks to Fraser Seely at Fifth House for realizing the merits of this project in the first place. And kudos to Penny Hozy for providing the finishing touches at the end.

I invite other researchers to expand on my research and continue to explore this alternative way of looking at history.

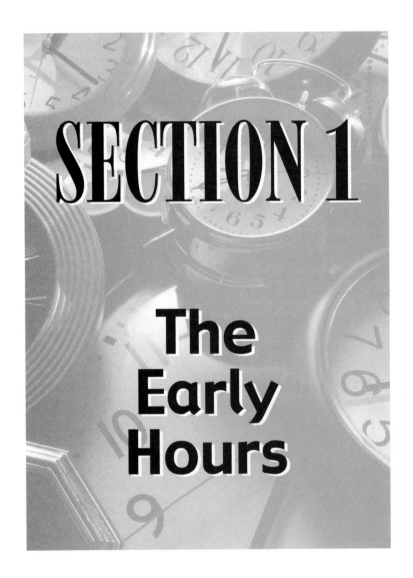

SECTION 1

The Early Hours

Midnight to 12:59 a.m.

- ⏱ **First test-tube baby born**
- ⏱ **Great Fire of London breaks out**
- ⏱ **The sun sets on the British Empire**
- ⏱ **Prohibition begins**
- ⏱ **Robert Kennedy shot**
- ⏱ **Princess Diana dies in a car crash**

12:00 **a.m., Sat., Jan. 1, 2000** – Millennium celebrations were held around the world as midnight moved east to west through each of earth's 24 time zones.

The first midnight celebrations began at Millennium Island in the Republic of Kiribati (at 5:15 a.m. ET), a normally uninhabited strip of land in the South Pacific. A few thrill-seekers made the journey just to be the first to greet the new year.

The first sunrise in the continental United States was observed at 7:04 a.m. ET over Porcupine Mountain, Maine, and Cadillac Mountain in Maine's Acadia National Park.

The last region on earth to ring in Y2K was Polynesia (at 5 a.m. ET on January 2, 2000).

All celebrations were a year early, though, considering that the start of the new millennium is actually January 1, 2001. Also, worldwide concerns about computer failures as the 2000s began turned out to be basically groundless due to intensive preventative measures taken by governments and financial institutions.

The first baby to be conceived outside the human body was a girl.

12:00 a.m., Sat., Jan. 1, 1977 – Guy Lombardo led his Royal Canadians through "Auld Lang Syne," their traditional celebration of New Year's Eve for the 48th and last time. Lombardo began performing his now classic rendition of the old Scottish song in 1929 at New York City's Roosevelt Grill. When the Grill closed, he moved his act to the Waldorf Astoria. Lombardo died November 5, 1977. The Canadian-born icon had played in a band, or led one, for 63 of his 75 years.

12:00 a.m., Tues., July 1, 1997 – One hundred and fifty-six years of colonial rule ended as Britain handed Hong Kong back to China. In doing so, Britain honoured the terms of a 99-year lease it made with the crumbling Manchu dynasty in 1898. China had refused to extend the lease another 50 years, as requested by the British. China had said it would repossess the territory by force if Britain did not return Hong Kong and end the "century of shame."

The takeover was carefully choreographed. Chinese troops crossed the border into Hong Kong at the same moment as the last British soldiers were jetting away. Hong Kong's last governor, Chris Patten, presided over the handover ceremony, held in the midst of a monsoon. Fears that China would violate civil liberties and take a heavy-handed approach were not realized in the first years of the post-handover period.

12:00 a.m. Sat., Jan. 6, 1878 – Carl Sandberg, who wrote of life in the U.S. Midwest, was born in Galesburg, Illinois. Sandberg won the Pulitzer Prize in 1939 for his six-volume work *Abraham Lincoln – the War Years*. The book took 16 years to write and is a quarter of a million words longer than the Bible. Sandberg also won a Pulitzer Prize in 1950 for poetry. He died at age 89 at 9:00 a.m., Saturday, July 22, 1967.

12:00 a.m., Tues., July 25, 1978 – Medical history was made as the first test-tube baby was born. The first baby to be conceived outside the human body was a girl named Louise, born to British couple, Lesley and John Brown. Louise weighed 163 grams (five pounds, 12 ounces) at birth and was pronounced healthy after being delivered by Caesarian section. Mrs. Brown had been unable to conceive because of a problem with her Fallopian tubes.

12:00 a.m., Sat., May 15, 1948 – Israel's history as an independent state began. It was a rocky start to a turbulent era.

The Jewish state found itself under attack from its Arab neighbours in the north (Syria and Lebanon), south (Egypt) and east (Transjordan and Iraq) hours after it gained its independence from Britain. Israel would prevail and actually expand its territory, but the lines were drawn for decades of bitterness and conflict. Since that troubled beginning, Israel has endured the Suez Crisis (1956), the Six-Day War (1967), invasion by Egypt and Syria (1973), bombing by Iraq (1991) and several other terrorist acts too numerous to mention. In 1977, Egypt and Israel signed a formal peace treaty and opened diplomatic relations.

Israel's history as an independent state began.

12:00 a.m., Thurs., Dec. 12, 1901 – From his listening post on Signal Hill, Newfoundland, Guglielmo Marconi faintly heard the letter "s" being repeated over and over. The message was being transmitted from Poldhu, England – some 3,218 kilometres (2,000 miles) away, and was the first successful transatlantic transmission. It was the first step in the 20th century's telecommunications explosion.

12:00 a.m., Tues., May 4, 1926 – The General Strike of 1926 began. Called by the Trades Union Council to protest a decision by British mine owners to lower wages, the strike involved four million workers and paralyzed the country for eight days. Among those taking part were transport and rail workers, printing and paper union members and many workers in the metal, engineering and building trades. The British government lessened the strike's impact by using volunteer workers. No newspapers were published, so the government printed its own short-lived daily, the British Gazette.

The Trades Union Council called off the strike, declaring a deadlock when the miners refused all attempts at compromise. It would be another six months before they returned to work. The General Strike was the largest labour action in British history.

12:00 a.m., Thurs., Feb. 12, 1880 – A band of about 20 men, all wearing masks and disguises, gathered on a farm on the outskirts

Liberia was proclaimed as the first independent African nation.

of Lucan, Ont. The men came armed with shotguns, rifles, hatchets, axes and even shovels to commit one of the most brutal acts in Canadian history, the Black Donnelly murders.

James Donnelly, 63, his wife Johannah, 56, sons John, 32, Thomas, 25, and niece Bridget, 21, were slaughtered in revenge for violent acts committed by members of the Donnelly family over the years, including murder, attempted murder and robbery. The Donnelly murders were particularly brutal – Thomas was bludgeoned with a pickaxe and nearly decapitated with a shovel; James, Johannah and Bridget were battered to death with shovels; John was riddled with bullets.

One man went to trial for murder and 11 others were charged, but no one was ever convicted. While many theories abound as to who perpetrated the crimes, the murders remain officially unsolved more than a century later.

12:00 **a.m., Sat., Jan. 18, 1936** – Rudyard Kipling, British author best known for his writings of children's books and verse, died in London at the age of 70. Kipling, who barely survived a youth of beatings and bullying in foster homes and boarding schools, became the first Englishman to win the Nobel Prize for literature in 1907. A generous man, Kipling gave the manuscript of his *The Jungle Book* to the nurse who looked after his first child, telling her to sell it if she needed the money. The woman is said to have lived comfortably from the proceeds.

Kipling is remembered for the famous phrase: "East is East and West is West and never the twain shall meet."

12:00 **a.m., Wed., June 23, 1847** – Liberia was proclaimed as the first independent African nation. Located on Africa's southwest coast, Liberia was founded in 1822 by freed former U.S. slaves. The country adopted a constitution similar to that of the U.S. and, unusual for Africa, established English as the official language. Even though former American slaves comprised only two per cent of the population, they formed the ruling class. Native inhabitants were reduced to second-class citizenship.

12:00 **a.m., Mon., July 7, 1952** – Train No. 1951, the last London tram in operation, began its final journey from Woolrich. It would end its eight-kilometre (five-mile) run outside New Cross depot. Almost everything that could be stolen from the car – light bulbs, seats, the trolley bell – was taken during this last run. Travellers even placed pennies on the track to be flattened as souvenirs.

Trams flourished in London early in the 20th century, at one point carrying around four million passengers a year. But patronage slipped with the introduction of the motor bus in the 1920s, and by 1952, only one section of track remained.

The Great Fire of London erupted in Pudding Lane.

12:00 **a.m., Sun., Sept. 2, 1666** –The Great Fire of London erupted at a wooden-frame baker's shop in Pudding Lane. By the time it subsided, over 80 per cent of the city lay in ruins. More than 13,000 homes and churches, including Saint Paul's Cathedral, were destroyed. Diarist Samuel Pepys wrote: "It made me weep to see it." King Charles II actually joined in the firefighting at one point. Incredibly, only eight people died during the four-day blaze but 200,000 were left homeless.

The Great Fire destroyed the last vestiges of bubonic plague that had stalked the city for a year. It also resulted in a new building code banning wooden construction which made the city safer for all after reconstruction.

12:00 **a.m., Sat., Dec. 29, 1979** – The seven-year civil war in Rhodesia officially came to an end as a truce went into effect. More than 21,000 people died in the conflict which pitted brother against brother, neighbour against neighbour. Following elections later that winter, white-ruled Rhodesia became black-ruled Zimbabwe, and the long-time British colony became an independent country.

12:00 **a.m., Sat., Jan. 1, 2000** – Control of the Panama Canal was officially transferred from the United States to Panama. A ceremony marking the transfer had begun just 12 hours earlier as the Panamian flag was raised to the cheers of several thousand onlookers. The American flag had been lowered the previous day, ending 85 years of U.S. control over the famous waterway.

Among those on hand for the transfer ceremony was Cecil Haynes, 86, an inventory management specialist who had worked at the Canal for 71 years and never missed a day of work.

The sun finally set on the British Empire.

The Panama Canal was built by the United States between 1904 and 1914 on land leased from Panama. Nearly 22,000 people died during its construction, either from work-related accidents or from malaria. The Canal, affectionately known as "The Big Ditch," connects the Atlantic and Pacific Oceans through the Isthmus of Panama.

Despite the transfer of control, the U.S. still retained the right of priority passage for its warships and those of its allies.

12:00 a.m., Mon., July 4, 1960 – America's flag, the Stars and Stripes, was raised with all fifty stars for the first time at Fort McHenry National Monument in Baltimore, Maryland. The 50th star had been added for Hawaii. Alaska accounted for the 49th star a year earlier. Incidentally, no known law designates the arrangement of the stars (historians have been unable to find the original flag law), and no star is specifically identified with each state.

12:00 a.m., Mon., Aug. 1, 1966 – The sun finally set on the British Empire as the British Colonial office in London closed, signalling a formal end to the once-vast domain.

At its height, the British Empire comprised one-quarter of the earth's surface, including such countries as Australia, Canada and India. But the Empire began to fall apart after the Second World War, as numerous British possessions declared their independence. British politicians, who had their hands full at home, were not displeased to see them go. The Empire's heritage lives on in the British Commonwealth of 48 nations, which includes Britain and Canada.

Midnight was a significant time in the history of the British colonies.

On Friday, August 15, 1947, British rule in India came to an end as the country became an independent nation. Pakistan also came into being at the same time. Jawaharlal Nehru became India's first prime minister, while in Pakistan, Muhammed Ali Jinnah became that country's first Governor General.

On Wednesday, May 31, 1961, South Africa officially became a republic, ending its 156-year tie to the British crown.

12:01 a.m., Sat., Jan. 17, 1920 – Prohibition, the "noble experiment," began as the 18th Amendment prohibiting the sale of beer, wine and alcohol went into effect. Many patrons took to the bars on January 16 to toast the end of legal drinking for the foreseeable future.

The 18th Amendment, or Volstead Act as it was also known, ushered in one of the worst decades of crime in U.S. history as bootleggers and speakeasies abounded. The Amendment was repealed nearly 14 years later and drinking became legal again in most states.

12:01 a.m., Sat., Aug. 1, 1981 – Founder John Lack intoned the words "Ladies and Gentlemen, Rock and Roll!" as MTV went on the air and a new era in television was born. The network, the first TV service devoted entirely to music videos, kicked things off – fittingly – with *Video Killed The Radio Star* by the Buggles.

From a base of 2.5 million subscribers in 1981, MTV (Music Television) grew to over 54 million subscribers by its 10th anniversary. MTV affiliates have been set up in Europe, Japan, Australia, Latin America and Brazil for a worldwide network of 38 countries on six continents. A sister service, VH-1 (Video Hits), was set up for adult audiences in 1985.

12:02 a.m., Dec. 11, 1962 – Canada exacted the death penalty for the last time as a double hanging was carried out at Toronto's Don Jail. Ronald Turpin and Arthur Lucas were executed: Turpin for murdering Toronto Police Constable Frederick Nash, and Lucas for killing a man named Thorland Crater.

12:04 a.m., Fri., Mar. 24, 1989 – The oil tanker *Exxon Valdez* ran aground on a reef off Alaska, spilling almost 60 million litres (11 million gallons) of crude oil. The impact of the spill was enormous: more than 1,294 square kilometres (500 square miles) of water and over 1,609 kilometres (1,000 miles) of coastline were affected. Searchers found and bagged 34,400 dead seabirds; at least 1,000 sea otters died and 151 eagles were lost; 150 civil lawsuits were activated.

A clean-up force resembling an invading army responded to the spill. Animal rescuers, beach cleaners, rock scrubbers, bureaucrats, experts,

Canada exacted the death penalty for the last time.

**Soviet space
probe Lunik II
crashed into
the lunar surface.**

local people and even tourists did what they could to help clean up the mess. Exxon was fined and the *Exxon Valdez*'s captain, found to be drunk at the time of the crash, was fired although he was cleared of most of the major criminal charges brought against him. Despite its efforts to pay and assist in the cleanup, Exxon was sharply criticized for reacting slowly to the spill, which poisoned the area for years.

12:07 a.m., Mon., Sept. 14, 1959 – Soviet space probe Lunik II crashed into the lunar surface. It was the first time a man-made object had made contact with the moon's surface. The earth-to-moon trip took 35 hours.

12:10 a.m., Sun., Sept. 24, 1967 – Cunard's two luxury liners *Queen Mary* and *Queen Elizabeth* passed at sea for the last time, trading blasts as they went. The two ships had criss-crossed the Atlantic hundreds of times. The *Queen Mary* was launched in 1937 and the *Queen Elizabeth* in 1940. However, air travel and the popularity of the French liners eventually forced the demise of steamship travel.

The *Queen Mary* was sold to the city of Long Beach, California, in 1967, where she remains docked as a tourist attraction. The *Queen Elizabeth* was purchased by a Hong Kong shipowner who wanted to refit her as a floating university. Renamed *Seawise University*, she caught fire, burned and rolled over on January 9, 1972 while docked at Hong Kong. Arson was suspected.

12:11 a.m., Mon., Apr. 28, 1969 – French President Charles de Gaulle announced his resignation after the French electorate rejected a referendum on decentralization and reform of the Senate. De Gaulle had promised he would quit if the referendum failed and kept his word. A month and a half later, France had its first new leader in 11 years – Georges Pompidou.

De Gaulle earned his place in history when he rallied the "Free French" to fight the Germans following France's surrender in 1940. He became head of the provisional French government following liberation but resigned in 1946 in a dispute over spending.

De Gaulle returned to the presidency in 1958. He was called to deal with opposition to Algeria's bid for independence. As president, he stabilized

France's economy and industry, but raised eyebrows when he withdrew France from NATO in 1966 and rejected Britain's bid to enter the European Economic Community in 1967. He enraged many Canadians when he openly supported Quebec separation during a visit to the province in 1967 in his famous "Vive le Québec libre" speech. De Gaulle, who survived 31 assassination attempts in his career, resigned after a year of industrial unrest and student riots.

De Gaulle died of a heart attack at 7:30 p.m., Tuesday, November 10, 1970. He was 79.

12:12 a.m., Mon., July 30, 1945 – The U.S. Navy cruiser *Indianapolis* sank just 15 minutes after being torpedoed by a Japanese submarine. All of the 1,198 men on board died. The *Indianapolis* had completed her last mission of the war, delivery of atomic bomb material to Guam, and was headed to the Philippines when she was sunk in the Philippines Sea.

12:13 a.m., Fri., May 20, 1977 – The original *Orient Express*, a luxury train which in its heyday symbolized the golden age of railroads, began its final run after 94 years of service. Few on the train were aware of the significance of the run, which was a two-and-a-half-day journey from Paris to Istanbul.

The *Orient Express* debuted June 5, 1883 with luxurious, plush surroundings and rich meals served by finely tailored waiters. Mystery novelist Agatha Christie used the train's sumptuous setting as the scene for one of her most popular novels.

The coming of air travel, however, forced cutbacks and by the late 1970s, passengers even had to supply their own food and water.

The *Orient Express*'s romance and mystery was not forgotten, and the train was revived in the 1980s by private entrepreneurs.

12:15 a.m., Wed., June 5, 1968 – Minutes after delivering his victory speech at the California primary, Senator Robert F. Kennedy was gunned down in a corridor of the Ambassador Hotel in Los Angeles. He died just over 24 hours later at 1:44 a.m. on Thursday, June 6. A 24-year-old Jordanian, Sirhan B. Sirhan, was charged with the murder and later received a life sentence.

The original *Orient Express* began its final run after 94 years of service.

Senator Robert F. Kennedy was gunned down.

The Kennedy shooting came just two months after the shooting death of civil rights leader Martin Luther King, and just four and a half years after Kennedy's brother President John F. Kennedy was assassinated in Dallas. Had Robert Kennedy lived, he would have been the favourite to capture the 1968 Democratic nomination, and face Republican Richard Nixon in the presidential race.

12:15 **a.m., Sat., Aug. 9, 1969** – Steven Parent unplugged his clock radio and prepared to leave the grounds of 10050 Cielo Drive in Beverly Hills, California. He would never make it. Seconds after getting into his car and starting to drive toward the exit gate, Parent was shot to death by Charles Watson, an associate of Charles Manson. Within the next hour, Watson, Patricia Krenwinkel and Susan Atkins brutally murdered four other people, including *Valley of The Dolls* star Sharon Tate, in one of the most shocking crimes of the century. The next night, Manson himself led his group of followers to a house in the Los Feliz section of Los Angeles, where they murdered grocery chain owner Leno LaBianca and his wife Rosemary.

The crimes, known as the Tate-LaBianca murders, are among the most sadistic in history. One of the victims, coffee heiress Abigail Folger, was stabbed so often her white dress appeared red. Her companion, Voycek Frykowski, was stabbed 51 times in addition to being shot and bludgeoned. Tate, eight months pregnant, was hanged from the rafters before being stabbed to death in a scene that sickened even the most case-hardened detectives. Jay Sebring, the other murder victim, and the LaBiancas also met with a violent end.

After a trial that made international headlines, Manson, Watson, Krenwinkel, Atkins and Leslie Van Houten were convicted of murder and sentenced to death for their involvement in the killings. The sentences were later commuted to life imprisonment. As the 21st century began, all remained in prison.

12:15 **a.m., Sat., Jan. 18, 1862** – John Tyler, the 10th president and the first vice-president to succeed to the Oval Office on the death of a president, died at age 71 in Richmond, Virginia.

Tyler's presidency started with controversy and he died in official disgrace. When he succeeded to the presidency on William Henry Harrison's death in 1841, the constitution was somewhat unclear as to whether Tyler should be president or acting president. Tyler left no doubt that he should be president, thus setting the important precedent that the vice-president be next in line for the presidency. Unfortunately for Tyler, many did not share his view. When the next election rolled around in 1844, he was a man without a party. Tyler declined to make a third-party bid but continued to make waves even in retirement.

On the eve of the Civil War, Tyler led an unsuccessful peace mission to Washington. Later that year, he was elected to the Confederate House of Representatives. Regarded as a traitor in the North for joining the Confederacy, Tyler's peace bid did nothing for his popularity in the South either. Tyler's death was not acknowledged by the White House, the only time the passing of a president has been officially ignored by Washington.

A half-century would pass before the U.S. Congress decided to erect a memorial stone over Tyler's grave.

John Tyler, the first president to become a widower in office, was also the first to remarry while president. He fathered 15 children, more than any other president. Tyler narrowly escaped death in 1844 when a gun exploded on a naval vessel, killing six people including two cabinet ministers and the father of his future wife. Tyler was below decks at the time.

Prior to the presidency, Tyler served as a representative, governor and later senator for Virginia.

12:15 a.m., Mon., July 1, 1974 – Juan Peron, twice the president of Argentina, died at age 79. Peron rose to power in a military coup in 1946. He owed much of his popular support to his charismatic wife Eva. Peron's fortunes declined after Eva died in 1952 and he was forced into exile in 1955. He took the body of his dead wife with him. Peron returned to the presidency in 1973 with a new wife, Isabel, as vice-president. When he died, Isabel became president.

12:17 a.m., Tues. Mar. 20, 1990 – Ceremonies recognizing Namibia as an independent country concluded, as the new Namibian flag replaced the South African ensign. Namibia had been a South African possession since 1915, when South African forces invaded the German colony

Tyler's presidency started with controversy and he died in official disgrace.

A Mercedes S-280 carrying Diana, Princess of Wales, crashed.

then known as South West Africa. Namibia was the last colony on the African continent to gain independence

12:25 a.m., Sun., Aug. 31, 1997 – A Mercedes S-280 carrying Diana, Princess of Wales, crashed in a Paris tunnel. Driver Henri Paul and Diana's boyfriend Dodi Fayed were killed instantly; the Princess died four hours later in a Paris hospital despite frantic efforts by doctors to save her. She was 36.

A fourth passenger in the car, bodyguard Trevor Rees-Jones, was badly injured and could only remember pieces of the last moments in the Mercedes. The driver of the car was found to have been legally drunk. In addition, prescription drugs and an abnormally high amount of carbon monoxide were found in his blood. The group was attempting to outrun photographers who wanted to take pictures of the Princess and her lover. Pictures of the crash scene were spread around the Internet within hours.

Di's death set off a worldwide outpouring of grief that reminded many of the sadness following President Kennedy's assassination in 1963. An estimated one million flowers were placed by mourners outside the Princess's residence at Kensington Palace and her temporary resting place at the Chapel Royal of St. James Palace. TV and radio worldwide went to 24-hour coverage of developments. Princess Diana's funeral at Westminster Abbey, the Saturday after her death, was the most witnessed event in 20th century television history. Elton John re-recorded his song "Candle in the Wind," with the lyrics rewritten in her honour. The tribute topped bestseller lists for months (with all proceeds going to charity).

12:25 a.m., Sat., May 20, 2000 – For the first time in 152 years, a sitting British prime minister became a father. Cherie Blair, wife of Prime Minister Tony Blair, gave birth to son Leo at a London hospital. Leo weighed in at six pounds, 12 ounces, and was the couple's fourth child.

The last time a British prime minister fathered a child in office was in 1848 when George Gilbert William Russell, fourth son of Prime Minister Lord John Russell, was born.

12:27 a.m., Sun., Oct. 26, 1986 – In one of baseball's greatest gaffes, Boston Red Soxer Bill Buckner fumbled a ground ball hit to him by Mookie Wilson of the New York Mets. The error allowed Ray Knight to score the winning run as the Mets completed an unbelievable rally in this, the sixth game of the World Series. Down 3 games to 2, the Mets trailed 4–2 in the bottom of the 10th. Red Sox pitcher Calvin Schiraldi retired the first two Met batters and got two strikes on Gary Carter. The Shea Stadium scoreboard in New York flashed congratulations to the "World Series Champion Boston Red Sox." Then the comeback began: Carter singled, Kevin Mitchell singled and Ray Knight singled to score Carter and make it 5–4. Bob Stanley came on in relief and promptly threw a wild pitch that scored Mitchell. Then came Wilson's dribbler toward Buckner who was unable to handle it.

The Mets went on to win game seven two nights later, while Boston, without a World Series victory since 1918, was snookered again.

12:30 a.m., Thurs., Aug. 4, 1892 – Francisco Franco, who would go on to become Spain's dictator for 36 years, was born in El Ferrol, Spain.

Franco became Spanish leader in 1939 following a three-year civil war. He ruled with an iron fist. Despite a policy based on the suppression of human rights, Franco provided Spain with a stability that led to a higher standard of living, industrial growth and an important alliance with the U.S.

Generalissmo Francisco Franco died at 4:30 a.m., Thursday, November 20, 1975 at age 82 from internal bleeding. He was succeeded by his hand-picked successor, Prince Juan Carlos, 37.

12:30 a.m., Sun., Apr. 4, 1841 – William Henry Harrison, ninth American president, whose one-month stay in office was the shortest of any chief executive, died of pneumonia at the White House.

Harrison, at 68 the oldest man to be inaugurated prior to Ronald Reagan, and the oldest to die in office, insisted on delivering his record-length one-hour-and-forty-minute inaugural speech in a brisk wind without hat or overcoat. He was later caught in a downpour and developed a cold which quickly worsened. Harrison died exactly one month after his inauguration, the first time a U.S. president had died in office. He holds the dubious record of being president-elect longer than he was president.

Harrison, the first of two Whigs to be elected president (Zachary Taylor was the other), was a military man who became a national hero after

Franco became Spanish leader in 1939 following a three-year civil war.

The greatest World Series game of all time came to a dramatic end.

scoring major victories in the War of 1812. He later served as a representative and senator from Ohio. In the election campaign of 1840, Harrison's campaign got an unexpected boost when the opposition belittled his supposed frontier, log-cabin manner (in fact he was born and lived on an estate). Harrison wisely did nothing to deter the popular but erroneous image of him as a frontiersman and it helped him defeat rival Martin Van Buren.

12:30 a.m., Tues., Apr. 4, 1933 – The Navy dirigible *Akron* crashed off the New Jersey coast with the loss of 73 lives. The accident, the deadliest airship disaster ever, was believed to have been caused by lightning. Oddly, the three survivors were virtually unharmed.

12:34 a.m., Wed., Oct. 22, 1975 – What has been called the greatest World Series game of all time came to a dramatic end. Carlton Fisk's bases-empty home run in the last of the 12th gave the Boston Red Sox a thrill-a-minute 7–6 victory over the Cincinnati Reds. The win forced a seventh and deciding game in the series, won the next night by the Reds.

The "game," as it has simply been called, had everything and more. Fred Lynn got things rolling with a three-run homer in the first inning, giving Boston a 3–0 lead. Cincinnati moved to a 6–3 lead before Boston's Bernie Carbo tied it with a two-out, three-run homer in the eighth. The Red Sox nearly won it in the ninth, but Cincinnati outfielder George Foster's perfect throw cut down Denny Doyle at the plate. In the 11th, the Reds had a chance to move ahead when, with Ken Griffey on first, Joe Morgan slammed a drive toward the right field fence. Dwight Evans made a brilliant catch and threw to first for the double play.

That set the stage for Fisk's game winner. He took the first pitch from Pat Darcy and crashed it off the left field foul pole. Fisk provided one of baseball's most memorable sights when he used all the body language he could muster to keep the ball fair, then pranced around the bases like a little kid.

12:40 a.m., Sun., Apr. 17, 1892 - Alexander Mackenzie, Canada's second prime minister and the first Liberal PM, died in Toronto after a long illness. The Scottish-born Mackenzie was 70.

Mackenzie helped build the nation in both a literal and figurative sense.

He was a stonemason and helped work on such projects as Fort Henry and the Welland Canal.

Mackenzie was self-educated, but his lack of formal education didn't stop his political rise. He held his first elected position in 1861, and by 1873 was leader of the federal Liberal party. He became prime minister in 1874 in the wake of a scandal involving Sir John A. Macdonald and the governing Conservative party.

Among Mackenzie's successes were establishment of the Supreme Court of Canada, reformation of the electoral system and introduction of the secret ballot. The Intercolonial Railway was completed and the Pacific line started during Mackenzie's reign. Mackenzie also presided over the completion of the Parliament Buildings.

The Liberals were turfed from office after an economic recession in the mid-1870s. Mackenzie quit as Liberal leader in 1880 but retained his seat in the Commons until his death in 1892.

12:40 :56 a.m., Wed., Dec. 13, 1972 – With the words "Godspeed to the crew of *Apollo 17*," Eugene Cernan became the last man to leave the surface of the moon. Cernan, fellow moon explorer Harrison Schmidt and Ronald Evans had blasted off from Cape Kennedy six days earlier on America's sixth trip to the moon's surface.

Cernan, as was customary for the commander of a moon mission, was the last to enter the lunar landing vehicle after he and Schmidt completed their explorations. As such, Cernan became the last man on the moon, a distinction he still held as the 21st century began.

12:42 a.m., Sun., Apr. 7, 1957 – The age of the electric trolley in New York ended as the Queensboro Bridge train completed its final run. One hundred and twenty-nine passengers, mostly rail buffs and teenagers, were aboard for the final 2.5-kilometre (1.6-mile) trip from Queens Plaza into Manhattan.

Horse-drawn street trolleys made their first New York appearance in 1832, and were electrified toward the end of the 19th century. But the development of the New York subway doomed the electric trolleys, and they were phased out beginning in the early 1930s.

Eugene Cernan became the last man to leave the surface of the moon.

Hughes spent the last decade of his 70 years as a total recluse.

12:42 **a.m. Tues., Jan. 14, 1936** – A plane piloted by Howard Hughes touched down in Newark, New Jersey, after a flight of nine hours, 27 minutes and 10 seconds from Burbank, California. At the time, it was a record for that route. Hughes flew in the $120,000 H-1 *Silver Bullet*. The expensive plane only flew for a total of 44 hours before it was retired, never to be flown again.

Hughes gained fame in the thirties as a pilot and a Hollywood producer of such films as *Hell's Angels*, *Scarface* and *The Outlaw*. He designed the $41 million plane *Spruce Goose* with its wing span of 97 metres (320 feet). *Spruce Goose* was flown only one time – by Hughes himself – and is now housed at a museum in Long Beach, California.

During the early seventies, a little-known writer named Clifford Irving caught the world's attention with a book he alleged to be Howard Hughes's autobiography. The work was proved to be a fake, and Irving and his wife were jailed for their deception.

On Monday, April 5, 1976 at 1:27 p.m., Hughes, by then a reclusive and mysterious billionaire, died during a flight from Acapulco, Mexico to Houston for emergency medical treatment. Hughes, in poor health during the latter part of his life, died of kidney failure. He left an estate estimated at more than $1.5 billion.

Hughes spent the last decade of his 70 years as a total recluse, often holing himself and his staff up on entire floors of luxury hotels for weeks on end. The few who actually saw Hughes in his later years described the billionaire as thin, pale and in the words of the pilot on the plane in which he died "very wasted."

12:45 **a.m., Mon., Dec. 29, 1856** – Woodrow Wilson, who would go on to become the 18th U.S. president and a champion of peace, was born in Staunton, West Virginia. His birthdate was mistakenly recorded as December 28. The confusion came from the fact he was born just after midnight at the end of the 28th day of the month.

Wilson may have been the most intelligent man to become president. He graduated from what is now Princeton University with a 90 average – the only president to earn a doctorate. Wilson became the first layman to become president of Princeton, a post he held from 1902 to 1910. In his only political post prior to the presidency, he served as governor of New Jersey from 1911 to 1913.

Wilson won the 1912 Democratic nomination and went on to capture the national election in a three-way battle with Republican nominee William Taft and former president Theodore Roosevelt, representing the Progressive or Bull Moose party. Wilson was the last president to ride to his inauguration in a horse-drawn carriage. He narrowly defeated Republican Charles Hughes to win a second term in 1916.

Wilson spent most of his administration trying to keep the U.S. out of the war in Europe. But after it was learned that the Germans had proposed an alliance with Mexico should Germany win the war, U.S. opinion leaned toward intervention. In April, 1917, declaring the "world must be made safe for democracy," Wilson officially committed his country to war. The American intervention turned the tide and the Germans surrendered in November, 1918.

After the war, Wilson campaigned for the League of Nations. While on a speaking tour promoting the League in 1919, the president suffered a physical breakdown. He had a stroke soon after and despite being virtually incapacitated, refused to give up the reins of power even temporarily. During that period, Wilson's second wife Edith virtually ran the country; she decided which issues to bring to her husband's attention and which not to. In the end, Wilson failed in his effort to have the U.S. join the League of Nations. Wilson was awarded the Nobel Peace Prize in 1919 for his efforts to achieve world peace and establish the League.

Woodrow Wilson died following a stroke at his home in Washington, D.C. at 11:15 a.m. on Sunday, February 3, 1924. He was laid to rest at the Washington Cathedral – the only president to be buried in the U.S. capital.

12:48 a.m., Sun., Sept. 1, 1985 – Scientists aboard the *Knorr* searching the bottom of the North Atlantic for any sign of the *Titanic* were rewarded: the ship's underwater video cameras spotted some wreckage. Moments later, a boiler appeared and scientists were certain – the *Titanic* had been discovered more than 73 years after she sank on her maiden voyage in April, 1912.

The find fulfilled a dream for Dr. Robert Ballard, an American oceanographer who first developed an interest in finding the *Titanic* during the early

The *Titanic* had been discovered more than 73 years after she sank.

They had become the first men to fly to the Pole and back.

1970s. After several setbacks, he obtained financing for a joint French-American mission to find the ship in 1985.

After the discovery, Ballard and crew sent a video probe down to film the *Titanic* as it rested on the ocean floor. The footage was breathtaking and eerie. No bodies were found but numerous relics from the ship were visible. Ballard took great care not to disturb the ship, and he removed nothing, out of respect for the more than 1,500 who had died in the sinking. However, another expedition following Ballard was not quite as respectful. It took several items including the ship's safe which was opened on a live TV show. Ballard's find re-ignited interest in the giant luxury liner, and that excitement exploded with the December, 1997 release of the movie *Titanic. (see 2:20 a.m.)*

12:50 a.m., Sun., May 9, 1926 – Richard Byrd and Floyd Bennett took off from Kings Bay, Spitzbergen en route to the North Pole. When they returned 15 and a half hours later, they had become the first men to fly to the Pole and back.

Byrd, the commander and navigator, and Bennett, the pilot, circled the Pole several times. They surveyed some 155,000 square kilometres (60,000 square miles) of previously uncharted land on the way back. The flight was completed despite a ruptured fuel tank that threatened to shut down one of the three engines.

1 a.m. to 1:59 a.m.

- 🕐 **Blood bath at Munich airport ends**
- 🕐 **First heart transplant operation begins**
- 🕐 **Truman fires MacArthur**
- 🕐 **Bomb explodes at Atlanta's Olympic Park**
- 🕐 **First transatlantic TV transmission sent**
- 🕐 **Janis Joplin dies of heroin overdose**

1:00 a.m., Wed., Sept. 6, 1972 – A blood bath at the Munich airport in Germany ended a terror-filled day of kidnapping and murder as four Black September terrorists, nine Israeli Olympic athletes, and a German policeman were shot to death. The terrorists had been trying to fly to Cairo for asylum along with their kidnapped victims.

The drama had begun shortly before dawn the previous day when seven Black September guerrillas broke into the Olympic building housing the Israeli team, killing two coaches. Some Israeli team members were able to escape, but the terrorists captured nine hostages. The terrorists demanded the release of 200 Palestinians from German jails, and safe passage out of West Germany. Israel refused to allow the prisoners' release. Tense negotiations continued throughout the day and into the night. Shortly before midnight, the hostages and terrorists were flown by helicopter to the airport. The shooting began after two of the terrorists stepped out of the helicopter.

Despite the tragedy, competition at the Olympics resumed after a 34-hour break. ABC sportscaster Jim McKay won an Emmy for his coverage of the events.

1:00 a.m., Sun., Dec. 3, 1967 – The world's first heart transplant operation began at Cape Town's Groote Schuur Hospital. Five and a half hours later, the transplant team led by Dr. Christian Baarnard had successfully placed a heart into the body of 53-year-old grocer

The world's first heart transplant operation began.

Louis Washkansky. The donor was a 25-year-old woman killed in an auto accident. Washkansky lived for 18 days with his new heart before dying of lung problems. He had made good progress up to his death. Washkansky, had suffered a series of heart attacks prior to his transplant, and was given only days to live at the time of the operation.

Heart transplants, events of front-page significance in the late 60s, are relatively routine and generally successful procedures today.

1:00 **a.m., Tues., July 29, 1890** – Dutch painter Vincent Van Gogh, considered one of the greatest artists of all time, died two days after shooting himself in the ribs in Auvers-sur-Oise, France. Van Gogh's death came just 18 months after he sliced off his left ear, in one of history's most famous acts of self-mutilation, following an argument with fellow artist Paul Gauguin.

Van Gogh never realized fame and fortune while alive. Only one of his 1,500 paintings and drawings was sold during his lifetime. One of Van Gogh's last works, *Cornfield with Flight of Birds*, pictures the spot where he shot himself to death.

On December 7, 1999, Sotheby's of London auctioned off Van Gogh's *Oliviers Avec Les Alpilles Au Fond* for US$8.45 million – a record price for a Van Gogh drawing. The winning bidder was the New York Museum of Modern Art.

1:00 **a.m., Thurs., Dec. 15, 1983** – The famous "1984" commercial for the new Macintosh computer was aired for the first time on KMVT Channel 11 in Twin Falls, Idaho to ensure that it would qualify for that year's advertising awards. (Apple Computer's advertising agency paid KMVT $10 to run the spot.) An estimated 96 million viewers would see the commercial for the first time on January 22, 1984 early in the third quarter of Super Bowl XVIII.

The controversial commercial showed an athletic young woman chased by storm troopers bursting into an auditorium full of workers watching a "Big Brother" image on a large screen. The woman smashed the screen with a sledgehammer and fresh air passed over the masses. A voice announced: "On January 24, Apple Computer will introduce the Macintosh. And you'll see why 1984 won't be like '1984.'"

Apple Computer paid $800,000 for the 60-second spot. It was part of a $15 million, 100-day advertising blitz for the Mac, which was officially introduced for the first time on January 24, 1984. The Macintosh was the most advanced personal computer of its time, and in the words of one critic, "one step closer to the ideal computer as appliance." The 128 K of RAM, 3.5-inch disk drive and 9-inch monochrome display seemed revolutionary. The Mac cost Apple $78 million to develop. List price for the original Mac was US$2,495.

1:00 **a.m., Mon., Sept. 17, 1923** – Hank Williams, who would go on to become one of country music's greatest legends, was born in Mount Olive West, Alabama. His birth name was Hiram.

Williams, known as the "Singing Kid" early in his career, recorded such country classics as "Cold, Cold Heart," "Jambalaya" and "Your Cheatin' Heart." He had 11 number one songs on Billboard's Country charts between 1947 and 1953. His son, Hank Williams, Jr., is a major country star in his own right.

Hank Williams, Sr. came to a sad end. At 5:30 a.m., on Thursday, January 1, 1953, he was found dead in the back seat of his car as he was being driven to a concert in Canton, Ohio. Williams's driver had pulled over in Oak Hill, West Virginia to ask directions when he noticed his passenger was still. A patrolman confirmed a few minutes later that the future member of both the Country and Rock and Roll Halls of Fame was dead.

During the drive, Williams had taken two morphine injections and washed down a chloral hydrate capsule with a hit of vodka. He knew his end was near, and wrote a goodbye letter to his wife shortly before lapsing into unconsciousness.

1:00 **a.m., Wed., Apr. 11, 1951** – At a rare, late-night news conference, President Truman announced the firing of World War II hero General Douglas MacArthur. MacArthur was relieved of his commands in the Far East after publicly challenging Truman's policies; he would be replaced by Lieutenant-General Matthew Ridgway. The ever-popular MacArthur gave an emotional farewell speech in the U.S. Congress before being hailed as a hero in a ticker-tape parade in New York City.

MacArthur was called "one of America`s greatest heroes" by President

...art was a child prodigy who wrote the first of his 600 works at age five.

Lyndon Johnson. MacArthur led the Allied victory over Japan in World War II and commanded the United Nations forces in the Korean war. He won virtually every military honour within his reach. The General savoured the excitement of war and the dangers of combat. He borrowed one of his best-known quotations from an army song: "Old soldiers never die – they just fade away."

General Douglas MacArthur died of kidney and liver failure at 2:39 p.m. on Sunday, April 5, 1964. He was 84.

1:00 **a.m., Mon., Dec. 5, 1791** – Wolfgang Amadeus Mozart, Austrian composer and creator of some of the world's most enduring music, died at age 35 of typhoid. Mozart was a child prodigy who wrote the first of his 600 works at age five. He produced such classic works as "The Marriage of Figaro," "Don Giovanni" and "The Magic Flute," and was working on a requiem mass when he died. Mozart, who was continually in debt and died broke, was buried in an unmarked grave after a sparsely attended funeral. His life story is told in the Academy Award-winning film *Amadeus*.

1:00 **a.m., Thurs., June 3, 1875** – Singer Mme Galli-Marie felt a strange chill and a shooting pain in her side as she performed during the first all-Bizet concert in Paris. The incident supposedly took place during the scene in *Carmen* where Carmen sees death in the cards. Galli-Marie left the stage, claiming she had seen a vision of Bizet looking deathly pale. At that very moment, so the legend goes, Bizet died at his home in Paris. He was 36. Fanciful observers have attributed his death to disappointment at poor reviews for *Carmen*, but medical evidence suggests it was a heart attack.

Sadly for Bizet, *Carmen* did not gain acceptance until after his death. It has gone on to become one of the most popular works in the history of opera.

1:00 **a.m., Tues., Apr. 23, 1946** – Two men who had been trapped in a mine in Moose River, Nova Scotia, emerged from the depths to safety. Dr. W.E. Robertson and Alfred Scadding came out 10 days after they were first trapped 36 metres (10.9 feet) below the surface in a cave-in. On-the-scene radio reporter J. Frank Willis announced the good news to a breathless audience.

Robertson, Scadding and a third man, Herman Magill, had gone below to determine the feasibility of resuming production at the Moose River Gold Mine. Six days after the cave-in, rescuers heard muffled taps that indicated there were lives to be saved. A shaft was drilled to the men and rescuers dug with their hands to create an opening large enough for the men to crawl through. Throughout it all, broadcaster Willis kept an estimated 50 million listeners informed with nearly 100 on-the-spot reports. Magill died of exposure before rescuers could reach him, but the other two men survived the incident relatively unscathed.

1:00 **a.m., Wed., July 11, 1962** – Satellite TV became a reality as the first trans-Atlantic television transmission was sent from Andover, Maine via the *Telstar I* satellite to Pleumeur Bodou, France.

The first image sent was a picture of Frederick R. Kappell, chairman of the American Telephone and Telegraph Company – owner of Telstar. The broadcast paved the way for instantaneous TV broadcasts from anywhere to anywhere on the globe.

1:00 **a.m. Fri., June 30, 1967** – The last round of drinks was served at the famed Astor Hotel, a New York landmark for 63 years and one of the world's great meeting spots. The Astor, a 10-story, 700-room structure with more than a mile of pale green corridors, was a gathering spot for many a show business personality. One of its more famous full-time guests was also the last: former general Omar Bradley. The Astor was torn down to make room for an office tower in 1967.

1:00 **a.m., Nov. 2, (year unknown)** – According to Mary Shelley's 1818 classic *Frankenstein*, this was the day and time Frankenstein's monster was created. Interestingly, the creation of Dr. Victor Frankenstein was never referred to in the book as "Frankenstein"; its real name was "Adam."

1:14 **a.m., Thurs., June 13, 1963** – Civil rights leader Medgar Evers died after being shot by a sniper in front of his Jackson, Mississippi, home. Evers, field secretary for the National Association for the Advancement of Colored People, had declared only 10 days before his

Six days after the cave-in, rescuers heard muffled taps.

The last recording session featuring all four members of the Beatles wrapped up.

death that if he died it would be for a good cause. His death led to riots in the South by supporters, heating up an already tense situation.

Byron de la Beckwith, a white supremacist, was convicted of murder in 1994 after two hung juries and a 31-year wait for justice for the Evers family.

1:15 a.m., Thurs., Aug. 21, 1969 – The last recording session featuring all four members of the Beatles wrapped up in Studio Two at the Abbey Road studios in northwest London. John Lennon, Paul McCartney, George Harrison and Ringo Starr were all on hand for a session that featured remixes and decisions on the order of songs for side two of the *Abbey Road* album.

It was the last time all four Beatles would appear in the same recording studio together. The final Beatles recording session before the breakup – featuring Paul, George and Ringo (John was on vacation in Denmark) – ended at 4:00 a.m. Monday, January 5, 1970. The song recorded during this session was "Let It Be."

1:17 a.m., Mon., May 4, 1981 – Imprisoned Irish Republican Army member Bobby Sands died at Belfast's Maze Prison after a 66-day fast. He was 27. Sands, who had recently been elected to Parliament to fill a vacancy, was one of several IRA members who fasted to protest the fact they were being held as criminals – not political prisoners. Ten IRA fasters died before the protest was stopped. Sands had been serving a 14-year sentence for firearms possession.

1:21 p.m., Sat., July 27, 1996 – Tragedy hit the Olympics as a homemade pipe bomb exploded at Atlanta's Centennial Olympic Park. One person standing next to the bomb was killed and a Turkish cameraman rushing to the scene died of a heart attack. The blast also injured 111. Hours after the explosion, IOC director general Francois Carrard pronounced, "the games will go on" and competition continued that day.

Police were tipped off to the potential tragedy when a caller phoned 911 at 12:58 a.m. About 1:00 a.m., security guard Richard Jewell pointed out an unattended knapsack to an FBI agent. He was questioned by the FBI and hounded by the media. However, in October the FBI cleared Jewell as a suspect and the case remained open.

1:24 a.m., Sat., Apr. 26, 1986 – Two workers were killed instantly when an explosion ripped through the No. 4 reactor in the generating plant at Chernobyl, Ukraine. It took four days for the Soviets to acknowledge the accident, and then only after European monitoring stations recorded higher than usual radioactivity levels.

All told, 31 people were killed by the accident but Soviet scientists suggested the death toll would ultimately stretch into hundreds – perhaps even thousands – because of radiation-caused diseases. Experts believe it will be many years before the total scope of the disaster is known. Chernobyl was the worst nuclear disaster in history.

1:30 a.m., Mon., Nov. 30, 1874 – Sir Winston Churchill, one of the greatest and most eloquent statesmen of the 20th century, was born in Oxfordshire, England.

Churchill's career in public service was unmatched. First elected to the British parliament in 1900, he served in the House of Commons for four decades before being elected prime minister in 1940. Declaring he had "nothing to offer but blood, toil, tears and sweat," Churchill was a pillar of perseverance during the Battle of Britain as England withstood the Nazi onslaught alone – a time Churchill called Britain's "finest hour." The tide turned when America joined the war in 1941. Britain, the U.S. and the Soviet Union led the alliance that finally defeated the Nazis in 1945.

After the war in Europe was won, Churchill became the victim of one of the greatest political upsets ever as his Conservative party lost to Labor's Clement Atlee. Churchill was re-elected Prime Minister in 1951 and served four years before resigning in 1955. During his second stint as Prime Minister, he won the Nobel Prize for Literature in 1953 for his historical writings. Churchill was heaped with honours in retirement, becoming the first man to be made an honorary citizen of the United States in April, 1963. He spent his final years producing his four-volume *History of the English-Speaking Peoples*.

Churchill died of a stroke at 8:00 a.m., Monday, January 25, 1965. He was 90.

1:30 a.m., Thurs., Dec. 23, 1948 – Hideki Tojo, Japan's prime minister during World War II, was hanged at Sagamo prison for war

An explosion ripped through the No. 4 reactor in the generating plant at Chernobyl.

Janis Joplin died in her room at the Landmark Hotel in Los Angeles.

crimes. Tojo had been arrested three years earlier at his Tokyo home, nearly dying after being shot during his capture. Six collaborators were hanged along with Tojo.

1:30 a.m., Sun., Apr. 17, 1966 – New York's old Metropolitan Opera House concluded its last performance. Fittingly, the final opera performed was *Faust*, which was also the first opera staged when Old Met opened in 1883.

An audience of 4,000 people, paying up to $200 a ticket, attended the closing night gala. On the way out, many patrons removed the metal seat numbers and one daring soul even got away with a chair. The Old Met was demolished nine months later despite attempts by preservationists to save it.

1:35 a.m., Thurs., Oct. 6, 1892 – Alfred Lord Tennyson, one of the most popular poets in the history of the English language, died at his home in Aldworth, England. He was 83, and had been poet laureate for 42 years, or more than half his life.

Tennyson is best known for his works "Charge of the Light Brigade," "In Memoriam" and "The Idylls of a King." The meaning of his last words, "I have opened it," remains a mystery.

1:40 a.m., Sun. Oct. 4, 1970 – Janis Joplin, who shrieked her way to rock and roll immortality with such hits as "Piece of My Heart" and "Me and Bobby McGee," died in her room at the Landmark Hotel in Los Angeles. Joplin, an alcoholic and heavy drug user, was killed by an overdose of heroin. Her death occurred less than three weeks after fellow rocker Jimi Hendrix died, also of an overdose. Joplin, who once predicted she wouldn't live to the age of 30, was 27.

1:45 a.m., Sat., Aug. 9, 1975 – Samuel Bronfman II, heir to the Seagram's fortune, was kidnapped from his home in Purchase, New York. Nine days later, Bronfman was rescued when police raided an apartment in Brooklyn. Police also recovered the $2.3 million ransom paid by Bronfman's father only the day before. Mel Patrick Lynch, a fireman, and Dominic Byrne, who ran a limousine service, were later convicted of extortion but not of kidnapping.

1:49 a.m., Mon., Sept. 12, 1994 – In a shocking breach of White House security, a light plane crashed just short of the presidential mansion. President Clinton and his family were staying at Blair House, a government guest house, when the crash took place and were unharmed. The pilot, Frank Corder, was killed. Corder had a history of mental and drug problems and had recently separated from his wife. It is believed his motive was suicide and that he did not mean to harm the president.

The crash was one of three major security breaches at the White House in 1994. On October 29, a gunman sprayed the White House with gunfire. On December 10, a lone bullet was fired at 1600 Pennsylvania Avenue.

1:52 a.m., Sun. Oct. 31, 1999 – Egyptair Flight 990 disappeared from radar screens as the pilot and co-pilot fought for control of the craft. All 217 passengers and crew aboard died when the plane plunged into the Atlantic Ocean off Nantucket, Massachusetts. Some investigators theorized that a backup co-pilot sent the plane into a suicide dive while the pilot was briefly out of the cockpit. It's believed the pilot made a valiant effort to save the plane – fighting with the backup co-pilot for control – but was unsuccessful.

1:55 a.m., Wed., June 30, 1971 – Soviet cosmonauts Viktor Patseyev, Vladislav Volkov and Georgi Dobrovolsky were found dead in their spacecraft *Soyuz 11*. They died as the craft was making an apparent normal re-entry, landing near Kazakhstan in the southern Soviet Union. The three were returning from space after setting a space endurance record (24 days). They were the first men to occupy an orbiting space station and had spent much of their time in space performing experiments.

An investigation revealed the cosmonauts died after cabin air escaped through an improperly sealed hatch. The men would have lived had they been wearing space suits, however Soviet space officials had felt such protection was unnecessary.

1:55 a.m., Fri., May 29, 1914 – The Canadian passenger ship *Empress of Ireland* sank just 14 minutes after being rammed in a dense fog by the Norwegian ship *Storstad*. One thousand and twenty-four of the 1,477 on board died in the accident off Father Point, Quebec –

Egyptair Flight 990 disappeared from radar screens.

The Canadian passenger ship *Empress of Ireland* sank.

Canada's worst peacetime maritime disaster. One crew member recalled: "She just rolled over like a hog in a ditch." None of the ship's crew was seriously injured. Captain Anderson of the *Storstad* was held responsible for the accident. A monument at Metis-Sur-Mer commemorates the dead.

According to one survivor, some of the doomed sang "God Be With You Till We Meet Again" as the *Empress* went down.

2 a.m. to 2:59 a.m.

🕐 **Columbus discovers the New World**

🕐 **The *Titanic* sinks on its maiden voyage**

🕐 **Longest game in NHL history ends**

🕐 **Watergate break–in discovered**

🕐 **Germany surrenders to Allies in World War II**

🕐 **Alarm sounds on the Morro Castle**

2:00 **a.m., Fri., Oct. 12, 1492** – Rodrigo De Triana, a sailor on board Christopher Columbus's ship the *Pinta*, saw a distant limestone cliff in the moonlight and discovered the New World. At dawn, Columbus claimed the island (part of what is now the Bahamas chain) and named it San Salvador, or "Saint of Salvation."

Columbus was attempting to find a westward route to China and believed he had landed near Japan. His Atlantic crossing from Spain lasted 71 days. He had received Spanish support for the voyage only after being rejected by Portugal, France and England. The 88-man crew for his three vessels was scraped together from the streets and prisons of Palos, Spain.

Columbus made three more voyages to the New World before he died, embittered, in 1506 at the age of 55. To his dying day, Columbus believed he had found the west coast of Asia and not the "New World." His efforts paved the way for a new era in exploration and earned him a lasting place in the history books. Paradoxically, the Spanish government never paid him for his epoch 1492 journey.

2:00 **a.m., Thurs., June 4, 1896** – Henry Ford and his friend Jim Bishop finished work on a peculiar-looking machine Ford called the "baby carriage." It was time for a road test. Ford smashed a hole in the wall of his workshop with a mallet and he and Bishop set out on a late-night tour

Construction of the Berlin Wall began on orders from Soviet leader Nikita Kruschev.

of the Detroit suburbs. The vehicle only stalled once! "Crazy Henry," as some called him, had created his first automobile.

Ford went on to parlay a $28,000 investment into a billion-dollar auto empire. He founded the Ford Motor Company in 1903, revolutionizing transportation with his Model T and Model A. He updated mass-production methods and was a hero to his workers, who received an unprecedented $5 for an eight-hour day in 1914. Ironically, Ford was against unions, although in 1941 he signed the first union shop and checkoff contract in the automotive industry with the United Auto Workers. The former machinist's apprentice once lost a bid for the U.S. Senate and considered a bid for the presidency.

Ford died at 11:40 p.m., Monday, April 7, 1947 at the age of 63.

2:00 a.m., Sun., Aug. 13, 1961 – Construction of the Berlin Wall began on orders from Soviet leader Nikita Kruschev. The ugly barricade of stone and barbed wire would remain standing for more than 28 years as a symbol of Communist repression.

Berliners could hardly believe their eyes when East German army and police officers began to build the Wall on the demarcation line between East and West Berlin, and within three hours, angry West Berliners gathered in protest at the Brandenburg Gate – but their demands went unheeded. By nightfall, the border was sealed, with more than 300 border guards and 1,181 dogs making escape difficult.

Not that people didn't try to get out. Hundreds attempted to flee to the West over and under the Wall; 80 were killed in the attempt. The first victim was killed just six days after the Wall went up; the final victim died eight months before the Wall was opened.

The announcement that the Berlin Wall was being opened was made at 7:19 p.m. on Thursday, November 9, 1989. Making the announcement was Gunter Schabowski, a member of the ruling Politburo of the German Democratic Republic. Within hours, frenzied Germans from both sides of the border were dancing on the wall, taking chunks out of it with hammers and staging a wild celebration.

Pieces of the Wall were sold around the world after its fall – a fitting end to one of history's ugliest landmarks. Official destruction of the wall began in June, 1990 and was completed by November of that year except for six segments kept as a memorial. Those segments were removed by

November, 1991. Today, the former location of the Wall is marked over a distance of 20 kilometres by a red line or double row of cobblestones.

2:00 a.m., Sun., Mar. 31, 1918 – Daylight saving time was introduced in the United States, as the clocks were advanced one hour to 3 a.m.

Daylight time was started as a wartime measure, to allow factories to open later and give farmers an extra hour of light in the evening. The practice proved popular and continued after the First World War ended. In 1966, the U.S. Congress established that daylight saving time would begin the last Sunday in April and end the last Sunday in October. In 1989, the start of daylight time was advanced to the first Sunday in April.

Daylight time is not observed in Arizona, Hawaii or in parts of Indiana, nor in Saskatchewan in Canada. An experiment to introduce double daylight time (advancing the clock by two hours) in Newfoundland in the 1980s was not well received.

2:00 a.m., Wed., Oct. 17, 1849 – Frederick Chopin, one of the world's most renowned composers and pianists in his day, died of tuberculosis at age 39. The Polish-born Chopin, whose most famous works include the "Poloniases" and the "Etudes," wrote his first composition at age seven.

Unhealthy throughout his life, Chopin died young of overwork and a frail constitution. Near the end of his life, he had to be carried to his piano for concerts.

As he requested, Chopin's heart was placed in the wall of a church in Warsaw. The rest of him is buried in Paris.

2:00 a.m., Thurs., July 24, 1862 – Martin Van Buren, the eighth president and the first man born an American to occupy the Oval Office, died of an asthmatic attack in Kinderhook, New York, at age 79. Van Buren was the first sitting vice-president to be elected president and the only one until George Bush in 1988.

Van Buren, dubbed the "Little Magician" for his small stature and skill as a politician, defeated William Henry Harrison in the 1836 election, but lost his bid for re-election to Harrison in 1840. During Van Buren's term,

Daylight saving time was introduced.

Rebel troops officially announced the surrender of Cuban leader Fulgencio Batista.

the country suffered through high unemployment, economic depression and many bank failures, earning the president the nickname Martin "Van Ruin." Van Buren lost his re-election bid in 1840, failed to win his party's nomination in 1844 and finished a distant third as head of the "Free Soil" party in 1848.

Van Buren was the first president to begin the practice of stationing police at the front door of the White House. Up to that time, anyone who wanted to see the president could walk right into the president's office unchallenged.

The expression "OK" is derived from Van Buren's nickname "Old Kinderhook," which itself stems from his hometown of Kinderhook, New York.

2:00 a.m., Wed., Apr. 4, 1979 – Former Pakistan Prime Minister Zulfikar Ali Bhutto was hanged. The Pakistani leader was convicted in 1978 of ordering the murder of a political rival in 1974.

The Bhutto political era did not end with his death. In 1988, his daughter Benazir Bhutto was elected prime minister and on January 25, 1990 became the first head of a major government to have a baby while in office.

Benazir Bhutto was dismissed by Pakistani president Farooq Leghari in 1996 on charges of mismanagement.

2:00 a.m., Fri., Jan. 2, 1959 – Rebel troops officially announced the surrender of Cuban leader Fulgencio Batista.

The ouster of the deposed Cuban leader, who fled to the Dominican Republic, set off wild celebrations in the streets. Batista had fallen into disfavour because of his corrupt and oppressive government. Rebel leader Fidel Castro had little trouble finding support for his revolution. At first, Castro and provisional president Manuel Urrutia were welcomed by the U.S., which expected Cuba to restore its democratic constitution. Their glee proved to be premature, as Cuba under Castro became a Soviet satellite and a Communist threat. The U.S. broke off diplomatic relations with Cuba on Jan. 4, 1961, almost two years to the day after the revolution.

2:00 a.m., Tues., May 19, 1795 – James Boswell, whose work *The Life of Samuel Johnson* is considered one of the world's outstanding biographies, died of venereal disease. He was 54. Boswell, a Scottish-born lawyer, finished *Life* in 1791 after working on it for seven years.

The name Boswell has become a general term for a biographer (i.e., Winston Churchill found his Boswell in Martin Gilbert).

2:00 **a.m., Thurs., Apr. 27, 1865** – America's worst maritime tragedy occurred when the *Sultana* sank not far from the Mississippi shore. Largely forgotten today, the disaster took at least 1,450 lives.

The *Sultana*, which was built to carry less than 400 passengers, took on an estimated 2,000 to 2,500 Union prisoners-of-war being shipped home, plus about 100 civilians and 80 crew. The ship was so heavily weighed down that it took 17 hours – twice the normal time – to travel from Vicksburg, Mississippi, to Memphis. After taking on freight, the *Sultana* resumed its journey north. Then disaster struck as a boiler exploded, shooting fragments of metal through the ship, killing and maiming soldiers. Two more boilers exploded, collapsing the ship's centre and setting the *Sultana* on fire. Many passengers fell into the hole caused by the collapse, while others were trapped in flames or drowned. Rescuers recovered 1,450 bodies and many more may have been lost downstream in the chilly Mississippi.

The *Sultana* disaster received little press, partly because it occurred the day after the Confederacy fell and John Wilkes Booth was shot. Like the Pestigo fire of 1908, it remains one of history's forgotten, yet significant, events. *(see 9 p.m.)*

2:00 **a.m., Mon., Dec. 16, 1811** – Residents of the Mississippi Valley were awakened by an earthquake – one of the strongest in U.S. history. The original shock, felt over two-thirds of the U.S., caused land levels to change by as much as nine metres (30 feet) and destroyed an estimated 60,000 hectares (150,000 acres) of timberland.

The damage led to the passing of the first national relief act in 1815, which stipulated that those who lost land would be compensated with land elsewhere. No definitive death toll has ever been established in the Mississippi Valley quake; however, it is believed to be low because of the sparse population in the area.

The initial shock was followed by many other shocks and tremors, the last at New Madrid, Missouri, on February 7, 1812.

America's worst maritime tragedy occurred when the *Sultana* sank.

An attempt to rescue American hostages in Iran ended in tragedy.

2:00 a.m., Sat., May 7, 1988 – Embattled New York Yankees manager Billy Martin was attacked in the men's room of a topless bar near Arlington Stadium in Texas. Martin said he was roughed up by three men, one of whom hit him over the head with a blunt instrument. Martin had his share of scrapes during his long career as a player and manager, but he was able to return and manage the Yanks the next day. Yankees owner George Steinbrenner told reporters he supported Martin, saying, "Billy Martin is my manager. Case closed." Steinbrenner fired Martin a month and a half later.

The high point of Martin's career came in 1977 when he managed the Yankees to the World Series championship. He was fired the following year after one of his many run-ins with Steinbrenner. Martin would return to manage the Yanks four more times, and get fired each time. He also managed the Texas Rangers, the Minnesota Twins and Oakland A's, and was fired each time. But you can't argue with his success: one World Series, two pennants and five divisional titles in 17 seasons as a manager.

Martin died in a car accident at 5:45 p.m. on Christmas Day, 1989 in Fenton, New York, when the car in which he was a passenger missed his driveway and slid down a steep ravine.

2:07 a.m., Sun., Oct. 5, 1930 – The airship R-101, plagued from the start by technical and political problems and largely untested for flight, crashed and burned in a field near Beauvais, France. Only seven of the 54 aboard the world's biggest airship survived the crash, which occurred after the heavily weighted craft failed to clear a small hill.

The dirigible, in operation for less than a year, was on a scheduled journey from England to India via Egypt. Among the dead was Britain's Air Minister, Lord Thomson, who, prior to the flight, had declared the airship would be "safe as a house, save for the millionth chance."

The cause of the crash was never established, but it ended Britain's involvement with airships. The sister ship, the R-100, was immediately grounded and later broken up for scrap.

2:10 a.m., Fri., Apr. 25, 1980 – An attempt to rescue American hostages in Iran ended in tragedy. Eight servicemen were killed when a U.S. army helicopter which had landed in the Iranian desert to refuel collided with a transport plane. The helicopters, eight in all, had been called back after three had suffered technical failures. President Carter took full responsibility for the failed rescue attempt. Secretary of State Cyrus Vance resigned.

2:12 a.m., Tues., Dec. 15, 1964 – Canadian legislators voted to give Canada a new flag, ending one of the longest and most bitter debates in the country's history. The Liberal-dominated House of Commons approved the measure by a vote of 163–78.

The final debate on the red and white flag with its emblematic maple leaf lasted nine and three-quarters hours. Total Parliamentary time spent on the issue was 46 hours. More than 100 Commons speeches were made concerning the flag, most of them by opposition Conservatives who wanted to retain the traditional red ensign.

Canada's new flag was raised for the first time on February 15, 1965 in a ceremony on Parliament Hill. Conservative leader John Diefenbaker wept as the old red ensign flag was lowered for the final time. The fate of that original Maple Leaf flag remained a mystery for many years until it was found on Valentine's Day, 2000 in the Prime Minister's office. It had been passed down from Liberal leader to Liberal leader without the public's knowledge.

2:15 a.m., Tues., Sept. 20, 1881 – Chester Alan Arthur was sworn in as the 21st president following the death of President Garfield. Arthur, whose previous highest post had been collector of the Port of New York, had been a compromise choice as Garfield's vice-presidential running mate in 1880. This unlikely candidate for the Oval Office then became president on the death of Garfield *(see 9:20 a.m.)*.

While in office, Arthur completely redecorated the White House, auctioning off many historic pieces of furniture dating back to Washington's days. His best-known accomplishment was the Pendleton Act, which created the modern civil service.

Arthur was born in North Fairfield, Vermont, but political opponents claimed that he was born in Canada and thus ineligible for the presidency or vice-presidency. No proof of Arthur's Canadian birth has ever surfaced.

Arthur was defeated for renomination by James G. Blaine in 1884 – the last time a sitting president lost his own party's nomination. He died of a stroke at 5:00 a.m., November 18, 1886, aged 57.

Canadian legislators voted to give Canada a new flag.

The *Titanic*, the so-called unsinkable luxury liner, sank on its maiden voyage.

2:20 a.m., Mon., Apr. 15, 1912 – The *Titanic*, the so-called unsinkable luxury liner, sank on its maiden voyage from Southampton, England to New York. More than 1,500 people died.

Luxuries on the giant ship included a theatre, four restaurants plus the main dining-room, tennis and squash courts and a Turkish bath. The *Titanic* sank just two hours and forty minutes after striking an iceberg in the North Atlantic; she had been speeding through the ice-infested waters despite numerous warnings from other vessels in the area.

Titanic's radio operator immediately issued distress signals, and in doing so sent out one of the first ever S.O.S. calls (previously, C.Q.D. had been used). Only one ship, the *Carpathia*, sped to the disaster site, arriving about 4:00 a.m. *Carpathia* spent the next three and a half hours taking on lifeboats, saving some 711 people. Another vessel, the *Californian*, just 16 kilometres (10 miles) away from the doomed *Titanic*, failed to respond to the S.O.S.

Titanic's death list included may of the elite of high society, including financier John Jacob Astor, Macy department store owner Isador Strauss and author Jacques Futrelle, who ironically had lectured about the dangers of North Atlantic sea travel. The ship's Captain Smith was among those who drowned, but White Star general manager Bruce Ismay saved himself. Ismay died years later, a broken man.

Among those saved was the ship's tennis professional, Norris Williams, who would go on to win the mixed doubles title with Hazel Wightman at the 1924 Olympics in Paris.

The disaster made a hero out of a previously unknown wireless operator, David Sarnoff, who kept the world up-to-date with news on the *Titanic* sinking from his listening post in New York City. His place in the history books established (although some have said his role was exaggerated), Sarnoff went on to found NBC.

Public interest in the disaster was revived in 1998 with the Academy Award–winning movie *Titanic*.

2:25 a.m., Thurs., June 29, 1967 – Jayne Mansfield, 1950s blond bombshell only slightly less popular than Marilyn Monroe, died in a car accident near Biloxi, Mississippi. Mansfield died when the car in which she was a passenger slammed into the back of a mosquito-control truck.

The driver and Mansfield's boyfriend-manager were also killed. Manfield's three children, also in the car, were not seriously hurt.

Mansfield lived in a pink house with a pink poodle and signed autographs with a pink pen. She made about a dozen movies, and had just finished a nightclub act in Biloxi and was on her way to a TV appearance in New Orleans when she was killed. Mansfield was 44.

2:25 a.m., Wed., Mar. 25, 1936 – The longest game in NHL history ended after nearly six hours of action. Mud Bruneteau, participating in his first Stanley Cup playoff game, scored to give the visiting Detroit Red Wings a 1–0 victory over the Montreal Maroons at 16:30 of the sixth overtime period. Detroit went on to sweep the semifinal and win the Stanley Cup four games to one over Toronto.

2:28 a.m., Thurs., Nov. 19, 1999 – A stack of logs being erected for the Texas A&M bonfire collapsed, killing 12 and injuring 27. The bonfire, a revered 90-year tradition at the home of the "Aggies," was cancelled for only the second time in its history. John F. Kennedy's assassination in 1963 prompted the first cancellation.

2:30 a.m., Tues., Oct. 18, 1977 – Eighty-six hostages were saved from their captors during a lightning raid on a hijacked Lufthansa airliner at Mogadishu, Somalia. A West German commando force stormed the jet to end a five-day hijacking ordeal that included six stops in a zigzag journey over southern Europe and the Middle East. The only hostage casualty was pilot Jeurgen Schumann, who was shot as the plane sat at the airport in Aden, West Yemen. Three of the four hijackers died as a result of the raid. They had been demanding freedom for 11 West German terrorists and two Palestinians jailed in Turkey, along with $6 million in ransom.

2:30 a.m., Sat., June 17, 1972 – Five men were arrested at the Democratic National headquarters at the Watergate hotel-office complex. Security guard Frank Wills caught the five crouched behind a wooden partition near a secretary's desk. The men were carrying electronic surveillance devices and had planned to "bug" the offices.

Five men were arrested at the Democratic National headquarters at the Watergate hotel office complex.

Irish-born Canadian legislator D'Arcy McGee was shot from behind.

Arrested were Bernard Barker, Frank Sturgis, Virgilio Gonzalez, Eugenio Martinez and James McCord. McCord's arrest raised eyebrows as he was the security coordinator for the Committee for the re-election of the President.

From this seemingly innocuous beginning emerged the worst political scandal in U.S. history.

2:30 **a.m., Tues., Apr. 7, 1868** – Irish-born Canadian legislator D'Arcy McGee was shot from behind as he entered his rooming house in downtown Ottawa after a late-night session of Parliament. The bullet went through the base of McGee's brain, knocking out two of his teeth and his half-smoked cigar, before coming to rest in the door McGee was attempting to open.

The Government offered a $20,000 reward for information leading to the arrest of the assassin, and shortly thereafter arrested Patrick Whalen. Whalen, who had boasted of killing McGee, was a member of a radical group called the Fenians. The Fenians wanted the British tossed out of Canada and McGee, a fervent Canadian nationalist from Ireland, emerged as a prime target.

Whalen was hanged February 11, 1869.

McGee, often mentioned as a successor to Canada's first Prime Minister Sir John A. Macdonald, was only 43. His statue stands on Parliament Hill in Ottawa.

2:30 **a.m., Sun,. Jan. 14, 1973** – The first live, worldwide satellite concert began in Honolulu, with Elvis Presley the star attraction. The Honolulu Arena was sold out despite the late hour. The concert was later made into an album *Aloha from Hawaii via Satellite*, which hit number one on Billboard's album chart for one week in February, 1973. It was RCA's first Quadra-Disc, a short-lived and unsuccessful attempt at bringing quadraphonic sound to the masses.

2:35 **a.m., Mon., Nov. 23, 1992** – Fiddler-singer Roy Acuff, "the king of country music," died of congestive heart failure at age 89. Acuff, who in 1962 became the first living person inducted into the Country Music Hall of Fame, sold more than 25 million records including "The

Wabash Cannonball." Such was his fame that Japanese troops are said to have yelled "To hell with Roosevelt, to hell with Babe Ruth, to hell with Roy Acuff" during one battle charge (one of Acuff's hits was "Cowards over Pearl Harbor," a reference to the Japanese surprise attack).

2:38 a.m., Sat., Sept. 17, 1949 – Fire was discovered near the cocktail bar on the cruise ship *Noronic* as it stood at its pier in Toronto. Within 15 minutes, the largest passenger ship on the Great Lakes was ablaze from stem to stern. Most of the 207 who died had little chance as the ship's hull completely burned out and the single exit was cut off. So quickly did the fire spread that there was no time to launch the lifeboats. Somehow 373 people survived the blaze. The *Noronic* had been making her last cruise of the season from Detroit to the Thousand Islands.

2:40 a.m., Wed., Oct. 24, 1945 – Vidkun Quisling, a Norwegian politician who worked on behalf of the Nazis, was hanged for treason.

In 1939, Quisling persuaded his hero Adolf Hitler to invade Norway. But the invasion was poorly planned and the Norwegian government was able to escape. Quisling then gained access to the radio station and announced he was seizing power. A week later, the Germans pushed Quisling out, but by February, 1942, he was reinstated as premier. He proved to be a Hitler puppet, ignoring German atrocities. Such is Quisling's notoriety that the word "quisling" appears in dictionaries as a synonym for traitor.

Quisling was arrested on the liberation of Norway in May, 1945 and was found guilty of treason after a short trial.

2:41 a.m., Mon., May 7, 1945 – Germany surrendered unconditionally to the Allies and Russia. The surrender took place in a little red schoolhouse in Reims, France that served as headquarters for General Eisenhower. Signing for the Germans was Colonel General Gustav Jodl, chief of staff for the German army.

The war in Europe cost the lives of 34 million people, including 18 million civilians. Untold millions were wounded or left unaccounted for. Although the U.S. didn't enter the war until December, 1941, 300,000 Americans gave their lives in battle. The man who started it all, Adolf Hitler, took his life in a Berlin bunker on April 30.

The largest passenger ship on the Great Lakes was ablaze from stem to stern.

A balloon carrying eight East Germans to freedom landed safely in West Germany.

Hostilities in the Second World War didn't actually end until Japan's surrender in September, 1945. *(see 9:07 a.m.)*

2:42 a.m., Sun., Sept. 16, 1979 – In one of the cold war's most daring escapes, a balloon carrying eight East Germans to freedom landed safely in West Germany.

Peter Strelzyk, Gunter Wetzel and their families reached the West defying incredible odds. Using plans found in library books, Strelzyk and Wetzel made a balloon with materials purchased in bits and pieces from cities and towns throughout East Germany. They secretly tested it late at night in fields. The first attempt – with just the Strelzyk family – ended in failure. But Strelzyk and Wetzel and their families teamed up for a successful second try. They landed just inside the border at Naila, West Germany. Their escape was later portrayed in the movie *Night Crossing*.

2:45 a.m., Mon., Mar. 24, 1603 – Elizabeth I, "The Virgin Queen," at 69 the longest-lived British monarch to that date, died at her castle in Richmond, England. She had reigned for 44 years. Considered by many to be the most effective monarch in history, the shrewd and forceful Elizabeth was in ill health for most of her life. She died of pneumonia after characteristically refusing to take medicine for her illness.

Elizabeth gained her nickname "The Virgin Queen" because she never married despite the efforts of many men to win her hand. Her lasting achievement was her decision to separate the Church of England completely from the Roman Catholic Church, and end the persecution of Protestants.

2:45 a.m., Sat., July 10, 1943 – In what General Eisenhower called "the first page in the liberation of the European continent," American and British forces established a beachhead at Sicily. The long-awaited invasion was preceded by a week of round-the-clock bombing.

Two weeks after the beachhead was established, General Patton captured Palermo, Sicily's largest city. Just two days after that, Italian leader Mussolini was placed under house arrest. The long march to victory had begun for the Allies.

2:45 a.m., Sun., Nov. 6, 1995 – Jean Chrétien's wife Aline was wakened by the sound of a rock smashing a window at their official residence overlooking the Ottawa River. Shortly after, Aline Chrétien came face-to-face with a knife-wielding intruder at the couple's bedroom door. Mme. Chrétien slammed the door and locked the man out. The slamming of the door awaked the prime minister, who got out of bed and armed himself with an Inuit soapstone carving. Minutes later, RCMP arrived and arrested the man, a 34-year-old convenience store worker with a history of psychiatric problems.

It marked the first major security breach involving a Canadian prime minister and raised major questions about the PM's security. The incident came just hours after the assassination of Israeli Prime Minister Rabin.

It marked the first major security breach involving a Canadian prime minister.

2:47 a.m., Fri., Aug. 3, 1923 – Calvin Coolidge was sworn in as America's 30th president. His father, John Coolidge, a notary public, administered the oath of office in the family living room in Plymouth, Vermont – the only time a father has sworn in his son as president. Coolidge succeeded to the office on the death of Warren G. Harding. *(see 7:30 p.m.)*

Coolidge gained prominence, when, as governor of Massachusetts, he called out the state guard in September, 1919 during the Boston police strike. He was nominated for vice-president under Harding in 1920 and, after succeeding to the presidency, won election to the nation's highest post in his own right in 1924.

"Silent Cal," whose reputation as a reluctant conversationalist is legendary, reduced the national debt by $2 billion in three years. Yet, he is generally regarded as a "do-nothing" president.

The only president born on the fourth of July, Coolidge was also the last to hold regular White House receptions for the general public.

Coolidge chose not to run for re-election in 1928. He died January 5, 1933 at 12:45 p.m. of a blood clot, aged 60. Just before his death, he had been working on a jigsaw puzzle of George Washington.

2:48 a.m., Fri., July 14, 1972 – George McGovern began his acceptance speech for the Democratic nomination long after

One hundred and thirty-four people would die largely as a result of incompetence by the crew.

most Americans had gone to bed. Only in Alaska and Hawaii was the speech seen in prime time.

McGovern was the victim of his own party in one of the worst fiascoes in U.S. presidential politics. First, the speech was delayed by a floor battle over the new charter for the Democratic Party. Then, the long drawn-out vice-presidential nomination and roll call dragged the agenda well past midnight. By the time McGovern spoke at the Miami Convention Center, the television audience had dropped from 17 million homes to just over three and a half million. Compare that to the 20 million who watched Richard Nixon's acceptance speech for the Republican nomination in August. That November, Nixon defeated McGovern in one of the biggest landslides in U.S. presidential election history.

2:56 a.m., Sat., Sept. 8, 1934 – A fire alarm sounded on board luxury liner *Morro Castle*, beginning what could have been termed a comedy of errors had not the result been so tragic. One hundred and thirty-four people would die largely as a result of incompetence by the crew.

The tragic chain of events began when *Morro Castle* Capt. Robert Wilmott collapsed at a banquet and died of an apparent heart attack. First Officer William Warms took command, and was on the bridge when the fire broke out in the writing room. Defying standard practice, the crew failed to shut the fire doors that could have sealed off the blaze. Flames spread through the ship via the ventilation shafts. Warms allowed the ship to steam ahead, which fanned the inferno. He also delayed sounding a general alarm until after the fire had burned through the middle of the ship, separating passengers from crew. The crew fended for themselves, leaving passengers to launch their own lifeboats.

Only one distress signal was sent – over an hour after the fire began. A Coast Guard cutter arrived within minutes and began rescue operations, but it was too late for many. More crew survived than passengers, and even the ship's mascot dog was saved. One man saved himself by swimming 3.2 kilometres (two miles) to the New Jersey shore.

An inquiry found the crew guilty of incompetence. Radio operator George Rogers was at first hailed a hero. But a subsequent book written on the disaster suggest that Rogers may have poisoned Captain Wilmott, then started the fire himself.

3 a.m. to 3:59 a.m.

🕐 **Tchaikovsky dies at age 53**
🕐 **Tet offensive begins**
🕐 **Great Train Robbery is staged**
🕐 **George Harrison is stabbed**
🕐 **First double-crossing of English Channel made**
🕐 **Three Mile Island accident takes place**

3:00 **a.m., Mon., Nov. 6, 1893** – Peter Ilyich Tchaikovsky, the most renowned of all Russian composers and arguably the most gifted, died after drinking infected water in St. Petersburg. Cause of death was cholera. His death came only nine days after the premiere of his sixth symphony, "Pathetique." Tchaikovsky, who did not start studying music until his early 20s, was 53.

Tchaikovsky's works included the ballets *Swan Lake, The Sleeping Beauty,* and *The Nutcracker.* He lived a tormented life plagued by a nervous disorder and whispers about his homosexuality. There were even rumours that Russian officials arranged the composer's death rather than risk embarrassment to the Russian court should word of his homosexuality become public knowledge.

3:00 **a.m., Wed., Jan. 31, 1968** – As part of what became known as the Tet offensive, a Viet Cong suicide squad invaded the U.S. embassy in Saigon, eventually capturing five of the building's six floors. Six hours later, the embassy was back in U.S. hands, and all 19 Viet Cong invaders lay dead. Five U.S. soldiers died when the Viet Cong blew a hole in the wall to enter embassy grounds and shot their way into the building.

The embassy attack was one of several on U.S. installations during Tet, the Vietnamese New Year. Eighteen U.S. servicemen and some 70 South Vietnamese troops were killed. These incidents raised deep concerns about the safety of U.S. personnel in the region, and helped turn the tide of U.S. opinion solidly against the war.

3:00 a.m., Sun., Jan. 27, 1901 – Guiseppi Verdi, Italy's leading composer of the 19th century, died following a stroke at the Grand Hotel in Milan. He was 88. Verdi burst onto the scene with the opera *Nabucco* in 1842 and remained an Italian national symbol for nearly six decades. His works *Rigoletto*, *La Traviata* and *Il Trovatore* are among the most popular operas to this day.

As a youth, Verdi was rejected by the Conservatory of Milan when the musician in charge decided the boy had no aptitude. Years later, when officials of the Conservatory asked if they could rename their school after him, Verdi told them no.

3:00 a.m., Wed., Dec. 11, 1963 – Frank Sinatra, Jr., 19-year-old son of the famous entertainer, was released after being held for three days by kidnappers. Sinatra, who was snatched at a Lake Tahoe casino, was drugged, blindfolded and held in a series of cars and trucks during his captivity. He was released after his father paid a $240,000 ransom. Although some claimed the kidnapping was a publicity stunt, two men were given life sentences for the crime.

3:00 a.m., Mon., July 4, 1904 – Anton Chekhov, leading Russian dramatist of the late 19th century, died of tuberculosis at a clinic in Badenweiler, West Germany. He was 44. Chekhov received acclaim for his revival of *The Seagull*, and for his plays *Uncle Vanya*, *The Three Sisters* and *The Cherry Orchard*. Chekhov, who originally trained to be a doctor and supported himself by writing stories for magazines, became so good at writing that he decided to make it his career.

3:00 a.m., Tues., Feb. 25, 1893 – Enrico Caruso, who would become one of opera's leading tenors, was born in Naples, Italy.

Caruso was the first singer to owe part of his fame to recordings of his

Frank Sinatra, Jr., 19-year-old son of the famous entertainer, was released after being held for three days by kidnappers.

A gang of masked bandits commandeered a train near Mentmore, England and stole more than $6 million in bank notes.

music – he made 154 of them. His most famous roles included Carnio in *Pagliacci* and Rudolpho in *La Boheme*.

Caruso died of peritonitis at 48 at 9:00 a.m., Tuesday, August 2, 1921. His body was on public display until 1927 when his widow finally tired of the spectacle.

3:03 a.m., Thurs., Aug. 8, 1963 – In what was dubbed the "Great Train Robbery," a gang of masked bandits commandeered a train near Mentmore, England, and stole more than $6 million in bank notes headed for pulping. The well-orchestrated theft took 42 minutes and so much cash was stolen that the bandits lit cigarettes with bank notes in celebration. Ten men were found guilty in the robbery and sentenced to a total of 300 years in prison. Only a fraction of the loot was ever recovered. One of the robbers, Ronald Biggs, escaped to Brazil where he avoided extradition by getting married. He remains a free man to this day.

3:04 a.m., Wed., Feb. 4, 1976 – An earthquake hit Guatemala, killing 12,000 people, and leaving over one million homeless. It was the worst recorded earthquake disaster in Central American history. Approximately one out of 10 buildings in the country was damaged, including half the construction in Guatemala City.

3:06 a.m., Sun., Jan. 16, 1927 – Toronto swimmer George Young made himself $25,000 and earned a place in the history books. The 17-year-old became the first person to swim the width of California's 35-kilometre San Pedro Channel. Young was the only one of the 95 swimmers who started the race to finish, and claim the top prize – offered by chewing gum magnate William Wrigley, Jr.

Young took 15 hours and 45 minutes to swim from Santa Catalina Island to the mainland at Wilmington, California. Oil slicks, seaweed, and tide changes hampered his progress throughout.

3:10 a.m., Fri., July 17, 1959 – Billie Holiday, legendary blues singer whose classics included "God Bless The Child" and "Strange Fruit," died in a Harlem hospital at age 44. Holiday, a long-time heroin user, had been suffering from cirrhosis of the liver and heart trouble. Holiday, of whom singer Carmen McRae once commented: "the only way she's happy is through a song," left an estate worth a mere $1,000.

3:30 **a.m., Tues., Sept. 27, 1988** – Canadian Olympic *chef de mission* Carol Anne Letheren visited sprinter Ben Johnson at his quarters in the Olympic Village and asked for his gold medal back. A few hours later, the International Olympic Committee stunned the world with the news it was stripping Johnson of his gold medal in the 100-metre dash at the Seoul Games. Evidence of steroid use was found in Johnson's urine given after the race. Ben Johnson was also stripped of his world record-setting time – 9.79 seconds. The gold went to his arch-rival Carl Lewis of the U.S., who had finished second in 9.92 seconds.

Appearing before a Canadian government commission, Johnson's doctor George Astaphan revealed that the sprinter had been taking steroids since 1981. Just 26 days before the Olympics, Astaphan had given Johnson an injection of Winstol-V, a compound used to fatten cattle.

Johnson was banned from competition for life in 1993 following his second positive test for steroids. He was reinstated in 1993 but in the fall of that year was banned again following a third positive test. Despite the third failed drug test, Johnson's agent arranged a three-month contract to provide fitness training to the soccer-playing son of Libyan leader Muammar Gaddafi.

3:30 **a.m., Wed., Apr. 26, 1865** – John Wilkes Booth, accused assassin of President Lincoln, died after being shot in a barn near Port Royal, Virginia.

Booth and accomplice David Herold hid out in the barn after 12 days on the run following Lincoln's assassination. Booth, a failed actor who sided with the South during the Civil War, broke his leg when he leapt from Lincoln's private box after shooting the president in the head during a play at Ford's Theatre in Washington.

Despite positive identification by a doctor who had operated on Booth, there is still speculation the man shot at Port Royal was not Lincoln's assassin. One report says the dead man was Captain James Boyd, who bore a striking resemblance to Booth and was also out to kill the president. Some believe Booth escaped to England or India. Another report contended that

Ben Johnson was also stripped of his world record setting time – 9.79 seconds.

George Harrison was attacked at his home in Henley-on-Thames outside London.

Booth died in 1903 in Enid, Oklahoma, while using the name David E. George.

Booth and Lincoln crossed paths at least twice before the assassination night. Booth was an invited guest at Lincoln's first inauguration in 1861. And Lincoln went to see Booth in *The Marble Heart* one week before the famous speech at Gettysburg in November, 1863. *(see 7:22 a.m.; 10:13 p.m.)*

3:30 a.m., Thurs., Dec. 30, 1999 – George Harrison was attacked at his home in Henley-on-Thames outside London. The reclusive former Beatle was hospitalized with a collapsed lung after being stabbed once in the chest by an obsessed fan who broke into the home during the pre-dawn hours. Harrison's wife Olivia was hit over the head by the intruder but suffered only superficial wounds. Harrison, 56, received his wounds as he fought to protect his wife.

The attack took place 19 years and 22 days after John Lennon was gunned down by obsessed fan Mark Chapman outside his New York apartment building.

Neighbours had described Harrison's 100-room mansion as "Fort Knox" because of its tight security, which included patrol dogs.

Michael Abram, 33, of Liverpool was charged with attempted murder and admitted to psychiatric hospital.

3:30 a.m., Thurs., Sept. 23, 1965 – A ceasefire ending hostilities between India and Pakistan took effect. The agreement quelled tensions that had led the two sides to war twice in the previous 17 years. The deal was overshadowed by the death, by heart attack, of Indian Prime Minister Lai Shastri just hours after the agreement was reached. Despite the deal, hostilities have continued between India and Pakistan in the long-standing dispute over border territories.

3:30 a.m., Fri., May 31, 1968 – Doctors at the Montreal Heart Institute completed Canada's first heart transplant, the world's 18th. The recipient was Albert Murphy, 58, a retired butcher from Chomedey, Quebec. Murphy received the heart of Therese Rondeau, 38, a pregnant mother of four who died May 30 of a cerebral hemmorhage. Dr. Pierre Grondin headed the 27-man surgical team that performed the operation.

Heart transplants are routine today but they were a brand-new and trail-blazing procedure in 1968. Murphy died just 46 hours after the start of the operation on June 1, 1968.

3:30 a.m., Wed., Sept. 29, 1943 – Lech Walesa, the father of the Solidarity Movement, was born in Popowo, Poland.

Walesa, an electrician, was working at the Lenin Shipyard in Gdansk when he was fired for taking part in protests against the government. In 1980, he gained worldwide attention as leader of the strikes that led to the formation of the National Solidarity Federation. In December, 1981, the Polish government suspended Solidarity and imposed martial law. Walesa was arrested and finally released in November, 1982.

Walesa won the Nobel Peace Prize in 1983. In 1989, he played a key role in the installation of a Solidarity-led coalition government in Poland. He was elected president in 1990 but was defeated in a bid for re-election in 1995 by Aleksander Kwasnieski.

3:30 a.m., Wed., Dec. 16, 1964 – T.S. (Thomas Stearns) Eliot, poet, dramatist, critic who helped usher in poetry's so-called modern movement, died at age 76. Eliot was one of a group of poets who wrote about modern life and in modern language. He burst into prominence with his work "The Waste Land," which dealt with the world after World War I. Eliot is perhaps best known for his poems "Four Quartets," "The Love Song of J. Alfred Prufrock," and "Old Possum's Book of Practical Cats," as well as the two plays he wrote in verse, *Murder in the Cathedral* and *The Cocktail Party.* Eliot, who worked in a bank prior to starting his literary career, was awarded the Nobel Prize for Literature in 1948.

3:30 a.m., Tues., Mar. 6, 1888 – Louisa May Alcott, U.S. novelist remembered for the children's classic *Little Women*, died at a Boston nursing home at age 55. Alcott, whose family's neighbours included writers Henry Thoreau and Ralph Waldo Emerson, was in ill health throughout her life after contracting typhoid while a nurse in the Civil War. She died on the day of her father's funeral.

3:45 a.m., Fri., Sept. 22, 1961 – Argentine swimmer Antonio Abertondo completed the first double crossing of the English Channel. He

Antonio Abertondo completed the first double crossing of the English Channel

The greatest nuclear accident in U.S. history occurred at the Three Mile Island generating plant.

arrived at St. Margarets Bay, England, to finish a journey of 43 hours and 10 minutes. The first part of the swim from England to France took 18 hours, 50 minutes. The second leg took 24 hours, 16 minutes.

3:46 a.m., Fri., Nov. 22, 1935 – The first Pacific airmail flight began when the *China Clipper* took off from San Francisco with 58 bags of mail aboard. After stopping off in Honolulu, Midway, Wake and Guam, the *Clipper* finally landed a week later in Manila at 4:34 p.m., November 29. The 13,212-kilometre (8,210-mile) trip took 59 hours and 45 minutes in air time. It was the first time a plane had flown from California to the Philippines.

3:47 a.m., Wed., Aug. 19, 1942 – The first shots were fired in the Canadian raid on the French coast at Dieppe. The operation, designed to attack German operations and probe the feasibility of an Allied invasion of France, proved to be a disaster. Thousands of Canadian soldiers died in a hail of German artillery and the RAF suffered heavy air losses.

3:58 a.m., Thurs., Mar. 29, 1979 – The greatest nuclear accident in U.S. history occurred at the Three Mile Island generating plant in Pennsylvania. The plant began emitting radiation when problems with its cooling system exposed part of the core, which caused a shutdown. Human error and equipment failure was blamed for the accident, which was brought under control within two days.

Fears that the reactor would explode were not realized. All pregnant women and children within an eight-kilometre (five-mile) radius of the plant were evacuated. But only a small amount of radiation was released, and that inside the plant. The accident set off a flurry of anti-nuclear protests in the U.S.

4 a.m. to 4:59 a.m.

- 🕐 **Dionne quintuplets born**
- 🕐 **Rumble in The Jungle begins**
- 🕐 **Avalanche at Frank, Alberta kills 70**
- 🕐 **First shots of Civil War fired**
- 🕐 **Mikhail Gorbachev under house arrest**
- 🕐 **The Great Escape is discovered**

4:00 **a.m., Mon., May 28, 1934** – The first of five babies was born to Olivia and Elzire Dionne at a farmhouse near Callandar, Ontario. Cecile, Annette, Emilie, Yvonne and Marie Dionne became instant celebrities. The multiple births provided a rare good-news story during a Depression-era time when people were starved for something uplifting. The Dionnes were the first quintuplets on record to survive more than a few days. They weighed a total of 13 pounds, six ounces at birth.

Less than four months after birth, the quintuplets were moved from their parents' home to a nursery where they were kept under guardianship of the Ontario government, officially for health and safekeeping purposes. The children were displayed at the Dafoe Hospital in Callandar, where thousands of visitors streamed by every day (an estimated 141,000 in July, 1934 alone). As the quintuplets grew up, they became increasingly resentful of their exposure to the public, and by the mid-1950s had broken off most contact with their parents. In 1958, however, Cecile found herself back in the spotlight when she became the first quintuplet in history to give birth.

The Ontario government reached a compensation settlement with the Dionne women in the 1990s.

Emilie died of an epileptic seizure in 1954. Marie passed away in 1970.

The world's first cloned mammal from an adult cell gave birth for the first time.

4:00 a.m., Mon., Apr. 13, 1998 – Dolly had a baby! The world's first cloned mammal from an adult cell gave birth for the first time, delivering a lamb named Bonnie. Dolly was naturally mated at the end of 1997 with a Welsh Mountain lamb.

The announcement of Dolly's birth in February, 1997 at the Roslin Institute in Scotland caused quite a stir, raising the issue of human cloning. Team leader Dr. Ian Wilmut added to the speculation when he said scientists could now produce unlimited numbers of identical clones of animals. However, many religious leaders and ethicists were shocked at the news and called for a ban on human cloning.

4:00 a.m., Wed., Oct. 30, 1974 – "The Rumble in the Jungle" began in Kenosha, Zaire. About two hours later, with dawn quickly approaching, Muhammad Ali knocked out George Foreman in the eighth round to regain the heavyweight title.

Ali joined Floyd Patterson as the only heavyweight to regain the world crown after losing it. Ali would lose the crown to Leon Spinks in February, 1978 only to regain it a third time when he beat Spinks in September of the same year. Ali retired in 1979.

The unusual starting time in Zaire was due to pay television commitments in the eastern time zone.

4:00 a.m., Sun., Jan. 28, 1596 – Sir Francis Drake, who captained the first ship to sail completely around the world, died of dysentery on a ship off the east coast of Panama. The great explorer and adventurer had been hunting for treasure in the region.

Drake was knighted by Queen Elizabeth I in 1580 after his historic three-year sail around the world. But he was not so highly regarded by the Spanish, whose ships he plundered for treasure during the voyage. All the money went into England's coffers, resulting in a lowering of taxes in Great Britain.

4:00 a.m., Tues., June 16, 1970 – Brian Piccolo, Chicago Bears running back praised for his courage in the face of terminal cancer, died in a New York hospital. He was only 26. Piccolo, former Wake Forest star who led the country in scoring and ground yardage in 1964, was stricken in November, 1969 – one year after his best pro campaign. Teammate Gale Sayers, his closest friend on the team, said just prior to Piccolo's death, he was "proud to have a friend who spells out the word courage 24 hours of the day every day of his life."

4:00 **a.m., Fri., Nov. 4, 1966** – The Arno river rose causing a flood to hit Florence, Italy, destroying numerous irreplaceable art treasures. A total of 1,400 works were lost, including Cimabue's *Crucifixion* and works by Uccello, Botticelli, Lorenzetti and Martini. Numerous records were destroyed, including the entire collection at the Music Conservatory library and 10 per cent of the state archives. More than 600,000 tons of debris were left in the wake of the Arno flood and 5,000 families were left homeless. Cleanup efforts were hampered by the fact oil storage tanks had broken open to create a sticky, black mixture of petroleum and sand.

Florence has been hit with over 100 moderate to major floods since 1333.

4:00 **a.m., Wed., Jan. 10, 1883** – One of America's worst hotel blazes erupted in Milwaukee's Newhall Hotel. Seventy-one people died in the firetrap structure, largely as the result of poor safety conditions.

Three years earlier, local fire insurance companies refused to offer insurance coverage to the hotel after finding dry woodwork, flimsy, unbricked partitions and no fire escapes. Among those who escaped the fire was General Tom Thumb, P.T. Barnum's famous midget, along with his wife. Firefighter Herman Strauss gained national fame when he personally carried 16 girls to safety.

4:10 **a.m., Wed., Apr. 29, 1903** – An avalanche roared down on the mining town of Frank, Alberta. Less than two minutes later, an estimated 70 people were dead and the town devastated in one of the worst landslides in recorded history.

The town of Frank had been built around the turn of the century at the foot of Turtle Mountain, a geologically unstable mountain which was primed for a slide. The town serviced coal mines in Turtle Mountain, and for a while times were very good. Then came the night of the avalanche. One eyewitness said he heard a strange whistling roar just before the landslide hit.

A flood hit Florence, Italy, destroying numerous irreplaceable art treasures.

Queen Victoria, whose 63-year reign is the longest of any British monarch, was born.

At that moment, a mass of limestone half a mile square separated from the mountain and headed toward Frank. It wiped out a bridge before burying the south side of Frank under 90 million tons of limestone. Amazingly, 17 miners who had been sealed into their mine by the slide emerged unharmed 13 hours later, having dug their way out.

Frank eventually recovered from the catastrophe, but the mine was closed in 1918 for safety reasons. To this day, the scar left by the limestone break is still visible on the east face of Turtle Mountain.

4:15 a.m., Mon, May 24, 1819 – Queen Victoria, whose 63-year reign is the longest of any British monarch, was born at Kensington Palace. Her father called her his "pretty little princess, plump as a partridge."

Such was Victoria's influence that the years she ruled the British Empire are known as Victorian Times or the Victorian Era. During her reign, Britain acquired many new colonies, establishing an empire "where the sun never sets." Queen Victoria's dignity and stability helped restore the popularity of the monarchy. Victoria never recovered from the death of her beloved husband Albert in 1861. She spent the last 40 years of her life in mourning. She survived seven assassination attempts during her reign.

Victoria died at 6:30 p.m., Tuesday, January 22, 1901. She was 82 and even though half blind with cataracts, insisted on carrying out her duties until the end. She was succeeded by her son, Edward VII.

4:15 a.m., Mon., March 11, 1867 – After four weeks of debate, Ontario and Quebec voted to unite with the colonies of Nova Scotia, New Brunswick and Prince Edward Island. The motion carried by a vote of 91–33. On July 1, 1867, the new Dominion of Canada was proclaimed. *(see 10:15 p.m.)*

4:20 a.m., Thurs., Aug. 8, 1918 – The Battle of Amiens, often called the "Black Day of the German army," began as Allied forces attacked German positions in dense fog. It was a surprise attack; Allied troops had assembled in the Somme region near the German 18th Army in secret. Success was almost instantaneous; German losses outnumbered Allied casualties more than 2–1. More than 30,000 Germans surrendered to the Allies after a month-long battle that broke the German will on the Western Front and all but sealed the Allied victory.

4:30 a.m., Fri., Apr. 12, 1861 – The opening shots of the Civil War were fired as Confederate forces began bombarding Fort Sumter in Charleston, S.C. Union commander Major Robert Anderson surrendered three days later, marching his 79 men men out of the fort with colours flying. In what must have been a surreal scene, women in gowns and men in evening dress watched the battle on Charleston's waterfront, unaware that America's bloodiest domestic conflict lay ahead.

4:30 a.m., 1980 – Terry Fox began each day of his Marathon of Hope across Canada at this early hour. But on September 1, 1980 – day 143 of his heroic attempt to run across Canada on one leg and an artificial limb – Fox had to abandon his run outside Thunder Bay, Ontario. He had completed 5,379 kilometres (3,339 miles) to that point. Fox's primary cancer had spread to a secondary location, his lungs. Fox died on June 28, 1981 at Royal Westminster Hospital in New Westminster, B.C. This brave and inspirational Canadian would have been 23 one month later.

Fox, a native of Winnipeg, discovered in 1977 that he had a malignant tumour in his right leg. As a result, the leg was amputated six inches above the knee. The night before his operation, Fox read about an amputee runner and the seed was planted for his fund-raising run across Canada.

On April 12, 1980, Terry Fox dipped his artificial leg into the Atlantic Ocean off St. Johns, Newfoundland. For the next five months, he would run an average of 43 kilometres (26 miles) a day, his artificial leg notwithstanding. The determined marathoner had already run over 5,000 kilometres (3,000 miles) in training for this difficult journey.

Fox was showered with awards both before and after death. Shortly after his run ended, he became the youngest Companion of the Order of Canada. After his death in 1981, he was posthumously inducted into the Canadian Sports Hall of Fame. Also in 1981, the first Terry Fox Run was held at 760 sites in Canada and around the world. More than 300,000 people participated and $3.5 million was raised; the Terry Fox Run has become an annual event. By the end of the 1990s, total monies raised in Fox's name were $250 million; annual participation in his run had topped one million.

The opening shots of the Civil War were fired.

The world's first communications satellite was launched from Cape Canaveral, Florida.

4:30 a.m., Fri., July 18, 1817 – Jane Austen, English novelist whose timeless works included *Pride and Prejudice*, *Sense and Sensibility* and *Emma*, died at age 41. Austin suffered from Addison's disease, a then-unknown malady. But she became the first person to describe the syndrome through notes. Her last words were "I want nothing but death."

4:30 a.m., Fri., Aug. 22, 1862 – Claude-Achille Debussy, an "Impressionist" often called the most French of all French composers, was born in Saint-Germain-En-Laye, France. Debussy, a quiet man who seldom performed or conducted his major compositions, nevertheless gained everlasting fame for such works as "l'Enfant Prodigue" and the opera *Pelleas and Melisande*. His advanced musical ideas were panned early in his career, but he gradually gained a public following and recognition as one of the foremost composers of the late 19th and early 20th century.

Debussy died at 10:00 p.m., Monday, March 25, 1918. He was 55.

4:35 a.m., Tues., July 10, 1962 – *Telstar*, the world's first communications satellite, was launched from Cape Canaveral, Florida. The next day, Americans saw their first live pictures from Europe (see 1:00 a.m.). A song about the satellite, "Telstar" by the Tornados, went to number one on the Billboard charts in December, 1962.

4:40 a.m., Tues., Aug. 17, 1920 – Ray Chapman of the Cleveland Indians became the only player to die from injuries received in a major league baseball game. Chapman succumbed to severe head injuries in a New York hospital. He was 29.

The previous afternoon, in the fifth inning of a game against the New York Yankees, Chapman was hit in the left temple by a ball pitched by submarine-style pitcher Carl Mays. Chapman had a reputation for crowding the plate and Mays was known for brushing back batters. Witnesses say Chapman seemed frozen to the spot as the fateful pitch sailed toward his head, hitting him with a resounding crack. Chapman was stunned but was able to walk off the field with the assistance of two teammates. Initial reports on his condition were favourable, but he did not survive the night.

Chapman's wife of less than a year committed suicide eight years later. A daughter born after Chapman's death died after catching the measles in

1929. Mays continued to pitch in the major leagues, retiring in 1929 and dying in 1971.

4:45 **a.m., Mon., May 1, 1978** – Japanese explorer and mountaineer Naomi Uemara became the first person to reach the North Pole solo. Uemara travelled 724 kilometres (450 miles) in two months, averaging nearly 12.8 kilometres (eight miles) a day with his sled drawn by 17 huskies.

4:50 **a.m., Mon., Aug. 19, 1991** – Soviet President Mikhail Gorbachev was placed under house arrest at his vacation home on the Crimean Sea. A mind-boggling series of events would follow.

Gorbachev was the victim of a coup led by a group of Communist hard-liners who believed his reforms had gone too far. The group put Vice-President Gennady Yanayev in charge of the country and the world held its breath as tanks and other military vehicles rumbled into Moscow.

What the plotters didn't count on was Russian Federation President Boris Yeltsin and the determination of a Soviet people used to democracy. In addition, support in the military was soft. By Tuesday, it became obvious the hard-liners faced an uphill battle. By Wednesday, they were on the run. Early Thursday morning, Gorbachev returned to Moscow and most of the plotters had been arrested.

The biggest news was yet to come. Within days, Gorbachev issued a decree outlawing the Communist Party, then watched as one by one, the Baltic states declared their independence followed by the other Soviet republics. By the end of the year, the Soviet Union, for all intents and purposes, had ceased to exist. *(see 11:40 a.m.)*

4:50 **a.m., Fri., Oct. 8, 1869** – Franklin Pierce, the 14th president, who once said the Presidency would be "utterly repugnant" to him, died at his home in Concord, Massachusetts. He was 64 and had been suffering from dropsy and inflammation of the stomach.

Pierce, a former U.S. senator and congressman, was a compromise choice for the Democratic nomination in 1852 when the convention dead-locked. After defeating Winfield Scott in the general election, Pierce quickly alienated many when he enforced the Fugitive Slave Act, which permitted slave owners to seize black people in the north as fugitives without due

Soviet President Mikhail Gorbachev was placed under house arrest.

The most famous of all World War II prisoner-of-war escapes, was discovered by German guards.

process of law. On the positive side, he purchased land from Mexico to give the U.S. its present southwest border.

Pierce, considered among the most handsome of presidents, fought a life-long battle with alcoholism that eventually led to his death. He holds two distinctions. First, he is the only elected president who ran and lost in a bid for re-nomination by his own party for a second term; Pierce lost to James Buchanan. All the other elected one-term presidents chose not to run again or died in office. Pierce is also the only president whose cabinet did not change in any way during his four-year term – he had the same advisors going in as when he left.

In 1863, Pierce was denounced by many as a traitor when he made a speech criticizing the Civil War.

4:50 a.m., Sat., Mar. 25, 1944 – "The Great Escape," perhaps the most famous of all World War II prisoner-of-war escapes, was discovered by German guards. The discovery was made eight hours after the breakout from Stalag Luft III began and after 76 Allied prisoners had escaped. Fifty of the escapees were recaptured and shot, while 23 others were sent back to prison camps. Only three made it back home – two via boat to Sweden; one through Spain with help from the Spanish resistance. The story is told in the 1960s classic movie *The Great Escape*.

4:50 a.m., Sun., Nov. 14, 1915 – Booker T. Washington, who like Martin Luther King half a century later devoted his life to advancing the African-American cause, died of hardening of the arteries at his home in Tuskegee, Alabama. He was believed to have been 57. Born into slavery in Malden, West Virginia, Washington became an outspoken champion of African-American advancement, founding two schools for black people, and writing numerous books on the problems faced by his people. In his eulogy, he was called "the Moses of his race."

4:50 a.m., Sat., June 17, 1939 – Eugene Weidmann, convicted of luring six women to their deaths, died in the last public guillotining in France. Weidmann, whose three accomplices escaped the death penalty, listened as the bloodthirsty crowd milling outside the jail waited for his execution. Every room, balcony and window overlooking the execution site outside the Palais de Justice was rented at high prices. However, the execution was completed so quickly most people missed it.

Negative public reaction to the execution led to a law outlawing public executions in France.

4:53 a.m., Tues., July 20, 1976 – On the seventh anniversary of Neil Armstrong's historic walk on the moon, another space first: *Viking I* became the first spaceship to land on Mars. The craft sent back surprisingly clear pictures that revealed a rocky, somewhat earth-like terrain. However, *Viking I* was unable to detect the presence of living things. Its sister ship, *Viking II*, reached the red planet three months later.

Viking I became the first spaceship to land on Mars.

5 a.m. to 5:59 a.m.

- 🕔 **Soviets begin crushing Hungarian revolt**
- 🕔 **Great San Francisco earthquake hits**
- 🕔 **Federal agents seize Elian Gonzalez**
- 🕔 **First nuclear bomb tested**
- 🕔 **Soviets shoot down Korean jetliner**
- 🕔 **Germany declares war on Russia**

5:00 **a.m., Mon., Oct. 16, 1995** – Ceremonies began for the Million Man March in Washington, D.C. Hundreds of thousands of African-American men converged on the Washington Mall for what Nation of Islam leader Louis Farrakhan called a "holy day of atonement and conciliation." The 12-hour rally was highlighted by a speech from Farrakhan. The National Park Service estimated that 400,000 people attended the event. That compares with an estimated 250,000 at the 1963 rally in Washington which featured Martin Luther King's famous "I Have A Dream" speech.

5:00 **a.m., Sun., Nov. 4, 1956** – Soviet troops moved into Hungary to crush a revolution in the Communist satellite. Thousands of Russian tanks poured into the capital of Budapest as Soviet planes roared overhead. Within hours, Premier Imre Nagy and most of his government were taken prisoner, and 10,000 Hungarians lay dead with another 30,000 wounded. Janos Kadar, who, as First Secretary of the Hungarian Communist Party, had only days before promised to negotiate a Russian withdrawal, changed stripes and announced he had formed a new government and wanted to help the Russian cause. The Hungarian revolution was over.

5:00 **a.m., Sat., Apr. 27, 1822** – Ulysses S. Grant, who would become the 18th president and a key figure of the Civil War, was born in Point Pleasant, Ohio. His parents did not give him a name until a month after his birth, when they called him Hiram Ulysses Grant. Grant did not like the initials, H.U.G. When he entered West Point, and was mistakenly enrolled as Ulysses Simpson Grant, he kept the name. The initials U.S.G. were preferable to those of his birthright.

Ulysses S. Grant was born.

Grant gained prominence in February, 1862, when he scored the first major Union victory of the Civil War by capturing Fort Donelson, Tennessee. He was promoted, and by March, 1864 had risen to the rank of commander of all the Union armies. In April, 1865, Confederate General Robert E. Lee surrendered to Grant at Appomattox, Virginia.

A national hero, Grant easily gained the Republican nomination in 1868, defeating Horatio Seymour in the general election. He defeated newspaper giant Horace Greeley in 1872 to win a second term as president but did not run in 1876. In 1880, he came within 66 votes of becoming the first president nominated for a third term, but eventually lost to James Garfield.

Grant, above-board himself, presided over the first presidential administration marked by major scandals. As a result, his tenure in office was considered a failure, even though he enjoyed high personal popularity. Nearly penniless during his late retirement years, Grant rushed to complete his autobiography so he could provide his family with financial security. He completed his *Memoirs* one week before his death, dictating the last part of the book in great pain because of throat cancer. He had, in fact, become addicted to cocaine during his last year of life because doctors had to swab his throat constantly with cocaine solutions to relieve the almost unbearable pain of his cancerous lesions.

Ulysses S. Grant died at 8:07 a.m., Thursday, July 23, 1885. Throat cancer, likely a product of his 20-cigar-a-day smoking habit, was the cause of death. The General was 53. An estimated one million people attended Grant's funeral procession in New York City. Grant's *Memoirs* are still considered a masterful account of military strategy.

5:00 **a.m., Sun., Oct. 7, 1849** – Edgar Allan Poe, master of the macabre, died of fluid accumulation in the brain. He was 40. Abandoned by family and friends, his last words were "Lord help my poor soul."

Mati Hari was awakened in her cell outside Paris and told she would be executed.

Poe, whose best–known works include *The Murders in the Rue Morgue* and *The Pit and the Pendulum*, wrote many of his books under the influence of opium. He also drank heavily, and is said to have gone on a five-day binge just before his death. While known chiefly as a writer of grotesque mysteries and horror stories, Poe was also a dramatic poet and a writer of detective stories.

Each year since 1949, on the night of the anniversary of Poe's death, a mysterious stranger has entered the Baltimore cemetery to leave a partial bottle of cognac and three roses as tribute on Poe's grave. The stranger, known as the "Poe Toaster," has never been identified, nor does anyone know his reason for leaving the cognac (which does not figure in any of Poe's works). No attempt is made to stop or hinder the stranger. In fact, his annual arrival is watched from a distance by several Poe fans.

5:00 a.m., Thurs., July 21, 1796 – Robert Burns, perhaps the most celebrated of all Scottish poets, died of heart trouble at the age of 37. He did not die, as many have supposed, of alcoholism. His sixth child was born just four days later on the day of his funeral.

Burns, who published his first works in desperation only when his family farm faced ruin, gained great popularity with a series of poems in ballad style. He is remembered annually every January 25 on "Robbie Burns Day." And New Year's revellers annually sing the words to his poem "Auld Lang Syne" every January 1.

5:00 a.m., Tues., Apr. 16, 1912 – In one of history's most overshadowed events, Harriot Quimby took off in her attempt to become the first woman to fly across the English Channel. She succeeded, but her achievement was quickly obscured by news of the sinking of the *Titanic* just the day before. Needless to say, Harriot Quimby received no ticker-tape parades.

5:00 a.m., Mon., Oct. 15, 1917 – Exotic dancer-turned-suspected-spy Mati Hari was awakened in her cell outside Paris and told she would be executed that very morning. A few hours later, the former stripper, who allegedly passed military secrets to the Germans, was shot by a 12-man firing squad.

So ended the life of Margaretha Gertruda Zelle, Dutch-born beauty who changed her name to Mati Hari in 1904 and became one of Europe's most famous exotic dancers – supposedly the first to perform totally naked. She picked up many "friends" along the way, one of which happened to be the German chief of intelligence in Spain. And while there is considerable doubt as to whether she actually passed along secrets to the enemy, she was arrested for espionage in February, 1917. Hari declared her innocence, but was executed within seven months of her arrest. She was 41.

In one of the most famous of all earthquakes, a seismic shock hit the San Francisco area.

5:00 **a.m., Wed., Sept. 1, 1557** – Jacques Cartier, legendary French explorer, died in St-Malo, France at the age of 65.

Cartier is credited with discovering Canada in 1535 and was the first to chart the St. Lawrence River. His discovery of the St. Lawrence – originally called the Rivière du Canada – enabled France to occupy the interior of North America. However, his original goal of finding a passage to India was not met. In 1541, Cartier helped establish the first French colony in North America at Roberval. He retired in 1542 after what he thought were gold and diamonds brought back from the New World proved worthless.

5:13 **a.m., Wed., Apr. 18, 1906** – In one of the most famous of all earthquakes, a seismic shock hit the San Francisco area. The surface displacement of 402 kilometres (250 miles) along the San Andreas fault remains the longest in U.S. history.

It was fire, not the quake that actually caused the most damage in San Francisco. Immediate damage from the quake was moderate, however the break of water, gas and electrical lines allowed fires to spread rapidly. By the time the fire burned out three days later, numerous landmarks were gone and 75 per cent of the city lay in ruins.

It is believed 700 to 800 people may have died in the San Francisco area from the quake and fire. The City Hall – built over a period of 20 years – was reduced to rubble in less than a minute.

5:15 **a.m., Sat., April 22, 2000** – Heavily-armed U.S. federal agents burst into a Miami house where relatives of six-year-old Elian Gonzalez had been holding the Cuban shipwreck survivor. After finding Elian hiding in a closet with one of his protectors, the agents whisked him

The first atomic bomb was tested near Bingham, New Mexico.

out of the house, bundled him into a minivan and flew him to Andrew's Air Force Base outside Washington for a reunion with his Cuban father. An Associated Press picture showed a clearly terrified Elian being seized at gunpoint. Riots continued in Miami for hours after the seizure.

The Elian saga began on November 25, 1999 when the boy was found floating on an inner tube near Fort Lauderdale, Florida. A boat carrying Elian, his mother and two others from Cuba to Florida had sunk, drowning all but Elian. The following day, the child was turned over to his relatives in Miami, and the long tug-of-war and public debate over his fate began. On March 22, a U.S. district judge ruled that U.S. Immigration had the authority to return Elian to his father, which they did on April 23.

5:29 :45 a.m., Mon., July 16, 1945 – The first atomic bomb was tested near Bingham, New Mexico. An electronic signal detonated the bomb, setting off the greatest explosion man had ever known. The desert lit up as if it were noon; a huge flame hurled rocks and debris into the air while sending out a shock wave and a deafening roar. A huge mushroom cloud hung over the site and the steel tower on which the bomb sat was vaporized. After the blast, project head J. Robert Oppenheimer quoted Vishnu from the *Bhagavad Gita*: "I am become Death, the destroyer of worlds."

Less than a month later, the bomb would be used for the first time in warfare, hastening the end of World War II. *(see 8:15 a.m.)*

5:30 a.m., Thurs., Sept. 1, 1983 – A Soviet jet fighter shot down an unarmed Korean civilian jumbo jetliner. All 269 people aboard KAL flight 007 died.

Soviet officials claimed the plane was on a spy mission because it flew over the strategic Sakhalin Island, straying far from its normal flight path. They said the plane's pilot did not respond to warnings. But U.S. Secretary of State George Schultz said there was no excuse for shooting an unarmed civilian plane out of the air. Sixty-one Americans were among those who died when the plane plunged into the Sea of Japan.

5:30 a.m., Fri., Apr. 7, 1972 – Joe Gallo, powerful Mafia figure nicknamed "Crazy Joe," was gunned down as he celebrated his 43rd birthday in a New York restaurant. Gallo had ordered a second helping of food when a dark-haired man appeared at the side door and started shooting. Gallo, mortally wounded, returned fire and staggered out the front door into the street where he died. His killer hopped into a getaway car and disappeared.

Many speculate the Gallo slaying was in retaliation for the shooting of Joseph Columbo about a year before. At 11:45 a.m., on Monday, June 28, 1971, reputed Mafia boss Joseph Columbo was shot and critically wounded at an Italian-American civil rights rally in New York City. His assailant, a 25-year-old black man, was shot and killed at the scene. Columbo, shot in the head and neck, spent his remaining years in hospital in a vegetative state.

5:30 a.m., Fri., Sept. 29, 1978 – Pope John Paul I, installed as leader of the Roman Catholic church just a month before, was found dead in his bed at the Vatican. John Paul was found by his secretary, who said the Pontiff was apparently reading a book when stricken with a heart attack. Albino Cardinal Luciani, the former Patriarch of Venice, had a history of poor health. He was 65.

Only Stephen II, who died two days after his election in 752, had a shorter reign than John Paul I. John Paul was succeeded by the first Polish-born Pope, Karol Wojtyla, who took the name John Paul II.

5:30 a.m., Sun., June 22, 1941 – Germany declared war on Russia. The Germans had amassed some two million men – the largest concentration of military force in history up to then – along the Russian border in what they called "Operation Barbarossa." Hitler confidently predicted the German army would make it all the way to Moscow in just eight weeks to begin dictating peace terms to the Russians. The determined Soviet army and the bitter Russian winter proved him wrong as the Germans were stopped 64 kilometres (40 miles) from their goal. After a defeat at Stalingrad in January, 1943, the tide turned in favour of the Russians. Following another setback at Kursk in the summer of 1943, the tattered and badly beaten German army was in full retreat.

5:30 a.m., Mon., Apr. 19, 1965 – WINS New York became one of the first radio stations in the U.S. to switch to an all-news format (third, behind a station in Rosarito, Mexico and another in Chicago). WINS, unlike

Germany declared war on Russia.

The first Canadian all-news station was CKO-FM in Toronto.

its predecessors, remained "all news, all the time" as the 21st century began.

Previously, WINS was one of the top rock 'n' roll stations in the United States. It was where the legendary Alan Freed began his career as a star in the 1950s. WINS played its last scheduled rock and roll song on Sunday, April 18, at 7:57 p.m - "Out In The Streets" by the Shangri-Las, introduced by deejay, Johnny Holliday.

Public-service programming filled the gap until the WINS all-news format began.

The first Canadian all-news station was CKO-FM in Toronto, which signed on at 6 a.m. Friday, July 1, 1977, and signed off without prior warning at noon, Friday, November 10, 1989, with a brief announcement by the station manager.

5:37 a.m., Sun., July 25, 1909 – French aviator Louis Bleriot became the first man to fly over the English Channel. Bleriot needed only 37 minutes to fly the 33 kilometres (21 miles) from Sangatte near Calais, France to Dover, England. He collected a $2,500 prize offered by the *London Daily Mail* for the first flight across the channel. He was also awarded the Legion of Honour for the flight, which was made in a 24-horsepower, single propeller monoplane. During the flight, a French destroyer remained on guard in the channel in case rescue was needed but the event went off without a hitch. Bleriot was the first man to reach the English continent by air.

5:40 a.m., Wed., Aug. 15, 1945 – U.S. Navy pilot Lieutenant Commander Reidy gunned down a Japanese reconnaissance plane for the last confirmed aerial victory of the war. Five minutes later, the war was officially declared over, and all Japanese warplanes were grounded.

5:40 a.m., Sat., Jan. 23, 1909 – In a mishap that unwittingly heralded the beginning of a new age in communications, steamships *Republic* and *Florida* collided 281 kilometres (175 miles) east of New York City. Shortly after the collision, the *Republic*'s radio officer, Jack Binns, sent out the first wireless distress call (C.Q.D.— or Come, Quick, Danger).

The SS *Baltic* was the first rescue ship to arrive on the scene. She took on passengers from both of the collision victims. All passengers survived.

Florida eventually made it to New York under her own steam, but *Republic* foundered under tow. Wireless was made mandatory on all ships after this incident.

5:45 **a.m., Fri., Aug. 14, 1936** – A 22-year-old black man was pronounced dead in the last public execution in the United States. Rainey Bethea, convicted in the death of a 67-year-old white woman, was hanged from a scaffold in a field near Owensboro, Kentucky. Thousands of whites, many of them drunk, cheered as the hangman sprang the trap. Many tried to tear off pieces of Bethea's clothing or flesh as he dangled from the scaffold.

Indignation at the incident was such that another state-scheduled hanging five days later was done in private.

5:51 **a.m., Tues., June 12, 1979** – Californian Bryan Allen began his quest to become the first man to fly the English Channel in a muscle-powered machine. Two hours and 49 minutes after taking off from Folkestone, England in the newly-designed Gossamer Albatross, Allen landed 37 kilometres (23 miles) away at Cap Gris-Nez, France.

Allen powered the craft with his feet, like a bicyclist, pedalling furiously to keep the propeller churning at a rate of 100 revolutions per minute. The craft travelled between 17 and 20 kilometres (11 and 13 miles) an hour.

Allen and his partner Paul McCready won a £100,000 prize put up by British industrialist Henry Kremer for becoming first to fly across the channel solely on muscle power.

The last public execution in the United States was held.

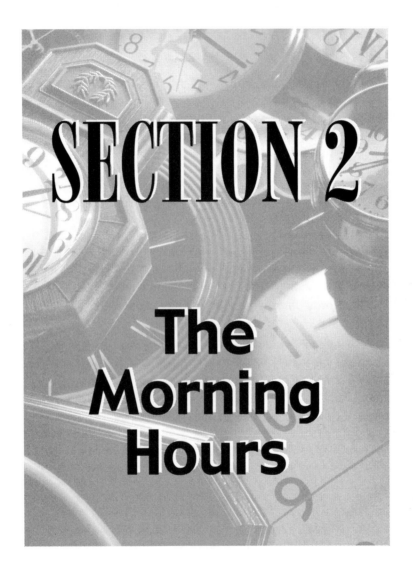

SECTION 2

The Morning Hours

6 a.m. to 6:59 a.m.

- ⊙ **Korean War begins**
- ⊙ **First subway opens in London**
- ⊙ **Black Hole of Calcutta opened**
- ⊙ **Battle of Midway begins**
- ⊙ **Elvis inducted into the Army**
- ⊙ **Amelia Earhart takes off on fateful voyage**

6:00 a.m., Sun., June 25, 1950 – The Korean War, which would last three years and take more than two million lives, began as North Korea crossed the 38th parallel into South Korea. Five days later, President Truman authorized the use of American ground forces to repel the invaders from the North. The United Nations agreed to the use of force and American General Douglas MacArthur was placed in charge of all troops, U.S. and U.N. The Soviet Union promised not to intervene militarily.

6:00 a.m., Tues., June 28, 1836 – James Madison, the fourth president, and the smallest Chief Executive at 5 feet 4 inches and 100 pounds, died of heart failure at his estate in Montpelier, Virginia. He was 85.

Madison was a veteran of Virginia politics who played a key role in the drafting of the Constitution in 1787. Hand-picked by President Thomas Jefferson to be his successor, Madison easily won the general elections of 1808 and 1812.

The chief event during Madison's tenure was the War of 1812, often called the second War of Independence. Unable to convince Britain to respect America's neutral rights at sea, Madison asked a badly divided Congress for a declaration of war June 1, 1812 and got it 17 days later. The war raged for three years and after a slow start, the Americans were able to

**The seige of
Oka, Quebec
began.**

hold off the British. During the conflict, Madison became the only president to engage in combat, albeit briefly, while in office. The war helped promote the U.S. from a largely agrarian nation to an industrial force no longer dependent on Europe.

Madison's wife, Dolly Madison, has gone down in history as one of America's most popular First Ladies, a vivacious woman who charmed the capital as few others have done. She was also brave. In 1814 she helped arrange for the safe transport of some valuable treasures from the White House, even as British troops advanced on the building. Among the items she saved before the White House was torched was Gilbert Stuart's famous full-length portrait of George Washington.

James Madison was the first president to be inaugurated outdoors, in 1817. Outdoor inaugurations are the standard practice today.

6:00 a.m., Wed., July 11, 1990 – The seige of Oka, Quebec began as, in what one witness compared to "a war movie," officers began moving into an area that had been seized by Mohawks from the nearby Kanasatake reserve. The officers lobbed tear gas and fired shots. When the smoke had cleared, one man – Corporel Marcel Lemay, 31 – lay dead. The Mohawks blocked off a municipal road to protect their claim to land that the town of Oka wanted in order to expand a nine-hole golf course.

The stand-off ended peacefully after about one month.

6:00 a.m., Fri., Sept. 22, 1989 – Hurricane Hugo, one of the most destructive hurricanes ever, was downgraded to a tropical storm by the U.S. Weather Service. While only 38 people died – a testament to advanced hurricane warning systems – the storm caused millions of dollars in property damage as it ripped through the Caribbean and then hit the Carolinas with winds of 217 kilometres (135 miles) an hour. Waves five metres (17 feet) high crashed into the coastal cities of Charleston, South Carolina and Charlotte, North Carolina The storm continued north before eventually dying out over Canada.

6:00 a.m., Thurs., Nov. 17, 1558 – Mary I, the English queen known as "Bloody Mary" because she revived laws for punishing heretics, died of degeneration of her heart and arteries at age 44. During her reign, many

Protestants were put to death as Mary hoped to return England to the Catholic faith. Among her victims was the Archbishop of Canterbury, Thomas Cranmer. Mary I reigned for five years following the death of her father, King Henry VIII. She was succeeded by Queen Elizabeth I, a Protestant.

6:00 a.m., Sat., Jan. 10, 1863 – The first underground railway, or subway, opened in London after four years of construction. The Metropolitan railway was 6.4 kilometres (four miles) long and contained seven stops in a 33-minute journey. Compare that to the London Underground of today, which contains more than 400 km (250 miles) of track and nearly 300 stations.

6:00 a.m., Tues., Aug. 30, 1988 – Marathon swimmer Vicki Keith waded out of Lake Ontario after successfully completing her summer-long quest to swim all five Great Lakes. Keith finished in style during her final lake swim of 51 kilometres (31.7 miles) when she set a world record for the longest swim by a woman using the butterfly stroke (38 kilometres/24 miles).

Keith began her quest by swimming Lake Erie July 1. She conquered Lake Huron July 17, Lake Michigan July 26 and Lake Superior August 15. She was the first person to swim the latter three.

6:00 a.m., Sat., Dec. 11, 1999 – One of Canada's greatest athletes – the beloved horse "Big Ben" – died. The show-jumping legend was euthanized at Millarbrooke Farm near Ottawa to ease his suffering after a bout of colic.

Big Ben, ridden by Ian Millar of Perth, Ontario, won $1.5 million and became the first horse to win two World Cup finals. The big horse competed in three Olympic Games, unusual in a sport where careers are short. Big Ben is one of only two animals inducted into the Canadian Sports Hall of Fame – Northern Dancer is the other. Both were honoured with their own Canadian stamps in 1999.

Big Ben, whose original name was Winston before Millar changed it, enjoyed incredible popularity. At one 1994 appearance in London, Ontario, some 3,000 fans waited two and a half hours in line to see Big Ben. The horse even received Valentines. Big Ben lived 23 years.

The first underground railway, or subway, opened in London.

The Battle of Midway, one of the greatest naval encounters in history, began.

6:05 **a.m., Tues., Oct. 23, 1917** – The first American shots were fired in World War I as the First Infantry Division of the 6th Field Artillery (Battery C) shelled a German trench 0.8 kilometres (a half mile) away near Nancy, France. There were no casualties.

6:05 **a.m., Mon., Nov. 7, 1910** – Count Leo Tolstoy, Russian novelist and philosopher who wrote the classic novel *War and Peace*, died of a fever in a railroad station in Astapovo, the Soviet Union. Tolstoy, who at the time was attempting to leave his wife Sonya, was 82.

War and Peace, the story of two Russian families at the time of the Napoleonic Wars, is considered by some to be the greatest novel of all time. It took Tolstoy seven years to write the more than 1,000-page masterpiece, and he followed that up with another famous novel, *Anna Karenina*. Tolstoy's interests turned to philosophy during his later years.

6:15 **a.m., Mon., June 21, 1756** – Surviving prisoners in the Black Hole of Calcutta were released after a horrific night. One hundred and forty-five men and one girl had been packed into a sweltering 5.4 x 4.5 metre (18 foot x 14 foot, 10 inch) cell with no food or water and only two small windows for ventilation.

The prisoners, all British, were entombed on orders of the Nabob of Bengal, Siraj-ud-duala who hated the English. Temporary British commander John Holwell told the Nabob that a secret fortune did not exist. Siraj-ud–duala did not believe the statement, and the imprisonment was his answer.

Only 23 of the 146 prisoners survived, including the girl, 15-year-old Mary Carey. Throughout the 10-hour ordeal, the men, packed together like sardines, died of thirst and suffocation. After the doors were finally opened, it took 20 minutes to clear the corpses so the survivors could get out. Carey and Holwell remained in custody until Siraj-ud-duala was killed by the British one year later.

6:15 **a.m., Thurs., June 4, 1942** – The Battle of Midway, one of the greatest naval encounters in history, began as Japanese fighter planes attacked the U.S. fortress on the strategic island of Midway. The mission proved to be a disaster for the Japanese, who were badly beaten in what turned out to be a turning point in the Pacific War. The Americans sank three Japanese aircraft carriers and another dozen or so vessels were damaged. American losses were slight. Within six months of Japan's defeat – its first major setback of the war – the Japanese were forced to give up their plan to isolate Australia, and found themselves on the defensive.

6:15 a.m., Mon., Apr. 19, 1824 – English poet Lord Byron died of malaria in Greece where he was helping the Greeks in their war of independence against the Turks. Byron, who was 36, was mourned in Greece as a national hero. He is best known for the poems "Childe Harold's Pilgramage" and "Don Juan."

6:15 a.m., Wed., Feb. 17, 1909 – Geronimo, legendary leader of the Apache Indians, died of pneumonia at Fort Sill, Oklahoma, aged 80. He had fallen off his horse into a creek a few days before.

Geronimo was a thorn in the side of the Americans and Spaniards during the latter part of the 19th century, organizing raids that supposedly killed 2,500 U.S. citizens. After escaping from captivity four times, he was finally confined to a reservation where he concentrated on ranching. Geronimo's name is Spanish for "Jerome."

6:20 a.m., Sun., Oct. 23, 1983 – Two hundred and eighteen U.S. Marines were killed when a terrorist drove a truck full of explosives into the Marine headquarters building in Beirut. The blast turned four stories of the structure into rubble. As one observer described it: "I haven't seen carnage like that since Vietnam." Moments after the attack, another bomb-laden truck crashed into the compound used by French peacekeeping forces, killing 58. Terrorist group Free Islamic Revolution Movement claimed responsibility for both attacks.

6:30 a.m., Wed., Dec. 13, 1939 – British ships opened fire on the German pocket-battleship *Graf Spee* at the Battle of the River Platte off Buenos Aires. The ship eventually escaped to Montevideo, Uruguay but was badly damaged. On December 17, German captain Langsdorff gave the order to scuttle the ship. Three days later, Langsdorff committed suicide.

Geronimo, legendary leader of the Apache Indians, died of pneumonia.

The first photos were taken of the dark, or hidden, side of the moon.

6:30 a.m., Mon., Aug. 23, 1926 – Rudolf Valentino, Italian-born silent screen star and idol to millions of female fans, died of a ruptured appendix and gastric ulcer in a Manhattan hospital. He was 31. Valentino, a former street beggar who starred in such films as *The Four Horsemen of the Apocalypse, The Sheik* and *Blood and Sand*, was deeply mourned. Actress Pola Negri sent 4,000 roses to his funeral while several other fans committed suicide. His funeral in New York was attended by thousands.

6:30 a.m., Fri., July 25, 1834 – Samuel Taylor Coleridge, who along with William Wordsworth started the romantic movement in English poetry, died of heart trouble at age 61. Coleridge, an opium addict since his teens, was supposedly inspired to write his famous poem "Kubla Khan" by an opium dream. He is also remembered for the poem "The Ancient Mariner," the story of a seaman cursed after shooting an albatross.

6:30 a.m., Wed., Oct. 7, 1959 – The first photos were taken of the dark, or hidden, side of the moon by the Soviet lunar probe *Lunik III*. The pictures showed that unlike the moon's visible portion, its far side had a regular pattern of craters, more rugged features, and fewer of the open spaces known as seas. The Soviets took advantage of their discovery to name many of the features, using names such as the Soviet Mountains and the Sea of Moscow.

6:30 a.m., Mon., May 21, 1917 – Adelaide Bunker, last survivor of history's most unusual quartet, died at age 94 in Mount Airy, North Carolina. Adelaide was the widow of Chang Bunker, one-half of the original Siamese twins.

Chang and Eng Bunker were born May 11, 1811 in Siam, joined at the breastbone by a ligament. They would remain attached throughout their entire lives. Despite their condition, Chang and Eng led an incredibly active life, touring the world as the original Siamese twins, then marrying in 1843 and fathering 21 children between them.

Chang, the dominant and more quick-tempered of the pair, died of pneumonia January 17, 1874, and his brother Eng died minutes later, apparently of shock. Doctors later determined that separating the twins would have killed them both.

Eng's wife, Sarah, died in 1892. The last of Chang's children died in 1945. Eng's last offspring died in 1950.

6:34 **a.m., Wed., Sept. 26, 1956** – Babe Zaharias, perhaps the greatest woman athlete of all time, died of cancer. The star of tennis, golf, track and field, basketball, baseball, bowling and diving was 45.

Born Mildred Didriksen (she married wrestler George Zaharias), the "Babe" got her nickname after hitting five home runs in a baseball game. At one time, she held or shared four track records including the javelin, 80-metre hurdles, high jump and long jump. She won two gold medals and one silver at the 1932 Olympics. Babe later turned to golf and won 17 amateur tournaments in a row during 1946 and 1947. She turned pro and promptly won 31 tournaments in eight years, including three U.S. Opens. She also captured the leading money-winning crown for four consecutive years. Seven of her tournament wins came after her first cancer operation in 1953.

A member of the LPGA Hall of Fame, she was voted Woman Athlete of the First Half of the 20th century in an Associated Press poll. As one writer put it: "She won everything but the Kentucky Derby."

6:35 **a.m., Mon., Mar. 24, 1958** – America's number-one rock star became army private #U.S.53310751. Elvis Presley, 23, with 10 number-one songs and four movies behind him, arrived at Local Draft Board 86 in Memphis to be inducted.

Presley spent two years in the army, was given no special privileges and was said by all concerned to have handled the situation well. During his absence, six Elvis songs made the national charts, two of which went to number one. A controversy arose in August, 1958, when Elvis asked for a special pass to visit his dying mother in Memphis. Amid cries of favouritism, he was allowed to see her on her deathbed. Favouritism it was not — such passes are routinely granted to soldiers in the U.S. military.

Elvis resumed his singing and acting career after being released from the army in the spring of 1960.

6:37 **a.m., Wed., Oct. 28, 1891** – One of the most powerful seismic shocks ever recorded hit the Mini-Owari region of Japan. An esti-

Elvis Presley arrived at Local Draft Board 86 in Memphis to be inducted.

Amelia Earhart took off from San Juan, Puerto Rico on an attempted around-the-world voyage.

mated 7,300 people died. In addition, 200,000 homes were destroyed along with about 10,000 bridges.

In the wake of the disaster, an important discovery about earthquakes was made. A researcher studying the quake advanced for the first time the theory earthquakes might be caused by faulting in the earth's surface, rather than faults merely being the after-effects of shocks. He turned out to be right, thus advancing greatly the science of earthquake detection and prediction.

6:51 **a.m., Wed., Aug. 6, 1890** – William Kemmler became the first victim of the electric chair. Kemmler, convicted of murdering his mistress with a hatchet, died in a botched, crude first attempt to use the chair for the purpose of capital punishment. His painful death took a total of eight minutes after the initial 17-second jolt of electricity failed to kill him. A second, stronger jolt finished him off. The chair was located at Auburn Prison in New York State.

Witnesses at Kemmler's execution were horrified at the sight of him convulsing and writhing while strapped to the chair throughout the ordeal. Many felt the chair should be abolished then and there, but its use as an execution device became commonplace by the early 20th century.

6:53 **a.m., Wed., Jan. 25, 1978** – A Soviet nuclear-powered spy satellite crashed into Canada's North West Territories, leaving a nine-foot wide crater and a radioactive trail across northern Canada. The satellite, known as *Cosmos 954*, carried a reactor with 45 kilograms (100 pounds) of radium. No injuries were reported. The Soviets paid $3 million of the $10 million it cost the Canadian government to clean up the mess.

6:56 **a.m., Mon., May 31, 1937** – Amelia Earhart took off from San Juan, Puerto Rico, on an attempted around-the-world voyage. Just over one month later, on July 2, the last message was received from the aviatrix as she flew toward tiny Howland Island in the Pacific. Earhart and her navigator Fred Noonan were never heard from again despite the largest air-sea rescue operation of the century. The duo had completed two-thirds of their around-the-world journey.

In a 1966 book, investigator Fred Goerner theorized that Earhart and Nooman were captured by Japanese after crash-landing on Saipan in the

Mariana Islands. One witness testified that she heard Earhart had died of dysentery. While Noonan's fate cannot be ascertained, he may have been executed. Another book, by U.S. Air Force Major Joe Gervais, suggests Earhart returned to the U.S. under a new identity and was still alive in 1970. There have been numerous other theories, but the true fate of the flyers remains a mystery.

Earhart, emulating Charles Lindbergh, became the first woman to fly the Atlantic as a passenger in 1928 and solo in 1932.

7a.m. to 7:59 a.m.

- 🕐 *Today* premieres on NBC
- 🕐 **Huge explosion strikes Siberia**
- 🕐 **Abraham Lincoln dies**
- 🕐 **Battle of the Somme begins**
- 🕐 **Salvador Dali is born**
- 🕐 **Japanese planes attack Pearl Harbor**

7:00 a.m., Sat., Dec. 22, 1849 – Fyodor Dostoyevsky was prepared for execution, or so he thought. The Russian writer and dissident was issued street clothes, placed in a guarded carriage and taken to a platform with several others where a firing squad awaited them. Names were read out, coffins aligned, and last rites offered. At this crucial point, a courier arrived in a carriage waving a reprieve. Suitably frightened, Dostoyevsky was taken to a Siberian labour camp where he served four years for anti-government activity. He had been convicted of circulating works against the government.

Dostoyevsky is best known for his novel *Crime and Punishment*, the latter of which he knew only too well. His life was marked by tragedy. At age 18, his father was murdered. Later, the writer had to flee Russia twice to escape his creditors. Not surprisingly, Dostoyevsky produced his best work in his later years, when his lifestyle was less precarious.

Dostoyevsky died of hemorrhaging at 8:38 p.m., Friday, January 28, 1881, at the age of 58.

7:00 a.m., Wed., Oct. 1, 1924 – Jimmy Carter, the 39th president, and the first president elected from the deep south since Zachary Taylor (1848), was born at Wise Hospital in Plains, Georgia. He was the first president born in a hospital and the first sworn in by his nickname. Carter's full name was James Earl Carter.

Jimmy Carter was virtually unknown nationally as recently as two years before his election. His main claim to fame was a term as governor of Georgia in the early 70s, and he nearly stumped the panel as to his profession on *What's My Line* in 1974. However, his bid for the 1976 Democratic nomination got off to a flying start with victories in the Iowa and New Hampshire caucuses. His bandwagon proved impossible to stop. Nationally, the candidate almost blew a 30-point lead in the polls but hung on to beat President Ford in one of the closest U.S. national elections ever.

The high point of Carter's administration came in March, 1979. In what became known as the Camp David Accord, Carter, Egyptian president Anwar Sadat and Israeli Prime Minister Menachem Begin worked out a deal to end the 31-year state of war between Egypt and Israel. Occupied Sinai was returned to Egypt.

Carter's credibility crumbled after Iranian militants seized the U.S. embassy in Tehran in November, 1979, capturing 52 hostages. A flurry of economic sanctions and embargoes failed to win their release; neither did an ill-fated "rescue" mission which resulted in the deaths of eight servicemen in the Iranian desert. The hostage crisis cost Carter his job as he was soundly defeated by Ronald Reagan in the 1980 election.

7:00 **a.m., Sun., Nov. 28, 1999** – Hsing-Hsing, one of two giant pandas donated to the U.S. by China in 1992, was euthanized at the Smithsonian's National Zoo in Washington, D.C. Hsing-Hsing was 28, considered quite old for a giant panda. He had been treated since May 15, 1999 for irreversible kidney disease.

Hsing-Hsing's partner Ling-Ling died on December 30, 1992 of heart failure. The two pandas were given to the National Zoo by the Beijing Zoo on April 16, 1972 following President Nixon's historic visit to China earlier that year. The two pandas produced five offspring in the 80s, none of whom lived more than four days. An estimated three million people a year went to see the popular pandas at the National Zoo.

7:00 **a.m., Mon., Jan. 14, 1952** – *Today* premiered on NBC. It is television's longest-running weekday program.

Today is television's longest-running weekday program.

The British Crown jewels were stolen from the Tower of London.

Morning network television was unknown when *Today* first appeared, and many critics were skeptical. But the show succeeded, largely because of its natural and ingenious original host Dave Garroway, whose relaxed style was perfect for the morning hours. The show's trips to other locales around the world proved to be a hit, as were the interviews with many of the world's most famous people.

Ironically, *Today* became a victim of its own success when one of its imitators, ABC's *Good Morning America,* eventually overtook it in the ratings.

Among those who succeeded Garroway in the host's chair were Barbara Walters, Hugh Downs, John Chancellor and Tom Brokaw. Dave Garroway committed suicide in 1982.

7:00 **a.m., Sun., Aug. 1, 1714** – Queen Anne, the last Stuart to rule Great Britain and Ireland, died at age 49. She reigned from 1702 to 1714, in an era dominated by the War of the Spanish Succession. No direct heir survived her, although Anne had five babies from 17 pregnancies. In her later years, Anne became so obese that pulleys were required to lift her from the drawing room to the bedroom.

7:00 **a.m., Tues., Sept. 13, 1814** – The bombardment of Fort St. Henry began. It would inspire Francis Scott Key to write the U.S. national anthem. Key, a volunteer in a light artillery company, wrote the words to "The Star-Spangled Banner" while British ship H.M.S. *Surprise* blasted away at Fort McHenry for more than 24 hours. The next day, Key gave the lyrics to his brother-in-law J.H. Nicholson, who suggested the music. The tune was adapted from "To Anacreon in Heaven," the anthem of the British Anacreontic Society of London, a club of amateur musicians. "The Star-Spangled Banner" was designated America's National Anthem on March 3, 1931.

7:00 **a.m., Tues., May 9, 1671** - The British Crown jewels were stolen from the Tower of London.

On the morning of the robbery, Colonel Thomas Blood managed to talk Talbot Edwards, keeper of the jewels, into showing them to himself and three companions. Once inside the room, the conspirators overpowered Edwards and began stuffing the treasures into their clothes. None of the robbers got very far, and all, including Blood, were caught quickly and sent to the Tower. Thomas Blood managed to talk the King not only into giving him a full pardon, but a $500 pension as well!

7:00 **a.m., Tues., Nov. 5, 1872** – Women's rights activist Susan B. Anthony arrived at a Rochester, New York, voting booth to vote in the presidential election. There was only one problem – women weren't allowed to vote. The two election inspectors on hand turned a blind eye and Anthony voted as did 15 other women at that location (a barber shop).

On June 17, 1893 in Canandiagua, New York, Anthony was convicted of voting illegally. Her 15 comrades-in-arms were not charged. Anthony was fined $100 plus prosecution costs. She promptly told the judge she would not pay. Normally, Anthony would have been jailed, but the judge ruled that she could not be incarcerated until she paid. Anthony never paid and was never jailed. Instead, the two election inspectors were jailed for five days in lieu of a $25 fine. Members of the women's voting movement supplied food during their brief prison stay.

Susan B. Anthony was an ardent speaker, writer and organizer. She devoted herself to women's rights and became a national hero. She died at 12:40 p.m., Tues., March 13, 1906 at the age of 86.

Anthony's name was revived in 1979 when the U.S. treasury attempted to introduce a new silver dollar, named the "Susan B. Anthony." The coin proved unpopular and an embarrassment to the Carter administration. Nevertheless, Anthony was the first woman to be depicted on American currency.

7:00 **a.m., Fri., May 1, 1970** – U.S. troops in Vietnam began to attack Communist military targets in neighbouring Cambodia. President Nixon claimed the action would save the lives of American servicemen and shorten the Vietnam War. His actions brought howls of protest from the rapidly-growing anti-war movement.

7:00 **a.m., Thurs., Aug. 16, 1979** – John Diefenbaker, "Dief the Chief," Prime Minister of Canada from 1958 to 1963, was found dead of a heart attack at his desk. Diefenbaker, the first Canadian prime minister from the prairies (brought up in Saskatchewan, although born in

Susan B. Anthony arrived at a Rochester, New York, voting booth to vote in the presidential election.

The world's first reusable space-craft, blasted off from Cape Canaveral.

Ontario), was 84. Just three months earlier, the champion of the common man had won his last election in a long and not always successful career.

In 1958, Diefenbaker's Conservatives swept into power with the largest majority in Canadian history at that time. But the economy was in poor shape and the Tories were unable to build support in French-speaking Quebec, so the majority fell to a minority in 1962. By 1963, "Dief" was Leader of the Opposition in the Liberal government of Prime Minister Lester Pearson. He was ousted as Conservative Party leader in 1967, but remained in Parliament as the member for Prince Albert until his death.

While Prime Minister, Diefenbaker appointed the first female cabinet minister, Ellen Fairclough, introduced legislation to improve social programs and opposed apartheid in South Africa. However, the cancellation of the Avro Arrow project was a major black mark during his term as prime minister. Finally, his bombastic style wore thin with voters.

7:00 **a.m., Sun., Apr. 8, 1990** – Ryan White, whose five-and-a-half-year struggle with AIDS attracted international attention, died of complications from the disease in an Indianapolis hospital. He was 18.

White contracted AIDS at age 13 through a blood-clotting agent used to fight his hemophilia. Ryan made headlines when he was barred from public school because of his disease. He was eventually allowed to attend classes. White later became a national spokesperson for children with AIDS, urging better understanding of the problem.

7:00 **:03 a.m., Sun., Apr. 12, 1981** – *Columbia*, the world's first reusable spacecraft, blasted off from Cape Canaveral in Florida, returning to earth two days later, with a picture-perfect landing at Edwards Air Force Base in California. Aboard *Columbia* for the 36-orbit flight were space veterans John Young and Robert Crippen. *(see 11:39 a.m.)*

7:05 **a.m., Thurs., Dec. 12, 1985** – A total of 258 people died when a DC-8 crashed on take-off from Gander, Newfoundland. All but eight of those who perished were American servicemen returning home for Christmas after serving in the international peacekeeping force on the Sinai Peninsula. The plane plowed a 1.6-kilometre (mile-long) path through forest before exploding. Canadian government investigations failed to find a reason for the crash, although terrorist sabotage was suggested.

7:06 **a.m., Sun., June 5, 1910** – O. Henry, secretive writer of short stories ending with an ironic twist, died nearly penniless at a hospital in New York. Henry, whose real name was William Sidney Porter (he is buried under that name) was born in 1862 in Greensboro, North Carolina. He began writing while serving time for bank embezzlement in the late 1890s. A heavy drinker, his intake was said to be 1.8 litres (two quarts) of whiskey a day.

O. Henry died of diabetes and cirrhosis of the liver. His many stories, including "The Gift of the Magi" and "The Last Leaf," live on.

7:14 **a.m., Mon., Aug. 11, 1919** – Andrew Carnegie, Scottish-born steel magnate and one of the world's richest men in his time, died of pneumonia at his estate in Shadow Brook, Massachusetts. He was 83. Carnegie, the first major public figure to propose that the rich share their wealth, donated about $350 million to various charities over the years. Despite his generosity, Carnegie was still worth over $500 million at his death.

7:15 **a.m., Tues., July 9, 1918** – One hundred and one people died in the deadliest rail collision in U.S. history. The head-on crash in Nashville, Tennessee, occurred when a train ran through a stop sign, entering the same track as another train. Both locomotives were destroyed, along with three baggage cars and six passenger carriages. Most of the victims were soldiers.

7:17 **a.m., Tues., June 30, 1908** – The Tunguska region of central Siberia was rocked by an explosion that flattened trees for 80 kilometres (50 miles). The blast was estimated to be equal to the detonation of 30 million tons of TNT or the equivalent of 1,500 atomic bombs of the type that devastated Hiroshima. For weeks afterward, the night sky glowed so brightly that it could be seen in western Europe.

Initially, the explosion was believed to have been caused by a giant meteorite. However, this theory was rejected when no crater and no meteor

Siberia was rocked by an explosion that flattened trees for 80 kilometres.

Abraham Lincoln, the 16th president and the first Republican Chief Executive, died.

fragments were found. Other theories range from an explosion of a comet head, to a blown-up alien spaceship, to the invasion of a "black hole" from outer space.

7:22 a.m., Sat., Apr. 15, 1865 – Abraham Lincoln, the 16th president and the first Republican Chief Executive, died – the first presidential assassination victim. The "Great Emancipator" never regained consciousness after being shot in the back of the head by actor John Wilkes Booth the previous night. Lincoln had been watching a play with his wife Mary in the presidential box at Ford's Theatre in Washington, D.C. Booth escaped but was later captured in a barn and shot to death. Lincoln was carried to a nearby boarding house where he died despite the efforts of several doctors. Secretary of State Stanton announced the death with the words: "Now he belongs to the ages."

Lincoln, the tallest president (at six foot four) and the first to wear a beard, rose to prominence largely because of a series of debates in several Illinois towns with fellow senator Stephen Douglas. The two men found themselves matched against each other in the presidential race of 1860, which Lincoln won easily, beating out Douglas and two other candidates. Lincoln was re-elected in 1864, defeating General George McClennan. The administration was dominated by one major event, the Civil War, which pitted North against South in a bitter conflict that killed an estimated 800,000. The conflict lasted four long years before the North won and slavery was ended forever in the United States.

A plain, simple but caring man, Lincoln proved to be the right leader for the right time, and in fact for all time. In 1982, he was ranked first in a historian's poll of presidents conducted by the *Chicago Tribune*.

7:28 a.m., Sat., July 1, 1916 – The Battle of the Somme began as 100,000 British soldiers began marching into the muddy fields of No Man's Land along the Somme River. Fifty-seven thousand of them would die that day in the worst day for British losses of World War I.

The British army began its march after a full week of shelling during which 1.7 million rounds were fired at German front-line troops. However, the German machine-gunners sat out the barrage underground and were waiting when the British began their advance.

Despite the failure of the first assault, a second major attack was launched July 14. Two months later, the battle featured the first tank action in history. The Battle of the Somme ended November 21 with the British having made only marginal gains. Six hundred thousand men died on each side.

7:30 **a.m., Fri., June 2, 1939** – Rescuers discovered the stern of the British submarine *Thetus* protruding from the water in Liverpool Bay. The sub became partially imbedded in the seabed and rose to stand almost vertically on her nose in 39 metres (130 feet) of water. Four men managed to escape from the doomed ship through an escape hatch but 86 died in one of Britain's worst peacetime naval disasters. Efforts to keep the stern afloat long enough to cut a hole into the sub's metal skin proved fruitless.

Experts estimated the sub's air supply ran out at about 2 o'clock the following morning. Faint tappings in Morse Code were heard from inside the ship late into the night.

7:30 **a.m., Thurs., June 10, 1937** – Sir Robert Borden, the "Grand Old Man of Canada," the last Prime Minister to be knighted, died in Toronto. Borden was 82 and had been suffering from heart problems.

Borden began his political career as an Imperialist. But he changed his stripes as prime minister and promoted an independent Canada within the British Empire. Borden's efforts as prime minister from 1911 to 1920 helped win Canada greater independence from Britain. In the process, Canada began building its reputation as a neutral party on the international front.

The most contentious issue during Borden's term in office was conscription. The issue came up after the First World War broke out in 1914 and enlistment in Canada was low. The issue of conscription proved to be divisive; Borden's Quebec ministers refused to support a draft. Without representation in cabinet, Quebec felt completely shut out. Borden imposed the Wartime Elections Act which deprived Canadians of German descent, and those from other foreign backgrounds, of the right to vote.

In February, 1916, Borden escaped – though slightly singed – as Parliament's centre block burned. The Prime Minister's office and everything in it was destroyed in the blaze.

Sir Robert Borden, the "Grand Old Man of Canada" died.

Salvador Dali, famed Spanish painter, writer, and member of the Surrealist movement, was born.

7:30 a.m., Wed., Sept. 21, 1921 – Oppau, Germany was shocked by a devastating industrial explosion. More than 1,000 people died and thousands more were injured when a generator burst at a dye plant. The blast left a crater 118 metres (130 yards) wide and 37 metres (45 yards) deep. The shock was felt as far as 80 kilometres (50 miles) away.

The Oppau factory was used for the manufacture of poison gas during World War I.

7:30 a.m., Fri., Jan. 22, 1943 – The fastest temperature rise in recorded history began at Spearfish, South Dakota when the thermometer rose from –20° Celsius (–4° Fahrenheit) at 7:30 a.m. to 7.2° Celsius (45° Fahrenheit) at 7:32 a.m. – a rise of 49° Fahrenheit in just two minutes.

7:45 a.m., Wed., May 11, 1904 – Salvador Dali, famed Spanish painter, writer, and member of the Surrealist movement, was born in Figueras, Spain. Dali caused controversy early in his career when, in 1929, he espoused Surrealism. His paintings, *The Persistence of Memory*, *Crucifixion* and *The Sacrament of the Last Supper*, are among the most famous in 20th-century art.

Dali also produced Surrealist films, illustrated books, handcrafted jewellery, and made theatrical sets and costumes. He wrote ballet scenarios and several books, including *The Secret Life of Salvador Dali* and *Diary of a Genius* – Dali, of course.

7:51 a.m., Sat., Dec. 21, 1968 – *Apollo 8* blasted off from its pad at Cape Canaveral, Florida. At 10:41 a.m., Saturday, December 21, 1968, *Apollo 8* broke out of Earth's orbit en route to the moon. It marked man's longest journey up to that time, and the first manned flight toward another body in the solar system. Christopher Kraft, Jr., director of flight operations for NASA radioed: "You're on your way. You're really on your way now." Commander Frank Borman replied: "Roger, we look good here."

Three days later, on Christmas Eve, astronauts James Lovell, William Anders and Frank Borman became the first men to orbit the moon. Millions of television viewers were able to watch the earth from 402,000 kilometres

(250,000 miles) away. The flight helped pave the way for the historic *Apollo 11* mission the next summer.

7:52 **a.m., Thurs., May 8, 1902** – On a date that one observer said "should be written in blood," Mont Pelee erupted, destroying the nearby city of Saint Pierre in Martinique. Within a few moments of the explosion, 30,000 people were dead or dying from the superheated gas and dust. Most were literally boiled to death. Trees were uprooted, buildings destroyed and most of the ships in the harbour sank.

Only two men survived the eruption: a shoemaker on the edge of town and a convicted murderer who had been sentenced to hang that morning. The reprieved murderer toured with Barnum and Bailey Circus until 1929, displayed in a replica of his jail cell. The shoemaker became a caretaker and constable guiding tourists through the ruins of Saint Pierre.

7:55 **a.m., Sun., Dec. 7, 1941** – Japanese planes attacked the U.S. military base at Pearl Harbor in the Hawaiian Islands. Over 2,400 people died in history's most famous surprise attack, dubbed "Operation Z." President Franklin Roosevelt declared war on Japan the next day and on its Axis partners, Germany and Italy, three days after that.

The attack on Pearl Harbor came as a shock, even though the Japanese had been planning the assault for some time. In addition to the dead and 1,300 injured, five U.S battleships were sunk or seriously damaged along with 14 smaller ships and 200 aircraft. By contrast, the Japanese had only 100 casualties while losing 29 planes and five midget submarines.

What shocked Americans almost as much as the death and destruction was the fact that the U.S. had left itself so vulnerable to attack. Even Roosevelt admitted the Japanese had pulled off a skilful deception, but the U.S. had just begun to fight.

Japanese planes attacked the U.S. military base at Pearl Harbor.

8a.m. to 8:59 a.m.

- 🕐 Six Day War begins
- 🕐 Ernest Hemingway born
- 🕐 Air India jet crashes off Ireland
- 🕐 Atomic bomb dropped on Hiroshima
- 🕐 The October Crisis begins
- 🕐 Mount St. Helens erupts

8:00 a.m., Mon., June 5, 1967 – The Six Day War began as Israeli planes raided airfields in Cairo and the Suez Canal Zone. At first, the Israelis met strong resistance from Egyptian forces, but the battle quickly turned into a rout as the Israelis won. Israel also turned back a Syrian challenge from the north. A cease-fire was signed on Sunday, June 11, less than a week after hostilities had begun. More than 15,000 Arabs died in the brief war.

While Israel made tremendous gains (their forces occupied territories four times larger than Israel itself), the Arab defeat only increased tensions in the Middle East.

8:00 a.m., Sat., Jan. 27, 1973 – A cease-fire went into effect in Vietnam after the signing of a peace treaty at the Hotel Majestic in Paris. The treaty ended U.S. fighting in the most divisive foreign war in American history. Nearly 56,000 Americans were killed in combat or non-combat action and more than 300,000 wounded. Thirteen hundred soldiers were listed as missing at war's end and some are still unaccounted for to this day. The Pentagon estimated the monetary cost of the war at $109.5 billion.

8:00 a.m., Sun., Feb. 14, 1779 – James Cook, one of the greatest explorers of the 18th century, died when he was stabbed by natives in the Hawaiian Islands. He was on his third voyage in search of the Northwest Passage. Cook was 50.

James Cook discovered Australia and Antarctica and mapped much of the South Pacific. He also discovered a way to prevent scurvy, the scourge of many a sailor. Only one of Cook's men died of illness during all his expeditions.

8:00 a.m., Fri., July 21, 1899 – Ernest "Papa" Hemingway, whose writings won him a Nobel Prize and a Pulitzer Prize, was born in Oak Park, Illinois. Hemingway's best-known works include *The Sun Also Rises*, *The Old Man and the Sea* and *Death in the Afternoon*. He died 19 days before his 62nd birthday. Hemingway shot himself to death at 7:30 a.m. Sunday, July 2, 1961 at his home in Ketchum, Idaho. Most of Hemingway's novels dealt with death, and to many, his violent, self-administered end seemed a tragic irony.

Hemingway was an ambulance driver during World War I, and the Paris correspondent for the *Toronto Star*. He continued his work as a journalist throughout the Spanish Civil War and the Second World War, winning the Bronze Star for his actions.

8:00 a.m., Sat., Apr. 14, 1759 – George Frederic Handel, German-born composer, died in London, England, his home for the latter part of his life. The composer of such classics as "The Messiah," "Fireworks Music" and "Water Music" was 74.

Handel, who worked for King George I, is said to have written "Water Music" to appease the King for dereliction of duty earlier in his career. Back in royal favour, he founded the Royal Academy of Music while managing the King's Theatre.

The composer created "The Messiah" in 1742, using a libretto taken from the Bible. Handel subsisted on virtually nothing but coffee during the 24 days it took him to compose the oratorio. King George is said to have risen to his feet in appreciation following the performance.

Handel went blind late in life but still managed to conduct "The Messiah" for the last time just eight days before his death. George Frederic Handel is buried in Poets' Corner in Westminster Abbey.

Ernest "Papa" Hemingway, whose writings won him a Nobel Prize and a Pulitzer Prize, was born in Oak Park.

**The United States
dropped an
atomic bomb,
the most powerful
weapon ever
used in war, on
Hiroshima, Japan.**

8:00 **a.m., Mon., Nov. 1, 1971** – The flag of the People's Republic of China was raised at the United Nations for the first time. A six-man delegation had arrived in New York the week before to establish a Chinese mission to the U.N. They were the first Chinese officials to visit the United States in 31 years. American ambassador to the U.N. and future president, George Bush, delivered the address welcoming the newcomers. The Republic of China, more popularly known as Taiwan, was expelled from the U.N. as part of the negotiated arrangement for China's entry.

8:00 **a.m., Sun., May 19, 1935** – "Lawrence of Arabia" died. T.E. Lawrence, British author and adventurer, succumbed to injuries suffered in a motorcycle accident in Dorset, England. He was 46. Lawrence is credited with leading the Arab revolt against the Turks in World War I. He also wrote several books, including *The Seven Pillars of Wisdom*, his account of the revolt.

8:00 **a.m., Tues., May 26, 1868** – England's last public execution was held outside Newgate Prison in London, when Michael Barrett was hanged for his part in a December, 1867 bombing in which 12 people died.

8:13 **a.m., Sun., June 23, 1985** – A bomb exploded aboard an Air India jumbo jet bound from Toronto to Bombay. All 329 aboard died when the craft plunged into the Atlantic Ocean off the west coast of Ireland. A Sikh extremist group claimed responsibility for the bomb.

8:16 **a.m., Mon., Aug. 6, 1945** – The United States dropped an atomic bomb, the most powerful weapon ever used in war, on Hiroshima, Japan. That action, and the dropping of a second A-bomb on Nagasaki three days later, hastened Japan's surrender and the end of World War II.

The bombs, about six years and $2 billion in the making, instantly killed 60,000 people in Hiroshima, and another 10,000 in Nagasaki. Many more would die later from injuries and radiation. Sixty per cent of Hiroshima was vaporized.

The bomb was dropped by the Superfortress *Enola Gay*, piloted by Capt. Paul Tibbets, Jr. "My God, what have we done!" cried Tibbets's co-pilot Robert Lewis, after the explosion.

American President Truman justified use of the weapon by saying it had the potential to save tens of thousands of American lives that would otherwise had been lost in conventional warfare. However, the A-bomb also ushered in a new and dangerous era in mankind's history, one that would be dominated by fear of global nuclear destruction.

8:19 **a.m., Sat., Mar. 16, 1985** – Terry Anderson, American-born correspondent for The Associated Press, was kidnapped by armed Shiite Muslim gunmen as he returned from a tennis game in Beirut. The ex-marine would be kept blindfolded and in chains for the next six and a half years as the longest-held western hostage in Lebanon. Anderson's father and brother both died during his captivity, and his wife gave birth to a daughter.

Anderson was finally released on December 4, 1991. His last word to his captors was "Goodbye."

Louis Riel was told that his end was at hand.

8:25 **a.m., Mon., Nov. 16, 1885** – Louis Riel, Métis leader accused of spearheading the Red River Rebellion of 1869-70, was told that his end was at hand. A few minutes later, one of Canada's most controversial and colourful figures was dead, hanged for his part in leading the unsuccessful rebellion in the North-West Territory. Riel, whose execution has contributed to more than a century of hostility among native and French-speaking Canadians, was 41.

8:25 **a.m., Fri., Apr. 13, 1917** – Diamond Jim Brady, turn-of-the-century railroad equipment salesman, better known for his love of the good life, died of a heart attack in his apartment in Atlantic City, New Jersey. He was 61.

Brady was a "fat cat" both literally and figuratively. The son of an Irish saloon-keeper was legendary for his expensive parties, gambling houses and a gem collection that included 20,000 diamonds. He was also a glutton, one who could put away double helpings of a 15-course dinner after consuming an enormous breakfast and lunch earlier in the day. His gastronomical excesses led to numerous problems, including gallstones, ulcers, diabetes, bad kidneys and chest pain. He was living in a $1,000 a week apartment in Atlantic City at the time of his death.

The nightmare known as the "October Crisis" had begun.

8:30 **a.m., Mon., June 1, 1868** – James Buchanan, America's 15th president, the only Chief Executive who never married, died of pneumonia and inflammation of the lining of the heart in Lancaster, Pennsylvania. He was 77.

Buchanan, a U.S. Representative and Senator from Pennsylvania prior to his presidency, gained stature as Secretary of State under President Polk, but lost bids for the Democratic presidential nomination in 1848 and 1852 before finally winning in 1856. He easily defeated the first Republican candidate, John Fremont, and former president Millard Fillmore in the general election.

Buchanan's administration was conducted in the shadow of the coming Civil War. During his term of office, seven states seceded from the Union to join the fledgling Confederate States of America led by President Jefferson Davis. Buchanan stood by and did nothing, maintaining the federal government had no right to force any state to remain in the Union. He feared confrontation would lead to civil war. Stripped of much of his support and credibility, Buchanan declined to seek a second term in 1860. Admittedly happy to be out of office, he strongly supported Lincoln and the Union effort during the Civil War years.

Buchanan's vice-president, John C. Breckinridge, was, at 36, the youngest man ever elected to national office. He died in 1875 at age 54, surviving the much-older Buchanan by only seven years. Breckinridge went on to become an ardent Confederate supporter, serving first as a general then as secretary of war for the South.

8:30 **a.m., Mon., Oct. 5, 1970** – The doorbell rang at the Montreal home of James Cross, senior British trade commissioner in Quebec. The maid opened the door to find two men who said they had a gift for Cross. The men were let in and, minutes later, burst out of the house with a handcuffed Cross in tow. The kidnappers sped off in a car. The nightmare known as the "October Crisis" had begun.

The kidnapping was the work of the FLQ, a radical separatist group that made headlines in the 1960s with a campaign of violence designed to promote their cause. But this was their first political kidnapping. A ransom note left at the scene demanded the release of 23 so-called political prisoners, $500,000 in gold and safe transport out of the country.

Five days later, another FLQ cell kidnapped Quebec labour minister Pierre Laporte from in front of his home. The federal government responded by declaring the War Measures Act, which outlawed the FLQ and gave police sweeping powers to search, arrest and detain without warrant. On October 17, the FLQ announced it had killed Laporte and told police where his body could be found. Laporte's corpse, strangled with the chain of a religious medal he wore around his neck, was discovered by police near a military base at St-Hubert, Quebec.

Early in December, police located the house where Cross was held. Following negotiations, Cross was released at 2 a.m. on December 4 after word was received that his kidnappers had arrived safely in Cuba with their families.

Laporte's kidnappers were tracked down and sentenced to long jail terms. Cross's captors returned to Canada from Cuban exile 10 years later to serve relatively light sentences.

8:30 a.m., Wed., Feb. 14, 1974 – Valentin Falov, Soviet ambassador to Germany, informed Paul Frank, undersecretary at the German foreign ministry, that the Soviet Union wanted to expel dissident Aleksandr Solzhenitsyn. He asked if the Germans would be willing to take the author. Frank contacted German Chancellor Willy Brandt, who immediately gave his approval. By day's end, Aleksandr Solzhenitsyn had been flown by the Soviets into Frankfurt, where he was released.

Solzhenitsyn's banishment from the Soviet Union followed publication of his book *The Gulag Archipelago*, a less-than complimentary look at the Soviet prison system. Solzhenitsyn was arrested and charged with treason (the charges were dropped in 1991).

The author received his first taste of the Soviet prison system in 1945, when he was arrested and jailed for eight years for criticizing Stalin. Released the day Stalin died in 1953, he then spent the next three years in exile.

In 1962, Solzhenitsyn published his first book, *One Day in the Life of Ivan Denisovitch*, which was critical of the Soviet prison system. That, and subsequent books were banned in the Soviet Union even though they were released abroad and circulated underground in the U.S.S.R. In 1970, Solzhenitsyn won the Nobel Prize for Literature but didn't travel to Stockholm to receive his prize for fear he would not be allowed to return.

Another FLQ cell kidnapped Quebec labour minister Pierre Laporte from in front of his home.

Mount St. Helens in southwest Washington state erupted.

8:32 **a.m., Sun., May 18, 1980** – Mount St. Helens in southwest Washington state erupted with a force of 10 million tons of TNT. Fifty-seven people died or were left missing by the eruption, which blew ash 20 kilometres (13 miles) into the air and blotted out the sun for hundreds of miles. The toll from the quake would have been much higher had most of the nearby residents not been evacuated. Scientists were warned of a possible eruption when the volcano, which had been dormant for 123 years, began emitting steam and ash about two months earlier.

8:34 **a.m., Wed., April 25, 1990** – The Hubble Space Telescope, which might more appropriately have been called the "Trouble Space Telescope," was launched aboard the space shuttle *Discovery*. The telescope was beset by problems almost from the outset, when scientists discovered it could not be focused properly. Apparently the lens had been ground improperly and the flaw was not discovered before launch. A space shuttle mission to fix the telescope was sent up in 1993, whereafter the telescope performed to expectations.

8:40 **a.m., Sat., June 14, 1919** – British pilots Captain John Alcock and Lieutenant Arthur Brown completed the first non-stop transatlantic flight. Their flight was made just days after Captain Albert Reed and a three-man crew completed the first Atlantic crossing, a flight that included stopovers.

Alcock and Brown flew non-stop in a Vickers Vimy from Lester's Field in St. John's, Newfoundland to Derrygimla Bog near Galway, Ireland. Six times during the flight Brown had to climb onto the wing to clear snow from the carburetor. Once the plane nose-dived to within 30 metres (100 feet) of the waves. The 3,154-kilometre (1,960-mile) trip took 16 hours and 27 minutes.

8:40 **a.m., Mon., Sept. 23, 1957** – A riot broke out outside Central High School in Little Rock, Arkansas, where nine African Americans were being admitted despite the bitter protests of some 1,500 white agitators. Federal troops had been brought out to enforce a directive by President Eisenhower to use whatever force was necessary to admit the students into the school. In the ensuing riot, seven people were arrested and one man struck down after trying to wrestle away a soldier's rifle.

The students had tried three weeks earlier to gain admission to the all-white school, but were turned back by state militia troops backed by an angry mob of about 400 whites. Arkansas Governor Orval Faubus, an opponent of racial integration, ordered the state troopers out in defiance of federal law. Faubus reluctantly agreed not to block the students' admission after a court order and a meeting with President Eisenhower.

8:45 a.m., Thurs., Sept. 1, 1715 – Louis XIV, the Sun King, whose 72-year reign as France's ruler was the longest ever by any monarch in recorded history, died of gangrene poisoning four days before his 77th birthday. During his reign, Louis XIV transformed France into an absolute monarchy and involved his country in four major wars. He is remembered for his famous quote, "L'état, c'est moi" or "I am the state."

8:45 a.m., Sun., July 6, 1919 – The first leg of man's first round-trip trans-Atlantic air flight was completed as British dirigible *R-34* arrived in Long Island. It took four days and 12 hours for the airship to cover the 5,149 kilometres (3,200 miles) between Edinburgh and Long Island. The return trip to Edinburgh lasted only 75 hours and was completed July 13.

8:46 a.m., Fri., Feb. 28, 1975 – A London underground train, gathering speed, slammed into the end of the tunnel at Moorhead Station. Forty-three people died in the accident. Rescuers battled dust, foul air, cramped conditions and temperatures of 48° Celsius (120° Fahrenheit) in efforts to free survivors. It took 13 hours to free the last 13 people, and four days to recover the body of engineer Leslie Newson – whose dead eyes stared straight ahead. No explanation was ever found for the disaster, although some people feel Newson was hypnotized by the route's sameness and fell into a trance.

A London underground train, gathering speed, slammed into the end of the tunnel at Moorhead Station.

9a.m. to 9:59 a.m.

- 🕐 **American U–2 plane shot down over Soviet Union**
- 🕐 **Siege of the Alamo ends**
- 🕐 **Explosion in Halifax harbour kills over 2,000**
- 🕐 **Japan signs articles of surrender**
- 🕐 **Indira Gandhi assassinated**
- 🕐 **First U.S. manned space flight blasts off**

9:00 **a.m., Sun., Oct. 23, 4004 B.C**. – This was the time and date of creation, as calculated by Bishop Ussher in the 1700s. Ussher calculated the date of creation from the Bible, using historical references in the Old Testament. He settled on the time because it was a "civil" hour of the day and he figured God would not be uncivil.

Ussher's calculation is mentioned in the movie *Inherit the Wind*. Scientists calculate creation at about 4,500,000 B.C.

9:00 **a.m., Thurs., July 4, 1776** – The American Continental Congress met to consider adopting the Declaration of Independence. Debate on the wording continued even on this day of decision as Thomas Jefferson's draft had been submitted only six days previously. All told, 86 changes were made to Jefferson's original document with 480 words deleted, leaving a total of 1,337. Late in the day, the Declaration was finally put to a vote, with the colonies voting north-to-south for independence. New Hampshire voted first. Georgia was last to vote. Twelve of the 13 colonies voted to form the United States. (New York abstained, its delegates having been forbidden to vote by the British government.) John Hancock signed the Declaration, as did the Congressional Secretary, and without fanfare or even cheers, the United States Declaration of Independence from Britain was complete. The Continental Congress then turned nonchalantly to other business, including a motion to sell 25 pounds of gunpowder to John Garrison of North Carolina.

July 4th would be the Fourth of July forever after.

9:00 **a.m., Sun., May 1, 1960** – A U-2 spy plane piloted by Francis Gary Powers was shot down over the mining town of Sverdlovsk in the Soviet Union. Powers ejected safely but was captured by the Soviets and held as a spy.

A furious Soviet Premier Khrushchev demanded that the U.S. apologize for its actions and punish those responsible. An equally furious President Eisenhower declined. What followed was perhaps the most dangerous era of the Cold War. Khrushchev cancelled a planned summit with Eisenhower, test ban talks collapsed and detente died as fears of a world-wide nuclear war reached a fever pitch.

Powers was subjected to a televised show trial in August, 1960 and sentenced to 10 years in a jail. He was released in exchange for Soviet spy Rudolf Abel 18 months later. Powers died in 1977 in a helicopter crash while working for a Los Angeles radio station.

9:00 **a.m., Sun., July 21, 1861** – The first battle of Bull Run began on a plain just outside Washington, D.C. Several civilians drove out from the nation's capital by horse and buggy to watch the conflict. They expected a short, decisive victory for the Union, but they were wrong. The first battle of Bull Run turned into a great military victory for the Confederacy as troops led by General Beauregard thoroughly routed northern soldiers under General McDowell. Confederate Colonel Thomas Jackson earned the nickname "Stonewall" for his brigade's strong stand against the enemy.

The second battle of Bull Run took place on August 30, 1862, pitting the Confederates under Stonewall Jackson against the Union army under General Pope. It too resulted in a victory for the South.

9:00 **a.m., Sun., Mar. 6, 1836** – The siege of the Alamo ended in San Antonio, Texas, and the cry "Remember the Alamo" became an American rallying slogan which is used to this day.

The Alamo fortress had been occupied for over three months, since the previous December, by a small force of Texan soldiers fighting in the

The siege of the Alamo ended in San Antonio, Texas.

The Battle of Hastings began.

revolution against Mexico's General Antonio Lopez de Santa Anna. General Santa Anna's 4,000 well-trained troops surrounded the fort on February 23, 1836. The Texans — all 184 of them — were trapped inside. With the rest of the Texan army too far away to help and General Santa Anna refusing to negotiate, the Alamo defenders knew they were doomed. The Mexican army besieged the fort on the evening of March 5. By the following morning, every man inside was dead, their bodies mutilated and burned as a final degradation. One woman, a few children and some slaves were allowed to live.

One month after the Alamo debacle, General Sam Houston defeated the Mexicans and the Republic of Texas was formed. Texas joined the United States in 1845 as the 28th state – the Lone Star state.

9:00 **a.m., Sat., Oct. 14, 1066** – The Battle of Hastings began as William the Conquerer of Normandy (France) attacked the Saxon (English) army of King Harold at Sussex.

William, commanding a motley crew of French, Breton and mercenary forces, about 7,000 strong in total, faced the well-trained English force. The English seemed to have the edge most of the day, but French cavalry hit the charging British on both flanks. Harold and two of his brothers were killed in the charge. By evening, the defeat of the Saxon troops was complete.

The victory enabled William to assume what he felt was his rightful place as King of England. Among his many accomplishments was the Domesday Book, a massive census that listed every man, woman and animal in England, all neatly recorded in two volumes. It became William's guide for levying taxes on his new subjects.

William the Conquerer died in 1087, at age 60, when his horse stumbled during a raid the King was leading against the French at Normandy.

9:00 **a.m., Tues., July 31, 1588** – The British navy began its attack on the massive Spanish Armada off the English coast. The battle lasted six weeks, and the English prevailed despite being outnumbered 2–1 in ships. The British ships were swifter and easier to move around in battle than the larger Spanish vessels, whose cannon proved to be virtually useless against their elusive enemy.

By battle's end, the Spanish had lost 65 ships and 10,000 men while the English lost less than 100 men and no ships. The rout could have been worse except that British ships pursuing the fleeing Spanish were forced to turn back due to lack of supplies.

9:00 a.m., Thurs., Dec. 6, 1917 – A seemingly minor collision between two ships in Halifax harbour set off the world's largest man-made explosion — prior to the Hiroshima apocalypse. More than 2,000 people died and 6,000 were injured. It was the worst catastrophe ever to occur on Canadian soil.

The accident took place when French munitions ship *Mount Blanc*, carrying 4,000 tons of TNT, collided with Norwegian relief ship *Imo*. Fifteen minutes later, the *Mont Blanc* exploded with a mighty roar. Two shock waves smashed buildings and shattered windows, blinding hundreds of people. A half-ton portion of the ship's anchor sailed right across the Halifax peninsula and landed four kilometres (two and a half miles) away. The waters of Halifax harbour parted right to its floor, creating a 9.1-metre (30-foot) tidal wave.

Among the many buildings destroyed in the explosion were a sugar refinery, a brewery and a school — where 200 children died. Many other Haligonians perished when the glass roof of the city's railway station caved in. At least one-sixth of Halifax's population was left homeless.

9:00 a.m., Thurs., Nov. 22, 1990 – Margaret Thatcher, the fiery, embattled Prime Minister of Britain, announced to her cabinet she was resigning as leader of the Conservative Party. Thatcher, a grocer's daughter who became Britain's first female prime minister, said she was stepping down in the interests of party unity, after a challenge by her former defence minister Michael Heseltine. Conservative finance minister John Major succeeded "the Iron Lady" after winning a three-way leadership race.

Thatcher was in office for 11 years, longer than any British Prime Minister of the 20th century. Both praised and criticized for her hard-line style, Thatcher came to power in 1979 and won subsequent elections in 1983 and 1987. She sent a force to the South Atlantic in 1982 to retrieve the Falkland Islands; she cut taxes, broke trade union power and privatized state industries by selling them to private investors. But Thatcher's popularity waned when Britain hit an economic slump. She became downright

A seemingly minor collision between two ships in Halifax harbour set off the world's largest man-made explosion.

The Toronto Industrial Exhibition, later known as the Canadian National Exhibition, opened its gates for the first time.

unpopular with the introduction of a "poll tax" on all British residents — which was rapidly scrapped by the Tories after her departure.

9:00 **a.m., Thurs., Feb. 2, 1922** – The James Joyce masterpiece *Ulysses* was made available for public viewing for the first time when Sylvia Beach, who had helped Joyce get the book published, displayed it at her Paris bookstore "Shakespeare and Company." Beach had picked up two copies – one for her and one for Joyce – at the train station just two hours before. The superstitious Joyce had insisted on February 2 as a publication date because it was his 40th birthday. He even had the cover done in the Greek style, with white lettering on a blue field because that supposedly brought him luck.

The Irish-born Joyce, considered one of the greatest writers of the 20th century, is also known for his works *Portrait of the Artist as a Young Man* and *Finnegan's Wake*. He was also an accomplished musician and even wrote a play. Plagued by eye problems throughout his life (he had 25 eye operations), Joyce wrote in large script and even then was usually unable to see the result. Although he spent most of his life abroad, most of Joyce's works were based in his native Dublin.

Joyce died of peritonitis at 2:00 a.m., Monday, January 13, 1941. He was 59.

9:00 **a.m., Wed., Oct. 2, 1985** – Rock Hudson, a Hollywood leading man for nearly three decades, died at age 59. He was the first major film star to acknowledge publicly that he had AIDS.

Hudson, whose real name was Roy Scherer, became a star in the 1950's with his roles in the films *Magnificent Obsession*, *Giant* and *Pillow Talk*. In the 70's, he starred on television as Commissioner Stewart McMillan in the highly acclaimed police show *McMillan and Wife*.

9:00 **a.m., Tues., Sept. 2, 1879** – The Toronto Industrial Exhibition, later known as the Canadian National Exhibition, opened its gates for the first time. More than 100,000 people paid 25 cents to attend the first "Ex" at what is now Exhibition Place. The event has been held there every year since, and is an annual Toronto fixture.

Many historic events have taken place at the Ex. In 1882, the Exhibition Grounds became the first in the world to be lit by electricity. In 1884, an electric railway – the first in Canada – was introduced. In 1888, Thomas Edison recorded a message by Lord Stanley (hockey fans might recognize the name). That message, sent to U.S. President Grover Cleveland, is the oldest existing sound recording in the world.

The name of the fair was changed to the Canadian National Exhibition in 1912 to reflect its evolution from an agricultural fair to an event nicknamed "Show Window of the Nation."

9:00 a.m., Tues., May 6, 1862 – Henry Thoreau, American writer, best known for the book *Walden*, died of tuberculosis at the age of 45. Thoreau was a nature lover who wrote *Walden* after spending two years at Walden Pond in a remote area of Massachusetts. The book was an account of his experience. Other Thoreau works included *Civil Disobedience*, which inspired Mahatma Gandhi, and *Week on the Concord and Merrimack Rivers*.

9:00 a.m., Tues., Nov. 10, 1970 – A low-depression area formed in the Bay of Bengal south of Madras, India. In two and a half days it would be history's worst cyclone. Packing winds of over 193 kilometres (120 miles) an hour, the cyclone hit the coast of East Pakistan just after midnight on November 13. Flood water wiped out houses, crops, animals and humans. In some cases, entire villages vanished as the water level near the coast rose to 4.5 metres (15 feet). More than one million people died. A civil war followed which led to the birth of a new country, Bangladesh.

9:00 a.m., Mon., Feb. 21, 1972 – President Richard Nixon arrived in Peking to begin his historic visit to China. The president met with Chairman Mao Tse-Tung on his first day in Peking and that night exchanged toasts with Premier Chou En-Lai. During the visit, American and Chinese officials discussed establishing better ties between the two superpowers and the problem of Taiwan. It was the first time a U.S. president had visited China and it opened the doors to improved Sino-American relations.

9:00 a.m., Fri., May 20, 1910 – A parade of all the world's great monarchs turned up in London for the funeral of England's King Edward VII. His successor, George V, and the kings of Denmark, Norway, Spain,

President Richard Nixon arrived in Peking to begin his historic visit to China.

Soviet air force Major Yuri Gagarin becomes the first man to be launched into space.

Greece, Portugal, Bulgaria and Belgium were there, as was German Emperor Wilhelm II and Archduke Ferdinand of Austria, along with royalty from Turkey, Japan, Russia, Italy, Sweden, Holland, Romania, Siam, Persia, France and China. Among those trailing the royals was former U.S. President Theodore Roosevelt.

Four years later, World War I began and the royal "age of innocence" would end forever.

9:02 a.m., Wed., Apr. 19. 1995 – One hundred and sixty-eight people were killed when a bomb destroyed the façade of the nine-story Alfred Murrah federal building in Oklahoma City. Nineteen of the dead were children in a daycare centre. Hundreds were injured, and the psychological toll on the victims' families can never be estimated. The blast took place just after the start of the workday, which maximized the casualties. It was the worst act of terrorism in U.S. history.

There were many poignant scenes on this tragic day. The image that stands out in most people's minds is that of a firefighter gently cradling the body of a one-year-old victim killed in the blast. Freelance photographer Charles Porter IV won a Pulitzer Prize for the photograph, which was distributed around the world by The Associated Press.

Timothy McVeigh, 29, was found guilty by a Denver jury on all 11 counts of his indictment, including eight counts of first degree murder, two of bombing the building and one of conspiracy. McVeigh, who believed that violence could ignite a second American Revolution, was sentenced to death for his crimes. An accomplice, Terry Nicols, 42, received a life sentence but escaped the death penalty.

9:02 a.m., Thurs., Aug. 27, 1896 – The shortest war in recorded history began, ending 38 minutes later with the United Kingdom "winning" over Zanzibar. The "war" started when the British battle fleet under Rear-Admiral Harry Holdsworth Rawson delivered an ultimatum to Sultan Sa'id Khalid to evacuate the palace and surrender. After steady bombardment, the Sultan gave in.

9:07 a.m., Wed., April 12, 1961 – Soviet air force Major Yuri Gagarin became the first man to be launched into space. The 27-year-old industrial technician orbited the earth in a craft named *Vostok*. His first words as he entered earth's orbit were, "I am in good spirits. The machine is working fine." Gagarin's historic flight lasted less than two hours and ended when he touched down in the Soviet Union.

Gagarin died in 1968 when a plane he was piloting crashed some 48 kilometres (30 miles) east of Moscow. Also killed in the crash was his co-pilot, flying instructor Vladimir Seryogin. The crash was caused when a military plane flew too close to Gagarin's, causing a violent airstream. Gagarin was unable to come out of the spin in time. Soviet officials did not release details of the crash until 20 years after the fact.

9:07 **a.m., Sun., Sept. 2, 1945** – Japan signed the articles of surrender officially ending World War II in the Pacific theatre. The signing highlighted a 20-minute ceremony on the deck of the American battleship *Missouri*. General Douglas MacArthur, in accepting Japan's surrender, said he hoped "a better world would emerge out of the blood and carnage of the past."

Japanese emperor Hirohito played a key part in ending the war, urging his countrymen to surrender rather than fight to the death after the atomic bombings of Hiroshima and Nagasaki. Cherished by the Japanese as a divine figure, but considered by some to be a war criminal, Hirohito was said to have agreed to war reluctantly after receiving information filtered by the military.

Hirohito reigned as Japanese monarch for 62 years, part of a line that by legend dated back to 660 B.C. He was the last surviving leader of the nations that fought the Second World War and the world's longest reigning monarch as the 1980s drew to a close. At 6:33 a.m., on Friday, January 6, 1989, Hirohito died of cancer at age 87. He was succeeded by his son Akihito, who became the 125th occupant of the Chrysanthemum Throne.

Time Warner and America Online agree to become one.

9:15 **a.m., Fri., Jan. 7, 2000** – One of history's biggest corporate mergers was created, as Time Warner and America Online agreed to become one. The deal was consummated the night before at a secret meeting between AOL boss Steve Case, Time Warner chief Gerald Levin, AOL vice-chairman Ken Novack and former Time Warner CFO Richard Bressler. After an evening that included a bottle of 1990 Chateau Leoville-Las Cases

"Bonnie and Clyde" were ambushed and killed by Texas rangers.

and chocolate mousse, Case and Levin tentatively agreed to a merger. They had a deal the next morning and made the announcement two days later on January 9.

The deal was seen as symbolic – the day the old media of print journalism finally surrendered to the new media of the Internet. The companies valued the deal at $350 billion. Influential Silicon Valley venture capitalist Roger McNamee called it "the single most transformational event I've seen in my career."

9:15 a.m., Thurs., Mar. 16, 1978 – Former Italian Premier Aldo Moro was kidnapped by Red Brigade terrorists in Rome. The Brigade offered to swap Moro for the release of some Communist prisoners, but the Italian government refused to negotiate. The decision was a death sentence for Moro, whose body was found in the back seat of a small car on May 9, eight weeks after his capture. Among those who attended his requiem service was Pope Paul VI, the first time a pontiff had attended a service for anyone other than a Cardinal.

9:15 a.m., Wed., May 23, 1934 – Legendary bank robbers Bonnie Parker and Clyde Barrow – better known as "Bonnie and Clyde" – were ambushed and killed by Texas rangers near Shreveport, Louisiana, their bodies riddled with 50 bullets.

Bonnie and Clyde terrorized the south for four years, committing numerous robberies and killing about a dozen people. A movie about their exploits was made in the late 60s, and the song "The Ballad of Bonnie and Clyde" by Georgie Fame was a moderate hit in 1968.

9:15 a.m., Sun., June 8, 1783 – Iceland's Lakagigar fissure erupted, producing the greatest outpouring of lava in recorded history. By the time the fissure finally died down eight months later, more than 517 square kilometres (200 square miles) of Iceland was covered in lava, in some places 182 metres (600 feet) deep. The lava did not kill anyone directly, but toxic gases from the eruption destroyed enough livestock and fish to cause a famine which took 10,000 Icelandic lives. The economic, environmental and emotional recovery took decades. Two centuries later, the event remains Iceland's worst disaster.

9:15 **a.m., Sat., July 26, 1986** – Publishing history was made as "The ITN Book on the Royal Wedding" — that of Prince Charles and Lady Diana Spencer — went on sale. Typesetting had begun just 43 hours and 15 minutes earlier at 2:00 p.m., July 24 – making it the fastest-published hardcover book in history.

9:19 **a.m., Mon., Oct. 25, 1999** – A Lear jet carrying reigning U.S. Open champion Payne Stewart and five others took off from an airport in Orlando, Florida. Just over four hours later (at 12:26 p.m. central time), the plane crashed into a field near Mina, South Dakota. The craft had flown 2,253 kilometres (1,400 miles) uncontrolled over the U.S. heartland. When told of the news, Billy Casper said: "Golf has lost a great man."

Investigators believe the pressurization in the plane failed during flight and the craft drifted and crashed when it ran out of fuel. It is believed the occupants died within seconds of the pressurization failure.

Earlier that year, Stewart had won his second U.S. Open by sinking a 15-foot putt on the final hole – the longest putt ever made to win the national championship by one stroke. Stewart, 42, winner of 11 tour events, was instantly recognizable by the knickers and tam-o'-shanter cap he had worn during tournaments since the 1980s.

9:20 **a.m., Mon., Aug. 25, 1919** – The first international air service began with Air Transport and Travel's flight from London to Paris. Only one passenger made the historic flight on the converted biplane bomber, a man named George Stevenson-Reece. The fare for the two-and-a-half hour journey was £21.

9:20 **a.m., Sat., July 2, 1881** – President James Garfield was shot from behind by rejected office-seeker Charles Guiteau at the Baltimore and Potomac railway station in Washington, D.C. He died two and a half months later.

9:20 **a.m., Wed., Oct. 31, 1984** – Indira Gandhi, four-time prime minister of India, was shot by two of her Sikh security guards as she walked to her office in New Delhi. Gandhi, aged 66, died four hours later. One of the assassins was shot dead at the scene and the other captured.

The first international air service began.

Canada was joined coast-to-coast by rail as the last spike was driven into a Canadian Pacific Railway tie.

Gandhi was succeeded by her son, Rajiv, 48, himself an assassination victim six and a half years later.

Gandhi, daughter of former Indian Prime Minister Jawaharlal Nehru, took over as Indian leader in 1969 on the death of Prime Minister Shastri. She fell from popularity in 1975 when she declared a "state of emergency" which enabled her to rule almost as a dictator. After being ousted at the polls in 1977, Gandhi returned to power in 1980.

9:22 a.m., Sat., Nov. 7, 1855 – Canada was joined coast-to-coast by rail as the last spike was driven into a Canadian Pacific Railway tie near Eagle Pass, British Columbia. The Honourable Donald Smith – cousin of CPR President George Stephen – drove in the final spike, but the great moment did not go smoothly. Smith's first effort bent the 81-centimetre (five-inch) spike and a foreman had to pull it out. On his second attempt, Smith slammed the iron home successfully and the four-and-a-half year transcontinental undertaking was finished. The location of the last spike ceremony was given the name "Craigellachie," which means "Rock of Alarm."

In 1927, Canadian Pacific erected a stone marker at the spot where the last spike was driven. An obelisk and a wooden sign on the Trans-Canada Highway also note the event.

9:27 a.m., Mon., Oct. 4, 1965 – Pope Paul VI stepped onto the tarmac at New York's Kennedy International Airport, the first time in history the leader of the Catholic church had set foot on North American soil. Later that day, the Pope met with President Johnson and made an appeal for world peace to the United Nations General Assembly. The Pontiff capped off his day with an ecumenical sermon to a packed house of 90,000 at Yankee Stadium.

9:30 a.m., Tues., June 1, 1926 – Marilyn Monroe, who would become a sex symbol of the silver screen in the 1950s and early 1960s, was born in a Los Angeles hospital. She would live only 36 years.

Monroe starred in films such as *The Seven Year Itch* and *Some Like It Hot*. An insecure woman prone to depression, she wed three times, including marriages to baseball star Joe DiMaggio and playwright Arthur Miller. She was also linked romantically with President John F. Kennedy and his brother Robert.

At 3:30 a.m. on Sunday, August 5, 1962, Monroe was found dead of an apparent drug overdose in her Los Angeles bedroom. The question as to whether it was a suicide or murder has never been completely resolved.

For years after her death, ex-husband DiMaggio regularly had red roses delivered to her resting place, a pink marble tomb at Westwood Cemetery in Los Angeles.

9:30 **a.m., Wed., Mar. 13, 1996** – A gunman walked into a school in Dunblane, Scotland and opened fire in the school's gymnasium. Sixteen kindergarten students and one teacher were killed. The shooter, Thomas Hamilton, was reported to be angry because he was not reinstated as a Boy Scout leader. Of the 29 children in the school, only one escaped injury.

The killings took place despite England's notoriously strict gun laws. However, Hamilton – a gun collector – carried four handguns into the school – all licensed.

9:30 **a.m., Wed., Feb. 2, 1881** – The longest sitting in the history of the British House of Commons came to a weary end. The 41½-hour sitting, on the question of better protection of person and property in Ireland, had begun January 31 at 4 p.m.

9:30 **a.m., Fri., Apr. 6, 1862** – Confederate soldiers began attacking General Grant's troops on the west side of the Tennessee River at Shilo. Grant was on the ropes by nightfall, but Confederate General Johnston failed to apply the killer blow. The Unionists eventually came back to drive the Southerners from the field and claim victory. The victory enabled the north to begin its conquest of the Mississippi.

9:30 **a.m., Sat., Apr. 3, 1897** – Johannes Brahms, renowned for his symphonies, "Requiem" and "Brahms Lullaby," died of liver cancer in Vienna at the age of 64. The German-born Brahms, who as a boy played in dockside inns to earn a living, was encouraged to create music by famed 19th-century composer Robert Schumann. Brahms was a perfectionist who did not complete the first of his four symphonies until he was 44. He destroy-ed many of his works because they failed to meet his own high standards.

A gunman walked into a school in Dunblane, Scotland and opened fire.

Amazon.com traded publicly on the New York Stock Exchange for the first time.

9:30 **a.m., Fri., May 28, 1937** – Alfred Adler, leading Austrian psycho-analyst, collapsed and died of a heart attack in Aberdeen, Scotland. He was 67. Adler is best known for a paper he published in 1907 that led to the concept of "inferiority complex."

9:30 **a.m., Fri., Apr. 28, 1967** – Expo 67, an international exposition celebrating Canada's centennial, opened to the general public in Montreal. The park, officially called the Universal International Exhibition, ran for six months before closing at 12:15 p.m. on October 27. More than 50 million people visited the site, including 60 heads of state and government. Among the dignitaries were Queen Elizabeth, U.S. President Lyndon Johnson and French leader Charles de Gaulle.

The fair covered 283 hectares (700 acres) on Montreal Island and included 100 pavilions from 62 nations. The La Ronde amusement park remained open after the rest of the fair closed.

9:30 **a.m., Thurs., May 15, 1997** – Amazon.com traded publicly on the New York Stock Exchange for the first time. One of the first major on-line retailers, amazon.com started primarily as a bookseller when it first appeared on-line in July, 1995. Since then, under the direction of founder and CEO Jeff Bezos, the company has expanded its shopping site to include CDs, videos, DVDs, toys and games, electronics, on-line auctions and free electronic greeting cards. By February, 2000, amazon.com was boasting that 17 million people in more than 160 countries had made it the leading on-line shopping site. Amazon.com also partnered with such sites as drugstore.com and pets.com (you can guess what they sell). Bezos was named *Time* magazine's "Man of the Year" in 1999.

9:34 **a.m., Fri., May 5, 1961** – *Freedom 7*, with Alan Sheppard aboard, blasted off from Cape Canaveral, Florida, in America's first manned space flight. Sheppard's flight lasted fifteen minutes and took him 241 kilometres (150 miles) above the earth. He landed in the Atlantic near the Bahamas. Three weeks after the flight, President Kennedy asked Congress to approve a program to send men to the moon by the end of the decade. *(see 10:56 p.m.)*

9:35 a.m., Wed., Feb. 4, 1970 – The oil tanker *Arrow* hit a rock off the Nova Scotia coast, causing one of North America's worst-ever oil spills. About 8.6 million litres (1.9 million gallons) of fuel escaped from the crippled ship into Chedabucto Bay, eventually covering 201 kilometres (125 miles) of coastline.

The ship was later abandoned and to this day sits in about 30 metres (98 feet) of water off Arichat, Nova Scotia. The cleanup took a decade and even then not all the oil was mopped up. The accident raised environmental awareness in North America and led to the creation of a Canadian coast guard department to co-ordinate oil spill cleanups.

9:35 a.m., Mon., Sept. 5, 1870 – Victor Hugo arrived at the Paris train station, returning home after 19 years away from the country of his birth. The French poet and novelist was greeted by supporters shouting "Vive Victor Hugo." Hugo had escaped to Belgium in 1851 after incurring the wrath of Napoleon for calling the emperor "Napoleon le petit," or "Little Napoleon."

Hugo, called the "most powerful mind of the Romantic movement," has a street named after him in every town in France. He is best known for his master work, *Les Miserables*. He was an incredibly prodigious worker, often starting his day by writing 100 lines of verse and 20 pages of prose.

Hugo died of old age Friday, May 22, 1885 at age 83.

9:46 a.m., Mon., Sept. 13, 1971 – The assault of New York's Attica prison began as more than 1,000 state troopers, sheriff's deputies and prison guards stormed the correctional facility in upstate New York in an effort to retake the prison seized by inmates four days earlier. Forty-two men – 10 hostages and 32 prisoners – died. Prisoners had rioted over conditions at the prison.

9:47 a.m., Thurs., Mar. 16, 1978 – The tanker *Amoco Cadiz* ran aground off the Britanny coast. More than 220,000 gallons of crude oil were spilled in an environmental nightmare that damaged over 112 kilometres (70 miles) of France's Britanny coast.

About 8.6 million litres of fuel escaped from the crippled ship into Chedabucto Bay.

A B-25 bomber, lost in cloudy skies over Manhattan, crashed into the Empire State Building.

9:47:39 a.m., Tues., Feb. 20, 1962 – *Friendship 7*, with astronaut John Glenn aboard, blasted off from Cape Canaveral, Florida. Eleven minutes later, he became the first American to orbit the earth. Glenn circled the earth three times and reported seeing the lights of Perth, Australia, whose residents had turned on all of their house lights.

The flight, which was delayed 10 times by weather, ended when the spacecraft splashed down at 2:43 p.m. near a recovery ship 338 kilometres (210 miles) northwest of Puerto Rico. Glenn later was feted with New York's largest ticker-tape parade since World War II.

After retiring from the space program, Glenn became U.S. Senator for Ohio and in 1984 made an unsuccessful bid for the Democratic presidential nomination. He was launched into space again in 1998 aboard the space shuttle *Discovery*. At 77, he became the oldest astronaut in history.

9:49 a.m., Sat., July 28, 1945 – A B-25 bomber, lost in cloudy skies over Manhattan, crashed into the Empire State Building. Pilot Army Colonel William Smith, his co-pilot and a passenger were killed instantly when the plane ripped a hole between the 78th and 79th floors of the world's tallest building. Because it was a Saturday and most people who normally worked in the building were off, only 10 people were killed. On a weekday, some 50,000 workers and visitors might have been in the building.

9:50 a.m., Tues., July 4, 1826 – Thomas Jefferson, the third president, and the man who drafted the Declaration of Independence, died at his Virginia estate on the 50th anniversary of the signing of the great document. Jefferson, who was 83, was in pain from an enlarged prostate and weakened by diarrhea. Ironically, the only other president to sign the Declaration of Independence, John Adams, died the same day about eight hours later.

Jefferson was the country's first secretary of state under Washington, and served as vice-president under John Adams. In the election of 1800, Jefferson and Aaron Burr were tied with 73 electoral votes each, just ahead of Adams at 65. The election was forced to the House, which chose Jefferson president. Burr became vice-president. Jefferson easily won a second term in 1804.

The key event of Jefferson's tenure was the Louisiana Purchase, a deal which saw the U.S. buy the Louisiana Territory from France for $15 million, or about three cents an acre. The Territory, a vast area between the Mississippi and the Rockies that includes all or part of 15 present-day states, doubled the size of the United States.

Jefferson also signed into a law a bill that banned the importation of slaves. The bill, however, did not end the influx of slaves.

When not tending to the nation's affairs, Jefferson invented things. He is credited with creating the swivel chair, the pedometer, a letter-copying press and an adjustable table that tilted for easy sketching. He also developed a plowing device that turned the soil more effectively than plows previously in use. Jefferson never patented his inventions, saying he wanted people to have free use of them.

During retirement, Jefferson established the University of Virginia, and helped create a new national library when he sold his 6,500-volume collection to the United States.

9:51 a.m., Fri., Feb. 4, 1983 – Karen Carpenter, who with brother Richard scored many pop rock hits in the 1970s and early 80s, died of cardiac arrest resulting from anorexia nervosa. She was 32. Karen and Richard first gained prominence with the Burt Bacharach tune "Close to You" in 1970. They followed that up with hits like "We've Only Just Begun," "Rainy Days and Mondays" and "Top of the World." Carpenter's obsession with weight loss is said to have begun when she read a magazine review that described her as "chubby."

9:54 a.m. (GMT), Sat., Mar. 20, 1999 – A hot air balloon circumnavigated the world for the first time. The Breitling World Orbiter passed over Northern Africa at the nine-degree west finish line – the exact point from which it began its trip 19 days earlier. Balloonists Bertrand Piccard of Switzerland and Britain's Brian Jones travelled 42,000 km (26,098 miles) in their history-making journey. The balloon touched down in Egypt the following day. "I am with the angels," said Piccard, who was making his third round-the-world bid.

A hot-air balloon circumnavigated the world for the first time.

The cry of "Gentlemen, start your engines" was heard for the first time at the Indianapolis Motor Speedway.

9:55 **a.m., Tues., May 30, 1911** – The cry of "Gentlemen, start your engines" was heard for the first time at the Indianapolis Motor Speedway. Moments later, the first Indianapolis 500, or Indy, began at the new "Brickyard." Local driver Ray Harroun emerged the winner just under seven hours later with an average speed of 120 kilometres (74.59 miles) per hour.

Harroun, whose car was the only one of the 43 in the race without a mechanic aboard, used a rear-view mirror of his own invention to keep an eye on his fellow competitors. Supposedly, it was the first time a rear-view mirror had been used in an automobile.

Indy 500 winning speeds have increased somewhat – they are now about two and a half times that of Harroun's.

10 a.m. to 10:59 a.m.

🕐 **Theft of "Star of India" discovered**
🕐 **O.J. Simpson verdict announced**
🕐 **Pierre Elliott Trudeau resigns**
🕐 **U.S. flag hoisted at Iwo Jima**
🕐 **Two planes collide over New York City**
🕐 **Wright brothers take first flight**

10:00 **a.m., Sat., Dec. 9, 1995** – New York radio station WQEW began playing 81 hours of some 1,200 Frank Sinatra recordings, alphabetically. The first song of the marathon was "A Baby for You and Me"; the last was "Zing, Went the Strings of My Heart." The broadcast was in celebration of Sinatra's 80th birthday with the 81st hour billed as "one to grow."

WQEW played 144-1/2 continuous hours of Sinatra within minutes of word of the singer's death at 3:22 a.m. EDT on Friday, May 15, 1998. Sinatra, "Old Blue Eyes," who has been called the greatest interpreter of American popular song, died of a heart attack at a hospital in Los Angeles. He was 82. Reportedly, his last words before he died at 10:50 p.m., Thursday, May 14, 1998 were "I'm losing."

Sinatra got his musical start in 1935 when his group, the Hoboken Four, won a 1935 *Major Bowes Amateur Hour* contest. His big break came when Harry James heard him sing on a New York radio station in 1939 and hired him. The next year, Sinatra joined Tommy Dorsey's band. By 1942 he was a soloist. Over 170 *Billboard*-charted singles would follow, including timeless classics such as "Young at Heart," "Witchcraft," "Strangers in the Night," "My Way" and "New York New York."

Sinatra was a rare combination of style and substance. Everything about him seemed to be legendary – his perfectionism, his temper, his charm, his sex appeal (The *New York Times* reported in 1943: "Mature ladies are as apt to grow as hysterical as teenagers"). He had animal appeal as well.

George Washington, America's first president was born.

A report out of New Zealand once said that cows there produced more milk when listening to recordings of Sinatra and the Andrews Sisters.

Sinatra was also a successful actor, winning the Academy Award in 1954 for best supporting actor for his role in *From Here to Eternity*. That role resurrected his career, setting his recording career back on the road to stardom.

"Everything he touched was a gem, and is to this day," said jazz great Joe Williams.

10:00 a.m., Fri., Feb. 11, 1732 – George Washington, America's first president, who would lead a poorly-trained force to victory in the American Revolution, was born on the family estate in Westmoreland County, Virginia.

Washington was a man of quiet courage who commanded respect from all. Under his command, American troops rallied from what seemed like certain defeat to triumph over the British. Washington was an undisputed choice to be the country's first president – but he had to be talked into taking the job. He swept all the electoral votes both in 1789 and 1792 – the only president ever twice elected unanimously by the electoral college.

Washington was well aware that his actions as president would set a precedent for future leaders to come. Among the many procedures he established was the right of the president to choose and consult regularly with his cabinet, and the right of a president to select the Chief Justice of the Supreme Court from outside that body. Washington retired after two terms, discouraging those who followed him from seeking a third term. The two-term limit, broken by Franklin Roosevelt's four-term presidency, was cast into law with the 22nd amendment in 1951.

Washington retired to his Mount Vernon estate after leaving the presidency in 1797. He was resurrected as Commander-in-Chief of the American forces in 1798 but his services were not required.

Washington died of laryngitis at 10:00 p.m. on Wednesday, December 14, 1799. He had caught a severe cold while riding around his estate in snow and rain two days earlier.

At his funeral, Washington was praised by General Henry Lee as, "First in war, first in peace, first in the hearts of his countrymen." Ironically, Lee was the father of Confederate General Robert E. Lee.

10:00 a.m., Tues., Apr. 3, 1973 – The first private cellphone call was made. Martin Cooper, a vice-president at Motorola Corp., was headed to a public demonstration of his company's new invention when he decided to test the device with a private call. Standing on a New York street, Cooper lifted the 2-1/2 pound box of wires, circuits and batteries to his ear and called an acquaintance at Bell Laboratories. "I don't remember my precise words. I do remember a kind of embarrassed silence at the other end," Cooper said. It was the first time the device had been tested outside the laboratory.

The sight of Cooper making a phone call on a hand-held box in 1973 must have been an odd one. Now cellphones are commonplace; in fact, in 2000, a survey showed that cellphone use had surpassed that of land-line phones in Japan for the first time. Cooper helped Motorola develop five generations of cellular handsets before placing one on the market in 1983. It took 15 years and $90 million but the end result was a popular communications form and a title for Cooper – father of the hand-held cellular phone.

The first private cellphone call was made.

10:00 a.m., Sun., June 28, 1992 – The Solomon R. Guggenheim Museum in New York City reopened following an extensive two-year restoration and expansion project.

The Museum originally opened in 1959 to house one of the world's finest collections of modern and contemporary art. Designed by Frank Lloyd Wright, the building contains the works of Van Gogh, Cezanne, Gauguin, Degas, Toulouse-Lautrec, Picasso and many others. As a result of the restoration, many of the original plans – including a rotunda – were opened to the public for the first time.

The original collection was founded during the late 1920s by Solomon R. Guggenheim. There are five other Guggenheim museums around the world.

Wright himself died six months before the Museum opened. He was 90. Among his more than 700 works are the Falling Water House in Pennsylvania and the Imperial Hotel in Tokyo.

10:00 a.m., Sat., Apr. 15, 1865 – Andrew Johnson, the 17th president of the United States, and the first to be impeached in the House, was sworn in 2-1/2 hours after the death of Abraham Lincoln.

One of the most daring of all robberies, the theft of the priceless "Star of India," was discovered.

Johnson himself had been tabbed for assassination, but the man assigned to shoot him changed his mind at the last minute.

Johnson is the only president to never receive any formal education. A tailor by trade, Johnson taught himself to read and at an early age was fascinated by political speeches. He soon entered politics and represented Tennessee as a Representative, Governor and Senator. In 1864, Johnson replaced Vice-President Hannibal Hamlin on the Republican ticket. Johnson made a somewhat poor first impression when he appeared drunk at the inaugural, having fortified himself with whiskey to battle a fever.

As president, Johnson fought to carry out Reconstruction in the war-scarred South, but his efforts were bitterly opposed and federal troops had to be called out to keep the peace. In 1868, Johnson opened up a hornet's nest when he dismissed Secretary of War Stanton without the required Senate consent. The House of Representatives voted almost 3–1 to impeach him for "high crimes and misdemeanors." The matter then went to the Senate, which came within one vote of achieving the necessary two-thirds majority for impeachment.

Johnson was denied re-nomination by his party in 1868. But his political career didn't end – in 1875 he became the only former president to be elected to the Senate. Johnson died following a stroke at 2 a.m., July 31, 1875.

10:00 a.m., Fri., Oct. 10, 1964 – One of the most daring of all robberies, the theft of the priceless "Star of India," was discovered at the American Museum of Natural History in New York. Stolen along with the "Star" were 21 other irreplaceable gems, all uninsured due to high premiums. The "Star of India" and eight other gems were eventually recovered in a Miami bus station on January 8, 1965.

10:00 a.m., Tues., Aug. 3, 1976 – Students at Makarere University in Uganda began to read a list of grievances, including a demand that Idi Amin's son, Taban, be removed from the university for illiteracy. Idi Amin responded by ordering his troops to the campus. In the melee that followed, more than 100 students died, some shot, some bayonetted, some thrown from upper storey windows. An estimated 700 to 1,000 students were injured and about 800 were taken prisoner. By week's end, the

Makarere campus was deserted, with students having returned to their villages in fear. This was not an isolated incident in Amin's barbarous reign, which ended with his exile in 1979.

10:00 a.m., Mon., July 13, 1863 – The New York City draft riot, one of the most violent anti-war protests in U.S. history, began outside a draft office on Manhattan's Third Avenue. The 500-strong mob, enraged that black people were excluded from the draft and that the rich could buy their way out, pelted the building with bricks and stones before forcing open the doors. As draft officials ran for cover, the demonstrators ransacked the building and set it afire.

Within two hours of the start of the riot, Third Avenue was filled with 50,000 rioters, most of them drunk. Homes, offices and shops were pillaged and burned as the mob ran wild. Police, under instructions to take no prisoners, fired on the rioters and by evening the street was strewn with dead and wounded. Gangs of rioters roamed the streets throughout the evening, torturing and lynching every black person in sight. By the time the riot was finally brought under control two days later, 1,200 had been killed.

10:00 a.m., Sat., Oct. 1, 1949 – China's Chairman Mao Tse-Tung and other top leaders appeared on a podium overlooking Tiananmen Square in Beijing. The occasion was a ceremony formally establishing the People's Republic of China. A huge crowd shouted slogans such as "Long Live the People's Republic of China" and "Long Live the Chinese Communist Party."

The celebration represented the culmination of a dream for Mao, the obscure peasant who became father of the Chinese revolution and China's leader for more than a quarter century. Mao, who helped build China's industrial and political base while staging a running feud with the Soviets, had undisputed power in China from the Communist takeover of 1949 on. His little red book, *Quotations from Chairman Mao,* was considered gospel and he became almost a living god to the 800 million Chinese he ruled. Two of his greatest triumphs came late in life, when he opened a relationship with the United States and won a seat in the United Nations at the expense of Taiwan. A humble man despite his enormous power, Mao preferred simple surroundings and dress, in keeping with his lower-class upbringing.

Within two hours of the start of the riot, Third Avenue was filled with 50,000 rioters.

The famous photograph used on the cover of the Beatles' *Abbey Road* **album was taken.**

Mao died after a long illness at 12:10 a.m., Thursday, September 9, 1976. He was 82.

10:00 a.m., Wed., Jan. 31, 1990 – The Soviet Union's first McDonald's Restaurant, the 11,201st in the world, opened in Moscow. Soviets flocked to the Golden Arches in droves despite an average lunchtime wait of 90 minutes, and the fact a Big Mac cost a little over two hours' pay for the average Soviet. The restaurant is the biggest and busiest in the McDonald's chain, with over 1,000 employees and more than 50,000 meals served daily.

10:00 a.m., Wed., Apr. 3, 1991 – The walls of Chicago's Comiskey Park came tumbling down, as a wrecking ball started swinging against the 80-year-old stadium. Up until the moment of demolition, Comiskey Park was the oldest standing major league baseball park, a Chicago landmark since 1910. The stadium was home to baseball's Chicago White Sox, as well as the old Chicago Cardinals football team and baseball's first all-star game in 1933. The old park was flattened to make way for a parking lot serving its successor, a new Comiskey Park located right across the street.

10:00 a.m., Fri., Aug. 8, 1969 – The famous photograph used on the cover of the Beatles' *Abbey Road* album was taken. The shot shows the four Beatles walking across a street in front of the Beatles' Abbey Road recording studios. The photo was one of six taken by photographer Ian Macmillan that day as a policeman held up traffic. Paul McCartney chose the photograph that wound up on the cover of the album.

The photograph later added fuel to the "Paul is Dead" theory which began circulating in late 1969. McCartney is barefoot in the cover photo, supposedly a symbol of death. And the licence plate on a Volkswagen in the background partially reads "28F," or that McCartney would have been 28 if he had lived (actually, he would have been 27 the day the photo was taken, a fact overlooked by almost everybody at the time).

Numerous other "clues" were found on other Beatles albums and within their songs (in some cases if played backwards). Suggestions that the Beatles did this as a publicity stunt have never been admitted or proven and have been strongly denied. The very-much alive Paul joked at the time, "If I had been dead, I probably would have been the last to know."

10:00 a.m., Mon., July 9, 1990 – More than 1,400 Moslem pilgrims died after power was lost in a tunnel near the holy city of Mecca in Saudi Arabia. The pilgrims were suffocated or trampled to death in the rush to find an exit from the darkened tunnel. Adding to the nightmare was the fact that the air-conditioning failed, sending temperatures to infernal levels. The tunnel was packed with 50,000 pilgrims at the time of the power failure.

10:00 a.m., Thurs., May 26, 1977 – George Willig, 27-year-old toy-maker dubbed "the Human Fly," completed his 3-1/2 hour climb up one of the 110-storey towers of the World Trade Center. He was prompt-ly arrested and later sued for $25,000 by the City of New York. Said Willig: "I just wanted the prize of getting to the top."

10:00 a.m., Sat., Dec. 18, 1999 – Julia Butterfly Hill came down from her tree. The 25-year-old climbed down from an ancient redwood tree in Monument Ridge, California, that had been her home for more than two years. The tree-sitting was a protest against the Pacific Lumber Company's plans to cut it down. Rather than allowing the tree she called "Luna" to die, Hill lived in its branches beginning December 10, 1997, remaining there for 738 days. She finally capitulated after the company agreed not to cut the tree down and she agreed not to visit Luna except on 48 hours' notice to the firm. Hill and her supporters also agreed to pay Pacific Lumber $50,000, which was donated to Humboldt State University for scientific research.

So what was it like to live in a tree? Cold and damp, said Hill, plus cramped – her living area was two 6 by 6 foot (1.8 by 1.8 metre) platforms. For company, she had her support team plus several visiting celebrities, including Joan Baez and Woody Harrelson. Hill noted that squirrels eagerly grabbed every morsel of food she dropped.

10:00 a.m., Thurs., Oct. 3, 1974 – Twenty-seven years after Jackie Robinson became the first black person to play major league

The tree-sitting was a protest against the Pacific Lumber Company's plans to cut it down.

**The island of
Krakatoa erupted.**

baseball, Frank Robinson became the game's first black manager. The former Baltimore Orioles star was named manager of the perennial also-ran Cleveland Indians, his first of three managerial stints.

Robinson was fired as Indians manager in 1977 despite leading the team to its first winning season in more than a decade the year before. Robinson surfaced as manager of the San Francisco Giants in 1981 before being sacked again in 1984. He began his third managerial job in 1989 with his old team the Orioles, and was named American League manager of the year for leading the team to a surprise second-place finish in the American League East. Robinson resigned as Orioles manager in 1991 and became the team's assistant general manager.

10:00 a.m., Mon., Apr. 3, 1882 – Jesse James, remembered as a hero but actually a cold-blooded killer and robber, was shot in the head in St. Joseph, Missouri. James had risen to clear cobwebs from a picture when he was shot by Robert Ford. Ford had been recruited by the local sheriff to capture James.

James became a post-Civil War hero for reasons that seem somewhat confused now. James and his accomplices killed bank clerks in cold blood during bank robberies; they derailed trains and then robbed injured passengers as they lay helpless; even innocent passersby were gunned down just for getting in the way. After numerous narrow escapes, James's luck ran out when a sheriff arranged to have Ford capture the outlaw. Ford went a step further and shot him.

James's open casket was viewed by more than 1,000 people; personal effects from his house were sold for $250, and years later his mother was able to charge people a quarter to look through the house where he grew up. His legend grew into the 20th century, when 20 films about his life were made.

10:02 a.m., Mon., Aug. 27, 1883 – The island of Krakatoa erupted. In a matter of seconds, five cubic miles of rock, ash and lava were ejected, resulting in a crater five miles (eight kilometres) wide and 243 metres (800 feet) deep. The final death toll may never be known as villages and settlements were wiped out, and ships capsized and sank without a trace. An estimated 36,000 were killed in western Java and southeastern

Sumatra alone when sea waves 18 to 36 metres (60 to 120 feet) high struck the coast.

Krakatoa's impact was terrifying. The shock wave of the explosion travelled seven times around the world and the sound of the explosion was heard 4,800 kilometres (3,000 miles) to the west off the coast of Madagascar. Ash and cinder were spread over a 776,000 square kilometre (300,000 square mile) area and fine dust particles in the upper atmosphere affected sunsets around the world for months. In some parts of the U.S., fire alarms were pulled as people mistook the red glow in the sky for fires. Krakatoa remains history's largest recorded explosion.

10:05 a.m., Thurs., Sept. 9, 1982 – Princess Grace of Monaco, the former Grace Kelly who went from actress to princess, died in a car crash in Monte Carlo. Princess Grace was travelling with her 17-year-old daughter Stephanie when the car plunged off a mountain road. Stephanie suffered only minor injuries.

Grace Kelly met her future husband Prince Rainier III in 1955 while making her 11th film, *To Catch a Thief* with Cary Grant. She completed two more films, *The Swan* and *High Society*, before her marriage in 1956. She married the prince in an elaborate royal wedding and retired from acting. Grace Kelly was 52 when she died.

10:07 a.m., Tues., Oct. 3, 1995 – O.J. Simpson was pronounced not guilty of first-degree murder by a jury in Los Angeles. The jury deliberated only four hours before finding the former football star innocent of charges he murdered his ex-wife Nicole Brown Simpson and waiter Ron Goldman outside Brown's condominium in the Brentwood section of Los Angeles.

Simpson's trial captivated the nation. TV networks like CNN and Court TV provided wall-to-wall coverage, and some radio stations carried the trial in its entirety so people could hear it in their cars. The issue of whether Simpson had carried out the murders was clouded by questions as to the integrity of Los Angeles police, in particular Detective Mark Fuhrman. The defence argued Fuhrman was a racist who planted evidence at the scene, presumably to frame Simpson. But the turning point in the trial came when the prosecution – in what was later viewed as a major blunder – agreed to

O.J. Simpson was pronounced not guilty of first-degree murder.

The last bare-knuckle championship heavyweight fight began.

let Simpson try on the once blood-soaked gloves he was purportedly wearing at the time of the murders. The gloves didn't fit and former actor Simpson appeared to wince as he attempted to put them on. That proved to Simpson supporters that he could not have been wearing the gloves at the time of the murders, although some pointed out the gloves may have shrunk because of the blood.

After the trial, Simpson vowed to "find the real killers" but no more arrests have been made. Simpson lost a civil suit in Los Angeles in February, 1997 when a jury ordered him to pay $25 million in damages to the Brown and Goldman families.

10:10 **a.m., Mon., July 8, 1889** – The last bare-knuckle championship heavyweight fight began in a clearing on a lumber estate in Richburg, Mississippi.

John L. Sullivan, who had lost 33 pounds for the match, faced the undefeated Jake Kilrain in what would be a lengthy contest. The bout was fought in secrecy due to the fact that prizefighting was illegal in all U.S. states at the time. A trainload of fight fans had left New Orleans the night before knowing they were headed to a championship fight, but not knowing exactly where it would be. When the train finally stopped in Richburg, a specially constructed wooden arena awaited the fightgoers.

The match lasted 75 rounds during which Sullivan established a considerable edge, but could not put his opponent away. Asked how long he would stay, Sullivan replied, "Till tomorrow morning, if necessary." By the end of the 75th round, Kilrain's back was covered with blisters, his head rolled loosely on his shoulders and he could no longer stand. At this stage, Kilrain's handlers threw in the towel, or in this case, a sponge.

John L. Sullivan was awarded the Police Gazette belt and had the honour of being the last man to win the heavyweight crown bare-knuckled.

10:12 **a.m., Mon., May 2, 1960** – Caryl Chessman, the so-called "Red Light Bandit," was pronounced dead after being executed in the gas chamber at San Francisco's San Quentin prison.

Chessman was convicted in 1948 on several charges including kidnapping with bodily harm, which carried the death penalty. However, he cheated death for 12 years, staving off scheduled execution dates eight times with his knowledge of the law. Chessman wrote four books on law during his incarceration and also read an estimated 10,000 law books in full or in part. He almost won a ninth stay of execution, but a secretary dialed the wrong number after a judge awarded him a last-minute reprieve. By the time she got the number right, the cyanide pellets had been dropped.

10:15 **a.m., Wed., Sept. 16, 1998** – A robotic device controlled by a heart surgeon began performing coronary bypass surgery for the first time, directed by Dr. Hermann Reichenspurner at a medical facility in Munich, Germany. The ZEUS™ Robotic Surgical System was developed by Computer Motion, Inc.

A robotic device controlled by a heart surgeon began performing coronary bypass surgery for the first time.

The procedure, which cuts recovery time by weeks, is performed without even cutting open the patient's chest. The ZEUS™ Robotic Surgical System acts like a microscope for the surgeon. The surgeon sees through a camera held by a voice-controlled robotic arm in the patient's chest. In the first operation of its type in the U.S., the doctor, with the help of ZEUS™, made three holes in the patient's chest, each small enough to insert the tools and camera.

The operation reduces recovery time from weeks to four to six days.

10:20 **a.m., Fri., Oct. 25, 1957** – Alberto "the Executioner" Anastasia was shot to death as he sat down for a haircut at a barber shop in New York City. Two gunmen fled from the scene and were never captured. The Mafia reportedly ordered Anastasia's murder when it was discovered he was selling "memberships" for $40,000 each.

Anastasia was a master killer for Murder Inc., a gang that plagued the city in the 1930s. He is "credited" with arranging 63 assassinations, doing the dirty work himself on 31 occasions.

10:22 **a.m., Tues., Jan. 17, 1966** – An American B-52 bomber carrying four hydrogen bombs collided with a K-135 tanker off eastern Spain. Three of the bombs landed on dry land near the village of Palomares while the other bomb fell into the sea.

Within 48 hours, authorities rounded up all three of the dry land bombs, one of which had been kicked by a curious farmer. The fourth bomb was discovered two months later on a narrow sea ledge at a depth of

Pierre Elliott Trudeau delivered his letter of resignation to Liberal party president.

685 metres (2,250 feet). The bomb was raised from the ocean and for the first time in history, cameramen had the opportunity to photograph an H-bomb. The U.S. removed nearly 2,000 tons of topsoil around Palomares because of radiation danger. Villagers began to suffer strange illnesses and claim the soil is still contaminated.

10:23 a.m., Sat., June 9, 1934 – The first successful field test of FM transmission was conducted. It was the culmination of 20 years of work on high fidelity transmission for FM inventor Howard Armstrong. The first FM station, Armstrong's W2XMN in Alpine, New Jersey, went on the air July 18, 1939, and many more stations soon followed. FM stereo was introduced in 1961.

10:30 a.m., Wed., Feb. 29, 1984 – Pierre Elliott Trudeau, both loved and hated by Canadians during his 15 years as Prime Minister, delivered his letter of resignation to Liberal party president Iona Campagnolo.

Trudeau rose to public prominence in 1968 following the retirement of Prime Minister Lester Pearson, creating a national frenzy that was dubbed "Trudeaumania." His charm, style, wit and intelligence led Trudeau to an easy victory in that year's election. Highlights of his first tenure (1968–1979) included passing a bill to make Canada officially bilingual, reduction of Canada's NATO commitment by half and the October crisis of 1970. During that crisis, British diplomat James Cross and Quebec cabinet minister Pierre Laporte were kidnapped. Laporte was murdered and Trudeau invoked the War Measures Act, calling out the troops to restore order.

After Trudeau lost to Conservative Joe Clark in 1979, he staged an amazing comeback to win a majority government in 1980. His second tenure (1980–1984) saw the defeat of a referendum that could have led to Quebec independence. In addition, Trudeau patriated the Constitution.

Trudeau had an active social life, dating numerous women before marrying Margaret Sinclair in 1971. They separated in 1977 and divorced in 1984.

Pierre Trudeau died at his Montreal home just after 3:00 p.m. on September 28, 2000. He was 80. Trudeau, who suffered from prostate cancer and Parkinson's disease, never recovered from the death of his youngest son, Michel, who died in a British Columbia avalanche in 1998.

10:30 **a.m., Sun., Mar. 11, 1888** – The U.S. weather office in New York City issued a "cautionary southeast storm warning." The next morning, New York was hit with the worst blizzard in its history. More than 60.9 centimetres (24 inches) of snow fell, and gale-force winds produced drifts up to six metres (20 feet). The city was paralyzed, as transportation and communication services were rendered useless.

For some people, the blizzard brought fun in the form of sled rides and skating on city streets. For others, it was a white death. More than 200 people died in metropolitan New York, many from the bitter -9° Celsius (15° Fahrenheit) cold.

10:30 **a.m., Tues., Jan. 3, 1967** – Jack Ruby, shadowy Dallas night club owner who shot accused presidential assassin Lee Harvey Oswald in front of a national TV audience, died of cancer at age 55. Ruby, who claimed he shot Oswald to protect the President's widow Jackie Kennedy, only further clouded the issue of President Kennedy's assassination. The official line was that Ruby acted spontaneously and on his own, but many investigators feel Ruby was hired to silence Oswald. Despite dropping numerous hints he knew more than he revealed, the man who as a teenager ran errands for Al Capone, carried his secret with him to the grave. During part of his incarceration, Ruby was held in a cell overlooking Dealey Plaza, site of the assassination. (see 12:30 p.m.; 1:07 p.m.)

10:30 **a.m., Fri., Jan. 12, 1945** – In one of the last major offensives of World War II, the Red Army infantry began its invasion of German lines in south Poland. Five days later, the Russian army occupied Warsaw as the noose slowly tightened on the Third Reich.

10:30 **a.m., Thurs., Feb. 23, 1945** – A group of six U.S. marines raised the American flag on the South Pacific island of Iwo Jima. Photographer Joe Rosenthal snapped the picture on the fifth day of an amphibious landing that saw 7,000 Americans killed and 20,000 wounded. Rosenthal's photograph, which won him a Pulitzer Prize, became a symbol of hope and strength to Americans demoralized by World War II.

Of the six servicemen in the picture, two, Mike Strank and Harlon Block, died in battle nine days later on March 1, 1945. Franklin Sousy was killed in

A group of six U.S. marines raised the American flag on the South Pacific island of Iwo Jima.

One of the greatest oil strikes in history was made near Beaumont, Texas.

action March 21, 1945. The other three made it home to heroes' welcomes. Ira Hayes died in 1955, Rene Gagnon passed away in 1979 and the last survivor – John Bradley – died in 1994. Four of the six were American-born; Strank was born in Czechoslovakia and Bradley was from the West Indies.

After the war, the Iwo Jima photo appeared on a stamp and a war-bond poster and became the inspiration for the Marine Corps Memorial in Washington, D.C.

10:30 a.m., Thurs., Jan. 10, 1901 – One of the greatest oil strikes in history was made near Beaumont, Texas when the "Spindletop Gusher," as it came to be known, spewed a tower of oil 60 metres (200 feet) into the air. The well was soon producing nearly 75,000 barrels a day – about half the U.S. oil consumption.

The "Spindletop Gusher" astounded many experts who did not believe oil would be found there. This strike, and numerous others, helped the U.S. move past the Soviet Union as the leading oil producer at the time.

10:30 a.m., Fri., Jan. 16, 1920 – The first meeting of the League of Nations began at the French foreign ministry in Paris. Nine men gathered at a green-covered table for a meeting of the executive council, while 100 diplomats looked on. An empty chair was reserved for the United States, which chose not to join the international group.

The League of Nations did not have a permanent home until 1936, when it moved into its headquarters at Geneva, Switzerland. Although the League had 60 member countries at its peak, it proved ineffective as a peacekeeping body. After failing to prevent Adolf Hitler's invasion of Poland in 1939, the 21st and last session of the League took place in April, 1946, disbanding the organization—four months after the United Nations held its first session.

Among the items left behind at the League's last meeting was tea-making equipment valued at $162.28.

10:30 a.m., Thurs., Aug. 2, 1945 – Toronto radio station CKEY began running "stroke-by-stroke" coverage of the Canadian Open golf tournament. The event ended two days later with Byron Nelson shooting 72 and 68 in the 36-hole windup at the Thornhill Golf and Country Club.

That, combined with earlier rounds of 68 and 72, gave Nelson a 280 total and a four-stroke victory over Herman Barron.

The win was significant in that it was the last in Nelson's incredible streak of 11 consecutive victories on the PGA tour. He showed signs of weakening in the first round when he blew a tee-shot. The ball hit a bridge and bounced forward about 50 yards (45 metres). Nelson claimed it was the first shot he'd muffed in 100 rounds. He won 18 PGA tournaments in that amazing 1945 season – a record that many believe may never be broken.

An interesting sidelight to the event was the fact that the six Canadian pros who survived the cut shared an additional purse of $800 set aside just for Canadians.

10:30 **a.m., Mon., July 12, 1954** – An avalanche hit Blons, Austria, destroying the entire central section of the city and killing over 200 people. Nine hours later, a second avalanche hit the town, killing 115 rescuers and survivors of the first avalanche.

10:30 **a.m., Fri., Dec. 6, 1907** – At least 362 men died when an explosion rocked a coal mine in Monongah, West Virginia. The force of the explosion, caused by a short circuit in the electrical system, rattled windows 9.6 kilometres (six miles) away. It took three weeks to recover the bodies and many miners claimed more dead remained below. Only one man survived, a Polish miner named Peter Urban, who was found unconscious in a side tunnel. Urban would die in a cave-in at the same mine 20 years later.

10:31 **a.m., Fri., Nov. 5, 1976** – The Toronto Blue Jays made Bob Bailor their first choice in baseball's expansion draft. Fifteen years, 11 months, 20 days, 12 hours and 19 minutes later, at 12:50 a.m. on Sunday, October 25, 1992, the Jays became World Series champions for the first time.

A ground out by Atlanta's Otis Nixon gave the Jays a 4–3 victory over the Braves and a four-games-to-two victory in the Series. It marked the first time a non-U.S. team had won the World Series, which is named for its original sponsor, the now-defunct *New York World* newspaper. The Jays were making their first appearance in the World Series after 16 seasons and three previous

At least 362 men died when an explosion rocked a coal mine in Monongah, West Virginia.

The British royal navy sank the *Bismarck* in the mid-Atlantic Ocean.

losses in the American League Championship Series. Toronto also won the World Series in 1993 and technically reigned as defending champions until 1995. No World Series was held in 1994 because of a players strike.

Toronto is not the northernmost city to win the World Series. That honour goes to Minneapolis–St. Paul, Minnesota, whose Twins won the Series in 1987 and 1991. Minneapolis–St. Paul is about 144 kilometres (90 miles) north of Toronto. *(see 11:39 p.m.)*

10:31 a.m., Wed., Mar. 2, 1949 – The first non-stop flight around the world was completed when a U.S. B-50 bomber, named *Lucky Lady II*, landed at Carswell Air Force Base near Fort Worth, Texas. The plane was refuelled four times in mid-air during its 94-hour, 37,741-kilometre (23,452-mile) journey.

10:32 a.m., Wed., May 24, 1978 – The British royal family's image was tarnished as Princess Margaret, younger sister of Queen Elizabeth II, and Lord Snowden were officially divorced. They had been married since 1960. Irreconcilable differences were cited as the reason for the breakup. Three of the Queen's four children would be divorced by the century's end.

10:33 a.m., Tues., May 27, 1941 – The British royal navy sank the *Bismarck* in the mid-Atlantic Ocean south-west of Ireland. Only three days earlier, the *Bismarck* had torpedoed the British ship *Hood*, with a loss of 1,300 lives. The royal navy chased the German battleship for more than 2,735 kilometres (1,700 miles) before dealing the avenging blow. An estimated 1,000 men died when the *Bismarck* went down.

10:34 a.m., Fri., Dec. 16, 1960 – Two planes collided over New York City, killing all 128 passengers and six people on the ground.

The tragedy occurred when a TWA Constellation from Dayton, Ohio and a United DC-7 from Chicago crashed in a blinding snowstorm. The TWA plane disintegrated, falling in three pieces onto the landing strip of an army helicopter base. The United plane continued flying for a few miles before plunging into Brooklyn's Park Slope section. The only passenger discovered alive was 11-year-old Stevie Baltz, found in a snowbank. Baltz died the next day.

In 1956, two planes of the same make and from the same airlines collided over the Grand Canyon. The death toll from that accident was also 128.

10:35 **a.m., Thurs., Dec. 17, 1903** – The Wright brothers made the first authenticated heavier-than-air flight on a beach at Kitty Hawk, North Carolina. Orville Wright had the honour of piloting *Flyer I* after winning a coin toss with his brother Wilbur. The flight began on top of a sand dune named Kill Devil Hill. It lasted just 12 seconds and covered 36 metres (120 feet). Orville and Wilbur made four flights that historic day, the longest lasting about one minute and covering 259 metres (852 feet).

Seven people witnessed man's first flight. In 1952, the last living witness, John Thomas Moore, shot himself to death. He was 65.

It took the Wright brothers nearly seven years to develop their airplane at a cost of more than $1,000. They received a patent for it in 1906 and went on to produce the plane commercially.

Wilbur Wright died at his home in Dayton, Ohio, at 3:15 a.m. on May 30, 1912 of typhoid fever. He was 45.

Orville Wright died at 10:40 p.m., Friday, January 30, 1948. Orville, 76, suffered from lung congestion and clogged arteries.

10:35 **a.m., Fri., Aug. 7, 1998** – A bomb exploded at the U.S. embassy in Nairobi. A few minutes later, another bomb went off at the American embassy in Dar-es-Salaam. Two hundred and twenty-four people were killed in the two explosions. All but 11 of the deaths took place in Nairobi. Many others were blinded by flying glass.

One of the sad tales to emerge from the Nairobi explosion was that of a Kenyan woman later identified as Rose Wanjiku. Rescue workers were able to talk to Wanjiku as she lay buried in the rubble, but were unable to reach her until five days after the blast. Doctors later determined that despite surviving the explosion uninjured, Wanjiku had died of dehydration and exposure on the Tuesday morning following the blast. Rescuers reached her on Wednesday.

10:35 **a.m., Sat., July 10, 1937** – George Gershwin, jazz composer best known for the classics "Rhapsody in Blue" and "Swanee," died of brain cancer. He was only 39. Gershwin was also known for his opera

The Wright brothers made the first authenticated heavier-than-air flight.

A Chicago jury reached a verdict in the tax evasion case of Al Capone.

Porgy and Bess and the orchestral suite "An American in Paris." He once said he had more tunes in his head than he had time to write them.

10:41 **a.m., Wed., Aug. 25, 1875** – Merchant Navy seaman Matthew Webb became the first person to swim the English Channel without a lifejacket. Webb swam the breaststroke from Dover, England, to Cap Gris-Nez, France, in 21 hours, 45 minutes. Because of strong currents, he swam an estimated 61 kilometres (38 miles) to make the 33-kilometre (21-mile) journey. The first France to England crossing was not made until 1923.

10:48 **a.m., Sat., Feb. 1, 1958** – America's first satellite to orbit the earth, *Explorer I,* lifted off from Cape Canaveral, Florida. The tiny 13-kilogram (30.8-pound) satellite put the U.S. into the space race four months after the Soviets stunned the world by sending *Sputnik* into orbit on October 4, 1957. A previous U.S. attempt to launch the satellite had failed December 5, 1957, when the ship blew up two seconds after takeoff.

10:51 **a.m., Sun., Oct. 18, 1932** – A Chicago jury informed Judge James Wilkerson that it had reached a verdict in the tax evasion case of Al Capone. Twenty minutes later, the jury announced Capone's conviction on five counts of tax evasion. The real shock came the next day, when Wilkerson sentenced the gangster to 11 years in prison and fined him $80,000. Capone and his defence team had been expecting a much lighter sentence.

It was quite a comedown for Capone, who had ruled Chicago with an iron fist during the Prohibition years, reportedly earning more than $100 million from bootlegging, gambling and prostitution. Over 300 men died during the Capone gang wars. Hollywood recreated the era in *Scarface* and *Public Enemy*.

Capone remained in prison for eight years and emerged a sick man. His former powerful status was long gone and he was mentally ill. Capone spent his retirement years at his estate, where he could be seen fishing from his dock in pyjamas. He died at 4:00 a.m., on Sunday, January 19, 1947.

10:54 **a.m., Sun., July 3, 1988** – A U.S. warship shot down an Iran Air jetliner over the Persian Gulf. Two hundred and ninety people, including 66 children died.

The U.S. defended the shooting, claiming the plane was outside its normal air corridor and did not respond to warnings. Iranian officials called the disaster a "barbaric massacre." President Reagan later offered financial restitution to the families of the victims.

A U.S. warship shot down an Iran Air jetliner over the Persian Gulf.

11 a.m. to 11:59 a.m.

- ⏱ **World War I ends**
- ⏱ **Julius Caesar assassinated**
- ⏱ **Charge of the Light Brigade begins**
- ⏱ **Gunmen shoot up Littleton, Colorado, high school**
- ⏱ **Verdict announced in Scopes trial**
- ⏱ **Mount Everest conquered for first time**

11:00 a.m., Mon., Nov. 11, 1918 – World War I, then known simply as the Great War or the War in Europe, officially ended as the armistice took effect. The eleventh hour of the eleventh day of the eleventh month is acknowledged annually by two minutes of silence to remember those who gave their lives in war – "lest we forget."

The armistice was signed at five o'clock that morning, and the cease-fire took effect six hours later. Germany's collapse and the war's end had been inevitable since the fall of the Austro-Hungarian Empire on November 3. The Germans were out of manpower, food and morale.

The human toll was staggering. More than 10 million people had been killed, another 21 million injured, and 7.5 million taken prisoner or listed as missing in action. A total of 407,316 U.S. and 46,542 Canadian soldiers were killed, a toll that pales beside the 1.8 million casualties suffered by Germany.

11:00 a.m., Mon., Nov. 11, 1929 – Eleven years to the minute after the end of World War I, filming began on *All Quiet on the Western Front*, a powerful anti-war film that featured mostly unknown actors and actresses. Now considered one of the most important films ever made, it is also one of the most-watched (some 100 million people had seen it by 1968). *All Quiet on the Western Front*, adapted from Erich Maria

Remarque's best-selling novel and directed by Lewis Milestone, won the Oscar for best picture in 1930. Milestone took the award for best director.

11:00 a.m., Sun., Sept. 3, 1939 – Britain declared war on Germany at the same hour armistice had been declared ending World War I two decades earlier. The announcement was in response to the German invasion of Poland on September 1, 1939.

11:00 a.m., Fri., Mar. 15, 44 B.C. – Julius Caesar was stabbed 23 times by a group of conspirators as he took his seat at the Senate House in Rome. Two of the stab wounds were inflicted by Marcus Brutus, the leader of the 60-man conspiracy. It was to Brutus that Caesar directed his famous last words "Et tu, Brute?" (You too, Brutus?) The Roman dictator was left to die at the foot of Pompey's statue.

Brutus and co-conspirator Cassius had Caesar killed because they believed the ambitious dictator was becoming too powerful. They miscalculated. The popular Caesar was deeply mourned and cries went out for Brutus' and Cassius' deaths. The two were killed in battle two years later, in 42 B.C., the same year Caesar was officially recognized as a god and a temple was erected in his honour.

Although Caesar was best known as a military strategist and politician, he was also a gifted writer. His book *De bello Gallico*, describing the conquest of Gaul, is considered a literary classic. Caesar also implemented the Julian calendar, which was widely used until its replacement by the Gregorian calendar (introduced by Pope Gregory XIII) in the late 16th century. While most of the world uses the Gregorian calendar, the Julian calendar is still followed by the Eastern Orthodox Church. Greece retained it until 1923.

11:00 a.m., Fri., Apr. 1, 1949 – Joey Smallwood was sworn in as the first premier of Newfoundland. Just a few hours earlier, Newfoundland officially became Canada's 10th province. The time of entry was set at a few seconds before midnight, April 1, so Newfoundland's entry into Confederation would not be on April Fools' Day. Newfoundland voters narrowly approved the new status in a referendum July 22, 1948.

Julius Caesar was stabbed 23 times by a group of conspirators.

Iranian students began their invasion of the U.S. Embassy compound in Tehran.

11:00 a.m., Sun., Nov. 4, 1979 – Iranian students began their invasion of the U.S. Embassy compound in Tehran. Fourteen and a half months of captivity followed for the 49 people inside (three more, including U.S. chargé d'affaires Bruce Laingen, were held in the Iranian foreign embassy where they had gone seeking security).

The Iranian students had been demonstrating outside the Embassy for two weeks, protesting the American decision to allow the Shah of Iran into the U.S. for medical treatment. The U.S. government – and most of the students – believed that the embassy occupation would last only a few days at most. But days stretched into weeks and then months as the Iranians refused to let the hostages go until the Shah was returned to Iran. This proved an impossible demand for the U.S. Even the Shah's death in July, 1980 did not result in the hostages' freedom. Neither did an ill-fated "rescue" mission in April of that year.

In January of 1980, six American embassy employees had escaped from Iran posing as Canadian diplomats. They had taken refuge in the Canadian embassy and their whereabouts were kept secret by ambassador Ken Taylor and his staff until Canadian passports could be prepared for them.

Finally, after 444 days, and exhaustive three-way talks involving the U.S., the Iranians and third-party intermediary Algeria, the hostages were released on January 20, 1981.

11:00 a.m., May 15, 1918 – The Winnipeg General Strike, one of Canada's largest and bloodiest labour actions, began. Rail workers, telegraphers, telephone operators and postal workers all walked off the job. Newpapers did not publish and there were no milk or bread deliveries. Sympathy strikes broke out all over western Canada.

The strike took a violent turn on June 21 when Royal North-West Mounted Police attacked a peaceful parade of strike sympathizers in downtown Winnipeg. Two marchers were shot to death and many others wounded. The parade had been organized when Ottawa refused to hear the case of 10 alleged strike leaders who had been arrested four days earlier.

The strike ended on June 25 at 11:00 a.m. – six weeks to the minute after it began. Many strikers had already broken ranks to return to their jobs.

11:00 a.m., Tues., Feb. 24, 1981 – Buckingham Palace announced that Prince Charles and Lady Diana Spencer were engaged and would be married that summer. Five months and five days later, on July 29, the two were wed in a ceremony viewed by 2,500 at London's St. Paul's Cathedral. Millions more around the world watched the wedding on television via satellite.

Charles, 32, wore a full-dress naval commander's uniform, with a blue sash emblazoned across his chest. Diana, 20, was radiant in a dress of pale ivory silk with a 7.6-metre (25-foot) train. In repeating her vows, Diana told the Most. Reverend Robert Runcie, Archbishop of Canterbury, she would take "Philip Charles Arthur George" in holy matrimony. The bridegroom's name is actually "Charles Philip Arthur George."

The couple divorced in 1996 after producing two sons, William and Harry. *(see 12:25 a.m.)*

11:00 a.m., Mon., Nov. 27, 1978 – San Francisco mayor George Muscone was shot to death in his City Hall office. Moments later, Supervisor Harvey Milk, the city's first acknowledged homosexual official, was also shot and killed in the same building. Dan White, who had tried to withdraw his resignation as City Supervisor, surrendered to police about an hour later and was subsequently convicted of murder.

Muscone was succeeded as mayor by Dianne Feinstein, who gained national attention in 1984 when she emerged as a contender for the Democratic vice-presidential nomination that went to Geraldine Ferraro.

11:00 a.m., Mon., Nov. 15, 1948 – Canadian Prime Minister William Lyon Mackenzie King arrived at Government House in Ottawa to resign his position as prime minister in the presence of the governor-general. King had been Canada's longest-serving prime minister and had led the country through depression, war and peacetime reconstruction.

King served three terms as prime minister in a 22-year period. He was first elected in 1921, defeating Arthur Meighen. King's minority government collapsed in 1926 and the reins fell to Meighen – for three days. Meighen lost a non-confidence vote and by the end of the year the electorate had given King another mandate. Defeated at the polls by R.B. Bennett

Buckingham Palace announced that Prince Charles and Lady Diana Spencer were engaged.

**The Charge of
the Light Brigade
began.**

in 1930, King returned to power in 1935 where he remained until his retirement.

King claimed his main strength was that he listened to the people, but he listened to other voices as well. After his death, it was revealed that King had visited mediums in an attempt to communicate with his dead mother and others. The eccentric leader also had a room full of scrapbooks packed with mementoes such as ribbons and placecards.

King died at 9:42 p.m, Saturday, July 22, 1950.

11:00 **a.m., Fri., Oct. 16, 1793** – Marie Antoinette, Queen of France during the French Revolution, arrived at the scaffold to be guillotined. The unpopular monarch had been convicted and sentenced to death by the revolutionaries six and a half hours earlier.

The French people hated the Austrian-born Antoinette almost from the moment she and her husband, King Louis XVI, were crowned in 1774. Strong-willed and extravagant, she opposed reforms to the French economy and ruled with an iron fist (she once had a man sentenced to 50 years in prison because he whistled at her). Marie Antoinette was caught and imprisoned in 1793 while trying to flee the country.

11:00 **a.m., Fri., Sept. 23, 1949** – The United States announced that it had evidence that the Soviet Union had the atomic bomb. American officials advised citizens to take the news calmly, but with the announcement, a new era of fear and distrust of the "enemy" began.

11:00 **a.m., Fri., Jan. 20, 1961** – Robert Frost, the American poet known as the "Voice of New England," began to read a specially composed "Dedication" at the inauguration of the 35th U.S. president, John F. Kennedy. Strong sunlight blinded him and Frost could not continue. Instead he recited from memory one his most famous works, "The Gift Outright." A native-born Californian transplanted to New Hampshire, Frost would later recall his inauguration reading as one of the high points of his life.

Frost died in 1963 at the age of 89.

11:00 **a.m., Wed., Oct. 25, 1854** – The Charge of the Light Brigade began at the Battle of Balaklava. Six hundred and seventy-five

British horsemen rode into the so-called "Valley of Death" not realizing that a barrage of Russian guns lay in wait for them. Only 195 British soldiers survived the colossal military blunder; 250 Russians were killed in the battle.

11:00 a.m., Fri., Sept. 2, 1864 – U.S. General William Sherman entered Atlanta after his troops had destroyed the city by setting it on fire. Little was left of the proud Georgia city after Sherman's troops piled tents, wagons and bedding at the local railroad station and torched them. The burning of Atlanta climaxed Sherman's five-month bid to claim it and did nothing to dispel his reputation as a ruthless commander.

11:00 a.m., Wed., Feb. 12, 1908 – The much-ballyhooed "Great Around-The-World Automobile Race" began in New York City. It would continue to Paris by way of Alaska and Siberia. Six cars representing France, Germany, Italy and the U.S. began the competition; three finished. The German car *Protos* arrived in Paris on July 30 moments ahead of the American entrant *Thomas Flyer*. However, the German car, driven by Lieutenant Koepens, was disqualified after officials discovered that *Protos* was shipped to Seattle by rail. The *Thomas Flyer*, driven by George Schuster, was declared the winner. The Italian car *Zust* arrived in Paris two weeks later.

President Theodore Roosevelt greeted the victorious American team at a White House reception on August 20.

The winning car averaged 244 kilometres (152 miles) a day and in an incredible one-day run, clocked 675 kilometres (420 miles).

11:00 a.m., Fri., June 25, 1993 – Kim Campbell was sworn in as Canada's 19th prime minister, becoming the first female to hold that office seventy-five years after Canadian women had won the right to vote.

Campbell, Canada's first "baby boomer" prime minister, took office after winning the Conservative party leadership on June 13. She faced a rough tenure. Voters were angry after two terms of Conservative government led by Brian Mulroney. The party was decimated in the fall election, winning only two seats as Canada turned to Jean Chrétien and the Liberals. Campbell failed to win her own seat. She resigned as party leader, quit politics and left the country to accept a teaching position in California.

Kim Campbell was sworn in as Canada's 19th prime minister, becoming the first female to hold that office.

Pitcher John Montgomery Ward faced 27 batters and retired them all.

11:00 a.m., Sat., Dec. 16, 1911 – A Norwegian party led by explorer Roald Amundsen reached the South Pole after a 53-day trek with dog sleds from Antartica's Bay of Whales. In reaching the Pole, Amundsen beat a British expedition led by Robert F. Scott. Amundsen died in 1928 in a plane crash while attempting to rescue the crew of a downed Italian dirigible.

11:00 a.m., Fri., July 1, 1859 – The first recorded intercollegiate baseball game began in Pittsfield, Massachusetts. The historic contest saw Amherst beat Williams College 73–72.

The game differed considerably from today's standards: the pitcher stood only 10.6 metres (35 feet) from the plate (now it is just over 18 metres or 60 feet). Each team had 13 players (the present number is 9) and the game lasted 26 innings compared to today's nine. The game took four hours to play, averaging nine minutes an inning.

11:00 a.m., Thurs., Jan. 17, 1991 – Richard Branson and fellow adventurer Per Lindstrand completed the first Pacific crossing in a hot-air balloon, landing in a blinding snowstorm in a remote area of the Northwest Territories. The pair completed the trip despite accidentally jettisoning half their fuel early in the flight, forcing them to travel at a much higher altitude than originally planned.

Branson, who had previously crossed the Atlantic in a balloon and later in a high-powered speedboat, was asked what inspired him to cross the Pacific in a balloon. His reply: "Pure stupidity."

11:00 a.m., Thurs., June 17, 1880 – More than 1,800 baseball fans – a large crowd for that era – looked on as the hometown Providence Grays began a rare morning game against Buffalo. The game had been moved from its original 3:30 p.m. starting time to avoid conflict with a local rowing regatta the same day. By the time the game ended, history had been made. In a 5–0 Providence victory, pitcher John Montgomery Ward faced 27 batters and retired them all. It was only the second perfect game in major league baseball history.

The first perfect game had been pitched by Worchester's J. Lee Richmond only five days earlier. Ward's feat was significant because it would be 84 years before another perfect game would be pitched in a regular season National League game – by Jim Bunning of the Philadelphia Phillies in 1964.

At the time of Ward's triumph, the term "perfect game" had not been invented – it was just a no-hit game. Between 1871 and 1998, there was one perfect game for every 12,111 major league games played.

11:00 a.m., Wed., Aug. 4, 1875 – Hans Christian Andersen, Danish writer of children's books, died of liver cancer at age 70. Andersen wrote 168 fairy tales, including "The Ugly Duckling" and "The Emperor's New Clothes." A lifelong hypochondriac, Andersen had an obsessive fear of being buried alive, and carried a note saying that anyone who found him unconscious must not assume he was dead and should have him re-examined.

11:00 a.m., Thurs., Nov. 7, 1940 – The Tacoma Narrows bridge, popularly known as "Galloping Gertie," collapsed during a 68-kilometre- (42-mile-) an-hour wind. It seemed like an accident waiting to happen. The bridge received its nickname because it rolled and undulated like a giant roller coaster when its structure caught the wind rather than allowing it to pass through. Motorists crossing the 853-metre (2,800-foot) centre span would see cars ahead momentarily disappear as if they had dropped into the trough of a giant wave. In the high winds of November 7, 1940, the bridge rolled and corkscrewed until it finally tore apart. "Gertie" had only been open four months.

The present Tacoma Narrows Bridge was completed ten years later and opened on October 14, 1950.

11:00 a.m., Fri., Mar. 30, 1951 – The last wooden streetcar in Toronto began its final run. Officials, streetcar buffs and even a barbershop quartet accompanied car #1326 on its final regular journey through the streets of Toronto. It was deemed surplus after the Toronto Transit Commission purchased 50 new cars in 1951.

The #1326 car was bought by a historical group and can still be ridden at a museum in Rockwood, Ontario.

The last wooden streetcar in Toronto began its final run.

U.S. *Apollo* spacecraft linked up with a Soviet *Soyuz* spacecraft.

11:04 a.m., Wed., Apr. 10, 1963 – The U.S. atomic submarine *Thresher* was officially noted as missing. Shortly after, it was discovered that all 129 men aboard had died when the sub's hull collapsed. The *Thresher* had been conducting diving tests about 321 kilometres (200 miles) east of Boston. It was found on the ocean floor at a depth of 2,560 metres (8,400 feet).

11:07 a.m., Wed., Jan. 10, 1951 – An Avro Jetliner took off from Chicago en route to New York. The world's first jet passenger trip averaged 711 kilometres (442 miles) an hour during the 102-minute journey.

11:09 a.m., Thurs., July 17, 1975 – A U.S. *Apollo* spacecraft linked up with a Soviet *Soyuz* spacecraft, approximately 225 kilometres (140 miles) above the Atlantic Ocean, marking the first such meeting in space. The U.S. and Soviet crews spent two days taking meals together and doing joint experiments.

11:15 a.m., Sun., June 28, 1914 – Serbian nationalist Gavrilo Princip shot and killed the Archduke Francis Ferdinand, heir to the Austrian-Hungarian throne, and his wife. Princip, a 19-year-old student, fired seven shots into the motorcar of the Archduke and Duchess as it passed through Sarajevo, Yugoslavia. The killer said he wanted to avenge Serb suffering and asked that he be torched "to light my people on their path to freedom."

The shots Princip fired have been called the first volleys of World War I. The assassination ignited a powder keg in Europe and by August, the First World War was underway.

Princip and two of his co-consipirators were sentenced to 20 years in prison. All died before the war ended in 1918. *(see 11:00 a.m.)*

11:15 a.m., Wed., Feb. 6, 1952 – The British Broadcasting Corporation announced that King George VI had died in his sleep earlier that morning. George VI had been Britain's ruling sovereign since the abdication of Edward VIII fifteen years earlier to marry American divorcée Wallis Warfield Simpson. George never expected to be King. Nevertheless, with his wife Elizabeth by his side, he did much to bolster British morale during the war years. George was succeeded by his daughter Elizabeth II – England's first reigning Queen since Victoria.

11:21 a.m., Tues., Apr. 20, 1999 – Two teenage gunmen began a shooting spree at Columbine High School in Littleton, Colorado, in which fifteen people died and 23 were injured. It was the latest in a series of bloody attacks at U.S. high schools in the 1990s, and one of the worst.

The nightmare began when students Eric Harris and Dylan Klebold arrived at the school and shot a couple of students. They then tossed bombs into the parking lot and onto the roof of the school. The pair proceeded to the cafeteria, shooting and throwing pipe bombs. After fatally shooting a teacher, Harris and Klebold went to the library where they killed 10 students before killing themselves.

11:29 a.m., Thurs., July 21, 1921 – The announcement of the Scopes trial verdict surprised no one. The defendant, Tennessee high school teacher John T. Scopes, was found guilty of teaching Darwin's theory of evolution to his science class and was fined $100. A law banning the teaching of Darwinism had been passed earlier that year.

The case garnered world wide attention and pitted America's top lawyers, Clarence Darrow for the defence, and William Jennings Bryan for the prosecution, against each other. Interest in the trial was so great that the proceedings were moved outside the crowded courtroom so more spectators could watch.

The trial's highlight came when Darrow called prosecuting attorney Bryan to the stand, allowing him to expose Bryan's relative lack of Biblical knowledge. The Scopes trial verdict was an afterthought; there was never any question that Scopes had broken the law. The real issue was the validity of the law, and whether humankind had really evolved from apes.

A victorious Bryan died less than a week after the trial ended.

11:30 a.m., Fri., Mar. 14, 1879 – Albert Einstein was born in Ulm, Germany. Physicist Einstein was best known for his Theory of Relativity, published during the early part of the century. His discoveries led to the development of the atomic bomb, a weapon Einstein urged the U.S. to manufacture but never use.

Two teenage gunmen began a shooting spree at Columbine High School.

Edmund Hillary and Tenzing Norgay reach the summit of Mount Everest.

The young Einstein was a slow developer and did not speak until he was four years old. He failed the entrance exams for the Federal Polytechnic of Zurich.

Einstein died of heart failure at 1:15 a.m., Monday, April 18, 1955, aged 76.

11:30 **a.m., Fri., May 29, 1953** – Edmund Hillary of New Zealand and his Nepalese Sherpa guide, Tenzing Norgay, reached the summit of Mount Everest – the world's highest mountain. It had taken five hours for the pair, part of a British team led by John Hunt, to reach the top of the 8,847-metre (29,028-foot) mountain.

Hillary and Norgay spent only 15 minutes at the peak. They left behind the flags of England, Nepal, India and the United Nations. Hillary's first words upon reaching his mates below were characteristically blunt: "Well, we've knocked the bastard off."

Hillary and Norgay were Hunt's second choice to reach the summit. Thomas Bourdillon and Charles Evans had made the first attempt and failed five days earlier.

Hillary was knighted by Queen Elizabeth for his achievement. Norgay died in 1986.

11:30 **a.m., Sun., June 18, 1815** – The Battle of Waterloo, one of history's most famous conflicts, began. It was a fateful mismatch pitting French Emperor Napoleon's 72,000 soldiers against a combined force of 140,000 men commanded by the Duke of Wellington and Prussian Field-Marshal Blucher. By nightfall, the rout of the French was complete. It was only Napoleon's second loss in 64 battles.

Napoleon became dictator of France in 1802 and expanded his territory by defeating Austria and Prussia. When he tried to invade Moscow in 1812, his army was virtually destroyed when it was forced to retreat during the freezing Russian winter. Napoleon finally abdicated in 1814 and was exiled to the island of Elba. He resumed power in 1815 but his defeat at Waterloo was the end of his dynastic ambitions. He was exiled again, this time to St. Helena, where he died of stomach cancer in 1821, aged 52.

11:30 **a.m., Thurs, Mar. 18, 1965** – Lt. Col. Aleksey Arkhipovich Leoniv left the spacecraft *Voshkod* and spent 12 minutes and nine seconds floating in space connected to his craft by a 4.8-metre (16-foot) cord. In that brief time, he travelled 4,827 kilometres (3,000 miles) at a speed of 28,162 kilometres (17,500 miles) an hour. It was the world's first spacewalk.

11:30 **a.m., Sun., Sept. 26, 1937** – Bessie Smith, legendary blues singer of the 1920s and 30s, died of shock a few hours after a car crash near Clarksdale, Mississippi, allegedly because she had been denied treatment because of her colour. Smith, who had a major hit with "Down Hearted Blues" in 1923, is credited with singlehandedly saving Columbia Records from bankruptcy because of the popularity of her records.

11:30 **a.m., Fri., March 28, 1941** – Virginia Woolf, British novelist whose best-known works include *A Room of One's Own*, *To the Lighthouse* and *The Waves*, drowned herself in the Ouse River. The writer had been depressed over German bombing of London and was unhappy with her latest novel, *Between the Acts*. Woolf's body was not recovered until three weeks later.

11:30 **a.m., Sat. Mar. 30, 1895** – George Bernard Shaw's famous play *Candida* was performed for the first time at the Theatre Royal in London, in what was known as a copyright performance. It was performed without costumes or scenery and read directly from the script to establish the author's ownership of the play. The public was informed of the performance by a poster outside the theatre, but those who paid to watch often got their money back. This unusual practice was abolished by the Copyright Act of 1911.

Shaw wrote more than 50 plays, including such classics as *Pygmalion* and *Major Barbara*. A force in the English socialist movement, Shaw spent his later years campaigning to simplify spelling and left much of his estate to that cause.

Shaw was 94 when he died at 4:59 a.m., Thursday, November 2, 1950.

11:30 **a.m.. Fri., May 1, 1931** – The Empire State Building, the world's tallest building at the time, at 86 floors and 379 metres (1,245 feet) was officially dedicated. President Herbert Hoover formally

The Empire State Building was officially dedicated.

The quiz show
Jeopardy!
debuted on NBC.

opened the structure when he pushed a button in his White House office to turn the building's lights on.

The Chrysler Building in New York (at 318 metres or 1,046 feet), completed in 1930, had previously held the honour. Before that, the Eiffel Tower in Paris (300.5 metres or 985.9 feet) held the record for nearly half a century.

At the beginning of the 21st century, the tallest free-standing structure in the world was Toronto's CN Tower, at 553 metres (1,815 feet). The tallest man-made structure in the world was a 664-metre (2,180-foot) radio tower near Warsaw, Poland.

11:30 a.m., Wed., Feb. 16, 1983 – Fires were reported outside Adelaide, Australia. By mid-afternoon, 20 major blazes raged out of control in one of history's worst brushfires.

The fire, fueled by scorching hot temperatures and 112-kilometre- (70-mile-) an-hour winds, moved like an express train across the Australian outback. An army of more than 20,000 volunteer firemen and forestry personnel supported by 800 fire trucks and tankers could do little to stop the inferno. One observer called it "a demon with a mind of its own." The blaze killed 74 people, caused property damage in excess of $450 million and reduced 5,179 square kilometres (2,000 square miles) of forest to ash.

11:30 a.m., Fri., Mar. 20, 1964 – The quiz show *Jeopardy!* debuted on NBC. It would become one of the most popular quiz shows in history.

Jeopardy! ran from 1964 to 1975 on NBC-TV with Art Fleming as host. But it was not until it was revived as a syndicated show in 1984 with Alex Trebek as host that it really took off. *Jeopardy!* gives contestants the "answers" and asks them to provide a suitably phrased "question." It has spawned *Jeopardy!* clubs, books, computer games and a host of imitators. The show is seen in virtually every North American market. It's comeback, neatly timed to coincide with the trivia craze of the 1980s, continues unabated into the 21st century.

11:35 a.m., Tues., Oct. 20, 1964 – Herbert Hoover, America's 31st president, the first chief executive born west of the Mississippi, died of massive internal bleeding at a New York City hospital. At 90 years, two months, Hoover was the second-longest-lived president after John Adams.

Hoover was the first self-made millionaire to become president. A native of West Branch, Iowa, he never finished high school but earned a fortune through mining enterprises in Australia and Burma. Hoover gained world-wide attention after World War I with his highly efficient methods of food and supply distribution in Europe. In 1921, he was named Commerce Secretary under Harding and kept the position during the Coolidge administration. Hoover easily won the Republican nomination in 1928 and swept past Democrat Alfred Smith to become the first engineer to be elected president.

Hoover's administration was marred by the stock market crash of 1929, which led to the greatest depression the United States has ever known. The crash mocked his campaign promise of "a chicken in every pot and a car in every garage." Hoover and his aides reacted slowly to the economic col-lapse. They believed that the worst was over and the good times would return. Hoover's image was not helped in May, 1932, when he called out federal troops to clear Washington, D.C. of thousands of war veterans who had camped there to demand World War I bonus payments.

Hoover was the last president to leave office on March 4; the transition date now is January 20. His retirement lasted nearly 32 years.

11:39:13 a.m., Tues., Jan. 28, 1986 – Seventy-three seconds after takeoff, American space shuttle *Challenger* exploded. The accident took the lives of seven astronauts including teacher Christa McAuliffe, who was to have been the first non-astronaut in space. Also killed were pilot Michael Smith and astronauts Ronald McNair, Ellison Onizuka, Gregory Jarvis and Judith Resnik. It was the worst space disaster in history.

Investigations revealed that hot gases leaked through *Challenger*'s two solid rocket seals, igniting the shuttle's fuel. It was also revealed that NASA had been warned that the seals were weak and could cause an acci-dent. This disclosure stained NASA's long-standing reputation for safety and forced cancellation of the 14 other space shuttle flights scheduled for 1986. It would be two and a half years before another space shuttle mission.

11:40 a.m., Thurs., Sept. 5, 1991 – The Soviet Union came to an end when its Congress of the People's Deputies voted itself out of

Seventy-three seconds after takeoff, American space shuttle *Challenger* exploded.

New Zealand became the first country to give women the vote.

existence, surrendering nearly 74 years of Moscow-dominated power to the nation's republics. The decision, on the heels of a failed coup against Soviet President Mikhail Gorbachev, effectively ended the old Union of Soviet Socialist Republics.

11:45 a.m., Mon., Aug. 27, 1979 – Lord Mountbatten of Burma, British World War II hero and the last Viceroy of India, was killed when Irish Republican Army terrorists blew up his fishing boat off the Irish coast. Mountbatten was 79. His 14-year-old grandson and a local boatman were also killed in the attack. Four other passengers were wounded, but recovered.

Two members of the IRA were quickly apprehended and charged with the attack, the boldest ever in the IRA's long history of terrorism. Lord Mountbatten was buried September 5 in the most elaborate British military funeral since that of the Duke of Wellington in 1852.

11:45 a.m., Tues., Sept. 19, 1893 – New Zealand became the first country to give women the vote when its governor signed the Electoral Act allowing women's suffrage. Women in the United States would not get the vole until August 26, 1920. Canadian women were given the vote in federal elections in 1918.

11:48 a.m., Mon., Aug. 1, 1966 – Charles Whitman, a former altar boy and Eagle Scout, began firing a rifle from a tower at the University of Texas in Austin. By the time police finally shot him 92 minutes later, Whitman had killed 12 and wounded 33 in one of the worst shooting rampages in U.S. history.

Whitman, who had killed his wife and mother at their homes before going to the tower, had no history of psychological problems and the motive for his actions was never conclusively explained. He was finally felled by six bullets fired by Romero Martinez, an off-duty policeman who had inched his way around a wall at the top of the tower.

11:50 a.m., Thurs., Nov. 21, 1991 – French adventurer Gerald d'Aboville became the first man to row across the Pacific west-to-east. D'Aboville, 42, reached the tiny fishing village of Ilwaco, Washington,

134 days and 10,138 kilometres (6,300 miles) after leaving Choshi, Japan. The French rower, whose craft capsized at least 34 times in the dangerous north Pacific, toasted his epic triumph with a glass of red wine.

In 1983, Peter Bird of Britain rowed 14,483 kilometres (9,000 miles) from San Francisco to Australia to become the first man to row the Pacific east-to-west.

11:55 a.m., Wed., Dec. 8, 1943 – Doors lead singer Jim Morrison was born in Melbourne, Florida, the same state where he would be arrested on obscenity charges 25 years later.

Morrison, the powerful voice on Doors hits like "Light My Fire" and "Hello, I Love You," lived a wild life dominated by drinking and drugs. He was arrested several times for drunken behaviour and for exposing himself and using profanity on stage (in March of 1969 in Miami).

At 9:24 a.m., on Saturday, July 3, 1971, paramedics were called to Morrison's Paris apartment. Within half an hour, the Doors lead vocalist was pronounced dead – drowned in his bathtub.

There are some who claim Morrison didn't die, that he faked his own death as a publicity stunt and is still alive. Nevertheless, a coffin supposedly containing his body lies in the same Paris cemetery where Edith Piaf and Oscar Wilde are buried.

11:57 a.m., Tues., Jan. 20, 1981 – Ronald Reagan was sworn in as the 40th president of the United States. He would leave office eight years later as the oldest president in U.S. history, just before his 78th birthday.

Reagan found his political roots in an unlikely place – Hollywood. The star of some 50 movies, mostly "B" pictures, Reagan showed an early interest in politics by twice being elected president of the Screen Actors' Guild. When his acting career began to fade, he turned to politics full-time. Reagan made 200 speeches in support of Republican nominee Richard Nixon in 1960, and in 1964 made a famous 30-minute address in support of Barry Goldwater. The speech supposedly drew more contributions than any political speech in history and boosted Reagan's political star.

In 1966, Reagan defeated two-time incumbent Pat Brown to become governor of California, and was re-elected for a second four-year term in

Ronald Reagan was sworn in as the 40th president of the United States.

With most music lovers moving to FM, many AM stations changed to talk and/or information programming.

1970. In 1976, he mounted a strong challenge to President Gerald Ford, who barely beat Reagan to avoid becoming the first incumbent president not to gain his party's nomination for a second term since Chester Arthur in 1884. By 1980, Reagan was the front-runner and easily won the nomination. He chose former rival George Bush as his running mate and defeated Democratic President Jimmy Carter and independent John Anderson in the national election.

Just two months into his administration, Reagan was shot in an assassination attempt that left his press secretary, James Brady, brain-damaged and two other men injured. The bullet entered Reagan's lung near his heart but he made a full recovery and was back at the White House less than two weeks later. His assailant, drifter John Hinkley, was arrested and later found not guilty by reason of insanity and confined to a mental institution.

One of Reagan's first tasks as president was to tackle the economy. He managed to bring the inflation rate down substantially and cut employment to its lowest levels since the Nixon administration. However, government spending increased to the point that the U.S. went from being the biggest creditor nation to the largest debtor nation.

Reagan's presidency was marred by the Iran-Contra scandal. In 1985, Reagan had agreed to secretly sell arms to Iran for the release of U.S. hostages held in Lebanon. The long investigation that followed concluded that Reagan was unaware of the fact that some of the profits from the arms deal went to support anti-Sandinista rebels fighting in Nicaragua. However, the President was criticized for creating an environment where such things could take place behind his back.

Reagan's administration was also marked by the U.S. invasion of Grenada in 1983, to put down a violent leftist coup, and by the thawing of relations with the Soviet Union, the beginning of the end of the Cold War.

Reagan retired as the most popular outgoing president since Eisenhower. It was disclosed in the early 1990s that he was suffering from Alzheimer's Disease. *(see 2:25 p.m.)*

11:57 a.m., Mon., May 10, 1982 –The final song of WABC's Musicradio era was played on the New York radio station. Veteran disc jockeys Dan Ingram and Ron Lundy followed a 36-minute montage of the great hits of the 50s, 60s, 70s and 80s with a short goodbye and a welcome to the talk-radio format. Then, Ingram intoned the words "WABC, New York" for the last time and played John Lennon's "Imagine." At the top of the hour, WABC Music Radio became WABC Talk Radio.

WABC's changeover, after 22 years of playing rock and roll, was typical of AM radio in the 1980s. With most music lovers moving to FM, many AM stations changed to talk and/or information programming.

11:58 **a.m., Sat., Sept. 1, 1923** – Japan's worst earthquake, centred 91 kilometres (57 miles) southwest of Tokyo, struck. The quake killed more than 140,000 people, destroyed half a million buildings and touched off fires that raged for three days in Tokyo and Yokohama.

Japan's worst earthquake struck.

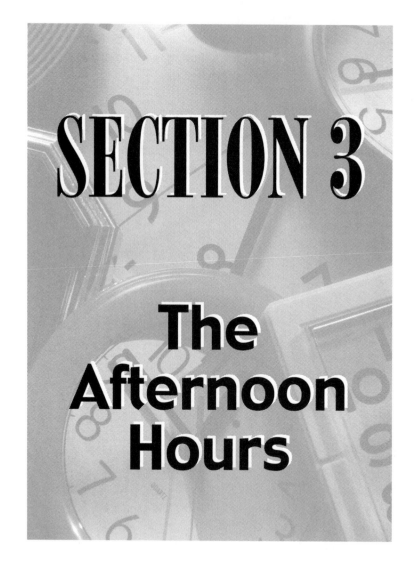

SECTION 3

The Afternoon Hours

Noon to 12:59 p.m.

- 🕐 **Stanley finds Livingston**
- 🕐 **Anne Boleyn beheaded**
- 🕐 **Shooting begins at Kent State, four dead**
- 🕐 **President Kennedy assassinated**
- 🕐 **Paris plane crash kills 346**
- 🕐 **Queen Elizabeth II crowned**

12:00 **p.m., Sat., Aug. 1, 1914** – World War I began as Germany's Kaiser Wilhelm II officially declared war on Russia. The declaration came after Russia refused to meet a deadline for ceasing troop mobilization near Austrian territory. The first shots of the war occurred on the Eastern front, as advancing Russians fired on German troops at Prostken, East Prussia. The war escalated August 4 when Germany invaded France, Luxembourg and Switzerland. By the end of the month, 17 million men from eight nations were involved in what would become known as "the war to end all wars."

12:00 **p.m., Tues., Mar. 5, 1946** – Winston Churchill arrived in Jefferson City, Missouri, and then travelled to nearby Fulton to deliver a nationally-broadcast speech at Westminster College. During his speech, the British Prime Minister warned of the danger posed by the Soviet Union and its allies, using the phrase "the Iron Curtain" to refer to the dividing line between the Communist east bloc countries and the democratic western nations in Europe.

12:00 **p.m., Tues., Aug. 1, 1944** – The American Third Army was officially declared operational with General George S. Patton at the helm. In just 21 days, the Patton-led army would advance eastward from

Bob Marley died of cancer in Miami.

Avranches, France, 320 kilometres (200 miles) to the Seine and westward 240 kilometres (150 miles) to Brest to liberate 116,550 square kilometres (45,000 square miles) of France.

Patton's tank units scored several other major victories during World War II as Patton led troops in North Africa. However, "Blood and Guts" Patton was demoted twice, once for outspokenness and another time for slapping a soldier in a hospital. The movie *Patton*, starring George C. Scott, won the Oscar for best picture in 1970.

Patton died of a blood clot following a December 9, 1945 car accident at 5:50 p.m., Friday, December 21, 1945, aged 60.

12:00 **p.m., Mon., May 11, 1981** - Bob Marley, one of reggae music's biggest stars died of cancer in Miami. He was 36. Marley was born in Nine Miles, Jamaica on February 6, 1945. His birth name was Robert Nesta Marley.

Marley, who had an electrifying stage presence, rose to international fame as he led reggae music to new heights of popularity in the 70s. Marley was also politically active in his native Jamaica, but left the country for good after an attempt on his life in 1976. His major hits included "Babylon by Bus" and "Roots, Rock, Reggae."

12:00 **p.m., Sat., July 13, 1985** – Live Aid, the worldwide charity concert for African famine relief, began at London's Wembley Stadium. More than 70,000 attended the concert to see musicians such as Paul McCartney, U2 and Phil Collins. Later in the day, the action switched to Philadelphia where 90,000 fans watched performances by Madonna, Bob Dylan, Joan Baez and Phil Collins. The veteran British rocker flew from England to the U.S. on the Concorde and performed on both sides of the Atlantic the same day.

The two-continent concert raised over £70 million for famine relief. An estimated 1.4 billion people in 170 countries watched the event, which was organized by Bob Geldof of the Boomtown Rats to heighten awareness of African famine.

12:00 **p.m., Sun., Feb. 18, 1979** – In a watershed move for the sport, CBS televised the entire Daytona 500 NASCAR race live for the first time. The race had been broadcast live nationally but not in its entirety from 1976 to 1978. The 1979 race proved to be a classic, with Richard Petty winning his sixth race – in a career total of seven wins – in a dramatic finish. An estimated 30 million fans watched the race on TV. The sport, which started as an under-publicized car-racing circuit popular only among aficionados, has grown dramatically.

Stanley's search ended when he discovered Livingstone alive at Ujiji in Central Africa.

12:00 **p.m., Mon., Nov. 13, 1871** – American newsman Henry Stanley uttered his famous question, "Dr. Livingstone, I presume?" The doctor responded, "You have brought me new life," ending one of history's greatest searches.

Stanley had been commissioned by the *New York Herald* to find Livingstone, who had been feared dead for four years. Stanley's search ended when he discovered Livingstone alive at Ujiji in Central Africa, on the edge of Lake Tanganyika. Stanley's were the first words Livingstone, 58, had heard a white man speak in five years. The frail explorer pressed Stanley for the latest news and learned of the opening of the Suez Canal and the transatlantic telegraph.

12:00 **p.m., Mon., Nov. 2, 1795** – James K. Polk, the 11th president and the only former Speaker of the House to advance to the Oval Office, was born on a farm in Mecklenburg, North Carolina. He died, aged 53, of cholera in Nashville June 15, 1849. Virtually forgotten today, Polk was voted the greatest one-term president ever in a 1982 historians poll conducted by the *Chicago Tribune*. Inaugurated at age 49, he is the first man to become president before his 50th birthday.

The Mexican War dominated Polk's presidency. The war started with Mexican troops confronting U.S. forces in a disputed region in what is now Texas. It ended with the U.S. army defeating the Mexicans and the U.S.–Mexico border established at the Rio Grande. U.S. territory was increased by more than 1.2 billion square kilometres (half a million square miles) and Mexico's size was reduced by approximately half.

Polk did not seek a second term, writing in his diary that he was "exceedingly relieved" at leaving the presidency. He died within three months of leaving office, the soonest a president has died after completing his term of office.

Standard time officially began in the United States.

12:00 **p.m., Sun., Mar. 14, 1999** – The 175th annual St. Patrick's Day parade began on the streets of Montreal and continued its tradition, unbroken since 1824, as the longest-running uninterrupted parade in North America.

The St. Patrick's Day Parade is held in honour of a Romanized young man named Patricius, who in 401 A.D. was seized by raiding Irish Celts and brought to Ireland. Patricius spent six years in isolation as a shepherd-slave, and because he had no one to talk to, prayed up to 200 times a day. Patricius eventually escaped back to England but found he was now more Irish than English. The man later to be immortalized as St. Patrick was ordained as a bishop – believed to be the first missionary bishop in history. He is also believed to be the first leading spokesman against slavery. Patricius set up a church in Ireland and spent the last 30 years of his life travelling the countryside, teaching pagans to embrace Christian values based on love and forgiveness. He is known as Ireland's Patron Saint.

12:00 **p.m., Sun., Nov. 18, 1883** – Standard time officially began in the United States. First proposed in 1870 by Canadian railway engineer Sir Sanford Fleming, the idea of standard time was advanced by the rail companies, who hoped it would make scheduling easier.

Prior to the advent of standard time, each community had its own clock, based on the positioning of the sun. It might be 12:00 in one town and 12:02 in another just a short distance away. While technically correct, these variations led to great confusion in scheduling when railroad tracks started to criss-cross the continent. The much simpler idea of standardized time zones was finally established in 1883.

The day standard time was introduced was called "the day of two noons." In the eastern part of each time zone, the "first noon" was based on the positioning of the sun, or sun time. Then, timepieces were set back so there was a "second noon" when twelve o'clock Standard Time occurred. To lessen the confusion, the changeover was done on a Sunday when fewer people would be at work or riding the trains.

12:00 **p.m., Wed., July 10, 1850** – Millard Fillmore, the first president born in the 1800s, was sworn in as the 13th president in the Hall of Representatives before a joint session of both houses.

Fillmore, who spent most of his pre-presidential years as U.S. representative from New York, was named vice-president on the Whig ticket under Zachary Taylor in 1848. Fillmore and Taylor did not meet each other until after the election and Vice-President Fillmore was ignored by Taylor's people. His days of obscurity ended on July 10, 1850, when Fillmore was sworn in as president following Taylor's death.

Fillmore's major act during his 20 months as president was to sign the Compromise of 1850, which included the controversial Fugitive Slave Law. The law required the federal government to help return fugitive slaves to their masters and it pleased few. Fillmore was not renominated for president in 1852.

Fillmore was not through with politics, however. He finished third in the 1856 presidential voting as a candidate for the anti-immigrant, anti-Catholic American, or Know Nothing party.

Fillmore died at 11:10 p.m., on Saturday, March 8, 1874 following a stroke at his home in Buffalo, New York. He was 74.

12:00 **p.m., Sat., July 10, 1976** – In Seveso, Italy, a valve burst under extreme heat at a chemical plant, and two kilograms (4.5 pounds) of dioxin began to spread around the city in a mushroom cloud.

While no human deaths were recorded, more than 50 people were sent to hospital and 400 children later developed cloracne, an affliction that temporarily disfigures the skin. In addition, some 40,000 animals had to be destroyed, and plants and crops shrivelled in one of Italy's worst environmental disasters. The long-term effects on the humans exposed to dioxin is not known.

12:00 **p.m., Thurs., Sept. 16, 1920** – An explosion rocked Wall Street. Thirty-three people died and 100 were injured in what remains New York's greatest murder mystery.

The blast came from a bomb located in a delivery wagon parked in front of the United States Assay Office. The roar was heard for 16 kilometres (10 miles) and windows were shattered for blocks around. Just prior to the explosion, a man leaving the wagon told a passerby to leave the area quickly. The man was never identified, and despite painstakingly reconstructing the wagon from 10 tons of debris, its ownership was never estab-

An explosion rocked Wall Street in what remains New York's greatest murder mystery.

William Wordsworth, one of the most famous English Romantic poets, died.

lished. All leads in the investigation have come to a dead end, and police are still at a loss as to motive and identity of the criminal or criminals involved.

12:00 p.m., Thurs., Sept. 16, 1971 – *Look* magazine announced it was folding and would publish its last issue October 19. Among the reasons given for the demise of the 34-year-old magazine were competition from TV and poor advertising revenues. *Look*'s collapse came just two years after the demise of the *Saturday Evening Post*. *Life* magazine would fold in December, 1973, publishing only annual issues for the rest of the decade. Both *Life* and the *Saturday Evening Post* were revived as monthlies during the 80s.

12:00 p.m., Wed., Apr. 3, 1850 – William Wordsworth, one of the most famous English Romantic poets, died of a breathing problem at the age of 80. Wordsworth, who collaborated with Samuel Taylor Coleridge on *Lyrical Ballads*, the first major collection of English Romantic poetry, is best known for his autobiographical poem "Prelude." In 1843, at the age of 73, he was named poet laureate of Britain. A cuckoo clock given to Wordsworth apparently sounded at the moment of his death.

12:00 p.m., Sat., Sept. 30, 1978 – Edgar Bergen, the famed ventriloquist who made millions laugh through his wooden dummy Charlie McCarthy, died in his sleep at the age of 75. Less than two weeks earlier, Bergen announced that he and his monocled, top-hatted dummy were quitting show business after 56 years.

Bergen, father of actress Candice Bergen, won a special Academy Award in 1937 for his many film shorts and appearances in movie musicals. After Edgar Bergen's death, Charlie McCarthy was put on display at the Smithsonian Institute.

12:00 p.m., Fri., Dec. 25, 1931 – Henry Fonda and actress Margaret Sullavan were married in a ceremony at the Kernan Hotel in Baltimore. The marriage was marked by constant bickering almost from the start. Fonda left within four months, having discovered Sullavan was having an affair with producer Jed Harris.

By 1936, Fonda had married his second of five wives, Francis Seymour Brokaw, who bore him both Peter and Jane Fonda. As for Sullavan, she married Fonda's agent the same year.

Fonda became one of America's favourite actors, starring in such films as *The Grapes of Wrath*, *Mister Roberts* and *My Darling Clementine*. He won his first and only Oscar for his performance in *On Golden Pond* with daughter Jane in 1981. It was the first time father and daughter had appeared together in the same film and Fonda remarked, "I thank God I lived long enough to play that role."

Henry Fonda died of cancer at 8:15 a.m., Thursday, August 12, 1982. He was 77.

12:00 **p.m., Wed., Aug. 25, 1999** – At exactly noon, in the Spanish town of Bunol, near Valencia, people began lobbing fresh, ripe tomatoes at each other in the annual "Tomatina" festival. The festival, held each year in late August, has been a tradition in Bunol since 1945. Tons of tomatoes are trucked into town from surrounding farms, and as many as 30,000 residents and visitors participate in the event, which lasts exactly one hour. The annual tomato war leaves participants and the town's streets drenched in red pulp.

12:00 **p.m., Mon., May 21, 1945** – The long-anticipated wedding of Humphrey Bogart and Lauren Bacall began with the strains of the "Wedding March." But a nervous Bacall had to rush off to the bathroom first! The suitably relieved actress was married to Bogart in a three-minute ceremony in Mansfield, Ohio.

Bogart's marriage to the glamorous Bacall further boosted his larger-than-life status. He was and remains an American icon. *Casablanca*, *The Maltese Falcon* and *The African Queen* are films that will be forever identified with "Bogie," Hollywood's first film-noir detective.

Bogart, who specialized in cons and gangsters but in real life was the prep-school educated son of a surgeon, got his break playing a lowlife in the movie *The Petrified Forest* in 1934. He went on to star in many other movies including *The African Queen*, for which he won his only best actor Oscar in 1951. He didn't win for his role as Rick Blaine in *Casablanca*, losing to Paul Lukas for *Watch on the Rhine*. Bogart's success came despite

The annual tomato war leaves participants and the town's streets drenched in red pulp.

Anne Boleyn, second wife of Henry VIII, was beheaded.

a lisp from a lip wound suffered while escorting a prisoner in the Navy.

Bogart died at 2:10 a.m. Monday, January 14, 1957 of throat cancer, aged 57. Close friend, director John Huston observed, "He is quite unreplaceable. There will never be anybody like him."

12:00 p.m., (date unknown) c. 1100 B.C. – According to Greek mythology, Icarus and his father Daedalus took flight off the cliffs overlooking the Aegean Sea, in an effort to escape the secret police of Minos. Both were equipped with wings made out of eagle feathers and beeswax. As the legend goes, Icarus – ignoring his father's warnings – flew too close to the sun and his wings began to melt. The intrepid aviator then plunged to his death in the blue waters of the Aegean as his father watched in horror. Daedalus could find no sign of his son; only scraps of eagle feathers bobbed on the water. The nearby island of Ikaria was named for Icarus, according to legend the first human casualty of flight.

12:00 p.m., Mon., May 19, 1536 – Anne Boleyn, second wife of Henry VIII, was beheaded in the Tower of London. Boleyn's crime was failure to produce a male heir. Henry was already eyeing a third wife, Jane Seymour, who eventually bore him a son, Edward.

Trumped-up charges of adultery, incest and plotting the King's death were brought against Anne. There was no chance of acquittal. On the day of her execution, she was almost hysterically cheerful, and expressed mock disappointment when the beheading was delayed three hours. Anne's life ended with a single stroke of the executioner's sword as she prayed for the King's long life.

Henry VIII had secretly married Anne Boleyn four months before his first marriage to Catharine of Aragon was annulled. Henry married six times before dying in 1547 at the age of 56. Anne Boleyn's only child by Henry would become Queen Elizabeth I.

12:00 p.m., Sat., Feb. 7, 1685 – Charles II, the Merry Monarch, King of England from 1660 to 1685, died of a brain hemorrhage at age 54. His last days were agony as 14 royal physicians tried everything known to 17th-century medicine to save him. Charles was bled almost bloodless, given numerous enemas, force-fed with oral purgatives, smeared with camphor and mustard plasters, had powder blown up his nose to encourage sneezing and treated with toxic quinine. The idea was to free the body of "ill humours," a common practice at the time. What is amazing is that he lasted five days from the beginning of the treatment to his death.

12:00 **p.m., Sat., Aug. 13, 1910** – Florence Nightingale, "the Lady with the Lamp" who led nursing reform in the 19th century, died at age 90. In 1907, she became the first woman to receive the Order of Merit. Ironically, the dean of nursing spent the last 54 years of her life bedridden.

12:00 **p.m., Sat., June 5, 1882** – Igor Stravinsky, one of the great composers of the 20th century, was born in St. Petersburg, Russia. Stravinsky revolutionized the music world with his progressive works. So outraged was an audience when his work "The Rite of Spring" was first performed in Paris in 1913, police had to be called to restore order in the theatre. His music quickly gained respect and he continued as a musical leader throughout the century with such works as the opera *The Rake's Progress* and the choral work "Symphony of Psalms."

Stravinsky died in 1971 of heart failure at age 88.

12:00 **p.m., Sat., Oct. 2, 1920** – The last scheduled tripleheader in major league baseball history began. Not seen since before the turn of the century, the tripleheader was revived for one time only because the Pittsburgh Pirates and Cincinnati Reds were fighting for third place in the National League and had to complete a full schedule. Cincinnati won the first two games 13–7 and 7–3. Pittsburgh was leading the third 6–0 when darkness set in.

12:00 **p.m., Wed., Jan. 10, 1917** – Buffalo Bill Cody, legendary sharpshooter, buffalo hunter, Pony Express rider and star of the touring "Wild West Show," died of uremic poisoning at Glenwood Springs, Colorado. He was 70.

Cody got his nickname after shooting more than 4,000 buffalo during an 18-month period beginning in 1867. He made millions with his "Wild West Show," an exhibition of Western life that toured America and Europe for three decades. Cody died shortly after reviving his "Wild West Show" as a

The last scheduled tripleheader in major league baseball history began.

The St. Lawrence Seaway officially opened.

morale-booster for Americans on the verge of U.S. involvement in World War I. To many, his death marked the end of the great frontier era.

12:00 **p.m., Oct. 18, 1960** – The New York Yankees held a news conference to announce the firing of manager Casey Stengel. He was axed despite leading the Yankees to 10 American League pennants in 12 seasons, and winning seven World Series titles. At issue was Stengel's age, to which he responded, "I'll never make the mistake of being 70 again."

Stengel managed a total of 17 major and minor league teams, most notably the Yankees and the New York Mets. Nicknamed "The Old Professor," he had a colourful way of expressing himself and was one of baseball's most quotable characters. While managing the woeful Mets during their inaugural year in 1962, Stengel was heard to say, "Can't anyone around here play this game?" He retired from managing in 1965.

Casey Stengel died of cancer at 10:58 p.m., Monday, September 29, 1975. He was 85.

12:00 **p.m., Fri., June 26, 1959** – The St. Lawrence Seaway officially opened as the royal yacht *Britannia* passed through two symbolic gates at St. Lambert Lock, Quebec. On hand for the historic occasion were Queen Elizabeth, Prime Minister John Diefenbaker, President Eisenhower and more than 15,000 spectators. Fireworks exploded and balloons were released into the air as *Britannia* entered the lock, the first ship to use the Seaway. More than 1,800 ships would pass through the lock during the first three months of operation.

12:00 **p.m., Thurs., Oct. 29, 1952** – Poet Dylan Thomas gave his last public reading at the City College of New York, an institution he called "the proletariat Harvard." Those who witnessed the reading saw the end of a literary era.

Thomas, a Welsh poet whose heavy drinking became uncontrollable near the end of his life (he called himself "the world's drunkest man"), packed his poetry with imagery and spirited language. Meticulous to the extreme, Thomas was known to rewrite a line 50 times before being satisfied with it. His works inspired a young Minnesota musician named Robert Zimmerman to change his name to Bob Dylan in the early 60s.

A week and a half after this last public reading, Thomas died of fluid on the brain at a clinic in New York, having drunk himself to death. He was only 39 when he passed away at 1:00 p.m., Monday, November 9, 1953.

12:00 p.m., Tues., Dec. 14, 1920 – An airliner, belonging to Handley Page Continental Air Services and headed for Paris, crashed into a London suburb, killing eight of the 12 passengers aboard. The four survivors jumped clear just before impact. It was the first airline disaster on a scheduled commercial flight.

12:00 p.m., Fri., Sept. 27, 1940 – Japan officially joined the Axis, linking its military might to that of Germany and Italy.

12:01 p.m., Sun., July 4, 1886 – Canada's first transcontinental train arrived in Port Moody, British Columbia, 139 hours after departing from Montreal. Some 1,000 people were on hand to watch as the Canadian Pacific Railway train completed its 4,670-kilometre (2,901-mile) journey. The first eastbound train would depart the following day.

12:03 p.m., Fri., Aug. 9, 1974 – Gerald Ford, who once said his career goal was to become Speaker of the House, was sworn in as the 38th president of the United States following the resignation of Richard Nixon. Ford, U.S. representative from Michigan for nearly a quarter century beginning in 1949, was named vice-president after Spiro Agnew resigned in October, 1973. When he succeeded Nixon, he became the first man to become president by appointment.

Ford was criticized just a month into his presidency when he gave Nixon a full pardon on September 8, 1974. His press secretary resigned in protest and some suspected that Nixon and Ford had cut a deal. Ford was also taken to task for his much-publicized "Whip Inflation Now" (WIN) campaign, which was abandoned during the recession of 1974–75. He survived two assassination scares in September, 1975. Ford barely escaped becoming the first incumbent president to lose his own party's nomination since Chester Arthur in 1884, when he edged out future president Ronald Reagan for the 1976 Republican nomination. Ford then lost to Democrat Jimmy Carter in one of the closest presidential elections in U.S. history.

Gerald Ford became the 38th president of the United States.

David Milgaard was released from prison.

12:03 p.m., Fri., Jan. 20, 1989 – George Bush became the 41st president as he was sworn in by Chief Justice William Rehnquist. Bush broke with tradition by wearing a blue business suit rather than a morning coat to the inauguration. Bush, the first sitting vice-president elected president since Martin Van Buren in 1836, was also the first president born in June to succeed to the Oval Office. Presidents have now been born in all 12 months.

Bush promised a "kinder, gentler nation," but his administration was marked by war – the U.S. involvement in the invasion of Kuwait in 1991. The invasion, and subsequent success in running the Iraqis out of Kuwait, raised Bush's approval rating to an unheard of 91 per cent by March 1, 1991. It was downhill for Bush after that as his administration was blamed for the country's continuing economic problems. He was also haunted by a campaign slogan: "Read my lips, no new taxes." Only a month after taking office, he disclosed a plan to bail out the thrift industry that would cost more than $300 billion over 30 years. Of that, $255 billion would be paid for by taxpayers. In 1990, Bush agreed to raise taxes in a budget compromise with Congress.

Bush was defeated in his re-election bid by Democrat Bill Clinton in 1992.

12:15 p.m., Apr. 15, 1992 – David Milgaard was released from prison after the Supreme Court ruled that he should have a new trial.

Milgaard was 17 in 1970 when he was imprisoned for the rape and killing of nurses' aide Gail Miller in Saskatoon, Saskatchewan in 1969. During his 22 years behind bars, he was raped and he attempted suicide. Twice he escaped, only to be caught. His freedom came after a long campaign by his mother, Joyce, to release him. The province of Saskatchewan refused to prosecute Milgaard again.

In 1997, DNA results exonerated David and overwhelmingly suggested another man, Larry Fisher, was the murderer. In 1999, David Milgaard was awarded $7 million by the federal and Saskatchewan governments, the largest amount ever awarded in Canada for a wrongful conviction.

Fisher was convicted of the Gail Miller slaying in 1999 and sentenced to life imprisonment with the possibility of parole after 10 years.

12:18 p.m., Fri., Feb. 26, 1993 – A bomb rattled the World Trade Center in New York. Six people died and more than 100 were injured. Five suspects were arrested in connection with the crime, which forced closure of the world's second and third tallest buildings.

On March 6, 1994, four men were found guilty of a total of 38 charges related to the bombing. All received prison terms of 240 years each without the possibility of parole.

12:19 p.m., Mon., Apr. 19, 1897 – The first Boston Marathon began, with a field of 15 starters at the corner of Hayden Rowe and Town Green in Hopkinton, Massachusetts. Two hours, 55 minutes and 10 seconds later, J.J. McDermott of New York City became the first to cross the finish line at Prudential Center Plaza in Boston. Starter Tom Burke had neither a starting gun nor a starting line. So he drew a line in the dirt with his boot and got the runners moving by shouting "Go."

The first marathon nearly met with disaster when McDermott ran into the middle of a funeral procession, causing two electric cars to stall. Undaunted, McDermott won the race by seven minutes.

It was the only time McDermott ever won the race, then 39.4 kilometres (24-1/2 miles). The current official distance is 41.8 kilometres, 322.3 metres (26 miles, 385-1/2 yards).

12:20 p.m., Mon., May 4, 1970 – National Guardsmen began shooting into a crowd of students protesting the Vietnam War at Ohio's Kent State University. Within minutes, four students lay dead and eight injured in the worst massacre ever at a U.S. university.

The students had yelled and tossed stones at the Guardsmen, who were called in when university officials suspected a demonstration would be held against the U.S. incursion into Cambodia. The Guardsmen, under orders to fire if provoked, unleashed a barrage of rifle fire.

The shooting shocked the nation, and further hardened opposition to the Vietnam War. The FBI later determined the National Guard was wrong to shoot at the demonstrators and said the protesters could have been repelled by tear gas.

The first Boston Marathon began, with a field of 15 starters.

The 26-second clip that followed has been called the most horrifying film in history.

12:20 p.m., Wed., Feb. 18, 1970 – After nearly 40 hours of deliberation, a Chicago jury returned a verdict of not guilty in the trial of the "Chicago 7." The seven defendants, who included activists Abbie Hoffman and Jerry Rubin, were acquitted of plotting to incite a riot during the 1968 Democratic convention. However, five of the men were convicted of seeking to promote a riot through individual acts.

12:26 p.m., Thurs., May 3, 1923 – The first non-stop transcontinental flight across the United States was completed. Lieutenants. Oakley Kelly and John Macready of the U.S. Army flew without a break from Hempstead, New York, to San Diego in 27 hours. At 4,506 kilometres (2,800 miles), it was the longest non-stop flight up to that time.

12:26 p.m., Thurs., Dec. 11, 1941 – Four days after the Japanese attack on Pearl Harbor, the United States declared war on Germany and Italy. *(see 7:55 a.m.)*

12:29 p.m., Fri., Nov. 22, 1963 – Dallas dress manufacturer Abraham Zapruder began filming the motorcade of President Kennedy as it arrived in Dealey Plaza. The 26-second clip that followed has been called the most horrifying film in history.

Zapruder had not planned to film the motorcade; he went home and got his eight-millimetre camera only at the suggestion of his secretary. With his back to the infamous grassy knoll, Zapruder climbed up on a 1.2-metre (four-foot) pedestal and started the camera rolling as two motorcyles at the start of the motorcade came into view. He continued to film until the presidential car disappeared under the triple underpass.

The Zapruder film has become the most famous record of the controversial murder. The film itself was purchased immediately after Kennedy's assassination by Time-Life, Inc., for $25,000 but was never released in its full form until after the original was returned to the Zapruder family in 1975. In 1999, the U.S. government purchased the film from the Zapruder family for $16 million. It is stored at -4° Celsius (25° Fahrenheit) at the U.S. national archives in College Park, Maryland. The Zapruder family still holds the copyright.

Zapruder died of cancer in 1970, aged 66. He was said to have been haunted by the images he filmed that November afternoon in 1963.

12:30 p.m., Fri., Nov. 22, 1963 – John Fitzgerald Kennedy, the 35th president, was shot along with Texas governor John Connally while riding in a motorcade through the streets of Dallas. Kennedy died of his wounds within 30 minutes; Connally recovered. Kennedy, the first Catholic and youngest man, at 43, to be voted into office, and also the youngest to die, was the fourth U.S. president to be assassinated. He had travelled to Texas in hopes of bolstering his popularity there for the 1964 presidential election. JFK was 46.

While Kennedy's stay in power was brief (less than three years), it was notable in many ways. His greatest triumph came in 1962 when he forced Soviet leader Nikita Khruschev to back down in what came to be known as the Cuban missile crisis.

The Americans had discovered Soviet missile bases on Cuba; Kennedy said he'd blockade the island until the missiles were rendered inoperable and shipments stopped; Khruschev said he'd withdraw the weapons if the U.S. withdrew theirs in Turkey. Kennedy stated there would be no negotiations until the missile threat was removed. With the world at the brink of war, Khruschev relented. The president's greatest failure also involved Cuba. The Bay of Pigs was an unsuccessful attempt by Kennedy to restore a democratic government in Cuba by backing an invasion by Cuban exiles to fight Castro.

Kennedy also made advances in civil rights and the reduction of trade barriers. During his tenure, American aid and presence in South Vietnam increased, a harbinger of things to come.

Kennedy's greatest assets were his youth and charm. The first president born in the 20th century, Kennedy and his wife Jacqueline brought to the White House a youthful, romantic presence it had long been lacking. The former Massachusetts senator was elected in 1960 when he edged out Republican Vice-President Richard Nixon in one of the closest presidential elections in history.

The circumstances of Kennedy's assassination have been the subject of much speculation over the years. In his book *Case Closed*, Gerald Posner estimated that more than 2,000 books have been published on the subject.

12:30 p.m., Wed., July 8, 1892 – Nelson Rockefeller was born into wealth in Bar Harbour, Maine. He would achieve almost everything he wanted except becoming president.

John Fitzgerald Kennedy, the 35th president, was shot.

Turkish Airlines Flight 509 crashed shortly after take-off from Paris.

Rockefeller, four-time Governor of New York, was unsuccessful three times in his bid for the Republican presidential nomination. The man who once said he never wanted to be vice-president of anything was sworn in as vice-president of the U.S. under Gerald Ford in December, 1974. However, Rockefeller opted not to run on the Ford ticket in 1976 and was replaced by Bob Dole.

At 10:15 p.m. on Friday, January 26, 1979, Rockefeller suffered a heart attack and died shortly after. Rockefeller, who was writing a book on art at the time of his death, reportedly passed away in the arms of a young female friend. The 70-year-old multi-millionaire had dined with his wife and two children earlier that evening.

12:30 **p.m., Sun., Mar. 3, 1974** – Three hundred and forty-six people died when Turkish Airlines Flight 509 crashed shortly after takeoff from Paris. The plane virtually disintegrated when it impacted at 764 kilometres (475 miles) an hour, and identification of the dead took four months to complete. Lawsuits from the crash totalled hundreds of millions of dollars. It was the worst-ever crash involving a single airplane.

An investigation revealed that the cargo door of the plane had flown open, causing the floor of the cabin to collapse into the cargo section, jamming the control cables and causing the plane to nosedive.

12:30 **p.m., Thurs., Nov. 12, 1936** – The Bay Bridge, the longest steel, high-level bridge in the world, opened to vehicular traffic. The 13.27 kilometre (8.25 mile) bridge took nearly three and a half years to build. Its foundations extend further below water than any other bridge. One pier is sunk at 73 metres (242 feet) below water and required more concrete than the Empire State Building in New York.

Six months after the Bay Bridge opened, the Golden Gate Bridge opened on Thursday, September 27, 1937. About 200,000 people walked across the bridge that first day; vehicular traffic started the next. The Golden Gate Bridge for years held the undisputed title as the world's longest suspension bridge at 1,200 metres (4,200 feet).

The twin triumphs of the Bay Bridge and the Golden Gate Bridge were celebrated at the Golden Gate International Expositions of 1939 and 1940.

12:30 **p.m. EDT, Wed., July 11, 1979** – The U.S. spacecraft *Skylab* crashed into the Indian Ocean several hundred miles west of Australia. Wreckage from the ghost ship, some pieces weighing more than 2,200 kilograms (5,000 pounds), was spread over 6,437.2 kilometres (4,000 miles). *Skylab's* orbit had decayed after six years in space, during which it circled the globe more than 34,000 times, travelling some 1.4 billion kilometres (874 million miles).

U.S. space officials had calculated the odds on one person being hit by a piece of *Skylab* debris at about 600 billion to one. As far as anyone knows, nobody was hit.

The U.S. spacecraft *Skylab* crashed into the Indian Ocean.

12:30 **p.m., Fri., May 16, 1975** – Female mountaineer Junko Tabei of Japan conquered Mount Everest — the first time a woman had accomplished the feat. Tabei, accompanied by a male Sherpa guide, took five hours to reach the summit of the 29,028 foot (8,219 metres) mountain. Prior to her conquest, 35 men had reached the summit of the world's highest mountain.

Tabei was also the first woman in history to climb the highest peaks on all seven continents. She has been involved with clean-up campaigns for mountains defaced by garbage and pollution.

12:30 **p.m., Fri., Feb. 2, 1979** – Punk rocker Sid Vicious was found dead of a heroin overdose in his Greenwich Village apartment. He was 21.

Vicious, born John Simon Ritchie in London, gained fame as the wild and unpredictable guitarist for the punk band The Sex Pistols in the late 70s. His act included vomiting and slashing himself on stage.

12:32 **p.m., Tues., Jan. 20, 1953** – Dwight D. Eisenhower was sworn in as the 34th president of the United States by Chief Justice Fred Vinson. Eisenhower would go on to become the first Republican to serve two full terms since Ulysses Grant a century earlier.

Eisenhower's background was entirely military, never holding elected office before the presidency. A West Point graduate in 1915, Eisenhower spent the next 33 years in the U.S. Army. As Supreme Allied Commander in

Queen Elizabeth II was crowned in the first televised coronation of a British monarch.

1944, he directed the greatest land-sea invasion in history, Operation Overlord, better known as the D-Day invasion. The Allies successfully landed at Normandy and proceeded inland toward eventual victory. Later promoted to five-star General, Eisenhower accepted Germany's surrender in 1945.

After retiring from the army in 1948, Eisenhower was wooed by both major parties as a possible presidential prospect. He finally chose the Republicans, and easily won that party's nomination for president in 1952. He defeated Democrat Adlai Stevenson by a landslide vote in the 1952 election, repeating his victory over the same opponent to win a second term in 1956.

Fittingly, Eisenhower's first major accomplishment in office was a military one – reviving the stalled Korean Peace Talks. His efforts led to the signing of an armistice in July, 1953. The next year, U.S. military involvement in Vietnam began, as Eisenhower sent aid and a handful of military advisors to the Diem regime in South Vietnam.

During Eisenhower's tenure, the so-called "Cold War" with the Soviet Union escalated as both countries built up their nuclear arsenals and relations between the two countries were strained.

Eisenhower died of heart failure at 12:35 p.m., Friday, March 28, 1969. He was 78.

12:35 p.m., Tues., June 2, 1953 – Queen Elizabeth II was crowned in the first televised coronation of a British monarch. Elizabeth had actually ruled as Queen since her father, George VI, died on February 6, 1952. Her reign was officially recognized in a lavish ceremony at Westminster Abbey in London. In this pre-satellite age, U.S. television networks arranged to have film of the coronation flown across the Atlantic and shown across the country the same day.

The former Princess Elizabeth repaired and drove trucks as a second lieutenant during the Second World War. Her reign of nearly half a century is the longest of any English monarch since Victoria.

12:39 p.m., Mon., Sept. 6, 1909 – The *New York Times* received a telegram from explorer Robert E. Peary informing them that he had reached the North Pole. News travelled slowly in those days – Peary claimed to have reached the Pole some five months earlier, on April 6. It was his eighth attempt in 23 years.

Earlier, Frederick Cook of Denmark claimed to have reached the Pole the year before Peary, but his claim was proven false. Later, serious doubts surrounded Peary's claim and it is the view of many historians that neither Cook nor Peary ever reached the North Pole.

Egyptian President Anwar Sadat was assassinated at a military parade in Cairo.

12:40 p.m., Tues., Oct. 6, 1981 – Egyptian President Anwar Sadat was assassinated at a military parade in Cairo. Sadat, who helped make peace with Israel during talks at Camp David, Maryland, died in a shower of gunfire when several men dressed as Egyptian soldiers stormed the reviewing stand. Ten other people were killed in the chaos and 40 injured. Three men involved in the attack were shot dead on the spot. Five other Moslem fundamentalists accused of killing Sadat were executed in April of 1982.

12:45 p.m., Fri., Mar. 5, 1982 – John Belushi, who rose to comic stardom on the TV show *Saturday Night Live*, was found dead of a drug overdose in a rented bungalow in Hollywood, California. His girlfriend, Cathy Smith, who allegedly obtained the drugs for Belushi, was later charged with murder. Belushi, whose repertoire included a wild Samurai warrior and a hilarious impression of Henry Kissinger, teamed with Dan Aykroyd in the movie *The Blues Brothers*. Belushi was only 33.

12:50 p.m., Fri., Sept. 1, 1972 – Soviet Boris Spassky resigned to American Bobby Fischer, ending one of the most memorable chess matches of all time. It took 21 games in Reykjavik, Iceland, for Fischer, 29, to defeat Spassky, the reigning world champion. The unpredictable Fischer was one hour late for the award ceremony and later refused to defend his title, eventually losing the crown in 1975.

12:50 p.m., Thurs., July 24, 1969 – *Apollo 11* splashed down in the South Pacific after the historic moon mission which saw Neil Armstrong and Buzz Aldrin become the first men to walk on the moon.

12:50 p.m., Sun., Dec. 29, 1963 – In what it called the first "important" U.S. airing of a Beatles song, New York radio station WMCA

Civil rights in the U.S. had taken a giant step forward.

played "I Wanna Hold Your Hand." The song spent seven weeks at the top of the Billboard singles chart in early 1964.

12:52 p.m., Sat., July 9, 1960 – Seven-year-old Rodger Woodward was discovered in the waters below Niagara Falls in what was later called a "one in a million" chance for survival. Deckhands on the *Maid of the Mist* found the slightly bruised and cut Woodward just minutes after he was swept over the brink of the Horseshoe Falls to the turbulent water and rocks below.

The accident occurred after a small boat carrying Rodger, his sister Deanne, 17, and family friend James Honeycutt, 40, overturned near the brink of the Falls. Deanne was grabbed in time by two American tourists. Honeycutt was swept over the Falls and his body was recovered the next day.

Experts attributed Rodger's survival to his light weight and the fact that he was wearing a life preserver. He was the first person to go over the Falls accidentally and live to tell about it.

12:52 p.m., Mon., May 17, 1954 – Chief Justice Earl Warren began reading the U.S. Supreme Court's decision in the case of Brown vs. Board of Education. When he was finished 25 minutes later, civil rights in the U.S. had taken a giant step forward.

The decision, read by Warren and approved unanimously by the court, banned segregation in U.S. public schools because of race. It was sparked by a suit filed by Oliver Brown, father of Kansas public school student Linda Brown. Oliver Brown was angered that his daughter had to travel two miles to school while there was an all-white elementary school much closer. Brown and other parents joined forces with the NAACP and sued the board of education. Future Supreme Court justice Thurgood Marshall took the case all the way to the Supreme Court where the historic decision was made.

12:54 p.m., Wed., Nov. 19, 1997 – An Iowa woman gave birth to the last of septuplets – the first set of septuplets in recorded history to survive more than a month. All seven babies were delivered by Caesarean section in six minutes. One of the attending doctors described the births as "a miracle."

The mother, Bobbi McCaughey, 29, of Carlisle, Iowa, had been taking a fertility drug. Doctors were amazed at how well-developed all the babies were. McCaughey (pronounced "McCoy") and her husband Kenny already had one child, daughter Mikayla, almost two at the time of the multiple births.

In January, 1998, a Saudi woman also gave birth to live septuplets. She had also taken a fertility drug.

12:56 **p.m., Thurs., May 11, 2000** – India's population reached one billion, according to computer-generated estimates. The running population count was displayed publicly on a large billboard-style digital counter at a busy road crossing in New Delhi. Just days before reaching the one billion mark, the clock stopped ticking. The clock was set up by the United Nations Population Fund as a reminder of the need to control population growth.

According to UN estimates, the population of the world reached six billion on October 12, 1999. It is estimated that the world's population increases by 77 million a year. The most populous country at the turn of the century was China with 1.25 billion people. In 1999, it was estimated that the world's population would be 9.2 billion by 2050.

India's population reached one billion.

1 p.m. to 1:59 p.m.

- 🕐 **Last passenger pigeon dies**
- 🕐 **Mount Vesuvius erupts**
- 🕐 **Lee Harvey Oswald dies**
- 🕐 **America enters World War I**
- 🕐 **The Beatles arrive in America**
- 🕐 **Eiffel Tower completed**

1:00 **p.m., Tues., Sept. 1, 1914** – Martha, the last passenger pigeon in existence, died at the Cincinnati Zoo. She was the last of a species that once numbered an estimated five billion in the United States.

As recently as the mid-19th century, it was not unusual for large flocks of passenger pigeons to block out the sun for hours on end. One mass nesting was estimated to have covered 1,942 square kilometres (750 square miles). The demise of the passenger pigeon was hastened by the fact they were slow on the ground and easy prey in the air for hunters who could kill dozens of them with one shotgun blast.

In 1900, the last passenger pigeon in the wild was killed. Finally, only three specimens remained, all at the Cincinnati Zoo. Two died, leaving only Martha. After Martha's death at the age of 29, her body was frozen and put on display at the Smithsonian Institution in Washington, D.C.

1:00 **p.m., Tues., Aug. 24, 79 AD** – Mount Vesuvius erupted. The ivy-covered volcano had been dormant for 3,000 years. The eruption buried the nearby city of Pompeii under nearly six metres (20 feet) of ash. Many of the 2,000 inhabitants died holding their hands or pieces of cloth to their mouths trying to block out the poisonous fumes. The smaller city of

Herculaneum escaped the worst of the ash fall but was buried when rain turned the ash into mud, resulting in an avalanche. The two cities of Pompeii and Herculaneum remain buried for 1600 years before being unearthed by archeologists.

Vesuvius has erupted several times since – the last in 1944.

The eruption buried the nearby city of Pompeii under nearly six metres (20 feet) of ash.

1:00 **p.m., Mon., Aug. 14, 1933** – Sparks from logging equipment touched off a blaze that consumed 97,000 hectares (240,000 acres) of forest near Tillamook, Oregon, almost as much lumber as was turned out by U.S. sawmills the previous year. In some places, the ash fall was more than a third of a metre (one foot) deep. The economic loss from this fire was staggering, with estimates ranging as high as $350 million.

1:00 **p.m., Sun., Dec. 31, 1967** – With a wind chill measuring -43° Celcius (-46° Fahrenheit) at game time, the "Ice Bowl" began. The game pitted two of the NFL's fiercest rivals, the Green Bay Packers and Dallas Cowboys, against each other in a classic matchup.

The game featured one of football's most memorable finishes. With 16 seconds left and the Packers trailing 17–14, it was Green Bay's ball, third down at the Dallas one-yard line. Passing up a possible field goal, Packer coach Vince Lombardi told quarterback Bart Starr to "run it, and let's get the hell out of here." Starr obliged, plunging into the end zone aided by a block by Jerry Kramer. The Packers won 21–17 and advanced to the Super Bowl where they beat the Oakland Raiders.

The Dallas win was a major career highlight for Lombardi, who coached the Packers to five NFL titles in seven years and an unprecedented three in a row from 1965 to 1967. Lombardi earned a well-deserved reputation as a taskmaster during his 10-year NFL coaching career – but he got results. In nine seasons with Green Bay and one in Washington, his teams won more than 73 per cent of their games and never had a losing season.

Lombardi, who studied for the priesthood as a boy, played guard for Fordham in the mid-1930s as one of the famed "Seven Blocks of Granite." A man obsessed with excellence, he is remembered for the quote: "Winning isn't a big thing. It's the only thing." He died at 7:12 a.m., on Thursday, September 3, 1970. He was 57.

Canada played Denmark in the first-ever Olympic curling gold medal game.

1:00 p.m., Sun., Feb. 15, 1998 – Canada played Denmark in the first-ever Olympic curling gold medal game. Two and a half hours later, Canada had won the first gold ever awarded in the sport, as Sandra Schmirler defeated Denmark's Helena Blach Lavrsen 7–5 in the women's finals. Later that day, Patrick Hurlimann of Switzerland would defeat Canada's Mike Harris 9–3 to win the first men's gold.

The gold medal capped a remarkable career for Schmirler and her team, consisting of third Jan Betker, second Joan McCusker and lead Marcia Gudereit. Formed in the early 90s, this close-knit squad won the 1993 Canadian women's curling championship, followed by a victory in the world championships. They repeated the feat in 1994. In 1997, Team Schmirler captured the Canadian championship for a record-tying third time, then won the world for the third time in as many attempts. A victory in the Canadian Olympic trials in the fall of 1997 earned Schmirler and company a trip to the Olympics and they didn't disappoint, winning eight out of nine games and taking the top prize.

In 1999, Schmirler was diagnosed with cancer and died at 3:00 a.m., Thursday, March 2, 2000. Less than a month earlier, she had appeared as a commentator for the Canadian Broadcasting Corporation for the finals of the Canadian junior championships. After Schmirler died, flags flew at half-mast in Saskatchewan for five days and her funeral was televised across Canada on two different national networks.

Less than a week before her death, Schmirler sent the following message to the competitors at the 2000 Canadian women's curling championship: "Keep things in perspective. There are other things in life besides curling, which I have found."

1:00 p.m. PT, Sun., Jan. 15, 1967 – The first Super Bowl telecast began from Los Angeles on CBS and NBC, the only time the big game was carried on two networks at the same time. An estimated 60 million people watched the first meeting between the National Football League and American Football League champions. The NFL Green Bay Packers won 35–10 over the AFL Kansas City Chiefs. Frank Gifford and Pat Summerall were the commentators for CBS. Curt Gowdy soloed for NBC.

At the time, the official name of the contest was the "AFL-NFL World Championship Game." The name "Super Bowl," coined by Chiefs owner

Lamar Hunt after his daughter's "Super Ball," wasn't officially adopted by the NFL until the third game. Commissioner Pete Rozelle thought it was undignified.

The Super Bowl was not a hit initially – only 61,946 fans attended the game at the 100,000-seat Los Angeles Memorial Coliseum. General interest in the game was low because most fans thought the NFL team would win easily. Media interest was also low compared to today's Super Hype. One major Toronto newspaper did not mention the upcoming game once in the two weeks from the NFL and AFL championships to the day before the game.

1:00 p.m., Mon., Aug. 12, 1940 – Air raid sirens sounded in Portsmouth as an estimated 300 German planes attacked the seaside community on England's south shore. Earlier, a British convoy had been attacked off Margate on the east shore. The Battle of Britain had escalated.

The Germans turned their attention to Britain following the invasion of Norway and the fall of France and the low countries in May-June of 1940. By early July, the Germans had 2,800 strike aircraft in various west European positions alerted and ready to strike. Six hundred and forty British fighters were readied for battle by the beginning of July, 1940. The British network of radar stations could detect coming raids from a distance of 160 kilometres (100 miles). In July, the Germans attacked several shipping and coastal targets in the south. By August, the Germans had started to raid inland and by mid-August, the Luftwaffe was mounting 1,800 sorties a day.

The Germans appeared to be winning at first, but the tide turned on September 7 when they changed strategies and began to bomb London instead of attacking the RAF. Reichsmarshall Hermann Goering was tired of Germany's continuing losses. By the time the Battle of Britain ended on October 31, the Germans had lost over 2,000 aircraft and 5,000 air crew. The British lost 500 men and sustained considerable damage to many key airfields, but had repelled the German advance, a major turning point in the Second World War.

1:00 p.m., Sat., Mar. 4, 1933 – Franklin Delano Roosevelt was sworn in as the 32nd president of the United States. In his inaugural

An estimated 300 German planes attacked the seaside community on England's south shore.

Canadian Prime Minister Brian Mulroney told an Ottawa press conference he was stepping down.

address, the 51-year-old Democrat told Americans suffering from the Great Depression that "the only thing we have to fear is fear itself." It would be the first of four inaugural speeches by Roosevelt, the longest-serving U.S. president. *(see 3:35 p.m.)*

1:00 **p.m., Wed., Feb. 24, 1993** – Canadian Prime Minister Brian Mulroney told an Ottawa press conference he was stepping down after eight years as Prime Minister and nearly 10 as Conservative party leader.

Mulroney was both praised and criticized for the two biggest moves of his administration, the introduction of a new trade deal with the United States and the establishment of a goods and services tax. Mulroney's risk-taking and decisiveness may have been a plus in dealing with Canada's problems, but these attributes also doomed him to record low popularity ratings. Mulroney was unsuccessful in two attempts to forge a constitutional deal between Quebec and the other provinces.

1:01 **p.m., Sun., Apr. 1, 1984** – Long-time Motown star Marvin Gaye died in a Los Angeles hospital. Gaye had been shot twice by his father just a half-hour earlier after the two had an argument, supposedly about an insurance deal. Marvin Gaye would have been 45 the next day.

Gaye had a string of hits beginning with "Pride and Joy" in 1963 and ending with "Sexual Healing" in 1982. His biggest hit was also one of Motown's biggest hits, "I Heard It Through The Grapevine" in 1969. Gaye, who once said, "just as Muhammad Ali was built to box, I was built to sing," was eulogized in two top-10 hits: "Missing You" by Diana Ross in 1984, and the Commodores' "Night Shift" in 1985.

1:02 **p.m., Fri., June 10, 1977** – Al Geiberger teed off in the second round of the Memphis Golf Classic. Four hours and 59 strokes later, the veteran linkster made history as the first golfer to break 60 on the PGA tour. Geiberger fired 11 birdies, one eagle and six pars in his incredible 13-under-par round of 59. He shattered the former PGA low round record of 60 shared by Sam Snead and five others. Geiberger went on to win the tournament by three strokes (without shooting a round in the 60s). It would be 14 years before the PGA witnessed another 59 – by Chip Beck in the second round of the 1991 Las Vegas International. Beck finished the tournament tied for third. In 1999, David Duval scored 59 in the final round of the Bob Hope Chrysler Classic at La Quinta, California, winning the tournament.

1:05 **p.m., Thurs., July 16, 1981** – Harry Chapin, rock's premiere storyteller and one of its great humanitarians, died in a Long Island hospital less than an hour after being involved in a car crash. Chapin was changing lanes on the Long Island Expressway when his 1975 Volkswagen was crushed from behind by a tractor-trailer. He was 39.

The New York-born Chapin, whose major hits included the narrative classics "Taxi," "Cat's in the Cradle" and "WOLD," was a humanitarian. Each year he performed about 100 concerts for political or social causes. Chapin co-founded the World Hunger Fund and helped raise $5 million for it. He lent his time to environmental and consumer causes and gave concerts for the Multiple Sclerosis Foundation. Chapin was scheduled to perform at a benefit concert the evening of the day he died.

Chapin was posthumously awarded the U.S. Congressional Medal of Honor for his environmental work in 1987.

1:05 **p.m., Mon., Apr. 18, 1983** – Forty people, including 16 Americans, died in an explosion at the U.S. embassy in Beirut. The blast resulted from a suicide attack when a man drove a car loaded with 136 kilograms (300 pounds) of TNT into the embassy compound.

1:05 **p.m., Mon., Apr. 19, 1993** – A fire raced through wooden buildings in Waco, Texas, where members of the Doomsday cult had been holed up for 51 days. The fire was set by the followers of Doomsday cult leader David Koresh as federal officials attempted to drive them out of their compound. Eighty-seven people died, including 24 children. Only eight people survived a mass suicide that rivalled the Jonestown massacre of 1978.

The standoff began February 28 when agents of the Federal Bureau of Investigation attempted to raid the building. Four agents died and 16 were injured in the raid.

1:06 **p.m., Fri., Apr. 28, 1967** – Cassius Clay, who had recently adopted a new religion, Islam, and the new name of Muhammad Ali,

Only eight people survived a mass suicide that rivalled the Jonestown massacre of 1978.

Lee Harvey Oswald, alleged assassin of President Kennedy, died of a single gunshot wound.

refused induction into the U.S. Army. Boxing officials stripped Ali of the world heavyweight championship and held a tournament later in the year to determine a successor. Ali won an appeal of his conviction as a draft evader and won back the title in 1974, knocking out George Foreman. Muhammad Ali won the title for a third time, over Leon Spinks in 1978, before retiring in 1979.

1:06 **p.m., Sat., Jan. 23, 1960** – The bathysphere *Trieste* reached the deepest known part of all the world's oceans – the Challenger Deep in the Mariana Trench in the South Pacific. At 10,917 metres (35,820 feet), this was the lowest spot ever explored by man. As the *Trieste* settled on the bottom, it was subjected to almost 200,000 tons of pressure in relatively mild temperatures of one degree Celsius (33° fahrenheit). The descent took four hours and 48 minutes. Aboard the *Trieste* were French scientist Dr. Jacques Piccard and Lieutenant Donald Walsh of the U.S. Navy.

1:07 **p.m., Sun., Nov. 24, 1963** – Lee Harvey Oswald, alleged assassin of President Kennedy, died of a single gunshot wound to the stomach. Oswald was shot by Dallas nightclub owner Jack Ruby as he was being transferred through the basement of Dallas police headquarters to a vehicle for conveyance to the county jail. Oswald, suffering from severe blood loss, died less than two hours after the 11:21 a.m. shooting which was carried live on NBC, and became the most widely watched murder in history.

Oswald's time of death was almost exactly 48 hours after Kennedy's. His funeral the next day was so poorly attended that reporters had to be asked to fill in as pallbearers.

As the mortally wounded Oswald lay on the floor of the police headquarters, a police detective asked him if he wanted to confess to the murder. Oswald, in great pain, shook his head firmly no. *(see 12:30 p.m.)*

1:07 **:25 p.m. (EDT), Fri., July 4, 1997** – The first faint signals were received from *Mars Pathfinder*, which had landed on the Red Planet earlier that day. *Pathfinder* came down on a flood plain near Ares Vallis. The probe's cameras sent out spectacular pictures of the rocky landscape to scientists and millions logging onto the Internet. *Sojourner*, the first mobile vehicle to explore another planet, conducted chemical studies of nearby rocks. One scientist called *Sojourner* "the robotic equivalent of Neil Armstrong for Mars."

1:10 **p.m., Sun., Nov. 11, 1945** – Jerome Kern, famed U.S. composer, died following a stroke at a New York hospital. He was 60. Kern had been in New York to co-produce with Oscar Hammerstein a revival of *Showboat*. Ironically, or perhaps fatefully, he had forgotten to play a few bars of his good luck charm "Old Man River" before leaving his house.

1:15 **p.m., Mon., Oct. 21, 1805** – Horatio Nelson, legendary British admiral, was shot in the chest during the Battle of Trafalgar. The heavily bemedalled Nelson proved an easy target as he was hit by a sharp-shooter aboard the French ship *Redoubtable* while he stood on the deck of his ship *Victory*. Nelson died three hours later, shortly after hearing of the *Victory*'s triumph. He was 47. Thousands attended his funeral in London.

1:15 **p.m., Mon., Dec. 20, 1860** – South Carolina voted to secede from the Union, splitting with the North on the issue of slavery and state's rights. The South Carolina vote was unanimous. Six other states would shortly join South Carolina to form the Confederate States of America.

1:18 **p.m., Fri., Apr. 6, 1917** – President Woodrow Wilson signed a war document making official America's entry into World War I. Earlier that morning, the U.S. House of Representatives had overwhelming-ly approved the measure after a 17-hour debate. Wilson had called for U.S. entry into the war only a few days earlier, saying, "the world must be made safe for democracy."

Contrary to popular belief, the U.S. did not enter World War I because of the sinking of the *Lusitania* in 1915. The U.S. went to war when it learned that Germany and Mexico were planning a military alliance.

1:20 **p.m., Fri., Feb. 7, 1964** – The Beatles arrived in North America for their first American tour to the screams of thousands of teenagers. On arrival, the Beatles thought the thousands packed into Kennedy Airport in New York City were there to greet an international

The Beatles arrived in North America for their first American tour.

Marie Curie became the first woman to lecture at the Sorbonne in Paris.

dignitary – but the reception was for them. Two days later, John, Paul, George and Ringo made their first U.S. appearance when they played on the *Ed Sullivan Show*. It drew what at the time was the largest audience in the history of television for an entertainment program.

1:25 p.m., Sat., Oct. 14, 1944 – The body of German general Erwin "The Desert Fox" Rommel was taken to a hospital in Ulm, Germany, following his death at age 53. Rommel gained recognition when he scored a number of early victories as commander of the Afrika Korps in Libya. But he was pushed back to Tunisia following a series of defeats.

The Desert Fox was given the choice of being shot or committing suicide after being found a conspirator in the July 20, 1944 plot to assassinate Hitler. It is believed he chose suicide.

1:30 p.m., Mon., Nov. 5, 1906 – Marie Curie became the first woman to lecture at the Sorbonne in Paris, as she began a lesson in physics. Curie picked up the lecture at the exact spot where her husband, Pierre, had left off the previous spring. Pierre Curie was killed when he was run over by a carriage in Paris on April 19.

The lecture theatre, which seated 200, was packed with reporters, the general public and students. Marie Curie taught the class 15 years to the day after she registered as a student at the Sorbonne. One newspaper called her elevation to lecturer as a "great victory for feminism."

The Curies made history with the discovery of radium and polonium and their pioneering research on radioactivity. However, the exposure to radioactive material had weakened Pierre prior to his accident and led to the death of Marie.

In 1903, the Curies won the Nobel Prize for physics. In 1911, Marie Curie won the Nobel Prize for chemistry, becoming the first person to win two Nobel Prizes.

1:30 p.m., Sun., Dec. 2, 1962 – The Grey Cup game that would come to be known as the "Fog Bowl" resumed at Toronto's CNE Stadium. The game had been halted with nine minutes and 29 seconds left in the fourth quarter on Saturday with the Winnipeg Blue Bombers leading the Hamilton Tiger Cats 29–28. The fog, which had enveloped the field from the start of the game, was so thick by the fourth quarter that officials had no choice but to call it.

There was no precedent for a game halted by fog. The Ti-Cats wanted the game replayed in its entirety the following Saturday. The Blue Bombers asked that a second game be played as part of a two-game total point series, or that it be picked up where it left off. CFL commissioner G. Sidney Halter opted for the latter.

About 15,000 fans attended the nine-minute, 29-second conclusion of the game. The Saturday crowd was listed as 32,655. Anyone who held a Saturday ticket was entitled to a refund, but only one person reportedly claimed it.

Neither team scored in the Sunday conclusion.

Sir John S. Thompson, Canada's fourth prime minister, collapsed and later died.

1:30 p.m., Wed., Dec. 12, 1894 – Sir John S. Thompson, Canada's fourth prime minister, collapsed and later died of a heart attack at a luncheon after visiting Queen Victoria at Windsor Castle. He is the only Canadian prime minister to die in office. Thompson was in London to be made a member of the Imperial Privy Council, a prestigious honour.

Thompson was one of four Conservatives who served briefly as prime minister after Sir John A. Macdonald retired in 1891. Macdonald was succeeded by Sir John Abbott, who held the job from June, 1891 to November, 1892. He resigned because of ill health and died in 1893. Thompson replaced Abbott in 1892. After Thompson's death in 1894, the job went to Sir Mackenzie Bowell whose own party forced him out for ineptitude in April, 1896. Sir Charles Tupper replaced Bowell, and kept the prime minister's chair warm for two months before losing to Liberal Sir Wilfrid Laurier in the election of July, 1896.

Of the 20 men and women to become Canada's prime minister, six have served less than two years in office – Abbott, Bowell, Tupper, Arthur Meighan, John Turner and Kim Campbell. Meighan served twice as prime minister without accumulating two years of tenure. Thompson lasted two years and one week in the job. Tupper's reign of 69 days is the shortest of all the prime ministers.

1:30 p.m., Fri., May 11, 1928 – The first regularly scheduled TV transmission was broadcast over station WGY in Schenectady,

Schubert wrote over 600 songs in his short lifetime, as well as 15 string quartets and 21 piano sonatas.

New York. It wasn't much of a show, as reported by *Television*, "Only the faces of men talking, laughing or smoking will be broadcast; no elaborate effects are planned at this stage." The half-hour transmission was broadcast every Tuesday, Thursday and Friday, supplemented by the broadcast of a play in September, 1928.

1:30 **p.m., Sun., Jan. 31, 1797** – Franz Schubert, Austrian composer best known for the "Unfinished Symphony," was born in Vienna.

Schubert, a squat, near-sighted, timid man, died nearly penniless with his works virtually unknown. The 500 musical transcripts found in his dingy apartment after he died were valued at $2.00 and are now considered priceless. Forty-three years after his death, a Viennese conductor named Johann Herbeck discovered the "Unfinished Symphony" in a dusty pile of Schubert's works and performed it to rave reviews. The "Unfinished," which contained two movements and only sketches for a third, remained uncompleted when Schubert put the piece aside and never got around to finishing it.

Schubert wrote over 600 songs in his short lifetime, as well as 15 string quartets and 21 piano sonatas. But the composer made only $3,000 from all his work and was so poor friends had to supply him with paper on which to write his music.

Schubert died in 1828 of typhus at age 31.

1:30 **p.m., Thurs., Jan. 21, 1932** – Lytton Strachey, English critic and satiric biographer of Queen Victoria, died of cancer of the colon at the age of 52. It was Strachey who reportedly said on his deathbed "If this is dying, I don't think much of it."

1:30 **p.m., Sun., Mar. 31, 1889** – Gustav Eiffel led French dignitaries to the top of the Eiffel Tower for a work-site party in celebration of the Paris landmark's completion. Eiffel placed an enormous French tri-colour on the tower's flagpole, signalling the opening of the tallest edifice ever built, up to that time. Begun in 1887 as the centre-piece for the Paris Exposition of 1889, the Eiffel Tower, built completely of iron with three platforms, was 300.51 metres (986 feet) high and cost $1,505,675.90 to build. Only one worker was killed during construction.

Eiffel, who was awarded the Legion of Honour, was a master builder of worldwide reputation, completing his engineering projects with clockwork precision. He was responsible for train stations and bridges in France, China, Hungary, Portugal and South America. Eiffel was also the designer of the internal iron skeleton supporting New York City's Statue of Liberty. Although he wrote his memoirs, Eiffel never published them, choosing instead to distribute only five mimeographed copies to his children.

Gustav Eiffel died on December 27, 1923. He was 91.

1:30 **p.m., Mon., Sept. 17, 1832** – Sir Walter Scott, Scottish poet and novelist who wrote the classic *Ivanhoe*, died of a brain disorder. He was 61. In addition to making his mark on the literary world, Scott also made medical history. At 18 months, he suffered what is believed to be the first recorded case of polio.

Sir Walter Scott, Scottish poet and novelist, died of a brain disorder.

1:34 **p.m., Sat., Sept. 14, 1901** – Vice-President Theodore Roosevelt arrived in Buffalo, New York, following the death of President McKinley. Two hours later he was sworn in as the 26th president. Roosevelt had rushed to Buffalo from a vacation retreat in the Adirondacks when told that the president was dying from an assassin's bullet. McKinley had already passed away by the time he arrived. At 42, Roosevelt was the youngest man to become U.S. president.

A former governor of New York and hero of the Spanish-American war, Roosevelt was the first president to tackle the environment. He also fought corruption in politics by big business and won the Nobel Peace Prize in 1905 for negotiating peace between Japan and Russia. The first president from a large urban area (he was born and raised in New York City), Roosevelt also paved the way for the construction of the Panama Canal.

He was re-elected in 1904 but declined to run in 1908. Unhappy with President Taft's leadership, Roosevelt ran for but lost the Republican nomination in 1912. He then ran on the Progressive ticket, dividing the Republican vote and handing the election to Democrat Woodrow Wilson.

Roosevelt was busy in retirement. In 1913, he led a 2,413-kilometre (1,500-mile) expedition through Brazil, almost dying of malaria in the process. The Brazil expedition came on the heels of an African safari in 1909–10. Roosevelt also wrote several books and magazine articles. His request to lead a group of volunteers in World War I was rejected by President Wilson.

Edward Whymper, a British climber, reached the top of the Matterhorn.

Roosevelt died at 4:00 a.m., Monday, January 6, 1919 of a coronary embolism at Oyster Bay, New York. *(see 8:00 p.m.)*

1:40 p.m., Fri., July 14, 1865 – Edward Whymper, a British climber, reached the top of the Matterhorn, a 4,477-metre (14,690-foot) mountain on the Swiss-Italian border. Making his seventh attempt at the peak that has challenged climbers for centuries, Whymper and a team of six were the first to reach the summit, just ahead of an Italian team. Four of Whymper's mates died on the descent, falling 1,219 metres (4,000 feet) to their deaths after a rope broke.

More than 100,000 people have followed Whymper to the Matterhorn summit, including a 76-year-old man and an 11-year-old girl.

1:40 p.m., Sat., May 27, 1905 – The battle of Tsushima, which led to the end of the Russo-Japanese war, began in the straight of Tsushima (between Korea and Japan). A fleet of Russian ships had attempted to make its way to safety through the narrow straight to the Russian port of Vladivostok. The Japanese intercepted, and in the battle that followed scored a rousing victory over the Russians. Five months later, the war ended with the Russian navy in tatters and the Japanese celebrating their greatest military victory. *(see 3:47 p.m.)*

1:42 p.m., Sat., June 18, 1960 – Arnold Palmer teed off in the final round of the 1960 U.S. Open golf tournament at the Cherry Hills course in Denver. Palmer, trailing by seven strokes after 54 holes, was angry after hearing sportswriter Bob Drum say a final-round 65 would not be enough for him to win the Open. Palmer proceeded to birdie the first four holes, shoot 30 on the front nine and play steadily on the back nine for a 65. This gave Palmer a 72-hole score of four-under 280.

Palmer watched as one by one his challengers faded. Third-round leader Mike Souchak ballooned to a final-round 65. Jack Nicklaus, struggling on the greens, shot 71 for second place, two back. Ben Hogan finished bogey-triple bogey when two pars would have given him a spot in a playoff. When the day was over, Palmer had leapfrogged over 14 players in the final round to win what would be his only U.S. Open title.

1:45 **p.m., Wed., Apr. 2, 1975** – Toronto's CN Tower was "topped off" as high-rigger Paul Mitchell lit a flare to signal to the crowds below that the tower's final height had been reached. The CN Tower is the tallest free-standing structure in the world at 533.3 metres (1,815 feet and five inches).

1:45 **p.m., Tues., Sept. 23, 1913** – French aviator Roland Garros became the first person to fly over the Mediterranean. His 897-kilometre (558-mile) journey (703 kilometres; 437 miles over sea) was the longest oversea flight of its time, and took just under eight hours from Cannes, France, to Bizerta, Tunisia. Roland Garros Stadium in Paris, site of the French Open tennis tournament, is named after the aviator.

1:45 **p.m., Tues., Jan. 23, 1968** – North Korea seized the U.S. navy intelligence ship *Pueblo* while it was on a surveillance patrol along the North Korea coast. Eighty-three crew members, including captain Lloyd Bucher, were held in custody for 11 months before being released Christmas Eve, 1968.

Bucher would admit that during his confinement he signed a confession that his ship was engaged in espionage, claiming that he signed the confession only to save the crew and only after he was beaten and threatened with death. In March, 1969, the U.S. Secretary of the Navy barred any disciplinary action against Bucher and the crew of the *Pueblo*.

1:47 **p.m., Sun., Mar. 2, 1958** – The first crossing of the Antarctic continent was completed by Dr. (now Sir) Vivian Ernest Fuchs and his 11 companions. They covered 3,472 kilometres (2,158 miles) in 99 days.

1:50 **p.m., Thurs., Jan., 14, 1954** – Former baseball star Joe DiMaggio and actress Marilyn Monroe were married at San Francisco City Hall, the second marriage for both. The two had met on a blind date two years earlier. Marilyn had never even seen a baseball game, and Joe had little interest in the movie scene. Love blossomed but the glamourous duo were divorced in 1955. For years after Marilyn's death in 1962, Joe had roses delivered to her grave every day.

Toronto's CN Tower was "topped off."

The operation, performed without the public's knowledge, was to remove a malignant tumour from the mouth of the Chief Executive.

1:50 **p.m., Fri., Nov. 30, 1900** – Irish dramatist Oscar Wilde, famed for his comedy of manners *The Importance of Being Earnest*, died of cerebral meningitis at age 46. Wilde, once imprisoned for homosexual offences, took the name "Sebastian Melmoth" after his release. He died in poverty in a Paris hotel.

1:52 **p.m., Wed., May 1, 1991** – Oakland's Rickey Henderson became baseball's all-time leading base-stealer when he stole his 939th base in a game against the New York Yankees. Henderson surpassed former St. Louis Cardinals great Lou Brock when he swiped third base, beating Matt Nokes's one-hop throw. After the historic steal, Henderson grabbed the base in both hands and told the Oakland Coliseum crowd, with characteristic immodesty: "I am the greatest of all time."

Henderson took only 13 seasons to set the record, six fewer than Brock.

1:55 **p.m., Sat., July 1, 1893** – A team of doctors led by Dr. Joseph Bryant began an hour-long operation on President Grover Cleveland. The operation, performed without the public's knowledge, was to remove a malignant tumour from the mouth of the Chief Executive. The doctors removed part of Cleveland's left upper jaw and part of his palate and fitted him with a rubber prosthesis. He was up and about two days later.

Amazingly, the operation, performed on a yacht cruising the East River off Manhattan, remained a secret until one of the physicians revealed all in a magazine article in 1917. The press in 1893 suspected the president was ill, but the White House denied it.

Cleveland was the governor of New York when he was chosen as the Democratic presidential nominee in 1884. Previously he had served as mayor of Buffalo, and after beating Republican James Blaine in the national election, he became the only ex-mayor to become president. Cleveland was defeated for re-election by Benjamin Harrison in 1888, but in a comeback unique in U.S. history, defeated Harrison in 1892 to reclaim the Oval Office. At his second inauguration he addressed the crowd before taking the oath of office.

During his first term, the 49-year-old Cleveland became the only president to be married in the White House. Cleveland tied the knot with Frances Folsom, a woman 28 years his junior, whom he had first met when she was a child. In 1913, Folsom became the first presidential widow to remarry.

Cleveland's second term was marked by a depression which saw thousands of businesses worth hundreds of millions of dollars go bankrupt. Known as the Panic of 1893, it was caused by poor harvests, industrial over-expansion, shrinking gold reserves and an economic slump in Europe.

Cleveland, the only man to serve two non-consecutive terms as president, died at 8:40 p.m., on Wednesday, June 24, 1908 at his home in Princeton, New Jersey. The man recognized as both the 22nd and 24th president was 71.

2 p.m. to 2:59 p.m.

- 🕐 **James Hoffa last seen**
- 🕐 **Scandal hits 1919 World Series**
- 🕐 ***Lusitania* torpedoed**
- 🕐 **Ronald Reagan shot**
- 🕐 **Roger Maris hits 61st homer**
- 🕐 **Karl Marx dies**

2:00 **p.m., Thurs., May 24, 1883** – The Brooklyn Bridge, one of the world's most famous spans, opened to the public for the first time. The suspension bridge took 13 years to build and saw its share of tragedy.

A total of 27 men, including its designer, John Roebling, Jr., died during construction of the bridge. Roebling was killed in 1869 while making observations to determine the exact location of the Brooklyn tower. His son, Washington, took over but was taken ill with Caisson Disease (the bends) in 1872 and supervised the completion of the bridge from his bedroom. Shortly after the bridge opened – on May 31, 1883, 12 people were crushed to death when a panic ensued on the bridge's promenade.

Washington Roebling never recovered from his illness and died in 1926 in Trenton, New Jersey, at the age of 89.

2:00 **p.m., Fri., Oct. 19, 1781** – The Siege of Yorktown, the decisive event in the struggle for American independence, ended in victory for the Revolutionary forces. Britain had lost its American colonies.

By mid-1781, General George Washington knew that things were turning in his favour. His opportunity to finish off the enemy came at Yorktown, where a French naval blockade hemmed in the British by sea. The American and French forces moved in on land, forcing a British retreat and cornering them at Yorktown, on the Chesapeake Bay. As the bands played "The World Turned Upside Down," the British surrendered their arms, bringing an end to the Revolutionary War.

2:00 p.m., Wed., July 30, 1975 – Teamsters Union president James Hoffa was seen for the last time outside a Detroit-area restaurant. Half an hour later, Hoffa called his wife and said the person he was supposed to meet hadn't shown up – and that was the last anyone heard of him. The most widespread speculation was that Hoffa had been kidnapped and murdered by underworld enemies – but his body has never been found.

At the time of his disappearance, Hoffa had been trying to regain leadership of the Teamsters Union, which he had built into the largest union in the U.S. before his 1967 imprisonment on mail-fraud and jury-tampering convictions. His 13-year term was commuted by President Nixon in 1971. Hoffa, whose 45-year union career was marred by violence and brushes with the law, was 62 at the time of his disappearance.

2:00 p.m., Thurs., July 12, 1804 – General Alexander Hamilton died at 47 one day after being shot in a duel with U.S. Vice-President Colonel Aaron Burr. Hamilton, secretary of the treasury under John Adams, and Burr were bitter political and personal enemies (at one time they shared the same mistress). The duel took place at dawn beneath the bluffs of Weehawken, New Jersey, just across the Hudson River from New York City. Burr challenged Hamilton to the duel as the result of a remark he had made against Burr some five months earlier.

Burr arrived first as had been previously agreed upon. Ten full paces were measured between them, and lots were cast for choice of position and who should give the word (General Hamilton's second won the "honour" in both cases). When the word was given, both parties fired at the same time and Hamilton fell instantly.

Burr was indicted for murder in both New Jersey and New York but his case never went to trial. He died at the age of 80 on September 14, 1836, the same day his divorce from his second wife was granted.

2:00 p.m., Wed., Nov. 28, 1979 – An Air New Zealand jet crashed into Mount Erebus in the Antarctic, killing all 257 aboard in the

Teamsters Union president James Hoffa was seen for the last time.

The first press telegram in communications history was sent.

world's southernmost air tragedy. Passengers had paid $359 each for what was supposed to be an 11-hour return flight from Auckland to the Antarctic.

2:00 **p.m., Mon., Feb. 18, 1952** – Willie Sutton, one of America's most notorious bank robbers, was arrested in Brooklyn, New York. The man known as "Willie the Actor" because of his many disguises offered no resistance.

Sutton had only a grade-eight education but was considered a criminal genius. He pulled off many carefully-planned, high-take robberies during a career that lasted nearly a quarter-century. His last robbery, a heist of $64,000 from a trust company in Queen's, New York, in March, 1950, was perhaps his most famous. The thorough Sutton spent over a month planning the job, and then pulled it off without a hitch.

Sutton disappeared into obscurity in Brooklyn before a salesman, Arthur Schuster, recognized him on a subway car and notified police. Sutton was arrested and sentenced to 50 years in prison for his many bank robberies. Schuster was shot to death outside his Brooklyn home two weeks after Sutton's arrest. His killer was never caught. Sutton was released from prison on Christmas Eve, 1969 after serving 17 years in prison. He died in 1980, aged 79.

2:00 **p.m., Sat., May 25, 1844** – The first press telegram in communications history was sent. The telegram, concerning a motion in the House, was dispatched by Morse code from a Congress reporter to the editor of the *Baltimore Patriot*. The *New York Daily Sun* commented: "This is indeed an annihilation of space."

2:00 **p.m., Tues., Sept. 28, 1920** – The "Black Sox" scandal hit major league baseball. A Chicago grand jury handed down indictments to six members of the Chicago White Sox baseball team and one former member. The players were indicted on charges they conspired with gamblers to lose the 1919 World Series to the Cincinnati Reds.

Among those charged were star left-fielder "Shoeless" Joe Jackson and standout pitcher Eddie Cicotte. None of the players charged was ever convicted, but all were banned from baseball for life by Commissioner Kenesaw Mountain Landis. Many have questioned Jackson's guilt but efforts to have him reinstated and thus become eligible for the Hall of Fame have failed.

2:00 p.m., Sun., June 20, 1955 – Ben Hogan and Jack Fleck teed off in an 18-hole playoff for the 1954 U.S. Open. The two were tied after 72 holes of regulation play at the Olympic course in San Francisco with matching scores of seven-over-par 287. In the playoff, the little-known Fleck shot a one-under-par 69 for a three-stroke win over Hogan.

Fleck's victory is considered one of the greatest upsets in golf history. It denied Hogan what would have been a record fifth victory in the U.S. Open. Hogan finished second in the 1956 Open and was in the running again in 1960 before finishing poorly and winding up four strokes out of a playoff. He played his last round in a PGA event in 1971.

Fleck went on to win two other tour events, the last in 1961. In 1979, Fleck won the PGA Seniors championship.

2:00 p.m., Sat., Mar. 2, 1980 – The first Labatt Brier, formerly known as the McDonald's Brier, opened with the round robin in Calgary.

The Canadian men's curling championship, which began in 1927 with McDonald's Tobacco as the sponsor, was thrown into turmoil when McDonald's withdrew its sponsorship in 1979. But Labatt stepped into the breech in 1980, retaining the name Brier, which was a brand of McDonald's tobacco. Another major change in 1980 was the introduction of a playoff system, in which the second and third place rinks met in a semi-final with the winner advancing to the final against the first place team. Previously, the team with the best record after the round robin won the championship; tiebreakers were played if necessary. In 1980, Northern Ontario beat Alberta 6–5 in the semifinal before losing 10–6 in the final to Saskatchewan's Rick Folk.

In 2000, it was announced that Nokia would take over as title sponsor but retain the Brier name.

2:05 p.m., Wed., Oct. 10, 1973 – Spiro T. Agnew became the first U.S. vice-president to resign under pressure. The former Maryland governor stepped down after pleading no contest to a charge of income tax evasion. Agnew was fined $10,000 and sentenced to three years' probation. Republican House leader Gerald Ford was chosen to replace him and became president the following year when Richard Nixon resigned.

Spiro T. Agnew became the first U.S. vice-president to resign under pressure.

Two ocean vessels, the *Queen Mary* and the *Curaçao* collided in the mid-Atlantic.

John Calhoun, vice-president under Andrew Jackson, was the first U.S. vice-president to resign when he quit in 1832 to seek election to the Senate.

2:12 p.m., Fri., May 7, 1915 – The British liner *Lusitania* was torpedoed by a German submarine off the southern Irish coast. The ship sank within 15 minutes with the loss of more than 1,000 lives, including 124 Americans.

The Germans defended their act, claiming the ship was carrying munitions intended for Britain, and that a newspaper advertisement had warned neutrals against travelling aboard ships flying the flag of countries involved in the war. The British denied the munitions charge, and former President Theodore Roosevelt called the sinking an "act of piracy."

President Wilson protested the German action and demanded that the safety of citizens from neutral countries be respected. However, the *Lusitania* sinking did not, as many believe, draw the U.S. into the First World War. It would be another two years before the U.S., fearing a German–Mexican alliance, joined the effort.

2:12 p.m., Fri., Oct. 2, 1942 – Two ocean vessels, the *Queen Mary* and the *Curaçao* collided in the mid-Atlantic. The *Queen Mary*, following a zig-zag pattern, sliced the *Curaçao* in half, apparently unaware it was following a straight course. The ships got too close and despite perfect visibility and the absence of World War II enemy craft, still managed to collide. There had been no voice communication between the ships.

After the collision, the *Queen Mary* did not stop in the submarine-infested waters for fear of endangering the 10,000 soldiers on board. That left the *Curaçao* to fare on its own and, although 101 men were saved by rescue ships, 338 died.

2:15 p.m., Tues., May 8, 1984 – Corporal Denis Lortie was taken into custody by police following his one-man siege of the Quebec National Assembly. Three people died and 13 were injured after Lortie, 22, wearing military fatigues and carrying a machine gun, entered the Assembly through a side door and started shooting.

Prior to the shooting, Lortie had delivered a tape to a Quebec City radio station in which he announced his plan to destroy the Quebec government.

National Assembly Sergeant-at-Arms René Jalbert talked to Lortie for four hours before the gunman finally surrendered. The legislature was not sitting at the time of the attack.

2:15 p.m., Thurs., Apr. 7, 1927 – Television was demonstrated in public for the first time at the Bell Telephone Laboratories in New York. It was "like a photo come to life," according to the *New York Times*. Highlighting the demonstration was a speech from Washington, D.C., 360 kilometres (200 miles) away, by U.S. Secretary of Commerce Herbert Hoover. The image that reached New York from Washington was one of Hoover talking on a telephone while smiling and nodding. The *New York Times* reporter observed that "time as well as space were eliminated."

Also shown in the demonstration was a vaudeville act from Whippany, New Jersey. A comedian named A. Dolan did a monologue portraying an Irishman and another routine in black-face. An engineer described technical aspects of the broadcast.

The following passage from the *New York Times* of April 8, 1927 was cautious but prophetic: "The commercial future of television, if it has one, is thought to be largely in public entertainment – super news-reels flashed before the audiences at the moment of occurrence, together with dramatic and musical acts shot on the other waves of sound at the instant they are taking place at the studio."

2:20 p.m., Wed., May 10, 1752 – A bolt of lightning proved one of Benjamin Franklin's scientific theories. The bolt struck an iron rod which had been set up in a garden in Marly, France, by scientist Thomas-François D'Alibard. Sparks flew and crackling could be heard. The experiment, witnessed by several terrified villagers, proved Franklin's contention that lightning was the same as electricity. Subsequent experiments confirmed Franklin's discovery.

Franklin was one of history's most gifted figures. As a politician, he helped write the Declaration of Independence; as a scientist, he invented the lightning conductor; as a journalist, he founded the *Pennsylvania Gazette* and *Poor Richard's Almanac*. Franklin also organized a fire brigade, worked as a postmaster and founded a university. As a meteorologist, he charted storm paths across America and the course of the warm sea current

Television was demonstrated in public for the first time.

President Ronald Reagan was shot as he left the Washington Hilton Hotel.

now known as the Gulf Stream. He was also American ambassador to France. One of Franklin's last acts was to help draw up the U.S. Constitution in 1788.

Franklin died of a lung ailment in Philadelphia at 11:00 p.m. on Saturday, April 17, 1790. He was 84.

2:20 p.m., Wed., July 25, 1973 – Louis St. Laurent, Canadian Prime Minister from 1948 to 1957, died at his home in Quebec City. He was 91.

St. Laurent's stay in office was an exciting time for Canada. Newfoundland was brought into Confederation, the Trans-Canada highway was begun and the first Canadian-born Governor General was appointed. St. Laurent, nicknamed "Uncle Louis" for his friendly, down-to-earth style, resigned as Liberal leader after losing the election of 1957.

2:25 p.m., Mon., Mar. 30, 1981 – President Ronald Reagan was shot as he left the Washington Hilton Hotel, where, just minutes earlier, he had finished a speech to a labour convention. Reagan was rushed to George Washington Hospital and was reported to be in stable condition after two hours of surgery. A single bullet had entered his left side, bounced off a rib, punctured and collapsed a lung and lodged just an inch from his heart. Doctors say the president might have died had he been admitted five minutes later.

Reagan's press secretary, James Brady, was shot in the head and suffered permanent brain damage. Also injured in the shooting were a Secret Service agent and a Washington policeman.

John Hinckley, 25, a drifter from Colorado, was apprehended at the scene but later found not guilty by reason of insanity. He said he shot the President in order to impress actress Jody Foster, with whom he had become infatuated. Hinckley was confined to a mental institution, but by the late 1990s was granted escorted day passes.

2:25 p.m., Mon., July 18, 1938 – Douglas "Wrong Way" Corrigan arrived in Dublin after taking off from Long Island 28 hours earlier. Corrigan, who had been barred from making a solo transatlantic flight, claimed he planned to fly west to California but flew east because of a faulty compass. He claimed he couldn't tell if he was flying over land or water because of clouds. It sounded like a tall tale, but forgiving American and Irish authorities declined to admonish Corrigan for his "error."

2:25 p.m., Sun., Sept. 26, 1999 – The United States took the lead for the first time in the 1999 Ryder Cup, winning their fifth straight match of the day 11–10. Two hours later, Justin Leonard sank a 40-foot putt on the 17th green at The Country Club at Brookline, Massachusetts, bringing the U.S. closer to victory in the biannual event. The Europeans were enraged when the U.S. team and supporters mobbed Leonard after his big putt while his opponent Jose Olazabal still had a 25-footer to tie. Olazabal missed and the U.S. took the Ryder Cup with a final score of U.S. 14-1/2, Europe 13-1/2.

The U.S. victory completed the greatest comeback in Ryder Cup history. The Americans erased a four-point final-day deficit by winning 8-1/2 of a possible 12 points in singles. It marked the first U.S. victory since 1993 and raised the final 20th century tally in the event to 24 victories for the U.S., eight for the team representing Britain and the rest of Europe, and two ties.

The tournament was started in 1927 at the urging of British seed merchant Samuel Ryder, a golf fan who commissioned the 7.4 centimetre (19 inch) solid gold trophy that is named for him. Originally, the tournament featured the best U.S. pros playing their counterparts from Britain. At the suggestion of Jack Nicklaus, it became a U.S.–European competition in 1979.

2:30 p.m., Sat., Dec. 12, 1925 – The Detroit Lions of the National Football League closed an offer to refund tickets for that day's game against the Chicago Bears. The refunds were offered because Bears star Red Grange was injured and could not play that day. It demonstrates the enormous drawing power of Grange even in his rookie season, and the way things were in pro sports in 1925. (According to the *Philadelphia Inquirer*, many of the 8,000 ticket holders came to Detroit's Navin Field to get their money back. Detroit won 21–0).

Grange starred as a running back for the University of Illinois where he set a record of five touchdowns in a 1924 game that stood for nearly half a century. The "Galloping Ghost" turned pro in 1925, helping the fledgling NFL to its feet first as a star player, then as a coach and promoter. He scored

The U.S. victory completed the greatest comeback in Ryder Cup history.

**The cornerstone
was laid for
the Smithsonian
Institution.**

56 touchdowns in 10 pro seasons, seeing action as a running back, wide receiver and defensive back.

Famed sportswriter Grantland Rice saved some of his best prose for Grange: "A streak of fire, a breath of flame, eluding all who reach the clutch; a gray ghost thrown into the game that rivals' hands may never touch."

Suffering from pneumonia, Grange died at 3:00 a.m., Monday, January 28, 1991 in a Lake Wales, Florida, Hospital. He was 87.

2:30 p.m., Wed., June 30, 1971 – The U.S. Supreme Court announced it was upholding the right of the *New York Times* and *Washington Post* to publish articles based on a secret government study of the Vietnam War. It marked the first time the U.S. government had been unable to prevent newspapers from publishing information on grounds of national security.

The Pentagon Papers, a 7,100-page secret history of the Vietnam War, was leaked to the *Times* by former Defence Department analyst Daniel Ellsberg. After carefully deleting military secrets, the *Times* began publishing the series on June 13, 1971. President Nixon, fearing his bargaining power in Vietnam might be undermined, had the Department of Justice issue an order barring the paper from continuing to publish the articles. Both the *Times* and the *Washington Post* appealed, leading to the Supreme Court decision.

2:30 p.m., Sat, May 1, 1847 – The cornerstone was laid for the Smithsonian Institution. Among those on hand were President James K. Polk, Vice-President George Dallas and several members of the U.S. cabinet.

The Smithsonian Institution was established with funds bequeathed to the United States by James Smithson. The museum has grown since its beginnings in the mid-nineteenth century, and now includes 16 buildings and galleries holding some 140 million artifacts and specimens. There is also a National Zoo and numerous research facilities in the United States and abroad.

2:30 p.m., Sun., Oct. 14, 1934 – *Lux Radio Theatre* debuted on NBC's Blue Network. In his book *The Encyclopedia of Old Time Radio*, John Dunning describes it as "the most important dramatic show in radio."

Lux Radio Theatre, sponsored by Lux Soap, was originally broadcast from New York and soon faced cancellation due to the lack of big name stars. But that all changed with the move to Hollywood in 1936. Famed movie director Cecil B. DeMille hosted the show; his austere opening, "Greetings from Hollywood, ladies and gentlemen," is legendary. DeMille signed off with equal flourish: "This is Cecil B. DeMille saying goodnight from Hollywood!" His presence helped the show draw many major stars, including Clark Gable, Gary Cooper, Fredric March, Spencer Tracy, Humphrey Bogart, Elizabeth Taylor and Bette Davis. Some of the dramas presented were *All About Eve*, *The African Queen*, *It Happened One Night* and *King Solomon's Mines*. The show's popularity was vast – some 30 million tuned in to listen at its peak.

During its 21-year run on network radio, approximately 52,000 pages of script were used in the Lux show, featuring 496 stars and 1,467 supporting players. Fred McMurray appeared the most times, 25. The show's last broadcast on network radio was aired June 7, 1955. A television version, *Lux Video Theatre*, ran from 1950 to 1957.

2:32 p.m., Mon., Mar. 1, 1954 – Five congressmen were shot, one seriously, in the U.S. House chamber in Washington, D.C., by Puerto Rican nationalists. All five survived and 200 others on the floor at the time of the attack escaped injury. Three men and a woman were arrested immediately after the incident and received maximum jail terms.

2:40 p.m., Thurs., July 6, 1944 – One hundred and sixty-eight people died when a fire swept through a Ringling Brothers and Barnum and Bailey circus tent in Hartford, Connecticut, signalling the end of the big-top era. One third of the victims were children.

The fire, probably caused by a carelessly discarded cigarette, set off a mad dash for the exits. During the scramble, the tent supports collapsed and the 19-ton tent, the largest single piece of canvas in the world, collapsed. It took only 10 minutes for all of the victims to die, most crushed or trampled by the crowd. No circus members or staff were killed. It was discovered later that the tent canvas, rather than being flame-proofed, had been made water-repellent with a coating of paraffin and gasoline.

Within a decade of the disaster, most major circuses had moved from tents to arenas or auditoriums.

Fire swept through a Ringling Brothers and Barnum and Bailey circus tent in Hartford.

Dodge City, Kansas, was hit by a "black blizzard."

2:40 **p.m., Sun., Apr. 14, 1935** – Dodge City, Kansas, was hit by a "black blizzard" – a raging dust storm. The dense, black cloud, more than 304 metres (1,000 feet) tall and stretching as far as the eye could see, slammed into Dodge City packing 96-kilometre- (60-mile-) an-hour winds and bringing 40 minutes of total darkness. The black wall, carrying tons of prairie topsoil from drought-parched fields, forced people to hide in cars, houses and other shelters until the worst had passed.

While few perished in this storm and others like it, the constant presence of dust-bowl conditions caused an epidemic of respiratory diseases and economic woes never before seen in U.S. history. Starting with the first dusters in 1932, farms, businesses and banks went under as crops failed and people abandoned their fields to the elements. Over a half-million people moved west from the Plains in the 1930s, and one in four homesteads was abandoned by 1936.

In 1938, the rain returned and, thanks to improved soil conservation techniques, harvests were bountiful once again.

2:45 **p.m., Sun., Oct. 1, 1961** – Roger Maris of the New York Yankees broke one of baseball's most coveted records as he smashed his 61st homer of the season off a pitch by Boston rookie Tracy Stallard. No hoopla followed the homer as many fans didn't want Maris to break the treasured record of 60 home runs set by Babe Ruth in 1927. In the half-empty Yankee Stadium, 23,154 spectators applauded as Maris circled the bases, his head down. The historic hit came in the fourth inning of the Yankees' 162nd, and final, game of the season. Brooklyn teenager Sal Durante caught the ball and sold it for $5,000 to California restaurant owner Sam Gordon. Eventually, the ball found its way to the Baseball Hall of Fame.

Maris's home-run total was one more than Babe Ruth hit in 1927 for the Yankees in a 154-game schedule, raising questions as to which should be the true record. Commissioner Ford Frick ruled that Ruth's total would hold as a record for a 154-game season, and Maris's as the record for a 162-game season. Maris's record was not, as many believed, accompanied by an asterisk – but by a reference to the length of the schedule. It was entered in the books as follows:

61 – Roger E. Maris, AL–NY, 1961 (162 G/S)
60 – George H. Ruth, AL–NY, 1927.

The Ruth distinction was quietly removed several years after the record-breaking homer. Maris never again approached his record season of 1961, retiring in 1968 from the St. Louis Cardinals. Mark McGwire, also playing for the Cardinals, broke the record in 1998 with 70 home runs. *(see 8:18 p.m.)*

2:45 **p.m., Wed., Mar. 14, 1883** – Karl Marx, father of "scientific socialism," died at age 65. The German-born Marx was the creator of "Marxism," the fundamental theory of Communism. He believed political, social and economic reality was based in the class struggle and predicted the downfall of capitalism. More than a century after his death, an estimated 1.3 billion adhere to his beliefs.

Karl Marx, father of "scientific socialism," died at age 65.

3 p.m. to 3:59 p.m.

- 🕐 **Jesus dies on the cross**
- 🕐 **U.S. House of Representatives impeaches Bill Clinton**
- 🕐 **China explodes its first atomic bomb**
- 🕐 **Don Larsen completes perfect game**
- 🕐 **Martin Luther King begins "I Have a Dream" speech**
- 🕐 **Elvis Presley dies**

3:00 **p.m., Fri., Apr. 7, 30 AD** – Jesus died on the cross. Jesus, called "The Son of God" or "Christ" by his followers, was crucified after a Jewish council convicted him on charges of blasphemy. A small crowd, including Jesus' mother, watched the crucifixion at Golgotha near Jerusalem. Two thieves were crucified with him.

Jesus won a great following as he preached the word of God, describing God as his father and performing numerous "miracles," such as raising the dead, curing people with fatal illnesses and turning water into wine. A charismatic preacher, Jesus was popular among the masses but ran into trouble with Jewish authorities, a conflict which led to his death.

According to the Bible, God raised Jesus from the dead three days after his death. Millions of believers today await his return.

3:00 **p.m., Sat., July 11, 1914** – Babe Ruth made his first appearance in a major league uniform, pitching the Boston Red Sox to a 4–3 victory over the Cleveland Indians at Fenway Park. Ironically, one of the greatest home-run hitters of all time was replaced by a pinch-hitter in the seventh inning.

Ruth, who hit 714 homers in a career spent mostly with the New York Yankees, transformed the game with his long ball power. After a few seasons as a pitcher, he switched to the outfield and set a major league record for home runs in one season with 29 homers in 1919. But the best was yet to come. Next season the Bambino cracked an unheard of 54 home runs, and he surpassed that with 59 in 1921. His watershed year came in 1927, when as part of the Yankees "Murderers Row," he hit 60 home runs to help the team win 110 games.

With Ruth in the lineup, the Yankees won seven American League pennants in 14 seasons. In addition, his colourful and outgoing personality helped promote the game to the greatest popularity it had ever known. He was also the game's highest paid player, earning $80,000 a year at his peak.

Ruth finished his career with the Boston Braves on May 30, 1935, leaving a game against Philadelphia with a knee injury, never to return. Five days earlier, in a game against Pittsburgh, Ruth had hit three home runs, including the last of his career. That final home run was the first ball ever hit out of Forbes Field. Pirates fans gave him a standing ovation after the game, not realizing they had witnessed the end of an era.

Ruth wore his famous number 3 for the last time on June 13, 1948, when, despite his failing health, he said goodbye in a raspy voice to a hushed crowd of Yankees fans. He would die two months later at age 53.

3:00 p.m., Sat., Oct. 3, 1914 – Canada sailed for war. Canada's first contingent of World War I troops left Gaspé, Quebec, for Britain. The 31,000 men were packed aboard 30 merchant ships along with weapons, vehicles, horses and an airplane. It took three hours for the 33-kilometre convoy to leave the harbour, heading for the "Great War."

3:00 p.m., Wed., Apr. 10, 1946 – London's Tate Gallery reopened after repairs to bomb damage from the Second World War.

The Tate Gallery, originally called the National Gallery of British Art, opened in 1897 with 65 British paintings. The building was donated by Sir Henry Tate. The first extension, the Turner Wing, opened in 1910. Three galleries for foreign modern art opened in 1916 followed by the John Singer Sargent Wing in 1926. In 1987, the Glore Gallery opened.

Collections in the Tate Gallery include works by William Blake, J.M.W. Turner and the pre-Raphaelites.

London's Tate Gallery reopened after repairs to bomb damage from the Second World War.

The Battle of Bunker Hill, one of the early battles of the Revolutionary War, began.

3:00 p.m., Mon., Mar. 25, 1896 – Opening ceremonies began in Athens for the first modern Olympic Games. More than 70,000 packed the reconstructed Panathenaic Stadion of Herodis to watch the historic event. Thousands more looked on from nearby hills.

The Olympic revival was the culmination of a dream for Baron Pierre de Coubertin of France, who first proposed the idea publicly in 1892. De Coubertin modeled the modern Games after the ancient Olympics, which were held in Olympia, Greece, from 776 B.C. until they were banned in 393 A.D.

One oddity of the 1896 Olympics was that no gold medals were awarded. Silver medals were presented for first place and bronze medals for second. The winners also received a diploma and a crown of olive branches. There was no presentation made to the third-place finishers. Of the 311 competitors, 230 were from Greece, 14 from the U.S. and none from Canada.

3:00 p.m., Fri., Sept. 3, 1658 – Oliver Cromwell, who led the parliamentary armies during England's civil war and ruled the country as Lord Protector, died at age 59.

Cromwell was one of the strongest opponents of King Charles I when the civil war broke out in 1642. The war, fought over religious differences and Charles's refusal to cooperate with Parliament, ended with troops led by Cromwell defeating the King's Royalist army at the Battle of Naseby in 1645. Charles fled to Scotland but was later brought back, tried and executed.

Cromwell's time in power was marked by numerous disputes between Parliament and the army which led to his becoming a virtual dictator. He proved to be a skilled administrator, however, and Scotland became prosperous through its union with England. The republic collapsed after Cromwell's death. His son, Richard, proved to be a weak ruler and by 1660, Charles II had ascended to the throne.

3:00 p.m., Sat., June 17, 1775 – The Battle of Bunker Hill, one of the early battles of the Revolutionary War, began near Charlestown, Massachusetts. The British emerged victorious, but only after a hard-fought battle during which they lost 1,000 men – three times the number of American casualties. The strong resistance of the American forces set the stage for a struggle that would last more than six years.

3:00 **p.m., Sat., Dec. 19, 1998** - House Judiciary Chairman Henry Hyde delivered the articles of impeachment against President William Jefferson Clinton to the Secretary of the Senate. Earlier that day, the U.S. House of Representatives – voting mainly across party lines – had approved two articles of impeachment against the President. The House impeached Clinton on charges of lying under oath to a federal grand jury and obstructing justice in the Monica Lewinsky affair.

It was the first time the House had chosen to impeach a president since Andrew Johnson in 1868. Johnson was spared conviction in the Senate by a margin of one vote. Clinton would also keep his job; the Senate did not convict him by the necessary two-thirds majority.

Clinton's troubles started in January, 1998 when it was reported that he had engaged in a series of sexual encounters with White House intern Monica Lewinsky. The fact that his wife Hillary still supported him and claims that he had "only" had oral sex with Lewinsky seemed to work in Clinton's favour. Also, many believed that the Republicans, led by Special Investigator Kenneth Starr, were "out to get" Clinton for political purposes. However, the fact that Clinton lied about the affair on national television and to his cabinet played against him. A half-hearted apology televised to the nation in August, 1998 didn't help.

Debate among Americans about what should be done with Clinton became quite heated at the time, although many others thought the whole matter was overblown. When the Senate acquitted Clinton of all charges in February, 1999, the news was greeted with a sigh of relief that it was finally over. Oddly, Clinton's approval rating rose during the year-long scandal.

3:00 **p.m., Fri., June 6, 1986** – CHUM Toronto ended 29 years as a Top 40 radio station with a montage of number-one songs from 1957 – the year the station debuted as a Top 40 station – to 1986. The last Top 40 deejay was Terry Steele. CHUM then switched to a soft rock format called "Hits of Yesterday and Today." The station went to a full-time oldies format in 1989.

The end of CHUM's Top 40 years also saw the cancellation of the legendary CHUM chart, a weekly compilation of the week's top tunes. It had been published every week without a break since May 27, 1957, a streak of over 1,500 charts.

3:00 p.m., Fri., Nov. 2, 1979 – Jacques Mesrine, France's public enemy number one, who was also wanted in Canada for murder and armed robbery, died in a hail of police bullets in Paris. Mesrine and his girlfriend were gunned down in his grey BMW in a carefully planned ambush by 80 police officers, including six sharpshooters. Mesrine, shot 18 times, died immediately. His girlfriend survived despite being hit by 21 bullets.

A suave, hard-bitten criminal with a sense of the dramatic, Mesrine was killed after two decades of murder, bank robbery and prison escapes. He became a folk hero in France, a Jesse James figure, thumbing his nose at the police with each successful crime. In an autobiography written in prison and smuggled out, he said he knew as a boy he would become a gangster and had decided at age 23 to become a killer. It all ended when a former cellmate tipped police to his location. In typical dramatic style, Mesrine left a final recorded message to his girlfriend, telling her they would meet again "not in paradise but maybe in hell."

3:00 p.m., Mon., Feb. 17, 1919 – Wilfrid Laurier whispered "C'est fini" to his wife and died following a stroke. Canada's first Quebec-born prime minister was 78.

Laurier was one of Canada's most respected prime ministers. Born in the tiny Quebec village of St. Lin, he used his strong powers of oratory to launch a political career that lasted nearly half a century. First elected to Parliament in 1874, Laurier worked his way up to national Liberal leader in 13 years. By 1896, he was prime minister, a position he held for 15 years – the longest uninterrupted tenure in Canadian history.

Under Laurier, Canada enjoyed some of its most prosperous years, thanks in part to a strong cabinet that included representatives from all regions. After a record four consecutive electoral triumphs, Laurier was defeated by Robert Borden in the election of 1911.

3:00 p.m., Thurs., Nov. 19, 1863 – With the words "four score and seven years ago," Abraham Lincoln began one of his most famous speeches.

The Gettysburg Address is known for its brevity as much as its content. At a time when long-winded speeches were the norm, Lincoln's succinct

269-word address came as a surprise to many who were expecting a much longer speech. In fact, just before Lincoln spoke, famed orator and former Massachusetts governor Edward Everett delivered a now forgotten two-hour speech. By contrast, Lincoln's speech lasted only two minutes; photographers didn't even have enough time to take a picture of him. Lincoln had written the speech on the back of an envelope while on the train to what is now known as Soldiers National Cemetery in Gettysburg, Pennsylvania. The president was there to honour the Union soldiers who died at the Battle of Gettysburg July 1–3, 1863.

3:00 p.m., Sun., Feb. 21, 1965 – Malcolm X, a black leader known as "The Angriest Negro in America," was shot to death as he spoke to a crowd of about 400 in New York City. Malcolm X, who had changed his name from Malcolm Little, was one of the principal spokesmen for the Muslim organization led by Elijah Mohammed. Three men were later arrested and convicted.

3:00 p.m., Wed., Aug. 2, 1876 – "Wild Bill" Hickok, legendary U.S. lawman, was shot dead from behind as he played poker in a Deadwood, South Dakota saloon. The hand he was holding – ace of spades, ace of clubs, eight of spades, eight of clubs, jack of diamonds – has been known since as "the dead man's hand."

Hickok first gained prominence as the rather flamboyant sheriff of Ellis County, Kansas. His shoulder-length hair, waxed mustache, European suits and colourful silk ties made him a memorable sight. He once boasted that he had killed 100 men, not counting Indians. As marshall of Abilene, Texas, Hickok gained more of a reputation as a card shark than for his ability to keep the peace. He was later ridden out of town after he accidentally killed two men, including his own deputy, in an effort to quell a drunken brawl. His badge forever stained, he became a full-time poker player and drifter.

The day he was shot, Hickok had ignored his own rule of always sitting with his back to the wall. Jack McCall, the man who shot Hickok, claimed the former lawman had killed his brother. McCall was hanged for murder March 1, 1877.

"Wild Bill" Hickok, legendary U.S. lawman, was shot dead from behind as he played poker.

Jules Verne, French adventure writer credited with inventing science fiction, arrived in New York.

3:00 **p.m., Tues., Apr. 9, 1867** – Jules Verne, French adventure writer credited with inventing science fiction, arrived in New York for his first visit to North America. He and his brother Paul had travelled from Europe for 14 days on the *Great Eastern*, known as the "Wonder of the Seas." Just a year earlier, the ship had been used to lay the first Atlantic cable between the United States and England. While in the U.S., the ever-curious Verne and his brother visited Broadway, took a cruise up the Hudson River and saw Niagara Falls.

Verne is one of history's great visionaries. In his books, he foresaw space travel, airplanes, automobiles – even the computer. His classics include *Around the World in 80 Days, 20,000 Leagues Under the Sea* and *A Journey to the Center of the Earth*. He got his start writing opera librettos.

Verne died at 8:00 a.m. on Friday, March 24, 1905 in Amiens, France. He was 78.

3:00 **p.m., Fri. Oct. 16, 1964** – China exploded its first atomic bomb and thus became the world's fifth nuclear power, joining the United States, the Soviet Union, Britain and France.

3:00 **p.m., Thurs., Nov. 7, 1991** – Magic Johnson announced to a stunned sports world that he was HIV-positive and was retiring. The Los Angeles Lakers star was the most famous sports figure to disclose that he had the virus that can lead to AIDS.

Johnson, one of the game's major stars who led the Lakers to five NBA titles, had recently married his college sweetheart Cookie Kelly. Kelly was seven weeks' pregnant at the time of the disclosure and tested negative for the HIV virus. Johnson said he wasn't homosexual and contacted the virus during a sexual encounter with a woman. Said teammate Kareem Abdul-Jabbar of Johnson, "His luck ran out on him."

3:00 **p.m., Mon., June 27, 1983** – Ballooning pioneers Maxie Anderson and Don Ida were killed when their balloon crashed at Schweinfurt, West Germany. The Americans were one of 18 teams from nine countries who had set out from France the day before.

Anderson made ballooning history by crossing both the Atlantic and

Pacific Oceans in separate voyages. In 1981, he and Ida failed in an attempt to circle the globe in a balloon.

The first scheduled transatlantic flight from the United States to Europe took off.

3:00p.m., Thurs., Feb. 25, 1909 – A biplane named the *Silver Dart* was wheeled out of its shed at Baddeck, Nova Scotia. Shortly after, the *Silver Dart* took off with John Alexander Douglas McCurdy at the controls – the first airplane flight in the British Empire. The plane flew 0.8 kilometres (half a mile) at 64 kilometres (40 miles) an hour before landing. Much of the credit went to Alexander Graham Bell, inventor of the telephone, who had worked with the Aerial Experiment Association.

3:00 p.m., Wed., June 28, 1939 – The long-awaited first scheduled transatlantic flight from the United States to Europe took off from Long Island, New York. Twenty-two people paid $375 each (about $3,500 at today's rates) for the historic journey on the *Dixie Clipper*. The plane needed only 42 hours and 10 minutes to fly to Europe, including stopovers, compared to six days on the *Queen Mary*.

The *Dixie Clipper*, the largest plane ever flown, measured 33 metres (109 feet) with a wingspan of 46 metres (152 feet). So large were its wings that an engineer could walk around inside them. The plane featured luxuries unheard of today: five main passenger cabins that converted into a sleeping compartment, and a honeymoon suite that included a daybed, loveseat and writing table. Its kitchen could turn out six-course dinners complete with turtle soup, filet mignon, Breast of Chicken Virginia and strawberry shortcake.

World War II soon brought an end to the luxury transatlantic flights of the *Dixie* and its sister craft. The last plane sank in Baltimore harbour in 1951 during a storm.

3:00 p.m., Thurs., May 15, 1941 – The New York Yankees met the Chicago White Sox in what appeared to be just another early-season American League game. It would be anything but.

A few minutes into the game, Yankees outfielder Joe DiMaggio hit a two-out single to centre off lefty Edgar Smith to drive in the only New York run in a 13–1 loss. It was the beginning of one of baseball's greatest feats. By July 17 in a game against Cleveland, DiMaggio had hit the ball in 56 consecutive games to set one of baseball's most enduring records. The streak, not even

**The battle
resulted in defeat
for Champlain
and his allies.**

noticed by reporters until game 13, garnered national interest that reached a fever pitch as DiMaggio closed on Wee Willie Keeler's 1897 record of 44 games. He broke Keeler's record on July 2 and kept on hitting until he was stopped by Cleveland pitchers Al Smith and Jim Bagby 15 days later. By the time the streak was over, DiMaggio had established a new standard in the game of baseball.

3:00 p.m., Sat., Apr. 15, 1989 – A stampede broke out in the standing-room-only section just before the start of a soccer game between Liverpool and Nottingham at Sheffield, England. Within minutes, 95 people had been killed and more than 200 injured. Most of those who died were either trampled underfoot or squeezed to death against the chain-link fence in the standing-room section.

3:00 p.m., Wed., Oct. 11, 1615 – French explorer and cartographer Samuel de Champlain stood before the Iroquois fort at Lake Onandaga near what is now Syracuse, New York. He was considering his options prior to attacking the fort with help from the Huron and Algonquin tribes. The battle – considered by many to be the beginning of the Indian wars in America – resulted in defeat for Champlain and his allies.

Defeat was rare for Champlain, who had played a major role in the exploration and development of the St. Lawrence River. Known as "The Father of New France," his first visit to what is now Canada had been in 1603, on a voyage up the St. Lawrence with François Grave Du Pont. In 1604, he arrived in Acadia accompanied by the Sieur de Monts, who was hoping to establish a French colony there. Later, in 1605 and 1606, Champlain continued his exploration, this time in New England as far south as Cape Cod. As yet, no location for a settlement had been decided on. Finally, in 1608 Champlain was sent by France to establish a colony in what became known as Quebec City.

Champlain organized a large fur trading network in the St. Lawrence, Ottawa River and Great Lakes regions. His detailed maps of the area were a benefit for many generations to come, but his main goal was to establish Quebec City as the centre of a powerful colony. That dream was interrupted in 1629 when Quebec was occupied by the British. But by 1633 – just two years before his death – he was able to see the beginnings of the Quebec colony he had long sought to establish.

Champlain died on Christmas Day in 1635. No authentic portrait of him is known to exist.

3:01 **p.m., Sat., May 27, 1995** – Actor Christopher Reeve, best known for portraying "Superman," left the starting box in a warm-up run for an equestrian competition in Virginia. Minutes later, the horse he was riding stopped cold at a jump, throwing Reeve, whose neck was broken when he landed on his head. He was left a quadraplegic, paralyzed from the neck down and unable to breathe without a respirator.

An active sportsman until his accident, Reeve refused to let the mishap get the best of him and became a spokesman for those paralyzed by spinal injuries. Despite the prognosis of doctors, he vowed to walk again, believing that a cure could be imminent. His bravery has made him a hero and given hope to others suffering from spinal chord injuries. He remains active in the entertainment field as a director and actor, most notably in a television remake of Alfred Hitchcock's *Rear Window*.

3:03 **p.m., Fri., May 25, 1979** – Two hundred and seventy four people died when an American Airlines DC-10 crashed shortly after takeoff from Chicago's O'Hare Airport. None aboard the plane survived and two men in a truck on the ground were also killed. The accident occurred after an engine broke off the wing, the result of a weakness in the wing's engine mounts. After the crash, the U.S. government ordered all DC-10s grounded until the flaw was corrected.

3:04 **p.m., Thurs., Apr. 18, 1946** – As 25,000 fans looked on at Roosevelt Field in Jersey City, New Jersey, Jackie Robinson stepped up to the plate for his first at-bat for the Montreal Royals. It was the first at-bat by a black man in baseball's previously whites-only International League. Until then, black players could only ply their trade in the Negro Leagues. Robinson grounded out against Jersey City pitcher Warren Sandell, but wound up going 4-for-5 with a homer to lead the Royals to a 14–1 victory.

A year later, after a stellar season with Montreal, Robinson crossed major league baseball's colour line as an infielder with the National League's Brooklyn Dodgers. Despite the pressure and frequent racial slurs,

Actor Christopher Reeve left the starting box in a warm-up run for an equestrian competition in Virginia.

The U.S. Congress voted Hawaii into the Union as the 50th state.

Robinson went on to star for a decade in the majors, paving the way for many other black players to follow. He led the Dodgers to six pennants, was named rookie of the year in 1947 and most valuable player in 1949. He retired after the 1956 season and was elected to baseball's Hall of Fame in 1962.

Robinson died of a heart attack at age 53 in 1972.

3:04 **p.m., Thurs., Mar. 12, 1959** – By a vote of 323–89, the U.S. Congress voted Hawaii into the Union as the 50th state. The vote came less than nine months after Alaska was admitted as the 49th state. Alaska and Hawaii marked the first American additions since New Mexico and Arizona became the 47th and 48th states in 1912.

3:11 **p.m., Fri., Oct. 19, 1956** – Journeyman pitcher Don Larsen of the New York Yankees became the first pitcher to toss a perfect game in the World Series. Larsen did not allow a single base-runner as the Yanks shut out the Brooklyn Dodgers 2–0.

Larsen seemed an unlikely candidate for immortality as he prepared to face Sal Maglie in the fifth game of the fall classic. The Yankees pitcher had a career record of 30–40 and was the team's fourth starter. But he proved untouchable and entering the ninth had retired 24 hitters. Just three outs away from history, Larsen opened the ninth by retiring Carl Furillo on a fly ball to right. Roy Campanella grounded to second for out number two. Only one man separated Larsen from perfection: Dale Mitchell, brought on to pinch-hit for Maglie. Larsen worked the count to 2–1, then, on his 97th pitch of the game, hit the outside corner for a called third strike and a perfect game. Catcher Yogi Berra of the Yankees leaped into Larsen's arms and Yankee players mobbed the field. Lost in the excitement was the fact that veteran home plate umpire Babe Pinelli had just called his last major league game.

Larsen retired with an 80–90 career record in 1967. Mitchell retired after the 1956 World Series.

3:12 **p.m., Sun., Apr. 30, 1939** – The New York World's Fair opened with an official theme of progress and peace. President Roosevelt made the opening speech to a crowd of 600,000, many of them servicemen.

By the end of the first week, one million people had passed through the turn-stiles. The Fair closed November 1, 1939 with a total of 26 million visitors.

New York also hosted another world's fair in 1964–65.

3:15 p.m., Mon., July 4, 1831 – James Monroe, the fifth president and the last Revolutionary War officer to occupy the White House, died of tuberculosis in New York City. He was the third of the first five presidents to die on Independence Day, John Adams and Thomas Jefferson having died exactly five years earlier.

Monroe was one of the most popular presidents in history. Easily winning election over Federalist Rufus King in 1816, he ran unopposed for re-election in 1820 – the only president other than George Washington to stand unop-posed. One elector voted against him, however, and Washington remained the only president to sweep the electoral college (in 1789 and 1792).

Like the four presidents who preceded him, Monroe was born in Virginia and had been involved in the formation of the country. A career politician and diplomat, Monroe served in several posts, including Secretary of State, Minister to France and later Great Britain, governor of Virginia and U.S. sen-ator from that state. By 1816, he was a shoo-in for the presidency.

Monroe enjoyed enormous personal popularity and his time in office was known as the "era of good feelings" (a phrase coined by a Boston newspa-per). His popularity was bolstered by the fact that the Republican Party dominated most sectors of society, leading to an unheard of lack of political conflict.

The fifth president is perhaps best known for a policy named the Monroe Doctrine. It was a message to Congress meant to warn European powers against intervention in the Western Hemisphere. To this day, the Monroe Doctrine remains a key part of U.S. foreign policy.

3:15 p.m., Fri., July 3, 1863 – The Battle of Gettysburg began to turn in the Union's favour as Confederate General George Pickett ordered an ill-advised charge against the Union ranks. Union artillery and musket fire destroyed the Southern fighters, and those who survived the ini-tial attack were repulsed in bloody hand-to-hand fighting. With the failure of what came to be known as Pickett's Charge, Confederate General Robert E. Lee turned tail and escaped into Virginia.

The Battle of Gettysburg began to turn in the Union's favour.

The New York Mets capped a miracle year by winning the World Series.

The Battle of Gettysburg began by accident July 1 when a Confederate brigade en route to Gettysburg to seize a supply of shoes, ran into a Union cavalry unit. In the unexpected battle that followed, the Confederates took Gettysburg and the Unionists retreated to the heights south of the town. After a series of skirmishes on July 2, Lee planned the disastrous charge of July 3. The loss at Gettysburg is considered the major turning point in the North's eventual victory over the South in 1865.

3:15 p.m., Wed., Dec. 30, 1903 – A blaze was ignited at the Iroquois Theater in Chicago. Despite the quick work of the fire brigade and the services of every ambulance in Chicago, 602 people died.

Close to 20,000 people had jammed into the theatre to watch the pantomime *Mr. Bluebeard*. The production was in full swing when a lamp overheated and set drapery near the stage ablaze. The flames quickly spread, setting off a panic. Within 10 minutes, 200 people were dead of smoke inhalation or from the flames. The other 400 were crushed or trampled to death, some with marks of boots or shoes on their faces.

3:15 p.m., Sun., May 10, 1863 – Stonewall Jackson, considered the best of all the Confederate generals, died at Guiney's Station, Virginia. Jackson succumbed eight days after he was accidentally shot by his own men at the moment of victory over Union General Joseph Hooker at Chancellorsville, Virginia. He was 39. Jackson's death was a major blow to the Confederate forces, which surrendered less than two years later.

3:17 p.m., Thurs., Oct. 17, 1969 – The New York Mets, baseball's laughingstock for seven seasons, capped a miracle year by winning the World Series. The clincher came when Baltimore's Dave Johnson flied out to Cleon Jones, giving the Mets a 5–3 victory over the Orioles, and a 4–1 triumph in the Series.

The win climaxed an incredible success story for the Mets, who had finished ninth the previous season, tying their best-ever finish. Before the season, oddsmakers posted their chances of winning the World Series at 100–1.

3:20 p.m., Tues., Apr. 22, 1997 – Peruvian commandos stormed the Japanese ambassador's residence in Lima, freeing 71 men after four months of captivity. One hostage and two soldiers died in the attack along with all 14 rebels who had taken the compound on December 17, 1996. Originally, 500 hostages were taken but by the time of the rescue, the rebels had released all but 72. The operation took place as the rebels were playing their daily soccer game. The successful rescue boosted the sagging popularity of Peruvian president Alberto Fujimori.

3:20 p.m., Wed., Aug. 20, 1980 – Italian mountaineer Reinhold Messner became the first man to scale Mount Everest completely alone, without oxygen, radio or supply relays. Messner, who had lost most of his toes in a previous team conquest of the mountain, took two and a half days to complete his solo journey to the summit.

Among the obstacles Messner faced and overcame were high gusting winds, soft, deep snow, loss of orientation due to a lack of oxygen, exhaustion, dehydration, and – most challenging of all – the lack of a partner or any outside help. His successful climb stands as one of the great feats in the history of mountain climbing.

3:28 p.m., Sun., Dec. 10, 1967 – Otis Redding, legendary rhythm and blues star, died when his twin-engine Beechcraft crashed into Lake Monoma, near Madison, Wisconsin. He was only 26. Also killed were the pilot, Redding's valet and four members of the vocal group the Bar-Kays.

Three months after his death, Redding hit number one on the Billboard charts with a song he had recorded just three days before his death, "(Sittin' On) The Dock of the Bay." It was the first posthumous number one single of the rock era and Redding's only top 10 hit. Redding also wrote Aretha Franklin's number one 1967 smash "Respect," and co-wrote "Sweet Soul Music" for Arthur Conley in 1967.

Redding's death came three years to the day after his idol, Sam Cooke, was shot to death in a Hollywood, California, motel.

3:30 p.m., Wed., Aug. 28, 1963 – Martin Luther King began his famous "I Have A Dream" speech at the Lincoln Memorial in Washington, D.C. More than 200,000 peaceful demonstrators – black and white – had gathered that day to demand the passage of civil rights legislation.

Martin Luther King began his famous "I Have A Dream" speech.

Elvis Presley, the number one solo artist of the rock era, was pronounced dead.

King was the fourth of 10 speakers to address the crowd. The U.S. civil rights leader held his restless and thinning audience spellbound with his 16-minute speech, considered a landmark in the civil rights movement. It was delivered with the passion and spirit of a church preacher, and the "I Have a Dream" section was said to have been improvised, not in the original text of the speech. Its closing words "Free at last, free at last, thank God Almighty, free at last" are among the most remembered in the history of oratory.

The thankless task of following King to the podium went to Roy Wilkins, executive secretary of the NAACP. Five more speakers appeared after Wilkins, but only the words of Martin Luther King are remembered.

3:30 p.m., Fri., Aug. 15, 1890 – Canada's first high-speed electric streetcar made its inaugural run in Toronto. The car, filled with politicians and well-known local citizens, took 12 minutes to travel from City Hall at St. Lawrence Market to the end of the line at North Sherbourne St. and Bloor.

3:30 p.m., Tues., Aug. 16, 1977 – Elvis Presley, the number one solo artist of the rock era, was pronounced dead after being found in the bathroom of his home in Memphis, Tennessee. Presley, 42, died of heart problems likely related to his drug addiction.

Presley was an unknown truck driver in the summer of 1953 when he recorded two songs at the Memphis Recording Service on his lunch break. The songs led to a recording contract with Sun Records and a few regional hits. By November, 1955, RCA had purchased his contract and by April, 1956, Elvis had his first national number one record – "Heartbreak Hotel." Seventeen more number one songs and 148 charted hits would follow that first smash release.

Elvis became more than just a popular singer – he became a hero, a symbol to a generation of young adults who were just discovering rock and roll. His popularity reached stratospheric levels in the latter half of the 1950s, and continued unabated until the early 60s. He had at least one number one song every year from 1956 to 1962, including such classics as "Don't Be Cruel." "All Shook Up" and "Stuck on You." By 1963, his popularity had begun to wane, but he made a strong comeback in the late 60s and early 70s with hits such as "Suspicious Minds" and "Burning Love."

Overweight and battling drug problems, Presley faded from the charts by the mid-70s but continued to be popular as a touring entertainer. His last performance was in Indianapolis on Sunday, June 26, 1977, just 51 days before his death.

Presley's legend has grown since his death. The anniversary of his passing is remembered annually by thousands of fans who flock to his Graceland grave to pay their respects to the man known simply as "The King."

3:30 p.m., Fri., Oct. 13, 1972 – A charter plane carrying members of an amateur Uruguayan rugby team, along with several friends and relatives, crashed into the Andes Mountains. An eight-day search for the plane proved fruitless, and it was assumed that all 45 on board had died. Ten weeks after the crash, two of the survivors reached civilization and the remaining 16 survivors were rescued shortly after.

In an admission that gained worldwide attention and sparked debate, the survivors admitted they had resorted to cannibalism after their food supplies ran out. The general opinion was that the survivors had nothing to be ashamed of – they simply did what was necessary to survive. Their incredible story is related in the Piers Paul Read book *Alive*.

3:30 p.m., Tues., Feb. 13, 1883 – Richard Wagner, one of the great German composers of the 19th century, died of a heart attack at age 69. His masterpiece, *The Ring of the Nibelung*, a cycle of four operas, took 25 years to complete. He was buried in Wahnfried, Germany in a tomb he had personally prepared.

3:30 p.m., Mon., June 1, 1964 – Mick Jagger's feet touched U.S. soil for the first time. The Rolling Stones had arrived in America four months after the Beatles. Describing their arrival, the *New York Times* noted that "the young men with shoulder length haircuts were greeted at Kennedy International Airport by about 500 teenage girls. About 50 Port Authority and New York policemen were on hand to maintain order."

The Stones spent 21 days in the U.S. on their initial tour. In San Bernadino, California, an estimated 4,000 girls threw jelly beans at their heroes. Interest was considerably less in Minneapolis, where they

The survivors admitted they had resorted to cannibalism after their food supplies ran out.

Jack Dempsey defended his world heavyweight title against "Gorgeous" Georges Carpentier of France.

performed to a house of 400. In Detroit, only 800 watched the Stones in a stadium that seated 13,000.

Things picked up considerably for original members Jagger, Keith Richards, Brian Jones, Bill Wyman and Charlie Watts when "Satisfaction" and "Get Off My Cloud" topped the charts in 1965. The Stones had eight consecutive Top 10 hits from 1965 to 1967. They went on to top the Billboard Hot 100 singles chart eight times and have more than 50 songs make the U.S. charts. The Stones were inducted into the Rock 'N' Roll Hall of Fame in 1989 and are considered by many to be the world's top rock and roll band.

3:30 p.m., Mon., July 31, 1944 – Interrogation officer Vernon Robison filed this report: "Pilot did not return and is presumed lost ... no pictures," as French aviator Antoine de Saint-Exupery, author of *The Little Prince*, *Wind, Sand and Stars* and numerous other works, disappeared while on a reconnaisance mission east of Lyon, France. His Lightning – number 223 – vanished without a trace.

3:30 p.m., Sat., July 2, 1921 – One of the most anticipated, ballyhooed and written about fights of the 20th century began, as American Jack Dempsey defended his world heavyweight title against "Gorgeous" Georges Carpentier of France.

The fight was a dream come true for promoter Tex Rickard. It matched Dempsey – an American with a reputation for being a "slacker" – against Carpentier, a bona fide war hero who had been wounded twice in World War I. Dempsey's reputation was not helped by his indictment in 1920 on draft evasion charges. He was acquitted, but the stigma remained.

Rickard foresaw a million dollar gate in the fight, but underestimated the interest. For a site, he chose a desolate lot near Jersey City, New Jersey, that was owned by a paper box manufacturer named Boyle. The press dubbed it "Boyle's Thirty Acres" and a makeshift stadium was built that would seat 90,000.

On the day of the bout, 80,123 fans showed up paying $1,789,238 – well over Rickard's goal. The fight – the first sporting event to be carried on radio – was decided early as Dempsey knocked out Carpentier at 1:16 of the fourth round. Famed sportswriter Grantland Rice observed "the

Lily of France lay stretched out upon the resin, now only one of the broken blossoms of pugilism."

3:30 **p.m., Wed., Apr. 25, 1792** – The guillotine was used in France for the first time. Its victim was a highwayman named Nicolas Pelletier who fainted when he first saw it and was executed while unconscious. The new machine became a popular device during the French Revolution, which saw nearly 2,500 heads roll, including those of France's King and Queen.

The guillotine was named after Dr. Joseph Guillotin, who, contrary to popular belief, did not invent the machine and argued it had been falsely named. Guillotin's involvement was that he had helped persuade the French National Assembly in 1789 to pass a law requiring capital punishment be carried out by a machine.

3:30 **p.m., Wed., July 9, 1969** – America began pulling out of its most controversial foreign war as the first of some 25,000 U.S. troops arrived from Vietnam at McChord air base near Seattle. The withdrawal came 19 years after a handful of American advisors arrived to work with French forces in July, 1950. U.S. troop strength had mushroomed to 539,000 before President Richard Nixon announced that U.S. troops would be gradually phased out starting in the summer of 1969. The last of the U.S. forces fled in April, 1975.

3:35 **p.m., Thurs., Apr. 12, 1945** – Franklin Delano Roosevelt, the 32nd president and the only president elected to four terms, died following a brain hemorrhage at his retreat in Warm Springs, Georgia. Roosevelt, who led America through its greatest Depression and its bloodiest foreign war, was 63.

Roosevelt seemed born to be president. At age five, his father took him to the White House, where he met President Grover Cleveland. The weary president patted Franklin on the head and wished, for the boy's own sake, that he never become president. Franklin didn't heed the advice, and embarked on a career that would land him in the Oval Office 46 years later. Roosevelt's first major appointment came in 1913, when President Woodrow Wilson named him Assistant Secretary of the Navy. After a losing bid as the

The guillotine was used in France for the first time.

Keller said her major disappointment was in not marrying.

Democratic vice-presidential nominee in 1920, he was stricken by polio, but in 1929 after a remarkable comeback, Roosevelt was elected Governor of New York. In 1932, he easily won the Democratic presidential nomination and then swamped Republican Herbert Hoover to win the presidency.

Roosevelt became president in the midst of the worst economic depression in U.S. history. To combat the problem, Roosevelt introduced the New Deal, a program of federal relief and regulation designed to put America back on its feet. Among the institutions created were the Security and Exchange Commission, which survives today as the nation's stock market watchdog, and Social Security, which provided retirement income for those over 65 years of age.

No sooner had the Depression passed into history, than the U.S. was faced with another problem: the rise of Nazism and World War II. At first, Roosevelt kept the U.S. out of the conflict, in line with national sentiment favouring neutrality. However, America was drawn into the war in December, 1941 when Japan launched a surprise attack on the U.S. base at Pearl Harbor, Hawaii. Shortly after, the U.S. declared war on Japan and Axis partners Germany and Italy. Things were going badly for the Allies at the time, but the tide turned within a year of the U.S. entering the war. By late 1944, the Allied victory was assured, but Roosevelt would not participate in the final celebrations. He died less than one month before Germany's surrender.

3:35 p.m., Sat., June 1, 1968 – Helen Keller, who overcame blindness and deafness to live a full and productive life and serve as a beacon of courage, died at age 87 in Westport, Connecticut.

Keller, who lost both her sight and hearing after an attack of scarlet fever at 18 months, learned how to talk and could even dance and ride horses. She eventually became a skilful writer. Keller said her major disappointment was in not marrying and said getting married was the first thing she would do if she regained her sight. Much credit in her development must be given to her first teacher, Anne Sullivan, who was partially blind herself. Keller spent most of her adult life trying to raise funds for the American Foundation for the Blind and raising awareness of the problems of the blind.

3:36 p.m., Thurs., Oct. 13, 1960 – Bill Mazeroski's solo home run in the bottom of the ninth inning gave the Pittsburgh Pirates their first

World Series title in 35 years. The home run off Ralph Terry broke a 9–9 tie and completed one of the fall classic's biggest upsets. It also marked the first time a World Series ended on a home run (it happened again in 1993 when Joe Carter won the World Series for the Toronto Blue Jays). The Pirates won the Series despite being outscored 55–27, out-hit 91–60 and out-homered 10–4 over the seven games.

The home run made Mazeroski a hero as a slugger – ironic for a player better known during his career for his defensive attributes at second base.

3:40 **p.m., Fri., Oct. 18, 1968** – Under gloomy skies, the long-jump final began at the 1968 Olympics in Mexico City. The first three of the 17 competitors fouled out, then American Bob Beamon stepped onto the runway. The 22-year-old New Yorker told himself not to foul and dashed to the takeoff board. Sailing 1.8 metres (six feet) into the air, Beamon landed so hard he bounced right out of the pit. Officials using a steel tape were stunned at the length of the jump – 8.9 metres (29 feet, 2-1/2 inches). It broke the existing world record by an incredible 55 centimetres (21-3/4 inches). The world record for the long-jump had advanced only 21.59 centimetres (eight and a half inches) in the previous 33 years.

Beamon's jump is considered one of the greatest athletic achievements of all time. It would be 23 years before Mike Powell broke the mark at the 1991 world championships. Beamon's jump was still an Olympic record as the 2000s began.

Beamon's jump is considered one of the greatest athletic achievements of all time.

3:41 **p.m., Fri., Jan. 25, 1889** – Pioneer muckraking *New York World* journalist Nellie Bly arrived in New York after completing a much-publicized around-the-world journey. It took Bly 72 days, six hours, 10 minutes and 11 seconds to complete her journey, which was inspired by the Jules Verne novel *Around the World in 80 Days*.

Bly, whose real identity of Elizabeth Cochrane was protected by her paper so she could pursue her stories anonymously, was greeted on her return by factory whistles, roaring cannons and a parade down Broadway. It was the highlight of a newspaper career that saw her become New York's top investigative journalist in the heyday of yellow journalism. Bly, 22 at the time of her around-the-world voyage, soon faded from prominence and died of pneumonia in 1922, virtually forgotten at 55.

The first controlled nuclear chain reaction was achieved.

3:42 **p.m., Wed., Apr. 23, 1969** – John Sinclair completed the greatest recorded feat of continuous marathon walking. He walked over 354 kilometres (215 miles) without a break over a period of 47 hours and 42 minutes near Simonstown, South Africa. A cold rain fell during the entire duration of the walk.

3:43 **p.m., Tues., Oct. 4, 1955** – The Brooklyn Dodgers, for years the hard-luck team of major league baseball, finally won their first World Series. Johnny Podres scattered eight hits and Gil Hodges knocked in both runs as the Dodgers beat the New York Yankees 2–0 in the seventh and deciding game. It was Brooklyn's first World Series win after losing in each of their seven previous appearances – twice in the final game.

3:45 **p.m., Thurs., Mar. 27, 1997** – The Toronto Stock Exchange, swamped by sell orders for Bre-X Minerals, closed down 15 minutes early. It was the day all Bre-X investors had dreaded.

Just two years earlier, Bre-X had been on top of the world as reports of a major gold find in Busang, Indonesia, transformed it from a penny stock into a $4 billion company. But on March 19, 1997, Bre-X geologist Michael de Guzman mysteriously plunged to his death from a helicopter en route to a meeting with a potential Bre-X partner, Freeport–McMoRan. Suicide was suspected. Then Freeport–McMoRan released a report stating that there was no significant gold at Busang. It also claimed that the original Bre-X gold claim had been falsified when samples were apparently tampered with.

Bre-X investors panicked and the company collapsed.

Facing a flurry of lawsuits and his reputation in tatters, company president David Walsh remained in the Bahamas, but insisted he had been duped and would clear his name.

Walsh died of a stroke on June 4, 1998. He was 52.

3:45 **p.m., Wed., Dec. 2, 1942** – The first controlled nuclear chain reaction was achieved on the squash court of the University of Chicago. The feat opened the door to the nuclear age and the dropping of the first atomic bomb in 1945.

3:45 **p.m., Sun., May 5, 1929** – For the first time in history, a two-way simultaneous conversation was held from a moving train. The demonstration took place on a Canadian National Railways train just outside Toronto. Reporters from the United States and Europe were on hand to witness this marriage of telephone and radio technology, which pre-dated the cellular phone by about half a century.

3:47 **p.m., Tues., Sept. 5, 1905** – The Russian–Japanese war ended half a world away from where it began. Officials from both sides signed the Treaty of Portsmouth in an unlikely venue for ending an Asian war – Portsmouth, New Hampshire.

The war began in February, 1904 after Japan staged a surprise nighttime torpedo attack on the Russian fleet off Port Arthur. Less than a year later, the Russians surrendered the city and the Japanese eventually took control of Korea and Manchuria. American President Teddy Roosevelt stepped in to mediate the dispute, which resulted in the Japanese achieving most of their original war aims.

3:50 **p.m. (GMT), Fri., Apr. 5, 1985** – More than 5,000 radio stations around the globe simultaneously played the song "We Are The World." The song, co-written by Michael Jackson and Lionel Richie, was recorded to raise awareness of starving people in Africa. Among the 45 artists who performed with the one-time-only group "USA for Africa" were Bruce Springsteen, Stevie Wonder, Tina Turner, Jackson and Richie. It was recorded at A&M's Hollywood, California, studios in a marathon 22-hour session that ended at 8:00 a.m. Wednesday, January 30, 1985. By April, 1985, it was the number one song on the Billboard charts, one of the fastest selling hits in recording history. Total estimated worldwide sales of the song and related products such as T-shirts and posters came to roughly $47 million. Sadly, the tragedy of famine in Africa continues.

3:52 **p.m., Wed., Sept. 14, 1994** – Stating that "there's an incredible amount of sadness," acting baseball commissioner Bud Selig announced the cancellation of the rest of the 1994 baseball season. It meant that there would be no World Series for the first time since 1904; the

More than 5,000 radio stations around the globe simultaneously played the song.

Bobby Thomson hit the "shot heard around the world."

baseball season would end prematurely for the first time since the formation of the National Association in 1871. A tradition that survived two world wars, a depression, an earthquake and previous labour problems was over. In a sport where the average salary was $1.2 million, money was the culprit as the owners and players remained at odds over a salary cap.

The early end to the season robbed San Diego's Tony Gwynn of his chance to hit .400 – he finished at .394 – and also ended the hopes of several players who had a chance to break Roger Maris's single-season home run record of 61. And then there were the Montreal Expos, robbed of a chance to win their first World Series, and on and on.

The baseball strike ended April 2, 1995 after 234 days, but not before baseball further tarnished its image by using replacement players during spring training. Baseball attendance was down markedly in 1995, and it would take several years to undo the damage.

3:58 p.m., Wed., Oct. 3, 1951 – Bobby Thomson hit the "shot heard around the world" – a three-run, ninth-inning homer that gave the New York Giants a 5–4 victory over the Brooklyn Dodgers in the third and deciding game of a playoff for the National League pennant. It completed an amazing comeback by the Giants, who rallied from 13-1/2 games off the pace to tie Brooklyn for first place at the end of the regular season.

Many baseball fans can recall the events of the ninth inning from memory. The Dodgers led 4–1 going into the bottom of the inning. But consecutive singles by Alvin Dark and Don Mueller put Giants on first and third. Monte Irvin then fouled out, but Whitey Lockman doubled to cut the Dodger lead to 4–2. Brooklyn pitcher Don Newcombe was then yanked in favor of Ralph Branca. The first, and only, batter he would face was Bobby Thomson, a Glasgow-born Scot who had hit .357 after being moved from centre field to first base in July. Thomson crashed a one-strike pitch into the lower deck of the left field stands and the "Miracle of Coogan's Bluff" was complete.

4 p.m. to 4:59 p.m.

- Jesse Owens sets sixth world record in 45 minutes
- Dow Jones Average tops 10,000
- Killer hurricane slams New England coast
- Civil War ends
- Nelson Mandela released from prison
- First woman launched in space

4:00 **p.m., Fri., Aug. 17, 1969** – This was the scheduled start time of the Woodstock Music and Arts Fair – known to most simply as Woodstock.

The festival started about two and a half hours late with Richie Havens as the first performer. Throughout the rainy weekend, some of the greatest acts in rock history appeared, including Jimi Hendrix, Crosby, Stills, Nash and Young, The Who, Grateful Dead and Country Joe and the Fish. An estimated 400,000 people – far more than organizers had expected – packed Max Yasgur's dairy farm in Bethel, New York, and the roads leading to it. Population-wise, Bethel became the third largest city in New York State that weekend (Woodstock is actually 128 kilometres [50 miles] to the northeast). Three people died, two from drug overdoses, and three babies were born. Despite problems with traffic, food, water, drugs, and sanitary facilities, Woodstock is remembered as the greatest rock festival in the world. An album highlighting the best performances was number one for four weeks in 1970 and a followup album reached number seven. A movie of the festival was a financial success.

Other Woodstock events were held in 1994 and 1999 in upstate New York. Neither of these was in Woodstock, New York.

Jesse Owens completed one of sports greatest feats, as he set or equalled four world records.

4:00 p.m., Tues., July 4, 1939 – New York Yankees legend Lou Gehrig delivered a speech in which he declared "Today, I consider myself to be the luckiest man on the face of the earth." The emotional address came at the end of a 40-minute ceremony held between games of a doubleheader between the Yanks and the Washington Senators at Yankee Stadium. Gehrig, who had written down the words the night before, delivered them only after some prompting from those on hand.

The speech came less than a month after Gehrig was diagnosed with amyotrophic lateral sclerosis, which would kill him two years later. The paralyzing disease is now commonly known as Lou Gehrig Disease.

Gehrig broke into the Yankees lineup on June 2, 1925 when regular first baseman Wally Pipp bowed out with a headache. Pipp would never play first for the Yanks again nor would anyone else until May 2, 1939. That day, Gehrig, who hadn't missed a game in nearly 14 years, took himself out of the lineup because he felt he was a detriment to the team. He was replaced by Babe Dahlgren and Gehrig called it quits at season's end.

Gehrig, who played most of his career in the shadow of Babe Ruth, won the American League batting title in 1934 and was voted the American League's most valuable player in 1927. He hit .340 during his career, slammed 494 home runs and was named to Baseball's Hall of Fame in 1939 – five years before he would normally be eligible.

Lou Gehrig died at 10:10 p.m., Monday, June 2, 1941. He was only 37.

4:00 p.m., Sat., May 25, 1935 – Jesse Owens, dubbed the "Black Antelope," completed one of sports greatest feats, as he set or equalled four world records in a span of only 45 minutes at Ann Arbor, Michigan.

Owens began his record-breaking hour at 3:15 p.m., when he tied the world mark for the 100-yard dash at 9.4 seconds. At 3:25, he set a world long-jumping record with a leap of 813 centimetres (26 feet, 8-1/4 inches) – a distance that was unsurpassed for a quarter-century. At 3:34, Owens ran 220 yards in a record 20.3 seconds. And at 4:00, he sped over the 220-metre low hurdles in a record 22.6 seconds.

A year later at the Berlin Olympics, Owens set the world on its ear by winning four gold medals – breaking or equalling 12 Olympic records in the process. He completed his stunning performance by winning the 200-metre race to thunderous applause. German leader Adolf Hitler had left the stadium by then.

4:00 **p.m., Mon., Dec. 25, 1989** – Deposed Romanian dictator Nicolae Ceausescu and his wife Elena were executed by a firing squad. One hundred and twenty bullets were fired into Ceausescu's body after a tribunal of the newly-installed provisional government found the couple guilty of genocide and several other crimes. Ceausescu's death signaled the success of a bloody two-week revolution that witnessed the end of the Romanian dictator's 24-year reign.

4:00 **p.m., Sat., Dec. 23, 1900** – Reginald Fessenden of Fergus, Ontario, sent out a voice message via radio from Cobb Island, 80 kilometres (50 miles) south of Arlington, Virginia. An assistant at a listening post in Arlington heard Fessenden say: "One, two, three, four. Is it snowing where you are, Mr. Thiessen? If it is, telegraph back and let me know." Fessenden's assistant telegraphed back. This initial transmission of speech over the airwaves was the beginning of radio.

Six years and a day later, at 9:00 p.m., Monday, December 24, 1906, Fessenden broadcast the first musical recording from Brant Rock, Massachusetts, to several ships at sea. The first song played (on an Ediphone) was Handel's "Largo." Next, Fessenden played "O Silent Night" on his violin, singing the last verse. He read seasonal passages from the Bible before signing off by asking listeners to write in. They did.

4:00 **p.m., Fri., Oct. 25, 1415** – The Battle of Agincourt ended as the English vanquished the French in one of history's biggest military upsets.

As the battle began, the French outnumbered the English five to one. The French were in a celebratory mood before what appeared to be almost certain victory. The English gained an early advantage by raining arrows on the French, causing them to panic, whereupon the English moved in with axes and swords.

4:00 **p.m., Mon., Oct. 19, 1987** – The Dow Jones Industrial Average closed down an incredible 508.32 points, or 22.64 per cent, on a day of unprecedented financial disaster.

An estimated $503 billion was erased from the value of U.S. stocks. The one-day point drop in the Dow was almost five times the previous record

This initial transmission of speech over the airwaves was the beginning of radio.

The Dow Jones Industrial Average closed over 10,000 for the first time.

drop of 108.35, set the previous Friday, October 16, 1987. It easily broke the previous percentage drop of 12.9, recorded on Black Tuesday, October 28, 1929. The volume, 604.4 million stocks traded, was also a record.

4:00 **p.m., Tues., Nov. 14, 1972** – Stock trading history was made as the Dow Jones Industrial Average closed above 1,000 for the first time. The key index had been above 1,000 in mid-session before but never at the final bell. On this historic day, the Dow closed at 1,003.16, up 6.09 from the previous day's trading.

4:00 **p.m., Mon., Mar. 29, 1999** – The Dow Jones Industrial Average closed over 10,000 for the first time in its 115-year history. It rose 184.54 on the day to finish at 10,006.78. This was the continuation of an incredible bull market for the Dow, which began after it closed at 792.43 on August 16, 1982. The Dow rose 38.81 the next day and almost 9,200 more points over the next 17 years. It took only four years for the Dow to go from the first 5,000 close to the 10,000 milestone.

4:00 **p.m., Sat., Mar. 12, 1938** – Adolf Hitler, who left Austria as a penniless young house painter, crossed the Austrian border as a conquering hero. Two days later, the German dictator announced in Vienna that Austria was henceforth united with the rest of Germany. He promised that the "German Reich shall never be broken by anyone again." The annexation, or "Anschluss," made "Der Führer" leader of over 70 million people.

4:00 **p.m., Wed., May 17, 1939** – A collegiate contest between Columbia and Princeton at Baker Field, New York City, became the first televised baseball game in history. Station W2XBS in New York City broadcast the play-by-play to New York audiences. A crew of three men did the show: announcer Bill Stern, director Burke Crotty and the lone cameraman, Dick Packard. The game, won 2–1 by Princeton in 10 innings, was difficult viewing for the few that watched because not every play could be recorded by the single camera.

W2XBS also televised the first major league game August, 26, 1939, using two cameras. Viewers saw both ends of a doubleheader between the

Cincinnati Reds and Brooklyn Dodgers at Ebbets Field. The managers and some players were interviewed between games. The announcer was Red Barber.

4:00 **p.m., Sun., Mar. 31, 1947** – Funeral services began in Sibbalds Point, Ontario, for Stephen Leacock. The renowned humourist, essayist, teacher, political economist and historian died at the age of 74. His last words were: "Did I behave pretty well? Was I a good boy?"

A native of Swanmore, England, Leacock grew up in Ontario on a farm near Lake Simcoe. A prolific writer with some 60 books to his credit, Leacock once joked: "I can write up anything now at a hundred yards." Two of his best known works, *Sunshine Sketches of a Little Town* and *Arcadian Adventures with the Idle Rich*, are Canadian classics. His work had significant influence on events of the time. His writings and public addresses on the issue of reciprocity played a role in the election defeat of Wilfrid Laurier in 1911.

Leacock's autobiography, *The Boy I Left Behind Me*, was never completed.

4:00 **p.m., Wed., Sept. 21, 1938** – A hurricane, packing winds of up to 289 kilometres (180 miles) an hour, slammed into the south coast of New England. More than 500 people were killed, 32,000 injured and 93,000 left homeless in what – in the days before hurricanes were officially named – became known as "The Great New England Hurricane."

It was by far the costliest such storm ever to hit the U.S. northeast. In addition to the human toll, property damage was estimated at $300 million. In New York City, the Empire State Building swayed as much as 10 centimetres (four inches) in the strong winds and the subways were flooded. In New Haven, Connecticut, an entire amusement park slid into the ocean and in Springfield, Massachusetts, 16,000 shade trees were felled. Adding to the scope of the disaster was the fact that virtually no warning of the hurricane's approach was given to the people of New England. Thanks to improved warning systems, the death toll was much lower when two hurricanes hit the region again in the mid-1950s.

4:00 **p.m., Sun., Apr. 9, 1865** – Victorious Union General Ulysses S. Grant shook hands with his defeated Confederate foe, General

A hurricane, packing winds of up to 289 kilometres (180 miles) an hour, slammed into the south coast of New England.

Samuel Johnson, one of the out-standing literary figures of the 18th century, was born in Lichfield, England.

Robert E. Lee, and the Civil War was over. With his handshake at Appomattox, Virginia, Lee formally surrendered the Confederate armies to the federal commander-in-chief ending a four-year struggle that took half a million lives.

The bloodiest war ever fought on U.S. soil pitted Americans against each other, brother against brother, in a conflict that threatened to tear the young country apart. Only the strength of the Union armies coupled with the moderating influence of President Lincoln, saved America from a permanent split. The Union victory led to the Civil Rights Act of 1866, which gave African Americans citizenship and led to the abolition of slavery.

4:00 **p.m., Wed., Apr. 19, 1882** – Biologist Charles Darwin, creator of the theory of evolution, died of a heart attack at his home in Down, England. He was 73. Darwin outlined his famous theory in his books *On the Origin of Species by Means of Natural Selection* and *The Descent of Man*. The great naturalist theorized that species developed by natural selection through survival of the fittest, and traced the development of man from apes.

4:00 **p.m., Wed., Sept. 18, 1709** – Samuel Johnson, one of the out-standing literary figures of the 18th century, was born in Lichfield, England. "The Hercules of Literature" suffered from a long list of illnesses throughout his life, including asthma, bronchitis, deafness, blindness in one eye, emphysema, gallstones, gout and manic depression. But his mind was brilliant, as evidenced by his 40,000 word Dictionary and his writings on Shakespeare.

Johnson was extremely superstitious. It is said he never stepped on cracks in the sidewalk and always touched each wooden post he passed.

Johnson died in 1784 at the age of 75.

4:00 **p.m., Mon., May 24, 1669** – This is the last hour noted in *Samuel Pepys Diary*, a record of life in London from January 1, 1660 to May 31, 1669. Pepys, an English civil servant, kept the personal log for nearly a decade before failing vision forced him to stop. The diary, which was more than 1.3 million words and 9,000 pages long, is considered an invaluable record of the events and customs of the day. Pepys wrote the entire diary in code and in complete secrecy (even his friends didn't know about it). The book wasn't deciphered and published until the 19th century.

Born 70 years earlier, Pepys died at 3:47 a.m., Saturday, May 26, 1703 of arterial disease.

4:00 **p.m., Mon., Mar. 31, 1732** – Franz Joseph Haydn, the "Father of the Symphony," was born in Rohrau, Austria. Haydn, who was largely self-taught, wrote 104 symphonies including the "Emperors Hymn," the national anthem of Austria. That work later became Germany's national anthem and retitled "Deutschland über Alles." The prolific Haydn also wrote over 80 string quartets and 20 operas. His brother, Michael, was also a gifted composer.

Haydn died at 12:40 a.m., Wednesday, May 31, 1809. He was 77.

4:01 **p.m., Wed., Aug. 29, 1877** – Mormon prophet Brigham Young died of acute appendicitis in Salt Lake City, Utah. Young, who declared polygamy a tenet of the church in 1852, married 27 women during his 76 years. His last wife, Anne Eliza Webb, left him after four years and went on the lecture circuit speaking on the "evils" of polygamous marriage. Sixteen of Young's surviving wives (only Anne Eliza was absent) and 44 of his children attended his funeral.

4:07 **p.m., Fri., Sept. 6, 1901** – William McKinley, the 25th president, was shot and fatally wounded by an assassin in Buffalo, New York. He was the third president to be assassinated; the first two were Lincoln and Garfield.

McKinley was shot as he was shaking hands in a receiving line at the Temple of Music at the Pan American exposition. Leon Czolgosz, 27, an unemployed millworker, approached the president with his right hand wrapped in a bandage concealing a gun and fired twice from point-blank range. The first bullet failed to penetrate the skin; the second went into McKinley's abdomen and lodged near the pancreas. Doctors were unable to find the second bullet and infection set in. He died at 2:15 a.m. on September 14, one week after the shooting. Ironically, the newly invented X-ray machine on display at the exposition was not used to find the bullet. Czolgosz, a self-avowed anarchist, was found guilty and electrocuted on October 29, 1901.

William McKinley, the 25th president, was shot and fatally wounded.

The United States declared war on Japan.

McKinley was elected president in 1896 after stints as representative and governor of Ohio. The key event during his presidency was the Spanish–American war, in which the U.S. intervened to free Cuba from Spanish domination and easily defeated the Spanish. Under terms of the Paris Peace Treaty, Spain relinquished Cuba and ceded Puerto Rico, Guam and, for $20 million, the Philippine Islands to the U.S.

After the McKinley assassination, Robert Lincoln – son of Abraham Lincoln – decided to avoid any future presidential functions. Lincoln had just arrived at the Pan American Exposition at the president's invitation when McKinley was shot. In 1881, Robert arrived at the Washington, D.C. railroad station to tell President Garfield he was unable to accompany him to Elberon, New Jersey, only to find that Garfield had just been shot. In 1865 when Robert was 12, he was sent to his father's bedside in Washington the evening President Lincoln was assassinated. Robert Lincoln, who died in 1926, is buried in Arlington Cemetery just a few metres from the final resting place of the fourth president to be assassinated, John F. Kennedy.

4:10 **p.m., Mon., Dec. 8, 1941** – The United States declared war on Japan, one day after the Japanese attacked Pearl Harbor. President Roosevelt signed the declaration after the Senate voted 82–0 ` and Congress 388–1 for approval. The only dissenting vote was cast by Jeanette Rankin, a Montana Republican, who had also voted against the declaration of war against Germany in 1917.

Earlier that day, Roosevelt had delivered his famous speech in which he declared the day of the Pearl Harbor attack was one "that shall live in infamy." The short – six minute and 30 second speech – was delivered to a joint session of the House and Senate.

4:10 **p.m., Mon., Apr. 30, 1945** – Benito Mussolini, "Father of Italian Fascism," was executed after a quick trial. His mistress Claretta Petacci and 11 others were executed along with him. The "Duce," Claretta and two compatriots were later hung by their heels in Milan in a gruesome public display.

Italian prime minister since 1926, Mussolini had set his sights beyond the borders of Italy in the 1930s with his conquest of Abyssinia (Ethiopia) in 1935. During World War II, he formed alliances with Germany's Hitler and Franco of Spain. A series of military disasters followed. With the Allies advancing in Italy, he was forced to flee to the north, where he was captured, tried and executed by Italian partisans near Azzano.

4:10 **p.m., Fri., May 31, 1889** — A roof-top-high wave of water, mud, rocks and other debris crashed into Johnstown, Pennsylvania with lightning speed. More than 2,200 people died in the Johnstown Flood.

The disaster had been in the making for years. The Southfork Dam — built across the Conemaugh River above Johnstown — had been deteriorating badly since its completion in the 1830s. Much-needed repairs had not been done, and when heavy rains in the spring of 1889 boosted water levels dangerously high, the aging, decrepit dam finally burst on the afternoon of May 31. Thousands of people disappeared under the avalanche of water and those who weren't drowned were killed in the fire that followed. In the aftermath, looters cut fingers and ears off corpses to get their jewellery.

4:14 **p.m., Sun., Feb. 11, 1990** — Nelson Mandela, 71, South African black nationalist leader, was freed after 27 years in prison. Given a life sentence in 1964 on charges of plotting against the government, Mandela walked hand-in-hand with his wife Winnie as hundreds of supporters cheered outside Victor Vester prison near Cape Town. It was the first time the South African public had seen Mandela in more than a quarter-century. No photographs of him were allowed during his captivity.

4:23 **p.m., Thurs, Oct. 24, 1901** — Anne Edison Taylor became the first person to go over Niagara Falls and live. The 50-year-old physical education instructor went over the Falls in a barrel outfitted with a blacksmith's anvil fixed to the bottom. She had a rubber hose that allowed her to breathe and packed pillows under each arm. Her last words before setting out were "Goodbye, boys." Her first words upon recovery were "Where am I?"

Taylor suffered only minor injuries.

4:23 **p.m., Sun., Apr. 14, 1968** — Argentinian golfer Roberto de Vincenzo birdied the 17th hole at Augusta National to take the lead

Nelson Mandela, 71, South African black nationalist leader, was freed.

Kit Carson, noted explorer, trapper, soldier and Indian agent, died.

at the Masters. While millions of golf fans viewed it live and on television, the birdie would not count.

De Vincenzo bogeyed the 18th to fall back into a tie for the lead with Bob Goalby. The distracted de Vincenzo quickly signed his card without noticing that playing partner Tommy Aaron had entered a "4" on the 17th instead of the "3" de Vincenzo had actually scored. Under the rules of golf, the higher score stood and put Goalby in the lead, unaware of the mistake on de Vincenzo's scorecard. Goalby then made a four-footer for par on the 18th hole. Goalby won the tournament with a 72-hole score of 11-under 277. De Vincenzo finished second at 278.

De Vincenzo, an experienced player who had won the British Open the year before, was stunned by his mistake and told reporters, "I am a stupid." Goalby said he would have preferred a playoff with Vincenzo for the title, but it did not happen. Unfortunately for both, the 1968 Masters has gone down as the tournament Roberto de Vincenzo lost rather than the tournament Bob Goalby won.

Ironically, Aaron — who had entered the wrong score in the first place — was almost victimized himself en route to winning the Masters in 1973. Playing partner Johnny Miller entered an incorrect score in the third round, but Aaron noticed the error before signing his card.

4:25 p.m., Sat., May 23, 1868 — Kit Carson, noted explorer, trapper, soldier and Indian agent who played a large part in the westward expansion of the United States, died of a ruptured aneurysm at Fort Lyon, Colorado. The man who helped claim California for the United States was 58.

Carson's fame came by accident after he met explorer and future presidential candidate John Fremont in 1842. Inspired by Fremont to explore the west, Carson eventually became a true American folk hero, hailed for his bravery, courage and loyalty. At the time of his death, he was serving as superintendent of Indian affairs for the Colorado Territory. His epitaph reads simply: "He led the way."

4:25 p.m., Wed., Jan. 1, 1975 — Four men, John Mitchell, H.R. Haldeman, John Erlichman and Robert Mardian, were convicted on all counts in the Watergate coverup trial. A fifth man, Kenneth Parkinson, was acquitted. Powerful officials in the Nixon administration, all four were out of prison before the end of the decade and writing bestsellers on their experiences.

4:30 **p.m., Tues., Dec. 29, 1170** – Thomas Becket, the Archbishop of Canterbury, was murdered in his own cathedral by four knights of the royal household. Becket was standing by the altar of the Virgin Mary when he was struck down.

The murder put an end to the long quarrel between Becket and King Henry II. Becket had been a thorn in Henry's side, once embarrassing the King by excommunicating six bishops who had helped Henry crown his son and heir. On another occasion, Becket shouted at the King that he had no right to judge him. Those actions, and others, sealed his death warrant at the hands of the royal knights.

4:30 **p.m., Sat., Mar. 25, 1911** – A deadly fire broke out at the Triangle Shirtwaist Factory in Manhattan. One hundred and forty-six employees, most of them young female immigrants, died as they were leaving work for the day.

Many of those who perished were unable to escape because management had locked the fire doors to prevent workers from stealing company property. Others died when they tried to leap down the elevator shaft. Many jumped to their deaths from windows to the street below.

The Triangle Shirtwaist fire led to a national movement for safer working conditions, and dozens of laws were passed governing everything from child labour to fire codes for factories.

4:30 **p.m., Tues., June 20, 1893** – Lizzie Borden was acquitted of the brutal axe murders of her father and mother in the quiet New England town of Fall River, Massachusetts. Debate over her guilt or innocence still rages.

On the morning of August 4, 1892, Lizzie claimed to have discovered her parents bludgeoned to death in their Victorian home. Both had received numerous blows with an axe. Borden was arrested after the murder weapon, its blade wiped clean, was found in the basement of the Borden home. Much of the evidence pointed directly at Borden, but during the trial,

Lizzie Borden was acquitted of the brutal axe murders of her father and mother.

**Four black
students sat
down at a
Woolworth's
whites-only
lunch counter.**

sympathy ran high for the gentle-looking, 33-year-old spinster. In what many still say was an outrage of justice, Borden was acquitted of the crime and set free. No one else was ever arrested for the murders. Borden continued to live in Fall River in her parents' house. She died in 1927, aged 67, and was buried in the family plot with her parents.

4:30 p.m., Mon., Feb. 1, 1960 – Four black students sat down at a Woolworth's whites-only lunch counter in Greensboro, North Carolina and were refused service. They left quietly when the store closed an hour later. The next day, a larger group of students sat down at the same Woolworth's lunch counter and again were refused service. Within days, sit-ins had spread to half a dozen other cities, in some cases resulting in riots and arrests. The fight for racial equality that would leave an indelible mark on the 60s had begun.

4:30 p.m., Fri., Apr. 9, 1965 – The Houston Astrodome, the world's first domed stadium, opened its doors to the public. A few hours later, the Houston Astros defeated the New York Yankees 2–1 in a 12-inning exhibition contest, the first baseball game ever played indoors.

Called "The Eighth Wonder of the World" by some, the covered stadium (its official name was the Harris County Domed Stadium), was built because of the stifling heat and humidity that marked Houston summers. Built at a cost of $31 million, the stadium revolutionized baseball, ending the game's long-time dependence on the elements. It also led to the establishment of artificial turf (originally designed because of the difficulty of growing grass indoors) as a fixture at many stadiums, indoor or outdoor. The Astrodome inspired imitation, and by the late 1990s, numerous domed stadiums of all shapes and sizes were packing in the fans.

4:30 p.m., Wed., Oct. 9, 1957 – Major league baseball headed to the West Coast with the announcement that the Brooklyn Dodgers, a New York institution for 67 years, would move to Los Angeles for the 1958 season. Later that fall, the New York Giants announced that they too were moving west – to San Francisco. It marked the first time major league baseball had teams west of St. Louis, Missouri. Fittingly, the two west coast pioneers played each other in their first game, April 15, 1958, with San Francisco winning 8–0.

4:30 p.m., Fri., Sept. 1, 1922 – The first-ever broadcast of a daily news program debuted on WBAY Radio in New York City. The hour-long show, known as *The Radio Digest*, was edited by George F. Thompson. In addition to news, the show also carried information about the new medium of radio.

4:30 p.m., Sun., June 16, 1963 – A 26-year-old former textile worker became the first woman in space. Launched in *Vostok 6* from Tyuratam, U.S.S.R., Valentina Vladimorova Tereshkova spent nearly three full days in space, orbiting the earth 48 times. Twenty years later, Sally Ride would become the first U.S. woman in space. Canada's first woman astronaut, Roberta Bondar, would not make her first trip until January, 1992 aboard *Discovery*.

4:30 p.m., Fri., Nov. 27, 1953 – Eugene O'Neill, one of America's greatest playwrights, died in a Boston hotel of a degenerative disorder. Three-time winner of the Pulitzer Prize, O'Neill is remembered for such classics as *The Iceman Cometh* and *Long Day's Journey Into Night*. His commitment and capacity for work were remarkable. He produced close to a play a year between 1920 and 1943, rewriting many of his manuscripts a half-dozen times. However, just prior to his death at age 65, O'Neill was too sick even to sign his own name.

4:31 p.m., Mon., Mar. 29, 1971 – Lieutenant William Calley was found guilty of murder for his role in the massacre of more than 100 civilians at My Lai, South Vietnam. He was sentenced to hard labour for life, later reduced to 10 years. The victims – all shot point-blank in cold blood – were mostly unarmed civilians, old men, women and children. President Nixon ordered Calley released a month after his conviction following a flood of public sentiment in favour of the lieutenant. Calley received a full parole in 1974.

4:35 p.m., Sun., Sept. 29, 1957 – The New York Giants finished their last home game at the Polo Grounds, losing 9–1 to the Pittsburgh Pirates. A crowd of 11,606 watched the end of a sports era. The next season, the Giants and the Brooklyn Dodgers left the Big Apple to settle in San Francisco and Los Angeles respectively.

A 26-year-old former textile worker became the first woman in space.

Pasteur is given much credit for the fact that life expectancies have doubled since the mid–19th century.

New York's Polo Grounds opened in 1889 at 155th Street and 8th Avenue. It had been home to many sports contests over the years, including baseball, automobile racing, and Gaelic football. Ironically, polo was never played at the Polo Grounds. The stadium nearly burned down in 1911 but was rebuilt to become one of America's premier sports arenas.

The Giants returned to the Polo Grounds as visitors in 1962 and 1963 to play against the New York Mets. The Mets moved to Shea Stadium in 1964 and the Polo Grounds was torn down for a housing complex.

4:40 p.m., Sat., Sept. 28, 1895 – The father of modern medicine, French chemist and biologist Louis Pasteur, died at age 71.

Pasteur brought medicine out of the dark ages when he convinced the medical world of the germ theory of disease. His efforts led to the development of immunization against rabies and the technique of pasteurization to destroy micro-organisms in beverages such as milk. He also introduced antiseptic procedures for physicians to lower rates of infection. Pasteur is given much credit for the fact that life expectancies have doubled since the mid-19th century.

4:45 p.m., Sun., July 26, 1925 – William Jennings Bryan, one of America's most famous lawyers and greatest orators, died of a brain hemorrhage in Dayton, Tennessee. The three-time Democratic nominee for president was 65.

Bryan's death came less than a week after his final and most famous courtroom victory when John T. Scopes was convicted of teaching evolution in contravention of Tennessee law.

Bryan, known as the "Silver-tongued Orator," could stir audiences with his speeches, but had trouble translating his popularity into votes. He lost the presidential elections of 1896, 1900 and 1908, and is the only man to lose three presidential races as nominee of a major party. Bryan served as Secretary of State during the first two years of the Woodrow Wilson administration.

4:45 p.m., Tues., June 14, 1988 – History's longest recorded sea ordeal ended. Fumiya Sato, an engineer aboard the Japanese tuna-fishing vessel *Kinei Maru 128*, glimpsed a dark object floating in the water. Upon closer inspection, Sato spotted two figures waving frantically in his direction. The *Cairo III* had been found 142 days after it foundered in a storm off the Costa Rican coast. The tiny vessel had drifted 7,200 kilometres (4,500 miles) through four time zones before finally being discovered 880 kilometres (550 miles) southeast of Hawaii. Previously, the longest anyone had survived being adrift was 133 days, when Poon Lim had floated on a raft off the north shore of Brazil after his ship was torpedoed in World War II.

The five men rescued were from the Costa Rican city of Puntarenas. Ironically, 22 of the men on the rescue craft were from Kesunnuma, Japan, which had been declared the sister city of Puntarenas in 1978.

History's longest recorded sea ordeal ended.

4:45 p.m., Wed., Mar. 13, 1901 – Benjamin Harrison, 23rd president, died of pneumonia in Indianapolis. He was 67. Harrison, the only grandson of a former president to become chief executive, was the first U.S. president to die in the 20th century.

The grandson of William Henry Harrison, he began his rise in the Republican Party when he campaigned for its first presidential candidate, John Fremont, in 1856. A lawyer by trade, Harrison became an active supporter of Republican candidates in subsequent presidential elections. He gained political office in 1881 when he began a six-year term as Ohio senator. His years as a political gadfly paid off in 1888 when he won the Republican nomination in eight ballots, then beat incumbent Grover Cleveland in the general election.

Harrison's administration was dominated by monetary issues. During his tenure, bills were passed raising tariffs on foreign imports and placing restrictions on monopolies. The former proved unpopular, and the latter ineffective.

Harrison's first wife was also involved in some monetary issues. She spent $35,000 of taxpayers' money to renovate the White House, laying new floors, installing electricity and new plumbing. In 1889 she initiated the tradition of setting up a Christmas tree at the White House.

Mrs. Harrison died just two weeks before her husband lost the 1892 presidential race to Grover Cleveland. Harrison later married a widow, Mary Dimmick. She survived his death by nearly half a century, dying in 1948 at the age of 89.

"Citation" became the eighth Triple Crown winner in history.

4:46 **p.m., Sat., June 12, 1948** – "Citation," with jockey Eddie Arcaro riding, broke from the gate in an effort to win the U.S. Triple Crown of thoroughbred racing. Two minutes, 28 and a fifth seconds later, Citation had completed a sweep of the Kentucky Derby, the Preakness and the Belmont Stakes with a six-length victory in the final leg. It was one of 19 races Citation would win that year in 20 trips to the post.

Citation became the eighth Triple Crown winner in history. The next would be "Secretariat" in 1973. There were 11 Triple Crown winners in the 1900s, the last being "Affirmed" in 1979.

Citation died Aug. 8, 1970 and is buried at Calumet Farm in Kentucky. Secretariat – the next Triple Crown champ after Citation – had been born just four months earlier.

5 p.m. to 5:59 p.m.

- London Blitz begins
- Earthquake hits Bay Area during World Series game
- 575 die when planes collide at Tenerife
- Australia wins America's Cup
- Pope John Paul II shot
- Foster Hewitt broadcasts first hockey game

5:00 **p.m., Sat., Sept. 7, 1940** – The London Blitz, the beginning of Hitler's planned invasion of England, started. The Blitz was Hitler's final link in his bid for ultimate control of Europe. What the Germans underestimated was the fierce resistance of Britain's people and its air force. A wave of German bombers struck the Royal Arsenal, power stations, gasworks and docks lining the River Thames in the first of 57 consecutive nights of bombing. The air assault would not end until the following May. An estimated 20,000 Londoners died and hundreds of thousands were injured. Prime Minister Winston Churchill eloquently described the British attitude with his words to the House of Commons: "Let it roar, let it rage. We shall come through."

By the time the Blitz ended, the tide had begun to turn against the Germans, whose failure to crack the English defences would ultimately cost them the war. The Blitz was truly England's "finest hour."

5:00 **p.m., Sun., June 25, 1876** – One of the most controversial battles in U.S. military history ended with the defeat of General George Custer and his troops at Little Bighorn.

The U.S. government wanted to relocate a large Sioux-Cheyenne village away from the mineral-rich Black Hills of South Dakota but the Indians

Custer then ordered his troops to stop and fight to the death.

refused to move. Custer, who had graduated last in his West Point class, ignored his scout's advice and decided to attack the Indian village on Little Bighorn River. The mission was a disaster, and the Indians soon had the General and his men on the run. Custer then ordered his troops to stop and fight to the death. Surrounded, all 267 of Custer's men perished in the battle. It's believed that Custer shot himself in the left temple before the Indians could finish him off. The blundering Custer emerged a fallen hero and received a full military funeral at West Point largely due to the efforts of his widow.

5:00 **p.m., Fri., Feb. 22, 1980** – The United States played the Soviet Union in a key hockey game at the Lake Placid Winter Olympics. It resulted in one of the greatest upsets of Olympic history.

The Americans entered the Olympic tournament seeded seventh out of 12 teams. Prior to the event, they had lost an exhibition game to the Soviets 10–3. The U.S. had won an Olympic gold in hockey only once – in 1960.

But the young (average age 22) American team wasn't going down without a fight. They began the tournament by scoring in the final minute to tie Sweden 2–2, then gained four more victories to reach the medal round.

The final game against the Soviets looked uncertain for the U.S. as they trailed 3–2 after two periods. At 8:39 of the final period, Mark Johnson scored to tie the game. Mike Eruzione gave the U.S. a 4–3 lead with only 10 minutes remaining. The Americans then fought off a furious Soviet attack in the final minutes to claim victory. ABC-TV announcer Al Michaels asked his audience "Do you believe in miracles?" as the final seconds ticked off and the players began a wild celebration.

The U.S. still had to beat Finland to claim the gold which they did two days later in a 4–2 victory. Another wild celebration ensued, highlighted by the crowd and players singing "The Star-Spangled Banner" at the medal ceremony.

5:00 **p.m., Thurs., Apr. 29, 1993** – Monica Seles began her quarterfinal match at the Citizen's Cup tennis tournament in Hamburg.

She won the first set 6–4 against Magdelena Maleeva and was leading 4–3 in the second set when she took a break. Seles sat on a chair, put a towel over her face and leaned forward. Then she felt an "incredible pain" in her back. Seles had been stabbed. The assailant, Gunther Parche, was only prevented from stabbing her again by a security guard. The blade missed Seles's spine by a few millimetres.

Parch said he wanted Steffi Graf, who was ranked below Seles at the time, to reclaim the number one spot in women's tennis.

Monica Seles recovered from the attack but did not return to competition until August, 1995. She won her first return tournament, beating Amanda Coetzer 6–0, 6–1 in the finals of the Canadian Open in Toronto.

5:00 **p.m., Sun., Aug. 2, 1903** – Calamity Jane, one of the legendary figures of the wild west, died in Deadwood, South Dakota.

Calamity Jane, whose real name was Martha Jane Canary, was a tough, hard-drinking firebrand whose legend far exceeded reality. Glamourized in the East as an Indian fighter, sharpshooter, nurse and heroine of the American West, Jane in fact was an alcoholic, part-time prostitute who engaged in numerous unlawful acts, including once shooting up a saloon. She was part of Wild Bill Hickok's gang, but reports of a romance between Jane and Hickok appear to be fiction. Worn out by years of debauchery and drunken behaviour, Jane appeared to be at least seventy when she died at the age of 51. Calamity Jane succumbed to pneumonia after a hard bout of drinking. She was buried beside Wild Bill Hickok, who was shot to death playing poker exactly 27 years earlier.

5:00 **p.m., Mon., May 11, 1812** – British Prime Minister Spencer Perceval became the only British prime minister to be assassinated. Perceval, prime minister for three years, was shot by a merchant named Richard Bellingham as he walked through the lobby of the House of Commons. He died soon afterwards. Bellingham, in financial ruin, had been pestering government offices for money. He was sentenced to death four days after the assassination and hanged three days after that.

On the morning of the murder, a man in Redruth, England told friends he dreamed of seeing a man shoot the prime minister in the lobby of the House of Commons. His friends had to restrain the man from travelling to London to warn Perceval. Shown pictures of the murderer and murder scene after the assassination, he claimed that every detail of the event and the dream coincided.

Perceval became the only British prime minister to be assassinated.

Howdy Doody Time, **the first hit children's TV show, debuted.**

5:00 **p.m., Sat., Dec. 27, 1947** – *Howdy Doody Time*, the first hit children's TV show, debuted on NBC television.

Howdy Doody was born in the mid-1940s when radio producer Martin Stone was asked by NBC to produce a TV show for children. He recruited Buffalo Bob Smith from radio's *The Triple B Ranch* to be the host, and Frank Paris and Rhoda Mann to be the puppeteers. The show, originally called *Puppet Playhouse*, was popular from the beginning. Smith's opener, "Hey kids, what time is it?" and the reply, "It's Howdy Doody time," set the tone for an hour of fun that featured both live and filmed slapstick.

Clarabell the clown, originally played by Bob Keeshan, enjoyed immense popularity and proved to be a good career move for Keeshan, who went on to star for 29 years as the host of *Captain Kangaroo* on CBS.

On September 8, 1954, Smith suffered a heart attack and was temporarily replaced by Gabby Hayes and Ted Brown. By January, 1955, Buffalo Bob was back via remotes and he returned full time in September, 1955. He died of cancer in 1998, just two months after his induction into the Buffalo Broadcast Pioneers Hall of Fame.

Howdy Doody aired for the last time in its original run on Saturday, September 24, 1960. At the end of the final show, Clarabell spoke for the first and only time, saying, "Goodbye, kids."

5:00 **p.m., Wed., May 27, 1896** – A deadly tornado slammed into St. Louis, killing 250 and injuring 1,200 in the worst tornado disaster in U.S. history. The storm, packing winds of 193 kilometres (120 miles) an hour, dumped two inches of rain on the city in just 10 minutes. The twister's 11-kilometre (seven-mile) path of destruction was similar to that of a previous tornado which hit St. Louis in 1872.

5:00 **p.m., Wed., Apr. 23, 1891** – Sergey Prokokiev, Russian composer and pianist best known for "Peter and the Wolf," was born in Sovka, Ukraine. Prokokiev wrote seven symphonies, seven concertos, and nine sonatas during a career hampered by Soviet government harassment. He died at the age of 61 in Moscow at 9:00 p.m., Thursday, March 5, 1953 of a cerebral hemorrhage, which some say was brought on by overwork. In 1957, Prokokiev was posthumously awarded the Soviet Union's highest honour, the Lenin Prize, for his "Seventh Symphony."

5:00 **p.m., Wed., May 27, 1840** – Niccolo Paganini, the leading violin virtuoso of his time, died of a pulmonary hemorrhage at his home in Nice, France. He was 58.

But the story does not end with his death. For the next five years, the church refused to accept his body amid rumors the violinist had made a pact with the devil. Paganini`s body was first moved to the basement of his house, then to a leper house, then to an unused vat at an olive oil factory, then to an estate. Finally, in April, 1844, he was buried at Polcevar. A year later, he was reburied at Parma. In 1893, the body was exhumed once again at the request of a curious violinist. Since then, Paganini's body has remained undisturbed.

5:00 **p.m., Mon., June 30, 1947** – Funeral services began for R.B. Bennett, Canada's prime minister during the Great Depression. Bennett had died of a heart attack four days earlier while taking a bath at his home in Mickelham, England. Richard Bedford Bennett, better known as "R.B.," was just a few days short of his 77th birthday. Laid to rest near his English estate, he is the only prime minister not buried in Canada.

Bennett, an off-and-on member of the House since 1911, was elected Conservative party leader in 1927. In 1930, running on a platform of aggressive measures to battle the Depression, he defeated William Lyon Mackenzie King.

Upon becoming prime minister, Bennett allocated $20 million to help the unemployed. However, the problems of the Depression were not easily solved and in time, Bennett's government was mocked for its attempts. Dissension spread in the Conservative party and people started making jokes about "Bennett buggies," cars pulled by horses or oxen because the owners couldn't afford gasoline. The Conservatives were soundly beaten by the Liberals in the election of 1935.

A generous man who gave $25,000 a year to charity, Bennett took the defeat hard and moved to England where he sat in the House of Lords. During the Depression, he had helped many who wrote to him for help with his own money.

5:00 **p.m., Wed., Nov. 29, 1967** – Prime Minister Lester Pearson was handed the first volume of a landmark report on bilingualism

sive earth-
ke hit the San
rancisco Bay
area as a national
TV audience
looked on.

and biculturalism by Andre Laurendeau, co-chairman of the Royal Commission on Bilingualism and Biculturalism, at a ceremony in Ottawa. The report urged that English and French be made the official languages of Canada.

The commission report was the culmination of Lester Pearson's five-year reign as prime minister. He resigned the following month and left office in April, 1968. Pearson had become Canadian prime minister in 1963 after a long and successful career as a diplomat. He won the Nobel Peace Prize in 1957 for his work in easing the Suez Canal crisis in 1956. Pearson was a genial man, who enjoyed personal popularity despite an administration rife with problems. The rise of Quebec separatism was a major concern of his administration. Pearson was unable to stem the movement despite efforts to give the primarily French-speaking province stronger representation in government. The Pearson administration is perhaps best remembered for giving Canada its own flag, which was approved after a long and bitter debate in 1965. Pearson was succeeded by his flamboyant justice minister Pierre Elliott Trudeau.

Pearson died of cancer at 11:40 p.m., Wednesday, December 27, 1972. He was 75. He died one day after U.S. President Harry Truman, the only time a former U.S. President and Canadian prime minister have died so close together.

5:04 **p.m., Tues., Oct. 17, 1989** – A massive earthquake hit the San Francisco Bay area as a national TV audience looked on.

ABC viewers had just tuned in to watch game 3 of the World Series at San Francisco's Candlestick Park. The picture shuddered and went blank just as commentator Al Michaels said "I think it's an earth – ." No one in the park was killed, but 63 other people in the Bay Area lost their lives. Forty-two died when they were crushed under a collapsed section of Interstate 880 in Oakland. Some of the cars were flattened to 15 centimetres (six inches). Longshoreman Buck Helms, 57, was pulled from his car 90 hours after the quake hit. Helms later died of complications.

Thousand were left homeless in San Francisco's Marina district. The quake lasted 15 seconds and registered 6.9 on the Richter scale. Three thousand people were injured and damages estimated at $10 billion.

World Series play resumed 10 days later. Oakland swept the series against the San Francisco Giants 4–0.

5:05 **p.m., Tues., Oct. 7, 1980** – West German car dealer Jaromir Wagner, 41, became the first man to cross the Atlantic on the wing of an airplane. Wagner completed the final leg from Greenland to Goose Bay, Labrador, in eight hours, claiming the worst part of the trip was the cold. He said the air was so thin he had trouble breathing.

Wagner wore a leather suit over a frogman's suit, a ski outfit, woollen sweaters, woollen underwear and a motorcycle helmet. Despite the protection, he still suffered frostbite on his chin.

The trip, which began in Glessen, West Germany, included stops in Aberdeen, Scotland, the Faeroe Islands, Iceland and Greenland.

5:07 **p.m., Sun., Mar. 27, 1977** – Two jumbo jets collided on the ground at Los Rodeos airfield in Tenerife, the Canary Islands, killing 575 people in history's worst airline disaster.

The accident occurred when a KLM jumbo began takeoff before it was supposed to, slamming into a Pan Am plane sitting on the runway. All 239 passengers aboard the KLM plane died; only 54 of the 380 on the Pan Am craft survived.

There were many theories about the cause of the accident. One is that the KLM pilot misunderstood a radio message and thought he was cleared for takeoff. It's also believed that the Pan Am plane was in the wrong place on the runway. Adding to the problems were poor visibility caused by drizzle and fog and the fact that air traffic at Tenerife was almost double the norm.

5:11 **p.m., Mon., Mar. 26, 1956** – Mount Bezymianny on the Kamchatka Peninsula in the U.S.S.R erupted in a shock that released 2.4 billion tons of material. Scientists estimate that the volume of rock and ash ejected from the volcano would be enough to cover the city of Paris to a depth of 14.9 metres (49 feet). No one was killed in the eruption, believed to be the largest volcanic action of the 20th century. It took place 48.2 kilometres (30 miles) from the nearest human habitation.

5:13 **p.m., Fri., Jan. 30, 1948** – Mohandas Gandhi, the "Great Soul," whose struggle led to the granting of independence to India in 1947, was shot to death by a Hindu extremist. Gandhi, 78 and weak from the

Two jumbo jets collided on the ground at Los Rodeos airfield in Tenerife.

The first vehicles began to cross the longest bridge over ice-covered waters in the world.

effects of one of his many fasts, was gunned down as he walked through the gardens of Birla House in New Delhi. His murderer, Nathuran Vinayak Godse, and an accomplice were hanged in November, 1949.

Gandhi preached passive resistance over violence and was imprisoned four times before achieving his goal of Indian independence. His life story was portrayed in the movie *Gandhi*, directed by Richard Attenborough and starring Ben Kingsley. It won the best picture Oscar in 1982.

5:15 p.m.. Sat., May 31, 1997 – The first vehicles began to cross the Confederation Bridge, a 12.9-kilometre (eight-mile) span joining Prince Edward Island and New Brunswick, the longest bridge over ice-covered waters in the world.

Construction on the Confederation Bridge began in 1994 after a referendum was held to ascertain that the residents of Prince Edward Island wanted the bridge. The vote was less than overwhelming – 59.4 per cent voted yes, 40.6 per cent said no to a permanent link to the mainland.

The opening of the bridge ended the ferry service that had started in 1917. An auto deck had been added in the 1930s but by the 1970s, the idea of a fixed crossing joining the Island to mainland Canada was being discussed.

5:15 p.m., Sat., Mar. 24, 1827 – Ludwig van Beethoven, the German-born composer whose "Fifth Symphony" may be the most recognizable musical work of all time, died of liver failure in Vienna at age 56. Legend has it that a thunderclap sounded just before he died.

Beethoven wrote nine symphonies from 1800 to 1824 culminating with the "Choral" or "Ode to Joy" symphony. From his late 20s, the composer battled increasing deafness that gradually became total. His handicap prevented him from playing in public after 1814. Ironically, many experts feel the quality of his composing improved as his deafness worsened.

Beethoven had reportedly begun outlining a 10th symphony when he died. Aware of his possible place in history, he once told a critic of his works: "They are not for you, but for a later age."

5:15 p.m., Sat., Mar. 8, 1930 – William Howard Taft, 27th president and the only man to serve both as U.S. President and Chief Justice, died in Washington at age 72.

Taft, a former governor of the Philippines and Secretary of War, ran for president on the Republican ticket in 1908 and defeated Democrat William Bryan. During his lone term in office, Taft dissolved the Standard Oil monopoly and tobacco trusts, started the Department of Labor, and drafted legislation for the direct election of senators and amendments to the income tax laws. He also became the first president to travel to a foreign country while in office, visiting Mexico in 1909.

Taft was the first president to throw the first ball on major league baseball's opening day (April 14, 1910), the first to play golf and the first to have a car provided for him. The 6-foot-2-inch Taft, who peaked at 150 kilograms (332 pounds), was the biggest man to occupy the Oval Office. A special bathtub large enough to hold four men was installed in the White House for him.

Taft lost to Woodrow Wilson in his 1912 re-election bid. The former president went on to serve as Chief Justice of the U.S. Supreme Court from 1921 to 1930 when illness forced him to resign. He died just one month later. Taft was the first president buried in the National Cemetery in Arlington, Virginia.

5:15 p.m., Sat., Sept. 14, 1968 – Detroit Tigers right-hander Denny McLain won his 30th game, the first major league pitcher to reach that plateau in one season since Dizzy Dean in 1934. McLain tossed a six-hitter as the Tigers beat Oakland 5–4 on Willie Horton's one-out single in the bottom of the ninth. It was McLain's 38th start of the season.

McLain finished the season at 31–6 with a 1.96 earned run average. He added another victory in the World Series and captured both the Cy Young pitching award and Most Valuable Player honours for the regular season.

5:15 p.m., Mon., Aug. 28, 1922 – The first radio commercial was aired when WEAF New York carried a 10-minute pitch for a new cooperative apartment house in Jackson Heights, New York.

The spot cost $100 per airing, ran for five successive days and, according to the sponsor, resulted in two apartments being sold. WEAF broadcast no programming of its own, just commercials and other paid messages. The station's owners called it "toll broadcasting" long before the advent of "infomercials."

The first radio commercial was aired.

Pope John Paul II was shot twice in the abdomen.

5:20 **p.m., Thurs., Mar. 25, 1965** – The March from Selma reached the State Capitol in Montgomery, Alabama, birthplace of the Confederacy. A 20-member committee leading the 25,000 marchers was turned away by Highway Patrol Major Walter Allan, Jr. The committee, led by James Lowery, vice-president of Reverend Martin Luther King's Southern Christian Leadership Conference, later returned and was admitted to the Capitol building. They were greeted by Governor George Wallace's executive secretary who informed them that the Capitol was closed for the night. They had hoped to personally hand the governor a list of grievances.

The march took place less than two months after Reverend King led a protest march around the county courthouse on February 1, 1965. Police arrested 770 of the protesters. In response, King organized the 80-kilometre march from Selma to Montgomery.

The first attempt was marred by violence, as police blocked the participants with clubs and tear gas. A white civil rights activist was killed. But on March 20, 1965, 3,200 people began the historic march protected by troops under orders from President Lyndon Johnson. During the course of the march, their numbers grew by eight times as more protesters – black and white – joined in to declare their opposition to segregation.

5:20 **p.m., Mon., Sept. 26, 1983** – Australia won the America's Cup yachting crown, ending the United States' 132-year reign – the longest monopoly in sports history. Australian skipper John Bertrand, in his yacht *Australia II*, beat the American boat *Liberty* skippered by Dennis Connor in the seventh and deciding race. It was the Australian's third straight win after trailing 3–1 in the series. Connor restored the Cup to the U.S. when his yacht beat an Australian opponent in 1986.

5:21 **p.m., Wed., May 13, 1981** – Pope John Paul II was shot twice in the abdomen as he attended his weekly general audience in St. Peter's Square. The Pope was rushed to a Rome hospital where he underwent emergency surgery for more than five hours. John Paul made a full recovery despite having sections of his intestine removed and resumed his busy schedule as the most travelled Pope in history.

Mehmet Ali Agca, 23, an escaped Turkish criminal, was arrested and sentenced to life imprisonment for the assassination attempt. He was later granted clemency by the Pope and released from Italian prison in 2000. Agca was returned to Turkey where he was re-incarcerated for the 1979 murder of a newspaper editor.

5:24 **p.m., Sat., June 20, 1964** – Highlighting a sensational season, "Northern Dancer" showed off for the home crowd by winning the Queen's Plate at Toronto's Woodbine Raceway.

Earlier that year, Northern Dancer had become the first Canadian-bred horse in history to win the Kentucky Derby, following up with a victory in the Preakness. The Winfields Farm horse won 14 of 18 career races, including 10 stakes. But he gained an even greater reputation after retiring from racing, producing 635 named foals, 467 of them winning races. His offspring won an estimated $27 million. As Winfields Farm vice-president Rick Waldham put it: "He was truly a sire of sires."

At 6:15 a.m., on Friday, November 16, 1990, Northern Dancer, 29 and suffering from colic, was put down at Northview Stallion Station near Baltimore.

5:27 **p.m., Tues, Nov. 9, 1965** – The biggest power failure in history struck nine northeastern U.S. states and two Canadian provinces. Power was out for 13 and a half hours, during which time 30 million people and 207,184 square kilometres (80,000 square miles) were plunged into darkness. Hotel rooms, a precious commodity during the blackout, were rented out in some cases at 10 times their normal price. Nine months later, hospitals reported a significant increase in births.

The blackout was triggered when a switch at a power station near Niagara Falls failed.

5:27 **p.m., Sun., Oct. 12, 1997** – Singer John Denver's plane was reported missing off Monterey, California. Later that night, authorities found Denver dead in the wreckage of his experimental craft. An investigation revealed that the plane had been low on fuel.

Denver, 53, was one of the leading pop-country crossover artists in the 1970s with hits like "Rocky Mountain High," "Take Me Home, Country Roads" and "Calypso." Two of Denver's hits, "Annie's Song" and "Calypso" were inspired after the singer-songwriter went skiing. Denver wrote "Calypso" – an ode to marine explorer Jacques Cousteau – in just 20 minutes after a

30 million people and 207,184 square kilometres (80,000 square miles) were plunged into darkness.

Fire broke out at Ohio State Prison, one of the largest and most over-crowded prisons in the United States.

brief ski outing in Aspen, Colorado. He also wrote the somewhat prophetic "Leavin' on a Jet Plane" for Peter, Paul and Mary in 1969.

In 1988, Denver made headlines when he offered Soviet officials $10 million to send him to the Mir space station. The offer was never accepted, but the Soviets reportedly considered it.

5:30 p.m., Wed., May 31, 1916 – The Battle of Jutland, the key naval encounter of World War I, began as British ships began firing on German battleships off Denmark's Jutland Peninsula. The Germans, led by Admiral Franz von Hipper, were attempting to break a British blockade which had prevented them from reaching the North Sea. However, the British, under Admiral Beatty, were able to force them back to Germany after an evening of confused battle. While the Germans technically won the Battle of Jutland (the British lost twice as much tonnage) the English navy still controlled the strategically important North Sea and continued the blockade until the war's end.

5:30 p.m., Wed, Apr. 30, 1930 – A fire broke out at Ohio State Prison, one of the largest and most overcrowded prisons in the United States. Fanned by a stiff breeze and fed by piles of wood scraps and tar paper left by construction workers, the flames spread quickly. The guards, fearing a break, were at first reluctant to open cell doors. By the time they decided to do so, the heat had warped the locks, rendering the keys useless. Three hundred and twenty men roasted to death in their cells. One prisoner managed to get out and freed 136 men by using a sledge hammer to batter open cell doors.

No action was taken against prison authorities despite the fact almost every fire regulation had been broken. It's believed the fire resulted from an electrical short circuit.

5:30 p.m., Fri., Dec. 20, 1968 – John Steinbeck, whose novels *The Grapes of Wrath* and *Of Mice and Men* are considered classics of 20th-century literature, died in New York City. The Pulitzer and Nobel Prize winning author was 66. Steinbeck, whose experience as a labourer gave him an insight into the problems of the working man, also served as a war correspondent during World War II.

5:32 **p.m. EST, Tues. Dec. 5, 1933** – It was the moment American drinkers had waited nearly 14 years for – the end of Prohibition. The so-called noble experiment passed into history when Utah became the 36th state to ratify the 21st amendment repealing the prohibitive 18th. The move ignited celebrations across the U.S. – cannons boomed in New Orleans, while other celebrants buried or hanged prohibition effigies. So ended an experiment that cost the lives of 92 federal agents and $129 million to enforce.

The end of Prohibition did not mean liquor was legal throughout the entire U.S. Several states remained dry. However, by the late 50s, only Oklahoma and Mississippi had a total ban against liquor. Oklahoma finally voted, after six tries, to repeal Prohibition in 1959. Mississippi voted for repeal in 1966. *(see 12:01 a.m.)*

It was the moment American drinkers had waited nearly 14 years for – the end of Prohibition.

5:36 **p.m., Fri., Mar. 27, 1964** – The most violent earthquake known to have hit North America (8.3 on the Richter scale) struck south Alaska. Over 517,960 square kilometres (200,000 square miles) were affected. The energy released by the quake was estimated to be twice that of the San Francisco earthquake and 10 million times greater than the atomic bomb that destroyed Hiroshima.

The death toll from the Alaska quake was relatively small – 131 – and 122 of those deaths were caused by tsunami resulting from undersea shocks. The effects were felt as far south as California.

5:40 **p.m., Sat., May 10, 1941** – Rudolf Hess, Hitler's high-ranking deputy, took off from a German airfield on a self-described mission of peace. Hess later crash-landed in Scotland where he was quickly captured and put in jail. The Nazi's third-in-command underwent psychiatric treatment and was sentenced to life imprisonment at Nuremberg in 1945.

From 1966 until his death at age 93 in 1987, Hess was the sole inmate at Spandau prison in Berlin. Much controversy surrounded his death. The official report was suicide by hanging, but some suspected murder. Others remain convinced it was not Hess who died at Spandau, but an imposter.

5:40 **p.m., Sat., June 9, 1973** – "Secretariat" became thoroughbred racing's first Triple Crown winner in 25 years. Canadian-born jockey

Foster Hewitt went on to become Canada's most famous hockey broadcaster.

Ron Turcotte rode the Kentucky Derby and Preakness winner to an incredible 31-length victory over runner-up "Twice a Prince" in the Belmont Stakes. Secretariat was timed at two minutes and 24 seconds for the 2.4 kilometre (one and a half mile) distance, a Belmont Stakes record that survives into the 21st century.

Secretariat became the first Triple crown winner since "Citation" in 1948. Only 11 horses have won the Kentucky Derby, Preakness and Belmont Stakes in the same year, "Sir Barton" being the first in 1919.

5:45 p.m., Thurs., Mar. 22, 1923 – *Toronto Daily Star* radio editor Basil Lake approached Foster Hewitt and said: "Foster, come here a minute. I've got a job for you tonight."

The "job" was to broadcast a hockey game that evening over the *Star*'s radio station, CFCA. Hewitt, who had been working since 7 a.m., reluctantly took the assignment and made his way to the Mutual Street Arena. The man whose name would become synonymous with hockey broadcasting in Canada proceeded to call his first hockey game on radio, an intermediate match between Kitchener and Parkdale.

Conditions were primitive. Hewitt broadcast the game from a tiny glass box that he could barely fit into. He called the game into a telephone receiver and every few minutes a woman's voice would come on and ask "What number is it that you're calling, sir?" It was so hot in the booth that Hewitt was constantly wiping the fogged glass so he could see the players. Not surprisingly, Hewitt said he couldn't wait for the game to end.

Foster Hewitt went on to become Canada's most famous hockey broadcaster. He died in 1985 at the age of 83.

5:45 p.m., Thurs., Aug. 29, 1907 – An unfinished bridge spanning the St. Lawrence River near Quebec City collapsed. Eighty-four men working on the 240-metre (262-foot) steel span died when the structure twisted and fell into the river. A locomotive and three cars are believed to have driven onto the bridge when it fell. Those who died had no chance to save themselves.

5:45 p.m., Fri., Sept. 30, 1955 – James Dean, the fast-living actor who became a symbol of youthful rebellion in the 1950s, was killed in a car crash. Dean, who became a legend despite appearing in only three movies, died when his Porsche careened off a country road between Los Angeles and Salinas, California. He was only 24. Ironically, he had filmed a safe driving commercial just before his death.

Dean burst into film stardom with his role in the classic *East of Eden*. The two other movies in which he appeared, *Giant* and *Rebel Without a Cause*, were released after his death. Dean's legend has grown in death, perhaps far exceeding the status he would have achieved had he lived.

5:49 **p.m., Sat., May 5, 1821** – Napoleon Bonaparte, Emperor Napoleon I of France, considered one of the great military geniuses of all time, died at the age 52.

Napoleon became dictator of France in 1802 and expanded its territory by defeating Austria and Prussia. He met his match when he tried to invade Moscow in 1812. His army was virtually destroyed in the retreat and he finally abdicated in 1814 and was exiled to St. Elba. Napoleon resumed power in 1815 but was defeated again, this time for good, at the battle of Waterloo. It was only his second loss in 64 battles. The five-foot, two-inch Napoleon was exiled to the island of St. Helena where he died of stomach cancer. His wife Josephine, Empress of France, had passed away seven years earlier at age 51.

5:56 **p.m., Sun., July 23, 2000** – Karri Webb qualified on points for the LPGA Hall of Fame by winning the biggest tournament in women's golf, the U.S. Women's Open in Gurnee, Illinois. Webb fired a final-round one-over-par 73 for a five-stroke victory over Meg Mallon and Cristie Kerr. It was Webb's 21st victory in just six seasons on the LPGA tour and third victory in a major event.

Fellow Hall of Famer Louise Suggs said of Webb, "Karrie is the best player of the modern era." But the humble Webb said, "There are far too many good players to put my name alongside them just yet."

Napoleon Bonaparte, Emperor Napoleon I of France, considered one of the great military geniuses, died.

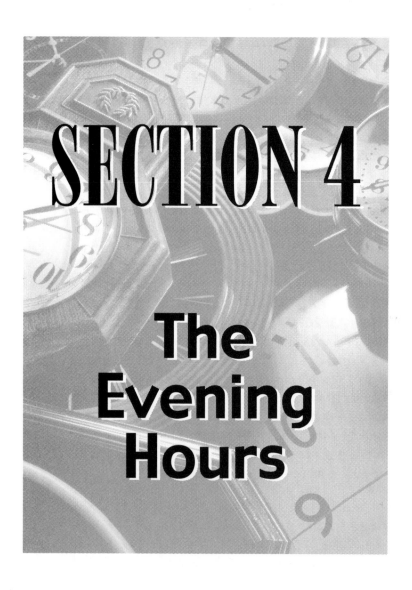

SECTION 4

The Evening Hours

6 p.m. to 6:59 p.m.

- ⏱ **CNN signs on**
- ⏱ **Martin Luther King shot**
- ⏱ **Adolf Hitler born**
- ⏱ **Three astronauts killed in *Apollo I* fire**
- ⏱ **Germans occupy France**
- ⏱ **Walter Cronkite signs off for final time**

6:00 **p.m., Thurs., Dec. 1, 1955** – Rosa Parks said no. That single action unwittingly sparked the modern civil rights movement in the United States.

Parks, then 42, had finished a long day at a Montgomery, Alabama department store where she worked as a seamstress. She could not find a seat in the black section of the bus and sat in an unoccupied seat in the white section. A white man asked for her seat. She refused to give it up. The man approached the bus driver, who told Parks to move or he'd call the police and have her arrested. Parks replied, "Have me arrested. I'm not going to move."

Parks was arrested at the next stop and taken to City Hall where she was fingerprinted and booked. At the time, it was a long established rule in the U.S. that African-Americans must ride in the back of the bus and surrender their seat to a white person if requested. A $100 bond was put up for her release. More than 50 people including some whites offered to pay, but Edgar Nixon, the head of the local NAACP paid the bail.

Four days after her refusal to move, Parks was found guilty of breaking the segregation code. An appeal was made, but Montgomery's black community began a boycott of the Montgomery bus system the very same day. Planned for 24 hours only, the boycott lasted 381 days, putting the bus

John Adams died on the 50th anniversary of the signing of the Declaration of Independence.

company out of business. The spokesman for the protest was a little-known local pastor with a knack for public speaking, named Martin Luther King.

The U.S. Supreme Court eventually ruled that discrimination on buses was a violation of federal law. The case against Parks was dropped and she eventually moved to Detroit. Today, Rosa Parks is regarded as "the mother of the civil rights movement."

6:00 **p.m., Wed., July 26, 1826** – John Adams, the second U.S. president and the longest-lived, died of old age in Braintree (now Quincy), Massachusetts. He was 90 years and seven months old. Adams, one of two signers of the Declaration of Independence to become president, died on the 50th anniversary of the document's signing. Coincidentally, the only other president to sign the Declaration of Independence, Thomas Jefferson, had passed away just five hours before Adams. Unaware of that fact, Adams's last words were "Thomas Jefferson still survives."

John Adams became the first and only future president to earn an MA when he graduated from Harvard in 1755. Soon, however, he abandoned his law career for the political arena. While a member of the Continental Congress, Adams played a key role in the drafting of the Declaration of Independence. He was appointed to several overseas posts, including that of the first American minister to Britain. In 1789, he became the nation's first vice-president, a post he held for eight years before narrowly defeating Thomas Jefferson for the presidency in 1796. Adams spent most of his term trying to keep the ill-prepared Americans out of a war with France; he eventually worked out a peace treaty – the Convention of 1800 – between the two countries.

Adams's wife Abigail was the first First Lady to preside over the White House, called the President's House at that time. (The Presidential home was not finished in time for Washington's tenure). During the independence year of 1776, Abigail urged her husband to give women a stronger role, noting "all men would be tyrants if they could."

Adams lost to Jefferson in 1800 and settled into a peaceful retirement. He lived long enough to see his son, John Quincy Adams, become president in 1825.

6:00 **p.m., Sun., June 8, 1845** – Andrew Jackson, seventh president, the first born in a log cabin, and the first subject of an assassination attempt, died at his home in Nashville, Tennessee. Jackson, who suffered from tuberculosis and dropsy, was 78.

Jackson's state of birth is in dispute (both North and South Carolina claim him). Jackson is considered the founder of the modern presidency because he exercised his authority freely, vetoing more bills (12) than the previous six presidents combined. A man who appealed to the common people, Jackson was elected to two terms, winning the elections of 1828 and 1832. In 1835, he escaped death when a deranged house painter named Richard Lawrence fired two pistols at close range, but both misfired. It was later calculated that the odds of two such weapons misfiring in succession were one in 125,000. Lawrence, who believed he was the King of England, was found not guilty by reason of insanity and died in a mental institution in 1861.

Jackson was also plagued by charges of adultery involving his wife Rachel. The two were "married" in 1791 but the union was invalid because Rachel's divorce from her first husband was not yet final. Even though Jackson and Rachel remarried in 1894, the matter was raked up in the national press during the presidential campaign of 1828. Rachel died on December 22, 1828 and President-elect Jackson blamed his political opponents for her death.

6:00 **p.m., Sun., June 1, 1980** – Cable News Network, the first TV network to carry news programming around the clock, went on the air. The first image on the screen was that of CNN founder and president Ted Turner, who had vowed earlier that CNN would remain on the air "until the end of the world. And we'll cover that live." After a speech dedicating the news channel to America, the scene cut to the anchor desk in Atlanta, where Dave Walker and Lois Hart delivered the first CNN newscast beginning at 6:04 p.m. The first story followed a visit President Carter paid to civil rights leader Louis Jordan, who was recuperating from a gunshot wound suffered the previous Thursday.

After a slow start both financially and artistically, CNN has become cable's most watched channel. It is available all over the world. CNN has been praised for its live coverage of breaking events. It is popular with world leaders attempting to keep up with the latest developments. A sister service, Headline News, was launched at midnight on January 1, 1982.

CNN, the first TV network to carry news programming around the clock, went on the air.

Mississippi author William Faulkner downed what he promised himself was his last drink.

6:00 p.m., Mon., Dec 4, 1950 – Mississippi author William Faulkner downed what he promised himself was his last drink before heading out to Stockholm to receive the Nobel Prize for literature. Faulkner, who shunned publicity, received his prize Sunday, December 10, delivering a speech inaudible to all present. Faulkner called the ceremony "as long as the Mississippi" and the end of his enforced abstinence.

Faulkner, who also won the Pulitzer Prize, wrote many classic novels including *The Sound and the Fury*, *As I Lay Dying* and *The Fable*. His stories told of violence and the decline of family and community in the American South. Faulkner did most of his writing in Oxford, Mississippi, and often went on marathon drinking binges. He died, aged 64, at 2:00 a.m., Friday, July 6, 1962.

In 1990, another well-known author took up residence in Oxford, Mississippi — John Grisham.

6:00 p.m., Sat., May 15, 1886 – Emily Dickinson, the reclusive American poet who would became famous only after death, died at age 56 of Bright's Disease. Although she wrote more than 1,700 poems, only two were published during her lifetime, and those anonymously. Many more of her works were discovered in a box after her death, and published posthumously. Dickinson was agoraphobic – she feared open or public places — and did not leave her bedroom for the last years of her life. She always wore white.

6:00 p.m., Wed., Aug. 4, 1792 – Percy Bysshe Shelley was born in Horsham, England. The poet earned the nickname "Mad Shelley" for his liberal views at the time concerning free love and atheism. He ran into so much opposition for his various affairs, including a failed marriage to a 16-year-old, that he moved to Italy from England in 1918 to concentrate on his poetry.

Shelley drowned at about 6 p.m., July 8, 1822 along with two friends when a squall overturned his sailboat off the Italian coast. Shelley was just one month shy of his 30th birthday.

Shelley's works included "Prometheus Unbound," "The River of Islam" and "The Lenci."

6:00 p.m., Tues., Oct. 15, 1844 – Johann Strauss, Jr., conducted his own orchestra in public for the first time. Much anticipation surrounded the debut at Dommayer's Casino in Vienna. Crowds gathered three hours before the concert was to begin and the police had to be called in to restore order. The first piece played by Strauss's orchestra was "La Muette De Portici" or "The Deaf Mute of Portici." By all accounts, the concert was well-received.

Strauss's many works include "The Blue Danube," which was featured in the 1968 movie *2001: A Space Odyssey*.

6:00 p.m., Sat., Dec 2, 1967 – The *Twentieth Century Limited*, at one time the biggest money-making train in the world, began its final run.

A rail version of the luxury ocean liners, *The Twentieth Century* was launched in 1902, and by 1962, had logged some 100 million kilometres (62 million miles) on its New York–Chicago run. Luxuries included a barber shop and a library. A red carpet was rolled out for every trip. Patronage dropped off by the 1960s, and the train was only half full on its final run, which was marred by the derailment of another train. *The Twentieth Century* arrived in Chicago nine hours late.

6:00 p.m., Tues., Nov. 14, 1922 – BBC Radio aired its first program – a news bulletin coupled with a weather report. The news-weather package was repeated three hours later. The next day, programming expanded with the broadcast of election news and the first entertainment program, an hour-long selection of vocal and instrumental items.

6:01 p.m., Fri., Apr. 5, 1968 – American civil rights leader The Reverend Dr. Martin Luther King, Jr. was shot in the head as he leaned over a railing just outside his room at the Lorraine Motel in Memphis, Tennessee. King was rushed to hospital where he died of his wounds about an hour later. He was 39 years old. A four-man police guard detailed to protect King had been lifted about one hour before he was shot. James Earl Ray was arrested two months later at Heathrow airport on charges of killing King and sentenced to life imprisonment.

American civil rights leader The Reverend Dr. Martin Luther King, Jr. was shot.

The four-minute mile barrier collapsed as Roger Bannister was timed at 3:59.4.

King was famous around the world for preaching non-violence and racial brotherhood in the 1950s and 60s. He is remembered by many for his powerful "I Have A Dream" speech at the Lincoln Memorial in 1963. More than 200,000 heard his words as part of a peaceful demonstration in support of civil rights legislation.

6:10 p.m., Thurs., May 6, 1954 – The four-minute mile barrier collapsed as Oxford medical student Roger Bannister was timed at 3:59.4 for the distance during a local meet. Bannister accomplished the feat despite crosswinds of 24 kilometres (15 miles) an hour.

Less than two months after Bannister's feat, John Landry of New Zealand broke the record again with a time of 3:58. In August, 1954, Bannister defeated Landry in a mile race in Vancouver. Both ran the distance in less than four minutes but neither set a record. Bannister retired from athletic competition in December, 1954 to practise medicine. He was knighted in 1975.

6:10 p.m., Thurs., June 9, 1870 – Charles Dickens, English novelist whose classics include *Oliver Twist*, *Great Expectations* and *David Copperfield*, died of a stroke at his home in Gad's Hill, England. He was 58.

Dickens, who began his career as a journalist, is considered one of the leading social commentators of the 19th century. His last work, *The Mystery of Edwin Drood*, was never finished and its ending has been the subject of speculation for over a century. The prolific Dickens wrote at least one book a year for the last 24 years of his life. Other works include *A Christmas Carol*, *The Pickwick Papers*, *Nicholas Nickleby* and *A Tale of Two Cities*.

6:10 p.m., Sun., July 6, 1975 – "Ruffian," one of history's greatest fillies, ran her last race. The horse broke her leg 7/16th of a mile into a one-and-one-quarter-mile challenge "Boy vs. Girl" match race against "Foolish Pleasure." The winner would receive a $350,000 purse.

Ruffian was put down at 2:20 a.m. the next morning.

She is buried near the flagpole at Belmont Park – the site of both her first and last races.

6:15 p.m., Mon., Sept. 28, 1970 – Gamal Abdul Nasser, President of Egypt for 14 years, died of a heart attack at age 52.

Nasser's achievements included the building of the Aswan High Dam and numerous social reforms. Considered a fire-breathing radical during his early years of power, Nasser later became a voice of moderation and peace. His death came only one day after he negotiated a deal to end fighting between the Jordanian army and Palestinian guerrillas.

6:15 p.m., Wed., Nov 7, 1962 – Eleanor Roosevelt, wife of America's 32nd president, and one of the most admired women of her time, died of tuberculosis in her New York apartment. She was 78, and had survived her husband Franklin by 17 years. Eleanor, a staunch supporter of liberal and humanitarian causes, spent most of her later life writing and lecturing.

6:18 p.m., Sun., Oct. 15, 1978 – The Catholic Church elected its first non-Italian pope in nearly 500 years. Karol Cardinal Wojtyla, Archbishop of Krakow, Poland, was chosen to become the 263rd Pope on the eighth ballot. Wojtyla, who took the name John Paul II, was the first non-Italian pope since Dutchman Hadrian VI died in 1523. Wojtyla was 58 and the youngest pope elected in the 20th century.

6:19 p.m., Sun., July 17, 1994 – Brazil won the World Cup, the first such competition to be staged in the United States. The Brazilians beat Italy 3–2 on penalty kicks after both teams battled to a scoreless tie during 90 minutes of regulation time and 30 minutes of overtime. The game at the Rose Bowl in Pasadena, California, ended when Italy's Roberto Baggio shot the ball over the net on his team's final shot. It marked the first time a World Cup final was decided in a shootout.

6:25 p.m., Fri., Aug. 4, 1922 – Bell Telephone suspended service for one minute in honour of Alexander Graham Bell, who had died two days earlier at the age of 75. The 60-second suspension of service took place during Bell's funeral in Baddeck, Nova Scotia.

Bell made history March 10, 1876 when, with the words "Mr. Watson, come here, I want you," he completed the first voice transmission over wire. Later that year, on August 10, 1876, he made the first long-distance telephone call, a one-way 12.8 kilometre (7.9 mile) transmission from Brantford,

The Catholic Church elected its first non-Italian pope in nearly 500 years.

P.T. Barnum, probably the world's greatest showman, died.

Ontario, to Paris, Ontario. Later that year, Western Union president William Orton turned down a chance to acquire the Bell telephone, calling it a toy.

Bell had two other claims to fame. An authority on speech, the Brantford inventor taught deaf children to speak. He also designed the Silver Dart, the first plane to fly in Canada. Douglas McCurdy completed that historic feat February 23, 1909 on Bras d'Or Lake in Nova Scotia.

6:30 p.m., Sat., July 27, 1946 – Gertrude Stein, American experimental novelist whose efforts were spurred by the example of modern painters like Picasso, died of abdominal cancer. She was 76. One of her most famous works was *The Autobiography of Alice B. Toklas*, her own career as told through the life of her secretary. Toklas, Stein's constant companion, died at age 90 in 1967. One of Stein's most requoted and enigmatic phrases is "Rose is a rose is a rose."

6:30 p.m., Wed., Aug. 19, 1812 – British frigate H.M.S. *Guerriere* surrendered to the U.S.S. *Constitution* ("Old Ironsides") off the Nova Scotia coast. The decisive battle lasted about an hour. When U.S. Captain Isaac Hull returned to Boston with his British prisoners, he was proclaimed the first hero in the War of 1812. Fifteen British sailors and seven Americans were killed in the battle.

6:30 p.m., Tues., Apr. 7, 1891 – P.T. Barnum, probably the world's greatest showman, the man who coined the famous line "there's a sucker born every minute," died of a stroke at the age of 80.

Barnum was 60 when *P.T. Barnum's Grand Travelling Museum, Menagerie, Caravan and Circus* made its debut in 1871. It was the largest circus in U.S. history at the time. Barnum's show grossed $400,000 during its first year of operation. In 1881, Barnum joined forces with James Bailey and James Hutchinson to form the *Barnum and Bailey Circus*.

In 1882, Barnum acquired the elephant "Jumbo," which he billed as "The Towering Monarch of the Human Race, Whose Like the World Will Never See Again." In 1883, Barnum walked Jumbo across the Brooklyn Bridge to test the structure's strength.

Barnum received his dying wish when the *New York Evening Sun* printed his obituary before his death. Barnum is said have relished the four-column report before dying a few days later in Bridgeport, Connecticut.

6:30 **p.m., Tues., May 6, 1856** – Sigmund Freud, father of modern psychiatry, was born in Freiburg, Austria.

Freud developed the theory of psychoanalysis, a method of helping disturbed people by having them talk about subconscious details of their lives. His ideas were controversial when they were first introduced, and books such as *Interpretation of Dreams* and *Studies in Hysteria* fueled the flames. In the 1930s, the Nazis condemned Freud's work as "Jewish propaganda," and publicly burned his books. Freud fled from his native Austria to England in 1938, after Princess George of Greece paid the Nazis 20,000 British pounds to allow him to do so.

Freud died at 3:00 a.m., on Saturday, September 23, 1939 of cancer of the jaw. He had battled the painful disease for the last 15 of his 83 years.

6:30 **p.m., Sat, Apr. 20, 1889** – Adolf Hitler was born on an overcast and chilly night in Branau, Germany.

Hitler grew up a lonely, frustrated artist. He moved to Munich, Germany where he began his political career with what later became known as the Nazi Party in 1919. A powerful orator and skillful politician, Hitler had become the German dictator by 1933. The reign of terror he created cost the lives of millions, many of them Jews systematically exterminated in German concentration camps. Hitler's three older siblings died in infancy. One wonders how different history would have been had the young Adolf not survived.

Hitler died at 3:30 p.m. Monday, April 30, 1945 when he committed suicide along with his wife Eva in his personal bunker in Berlin. He died after taking a poison capsule and being shot in the mouth. Eva, who had married Hitler one day before, took cyanide. The bodies were doused with gasoline and set ablaze. Their charred remains were discovered by Russian soldiers a few days later.

6:31 **p.m., Fri., Jan. 27, 1967** – Astronauts Virgil Grissom, Edward White and Roger Chaffee died when a fire engulfed their *Apollo I* spacecraft. The three were participating in a simulation of a scheduled February 21 launching.

NASA officials said an electrical spark ignited pure oxygen inside *Apollo*'s cabin. The men were unable to exit because *Apollo*'s escape system was blocked by a gantry.

Sigmund Freud, father of modern psychiatry, was born in Freiburg, Austria.

**The final NHL
game at the
Maple Leaf
Gardens arena
began.**

Grissom was one of the original seven astronauts selected for the space program. White made America's first space walk in 1965. Chaffee was preparing for his first space journey.

6:40 p.m., Sat., Feb. 13, 1999 – The final NHL game at the Maple Leaf Gardens arena began when the Toronto Maple Leafs faced off against the Chicago Blackhawks. The Hawks won the game 6–2, duplicating the feat of the Chicago team that opened the Gardens in 1931 with a win over the Leafs. Toronto moved into the spanking new Air Canada Centre, leaving the place known as the "Carlton Street Cashbox" after a 68-year stay.

Maple Leaf Gardens was the last of the six arenas still in use by an NHL team from the pre-expansion era before 1967. The New York Rangers vacated Madison Square Garden (for a new arena of the same name) in 1968; the Detroit Red Wings closed up shop at the Olympia in 1979. In the 1990s, three other heritage arenas were abandoned: Chicago Stadium (1994), Boston Garden (1995) and the Montreal Forum (1996).

6:40 p.m., Sun., Apr. 6, 1986 – Jack Nicklaus won his sixth Masters and 20th major championship as his last challenger, Greg Norman, bogeyed the final hole. It was the crowning triumph for the Golden Bear, who at age 46 became the oldest man to win the green jacket. Nicklaus – widely considered to be the greatest golfer in the history of the game – fired a seven-under-par 65 on this day to edge Norman and Tom Kite by one stroke. It was the 70th tour victory for Nicklaus, who dominated the senior tour in the 1990s and contended on the regular tour after his 50th birthday.

6:40 p.m., Mon., June 13, 1910 – Charles Keeley Hamilton flew from Governors Island, N.Y., to Philadelphia and back to claim a $10,000 first prize offered by the *New York Times* and the *Philadelphia Ledger* for the first airplane round trip between two large cities.

Hamilton's flying time for the 162-kilometre (101-mile) flight was three hours and 34 minutes. However, the historic journey took more than 11 hours to complete because of detours and a delay due to mechanical problems.

6:45 **p.m., Tues., Dec. 6, 1966** – The Beatles began their first recording session of *Sgt. Pepper's Lonely Hearts Club Band*, as they taped Christmas messages for Britain's offshore (or pirate) radio stations. That task completed, the Beatles recorded the first two instrumental takes of "When I'm Sixty–Four," planned as the second song for the as-yet unnamed album. The first song planned, "Strawberry Fields Forever," was released as the "B" side of "Penny Lane" and never made the album.

Sgt. Pepper's was released six months later (June 1, 1967) and is recognized by many as the greatest album in rock music history.

6:45 **p.m., Sun., July 23, 2000** – Tiger Woods became the fifth man to win all of golf's four major professional tournaments, as he captured the British Open. Woods fired a final-round three-under-par 69 on the ancient St. Andrews golf links in Scotland to win by eight shots over Ernie Els and Thomas Bjorn. It was the largest winning margin at the British Open in 87 years, and his 19-under-par total of 269 for 72 holes was a record for St. Andrews. Five-time British Open champ Tom Watson said of Woods "he is something supernatural."

The victory came about a month after Woods stunned the golf world by winning the U.S. Open at Pebble Beach by 15 shots – a record winning margin for a major tournament. Woods won the first of his major titles in 1997 when he won the Masters tournament by a record 12 shots. In 1999, he won the PGA Championship by one shot. He also won the 2000 PGA in a playoff over Bob May. Woods achieved the career Grand Slam at age 24, besting Jack Nicklaus who completed the feat by winning the British Open in 1966 at age 26. Gary Player and Gene Sarazan are the only other players to win all four of the modern professional majors.

6:50 **p.m., Mon., Jan. 21, 1924** – Vladimir Ilyich Lenin, leader of the Bolshevik revolution which created the Soviet Union in 1917, died at his retreat in Gorky at age 54. Cause of death was paralysis of the respiratory organs.

Lenin, a disciple of the German communist Karl Marx, spent years laying the foundation for the 1917 revolution. When the time was right, he seized control with relative ease and established the first Soviet government with himself as chairman.

Vladimir Ilyich Lenin, leader of the Bolshevik revolution which created the Soviet Union in 1917, died.

The longest game in the history of major league baseball was called because of darkness.

Lenin's five years in office were marked by civil war, famine and unrest – problems he answered with repression. Lenin also survived an assassination attempt in 1918 when he was shot and critically wounded by Fanya Kaplan, a 28-year-old Soviet revolutionary, who was executed four days later.

Following his death, doctors removed Lenin's brain and cut it into some 20,000 pieces for study at the Soviet Brain Institute. Scientists found that it had shrunk to one-quarter the normal size. Doctors were astounded that Lenin lived as long as he did.

6:50 p.m., Sat., June 22, 1940 – In the same rail car where Germany made its World War I surrender in 1918, France and Germany signed an armistice – one week after the Germans overran Paris. Under terms of the agreement, French forces were disarmed and demobilized. Germany would occupy the northern part of France and the Atlantic coast. British Prime Minister Winston Churchill, realizing his country was next on Hitler's list, appealed in vain for the French to continue fighting. One man who heeded Churchill's plan was General Charles de Gaulle, who helped lead the French resistance and later would become President of France.

6:50 p.m., Sat., May 1, 1920 – The longest game in the history of major league baseball was called because of darkness after 26 innings, with the hometown Boston Braves and the Brooklyn Dodgers locked in a 1–1 tie. This was also the longest pitching marathon in history, as both Leon Cadore of Brooklyn and Boston's Joe Oeschger went the distance. Cadore allowed 15 hits to Oeschger's nine. It is estimated that the pitchers fired more than 500 pitches between them.

The contest, which lasted just three hours and 50 minutes, ended when Boston third baseman Tony Boeckel was retired for the last out in the 26th inning. Umpire Barry McCormack then called the game despite protests from Brooklyn second baseman Ivy Olsen, who wanted to play a 27th inning so he could say he played three games in one day.

6:57 p.m., Sun., May 26, 1940 – "Operation Dynamo," the greatest evacuation in military history, began as a fleet led by Admiral Bertram Ramsay moved to evacuate Allied troops trapped on the beach at Dunkirk.

Anything that could float was utilized in the operation: paddle steamers, tugs, barges, pleasure craft, lifeboats and fishing vessels. A diverse group of doctors, truck drivers, retired businessmen and seamen including Charles Lightoller, Second Officer on the *Titanic*'s fateful maiden voyage in 1912, manned the evacuation fleet. Defying long odds and a steady German bombardment, the makeshift 848-craft armada successfully evacuated 338,226 men to England. Two hundred and forty boats were lost in the nine-day operation.

Walter Cronkite signed off his final CBS newscast.

6:58 **p.m., Fri., Mar. 6, 1981** – Anchorman, and for many the voice of the news, Walter Cronkite signed off his final CBS newscast.

Cronkite, for 19 years the evening newscaster at CBS, was also regarded as the "most trusted man in America." He replaced Douglas Edwards in the anchor seat in 1962 and was lifted to prominence with his emotional yet professional coverage of President Kennedy's assassination in 1963. Cronkite signed off his newscasts by saying "And, that's the way it is ..." followed by the date and his name.

7 p.m. to 7:59 p.m.

- 🕐 **Bomb blast downs plane at Lockerbie, Scotland**
- 🕐 **U.S. announces "liberation of Kuwait has begun"**
- 🕐 **Edmund Fitzgerald sinks**
- 🕐 **First ride of the Pony Express begins**
- 🕐 **Berlin Wall comes down**
- 🕐 **Hindenberg burns**

7:00 **p.m., Tues., Dec. 8, 1983** – The deadliest blaze in recorded history began at a church in Santiago, Chile. An estimated 2,500 women and children died when a fire tore through the building which was packed for ceremonies commemorating the Feast of the Immaculate Conception. The priests shut the only door of escape when the fire broke out so they would not be inconvenienced while they removed the church silver to a place of safety. Their decision condemned worshippers in the church to being burned or trampled to death – some just centimetres from safety. The devastation was over in 15 minutes.

More than 200 cartloads of human remains were taken away the next day. The church was never rebuilt.

7:00 **p.m., Tues., Aug. 4, 1914** – England declared war on Germany following the latter's declaration of war on Russia three days earlier. On the same day, the Germans pushed into France, Luxembourg and Switzerland as World War I – the "Great War" – began to escalate.

7:00 **p.m., Sun., Nov. 17, 1968** – NBC-TV cut short its coverage of a New York Jets–Oakland Raiders NFL game to broadcast the movie *Heidi*. There were 50 seconds remaining in the game and the Jets led the Raiders 32–29. Following the NBC cutaway, the Raiders scored two touchdowns to capture a thrilling 43–32 victory. NBC's switchboard was swamped with irate callers protesting the network's decision to cut away from the contest, which would later be immortalized as the "Heidi Game." As a result, NBC – and the other networks, regardless of scheduling time – have since broadcast games to completion.

7:00 **p.m., Mar. 17, 1894** – The doors to Montreal's Victoria Rink opened for the first Stanley Cup playoff game. Reserved ticket holders were allowed in first. The game was between the Montreal Amateur Athletic Association and the Montreal Victorias. Montreal AAA were named the first Stanley Cup champions in 1893 because they won the Amateur Hockey Association championship that year. Any hockey team in Canada was allowed to challenge for the Cup, and two teams did in 1894. On March 17, Montreal AAA defeated the Victorias 3–2. On March 22 in Montreal, Montreal AAA turned back the Ottawa Capitals 3–1.

7:00 **p.m., Fri., July 3, 1970** – American Top 40, one of the landmark rock 'n' roll countdown shows in radio history, aired for the first time. The show, recorded during an 18-hour all-night session earlier that week, was carried by seven U.S. affiliates during its first week. KDEO San Diego elected to carry the show Friday, July 3. The other six original affiliates carried it later that weekend.

By 1977, AT-40 was being aired by 425 U.S. stations as well as 400 stations of the Armed Forces Radio Network. Host Casey Kasem's warm on-air personality, the great wealth of facts he imparted on the show, plus the music, made it a winner. Kasem left the show in 1988 to start his own countdown show (he was replaced by Shadoe Stevens) but returned to American Top 40 ten years later.

7:00 **p.m., Mon., Sept. 8, 1952** – CBLT, the Canadian Broadcasting Corporation's Toronto television station, began its initial broadcast. Officially, the first image shown was that of a test pattern (so viewers could

American Top 40, one of the landmark rock 'n' roll countdown shows in radio history, aired for the first time.

CBLT–TV began its initial broadcast with a test pattern.

"line up their sets"). After 15 minutes of test pattern, the puppet "Uncle Chichimos" introduced the night's lineup. Percy Saltzman reported on the weather during that segment.

Here's the schedule for the first night at CBLT–TV.

7:00 p.m. – Test pattern
7:15 p.m. – *Let's see* (preview of that night's programming and weather)
7:30 p.m. – *CBC Newsmagazine*
8:00 p.m. – *Opening ceremonies* (with Prime Minister Louis St. Laurent)
8:15 p.m. – *Opening night* (variety show featuring musical talent, comedians and various speakers)
9:00 p.m. – *Leslie Bell Singers*
9:30 p.m. – Kinescope of greetings from CBC-TV Montreal (that station signed on two nights earlier as the first CBC-TV outlet)
10:00 p.m. – *CBC Newsmagazine*

7:00 p.m., Wed., Aug. 11, 1948 – ABC News made its first appearance, titled *News and Views.* The show was only 15 minutes in length, with an anchor position shared by H.R. Baughhage and June Gibbons.

News and Views lasted three years, and was succeeded by *After the Deadlines*, which in turn was followed by *All-Star News* in October, 1952, which featured 4-1/2 hours a week of prime time news, competing against NBC and CBS entertainment programs. *All-Star News* fared poorly in the ratings and was returned to the early evening slot with John Daly as anchor.

The position of ABC News anchor has been held by such luminaries as Harry Reasoner, Howard K. Smith, Frank Reynolds and Barbara Walters. Peter Jennings took on the role for *World News Tonight* in the early 1980s, remaining with the show into the new millennium.

7:00 p.m., Tues., Dec. 2, 1919 – Theatrical magnate Ambrose J. Small bought a newspaper as he was leaving Toronto's Grand Opera House. The newsboy was the last known person to see him alive. Small, who owned a string of theatres across Canada, disappeared off the face of the earth in one of history's most baffling disappearances of a prominent figure. Despite large cash rewards and a diligent police investigation, not a single trace of the theatre owner ever turned up.

On the day he vanished, Small had completed the sale of his theatre interests to Trans-Canada Theatres, Inc. for $1.75 million. He deposited a cheque for $1 million in the bank that day and proceeded to the Grand Opera House to wrap up some business with his lawyer. After Small's disappearance, sightings were reported from as far away as Japan, but all leads led nowhere. Ambrose J. Small is still officially listed as missing.

7:01 p.m., Wed., June 12, 1985 – Karen Anne Quinlan died at a nursing home in Morris Plains, New Jersey. She was 31.

Quinlan had lapsed into a coma more than 10 years earlier, apparently having consumed gin and tonic at a New Jersey bar subsequent to taking a mild tranquillizer and aspirin. She never awoke. In 1976, her parents won a landmark court order allowing them to remove their daughter from her respirator, and it was disconnected May 22, 1976. Contrary to doctors' predictions, Karen Anne lived another nine years. She weighed only 29.4 kilograms (65 pounds) at death. Karen Anne Quinlan spent the last decade of her life in a fetal position with no expression on her face other than an occasional frown.

7:04 p.m., Wed., Dec. 21, 1988 – A Boeing 737, bound from London to New York, exploded and crashed near the little town of Lockerbie, Scotland. All 258 aboard Flight 103 died, as well as 13 people on the ground. Investigators later determined that one of the suitcases in the baggage compartment of the plane contained a bomb. Two Libyan intelligence agents were accused of the bombing and finally brought to trial in 2000.

Among the dead were 38 students from Syracuse University and several U.S. servicemen heading home for the holidays. The UN commissioner for Namibia, Bernt Carlsson, also died.

7:05 p.m., Mon., July 7, 1924 – British runner Harold Abrahams captured the 100-metre dash at the 1924 Olympics in Paris.

Abrahams's story was one of dedication and perseverance. Better known as a long-jumper (he held the English record until 1956), Abrahams was an underdog in the 100-metre event. He trained hard under the direction of coach Sam Mussabini. Remembering his coach's advice to concen-

A Boeing 737, bound from London to New York, exploded over Lockerbie, Scotland.

U.S. bombers launched their first air assault on targets in Iraq and Kuwait.

trate on the starter's pistol and "run like hell" when it went off, Abrahams crossed the finish line about 0.6 metres (two feet) ahead of American Jackson Sholz. Arthur Porritt of New Zealand took the bronze.

Abraham retired after injuring his thigh a year later and went on to a successful career as radio commentator, lawyer, writer, statistician and president of the British Amateur Athletic Association. Until his death in 1978, Abrahams, Porritt and their wives met every July 7 at 7:00 p.m. to commemorate the victory. The race was remembered in the movie *Chariots of Fire.*

7:06 **p.m. EST, Wed., Jan. 16, 1991** – With the words "the liberation of Kuwait has begun," White House press secretary Marlin Fitzwater announced in Washington that the U.S. had launched air attacks against Iraq. As he spoke, U.S. bombers were launching their first air assault on targets in Iraq and Kuwait. The air attack followed Iraq's failure to withdraw from Kuwait on or before the UN-sanctioned deadline of midnight EST, January 15. Iraqi forces had occupied oil-rich Kuwait since August 2, 1990. Iraq's president Saddam Hussein claimed Kuwait as his country's 19th state.

After six weeks of air bombardment, the U.S. and its allies launched a ground offensive. The coalition forces met virtually no opposition as exhausted, half-starved Iraqi soldiers were eager to surrender to the NATO alliance. On February 27, President Bush announced that "Kuwait is liberated. Iraq's army is defeated." All allied offensive operations stopped at midnight that day.

Coalition losses were amazingly low; about 200 allied soldiers died. Iraqi losses, both military and civilian, (unofficially) numbered in the tens of thousands.

7:07 **p.m., Mon., Sept. 27, 1999** – The final game at Tiger Stadium ended as Detroit's Todd Jones struck out Carlos Beltran of the Kansas City Royals. The Tigers beat the Royals 8–2 behind Robert Fick's grand-slam home run in the eighth inning. So ended 77 years of baseball at Michigan and Trumbull.

Tiger Stadium was considered one of the great cathedrals of baseball. On a site originally used as a hay market, Bennett Park opened for minor league play in 1896. The park became Navin Field in 1912, Briggs Stadium in 1938 and finally Tiger Stadium in 1961. In 1988, it became the first major league stadium to be "hugged" by its fans. It was "hugged" again in 1990 as part of a campaign to save the building from demolition. The efforts were in vain as the Tigers moved into a new stadium for the 2000 season. The abandonment of Tiger Stadium meant that Boston's Fenway Park, opened in 1912, was the oldest major league ballpark still in use as the 21st century began.

War, peace, and more war dominated Truman's presidency.

7:09 **p.m., Thurs., Apr. 12, 1945** – Harry Truman was sworn in as America's 33rd president, three and a half hours after the death of Franklin Roosevelt. Truman, a former Missouri senator noted for his down-to-earth manner, was the seventh vice-president to succeed to the presidency on the death of the Chief Executive.

War, peace, and more war dominated Truman's stay in the White House. Although he had been told nothing about the development of the atomic bomb, Truman was forced, early in his administration, to make the historic decision whether or not to use the ultimate weapon against the Japanese. Truman approved its use, and the American bombings of Hiroshima and Nagasaki brought a quick, but devastating, end to World War II.

Truman led the U.S. in helping to create the United Nations. He helped formulate the Marshall Plan, which provided much needed aid to a Europe recovering from the Second World War. The NATO alliance was formed as a united front against Soviet aggression in 1949. In 1950, Truman won UN approval to expel Communist North Koreans following their invasion of South Korea. The resulting Korean War would last three bloody years before ending in a stalemate.

In 1948, Truman pulled off one of the greatest upsets in U.S. political history when he defeated Republican Thomas Dewey to win a second term. During that campaign, a supporter yelled "Give 'em hell, Harry," a cry that summed up the President's underdog status. His inauguration on January 20, 1949 was the first to be televised. An estimated 10 million people tuned in.

Harry Truman did not seek re-election in 1952. He died of kidney malfunction and other complications in a Kansas City hospital December 26, 1972 at 7:50 a.m., aged 88.

The final radio message from the *Edmund Fitzgerald*, was sent.

7:10 **p.m., Mon., Nov. 10, 1975** – The final radio message from the *Edmund Fitzgerald*, was sent. The ship sank in Lake Superior shortly after. All 29 men aboard the *Fitzgerald*, largest ore boat on the Great Lakes, were presumed dead after the vessel disappeared in a raging storm just 24 kilometres (15 miles) from shelter. The *Edmund Fitzgerald* went down in more than 152 metres (500 feet) of water – one of the deepest areas of Lake Superior – a lake known for its reputation as a graveyard of ships.

The event was immortalized in Gordon Lightfoot's 1976 ballad "Wreck of the Edmund Fitzgerald."

7:10 **p.m., Tues., Jan. 17, 1950** – Seven masked men stole more than $2.7 million from a Brink's vault in Boston. The bandits overpowered five Brink's employees and completed their well-planned crime within 20 minutes.

Six men were arrested for the holdup in 1956, but the money was never recovered.

7:10 **p.m., Wed., July 24, 1929** – The longest footrace in recorded history, from New York to San Francisco, was won by Abraham Lincoln Monteverde. Monteverde, 60, was the oldest contestant in the race and the only man to finish the 5,045 kilometre (3,135 mile) course. It took him 73 days, 10 hours and 10 minutes to make it on foot across the U.S.

7:15 **p.m., Sept. 2, 1931** – *Fifteen Minutes with Bing Crosby* debuted on the CBS radio network. The show had been delayed for a month because Crosby had laryngitis. *Fifteen Minutes* would appear six days a week, and Bing Crosby would remain on network radio for more than 25 years.

Crosby was one of the biggest entertainment stars of the 20th century. As a singer, he had more than 300 charted hits, including the best-selling record of the century, "White Christmas," which was originally released in 1942, and has sold over 30 million copies.

As an actor, Crosby was one of the most-loved stars in film, the "epitome of niceness" according to historian David Shipman. Bing Crosby starred in such classics as *Going My Way*, *Holiday Inn*, and *The Bells of St. Mary's*. He also made a series of films with Bob Hope, wherein the dynamic duo travelled to exotic destinations, accompanied by attractive co-stars, and romantic melodies.

In 1936, Crosby became the host of the *Kraft Music Hall* where he remained for 10 years. The once-a-week, 30-minute broadcast featured casual conversation, jokes and music. When he left the program, Crosby went on to host his own entertainment show which was pre–taped – a novelty for the times, and one that caused considerable controversy.

Bing Crosby died October 14, 1977 of a heart attack on a golf course in Spain. He was 74.

7:15 **p.m., Sat., Apr. 3, 1860** – Pony Express rider William "Billy" Richardson left St. Joseph, Missouri, travelling west. At about the same time in San Francisco, his counterpart James Randall rode for points east. Eleven days later on April 14, William Hamilton, last of some 30 westward bound riders riding in relay, had the honour of delivering the first Pony Express mail from eastern locales to San Francisco. The final east-bound rider on that initial run was Johnson William Richardson, who reached St. Joseph on April 13.

The Pony Express, founded by businessmen William H. Russell, William Bradford Waddell and Alexander Majors, lasted only 18 months, and employed between 80 and 100 riders all under the age of 18. Each rode a route of between 40 and 60 miles – sometimes more under hostile attacks. Fresh horses were provided at way stations every ten miles or so. Only one mailbag was lost, and one rider killed throughout the entire duration of the Pony Express, even though the mail route included treacherous mountains, desert, and dangerous Indian territory. The last of 34,753 pieces of correspondence handled by the Pony Express was delivered in November, 1861. Transcontinental telegraph lines, joined in October, 1861, eliminated the service.

7:15 **p.m., Thurs., July 25, 1963** – Agreement was reached in Moscow on a limited test ban treaty between the United States and the Soviet Union. President Kennedy called the achievement "a victory for mankind." The agreement banned nuclear testing in the atmosphere and underwater, although it permitted both nations to continue underground tests.

7:19 **p.m., Thurs., Nov. 9, 1989** – German officials announced the opening of the Berlin Wall. The stunning news was made rather

Agreement was reached in Moscow on a limited test ban treaty.

German officials announced the opening of the Berlin Wall.

casually in the middle of a news conference by Gunter Schabowski, a member of the ruling Politburo of the German Democratic Republic.

Within hours, frenzied Germans from both sides of the border were dancing on the wall, and smashing out chunks with hammers. The result: a wild celebration unprecedented in recent German memory. The Wall had fallen after 28 years, and very soon thereafter, the two Germanys would be one again.

7:20 p.m., Wed., Feb. 23, 1848 – John Quincy Adams, sixth American president, and the only son of a former president to be chief executive, died of a stroke in the U.S. Capitol Building in Washington, D.C. "Old Man Eloquent" was 80. He had served in the House of Representatives for 17 years after leaving the White House – the only former president to do so.

Adams, son of the second president John Adams, became president by defeating three other candidates in 1824. His earlier presidential candidacy had ended in failure when, in 1820, he suffered a humiliating defeat, winning only one electoral vote to James Monroe's 231.

A veteran diplomat and U.S. Senator, Adams spent probably his least successful years of public service in the White House, where much of his time was spent feuding with unsuccessful presidential contender Andrew Jackson. Jackson, however, had his revenge when he defeated Adams for re-election in 1828. Adams did not attend his successor's inauguration.

John Quincy Adams was elected to the House in 1831 and ran unsuccessfully for governor of Massachusetts in 1834.

One of the more interesting sidelight dramas of Adams's presidency concerns a woman named Anne Royall – possibly the first female reporter, newspaper editor and publisher in the United States. Legend has it that Royall extracted the first political interview in American history when she discovered the President swimming *au natural* in the Potomac River and refused to yield up his clothes until she had her story. The fact that Adams remained a firm supporter of Royall and her various broadsheets is cited by historians as an indication that the interview never took place.

7:20 p.m., Tues., June 26, 1945 – The signing of the United Nations charter was completed in San Francisco, climaxing a 63-day conference of delegates from 50 nations. The first session of the UN general assembly was held on January 10, 1946 in London, coincidentally the 26th anniversary of the ratification of its ill-fated predecessor, the League of Nations.

7:25 p.m., Thurs., May 6, 1937 – The airship *Hindenberg* burned while docking at Lakehurst, New Jersey. Amazingly, only 36 people died in the crash, while the majority of the craft's 98 passengers simply walked away unhurt from the vessel as it burned and slowly sank at its pier. It would be the end of an aviation era.

Hindenburg, pride of Nazi Germany, was about to complete its first scheduled transatlantic flight of 1937 and media coverage was greater than normal.

The *Hindenburg*'s fate was captured on a chilling radio broadcast made by the late Herb Morrison of WLS in Chicago, who sobbed as he described the event: "It's broken into flames, it's flashing, flashing, flashing terribly, it's bursting into flames. Oh, the humanities." Morrison's broadcast was not carried live; it was taped for later broadcast that evening.

No definitive answer has been found as to why the *Hindenburg* crashed. Theories have ranged from an electrical discharge to sabotage.

7:25 p.m., Wed., Aug. 21, 1940 – Soviet revolutionary, Leon Trotsky, bitter rival of Josef Stalin, died about 24 hours after an assassin plunged an ice pick into his brain. He was 60. Ramon Mercader, a Stalinist agent, attacked Trotsky in his study as his quarry was reading an article Mercader claimed to have written. Mercader was subdued by guards just moments after the attack at Trotsky's Mexico City home. He served 20 years for the murder, and died in 1978.

Trotsky, credited with founding the Red Army, lost a power struggle to Stalin for the Soviet leadership after Lenin's death in 1924. He was later exiled to Mexico and was condemned to death in absentia in 1937.

7:28 p.m., Fri., Nov. 25, 1949 – Bill "Bojangles" Robinson, "King of the Tap Dancers," died of a heart ailment at age 71. Robinson, known almost as much for his kindness as for his dancing, gave most of his earnings away to schools and orphanages. He performed countless free benefit concerts. He was also a star on Broadway, and in films.

The airship *Hindenberg* burned while docking at Lakehurst, New Jersey.

**Harding's adminis-
tration was marred
by scandal.**

More than 500,000 fans lined the streets of New York to watch Robinson's funeral procession, paid for by entertainment entrepreneur Ed Sullivan.

7:30 **p.m., Thurs., Aug. 2, 1923** – Warren G. Harding, America's 29th president, died of a stroke at the Palace Hotel in San Francisco. He was 57.

Harding's death came in the midst of a gruelling cross-country voyage during which he hoped to explain his administration's policies. However, the trip exhausted the chief executive, and probably hastened his demise. He was the first president outlived by his father, who died five years later.

Harding, a former newspaper publisher and Ohio senator, won the Republican nomination as a dark horse candidate in 1920. He defeated Democrat James Cox in the general election. Harding's administration was marred by scandal. His Secretary of the Interior, Albert Fall, sold the nation's oil reserves for profit in what became known as the "Teapot Dome" scandal. Another Harding official, Thomas Miller, was convicted of taking bribes.

Harding himself was above this sort of behaviour, but took a somewhat casual attitude toward his office. In 1921, he was called off the golf course to sign a treaty formally concluding World War I. Harding signed willingly – still in his golf clothes – and then quickly returned to his game. On another occasion, he gambled away a set of china dating back to the Benjamin Harrison administration in a single hand of poker. And despite an official stand in favour of Prohibition, the President kept a constant supply of bootleg liquor on hand at the White House.

On July 26, 1923, Harding became the first president to travel to Canada while in office when he visited Vancouver. Harding passed through Vancouver on his way to Alaska. He was conducting a cross-country tour during which he hoped to meet ordinary citizens and explain his administration's policies.

A 1982 presidential poll of historians, conducted by the *Chicago Tribune*, ranked Harding last in effectiveness. Few dispute this judgement.

7:30 **p.m., Fri., Oct. 4, 1957** – A U.S. television network interrupted regular programming to bring viewers signals from the world's first man-made satellite – a Russian satellite. Americans learned that the Space Age race had begun. Earlier that day, the Soviet Union had launched *Sputnik I*, a move that caught U.S. officials by surprise. It would be another three months before America would launch its first space probe.

Sputnik, just 55 centimetres (22 inches) in diameter and weighing only 83 kilograms (184 pounds), proved to be a propaganda success, as well as a technological achievement for the Soviets. Premier Nikita Kruschev noted that "people of the whole world are pointing to the satellite. They are saying the U.S. has been beaten."

A month later, on November 3, the Soviets scored another first when they launched a dog, "Laitka," into space – the first time a living creature had been sent into orbit. "Laitka" did not survive the journey as the dog's lifesupport system ran out a few days into the mission.

7:30 **p.m., Mon., May 3, 1948** – CBS TV debuted its News show — one that would become the most stable and, for years, the highest-rated of early evening TV news shows.

Douglas Edwards, anchor of the local news on CBS's New York affiliate, became the network's first anchor. He lasted nearly 14 years, before being replaced by Walter Cronkite in 1962.

7:30 **p.m., Mon., Nov. 5, 1956** – Crooner Nat King Cole became the first black man to host a network television series, the *Nat King Cole Show*. Cole's pattern was straightforward: he would sing a couple of songs and sometimes have a guest vocalist. Initially, the show lasted 15 minutes, but was expanded to a half-hour in July, 1957.

Despite the support of artists such as Count Basie, Sammy Davis, Jr., and Peggy Lee, the show failed to make a significant dent in the ratings, and was cancelled in December, 1957.

Nat King Cole's velvet voice gave life to such hits as "Mona Lisa" and "Ramblin' Rose." He started out as a jazz pianist but vaulted to stardom when he began to sing. Nat King Cole had 118 songs on the Billboard singles charts between 1942 and 1966.

His daughter, Natalie, followed her father's lead, singing "Pink Cadillac" and "This Will Be," among other hits. In 1991, through the magic of video editing, she was able to record the duet "Unforgettable," with her father. It became a smash success.

Nat King Cole died of cancer at 5:30 a.m., Monday, February 15, 1965. He was 47.

Crooner Nat King Cole became the first black man to host a network television series.

The Walt Disney Show premiered on ABC television.

7:30 p.m., Wed., Oct. 27, 1954 – *The Walt Disney Show*, longest-running prime-time series in the history of network television, premiered on ABC. The debut marked the first time a major Hollywood studio had taken a major plunge into the new medium of television. *The Walt Disney Show* was also ABC TV's first hit.

Walt Disney, creator of such classic figures as Mickey Mouse, Donald Duck and others, introduced the weekly program personally until his sudden death at age 65 in December, 1967. Appropriately, the first show after his death featured a tour of Disneyland led by Walt himself.

Disney did not come cheap. ABC paid him $500,000 up front and $50,000 per program to acquire the series. The show was a rousing success, lasting a record 34 years in prime time before exiting in 1990.

Disney achieved a lifelong dream in the 1950s with the construction of Disneyland, his fantasy paradise in Anaheim, California. After Walt's death, his brother Roy Disney expanded the operation to include Disney World and the Epcot Center in Orlando, Florida.

7:30 p.m., Sun., Oct. 28, 1950 – *The Jack Benny Show*, for years a staple of Sunday night radio, debuted on CBS television. It would remain on CBS for 14 seasons before moving to NBC for one last season in 1964-65.

Benny, one of America's favourite comedians, established his fame largely through radio. The show debuted in 1932 in the 7 p.m. time slot on Sunday nights. It would continue even after the star moved to TV. Benny was also a vaudevillian who made several movies.

Jack Benny died of cancer of the pancreas on December 26, 1974 in Beverly Hills, California. He was 80, even though his public knew the man never admitted to being over 39. Blessed with masterful timing and dramatic facial expressions, Benny is remembered as the perennial tightwad and terrible violin player who seemed always at ease with himself

7:30 p.m., Tues., Sept. 2, 1969 – *Star Trek* was televised for the last time on network prime-time television, although that was hardly the end of the futuristic space series. *Star Trek* ran for three seasons on NBC with little ratings success, but developed a fanatical following through re-runs in the 1970s. The resurgence of interest led to the first *Star Trek* movie in 1979, featuring most of the original cast. Many sequels followed.

7:30 **p.m., Tues., Nov. 25, 1952** – Agatha Christie's *The Mousetrap* opened at the Ambassadors Theatre in London, England. The mystery has been playing continuously on London stages ever since – the longest-running production in the history of theatre. The play was staged at the Ambassadors Theatre until 1974 when it relocated next door to St. Martins Theatre – where it remains.

By April, 1999, more than 19,000 performances had been presented to nine million theatre-goers. No fewer than 297 actors and actresses have appeared in the play.

Agatha Christie is one of the best-selling authors of all time, her works outsold only by the Bible and Shakespeare. She wrote 94 books – 83 of which were mysteries. Her works have been translated into 103 languages. Christie's first novel, *The Mysterious Affair at Styles*, was published in 1920 and featured her eccentric Belgian detective, Hercule Poirot – the most famous of her literary creations. Miss Jane Marple, the inquisitive spinster, another beloved Christie creation, first appeared in *Murder at the Vicarage* in 1930. Marple was also the detective in Christie's last published novel, *Sleeping Murder* in 1976.

Several successful films were made from Christie's works including: *Murder on the Orient Express* (1974); *Witness for the Prosecution* (1957); *And Then There Were None* (1957); and *Death on the Nile* (1978).

Christie died January 12, 1976 at the age of 85.

7:33 **p.m., Wed., July 14, 1965** – *Mariner 4* circled Mars, taking the first close-up photographs of the red planet. The satellite photographed 70 per cent of the planet's surface, studying Mars's atmosphere, clouds and surface composition. It was the first time a man-made object entered the orbit of another planet.

7:40 **p.m., Fri., June 19, 1964** – In a move hailed by civil rights activists and scorned by segregationists, the U.S. Senate approved the Civil Rights Bill. The vote was 73–27. The bill outlawed discrimination in places of public accommodation, publicly owned facilities, employment, union membership and federally aided programs. It also gave Washington new powers to speed school desegregation and enforce the rights of African Americans to vote. President Johnson signed the bill into law June 2

Agatha Christie's *The Mousetrap* opened at the Ambassadors Theatre in London.

Phantom of the Opera debuted at Her Majesty's Theatre in London.

after House approval the same day. As he signed the bill, Johnson said "Let us close the springs of racial poison."

7:45 p.m., Wed., Nov. 22, 1916 – Jack London, U.S. author of *Call of the Wild* and, at one time, the most popular and highest-paid writer in the world, died of uremia at his ranch near Glen Ellen, California. London was a one-time physical fitness addict who drifted into alcoholism and drug use. He is best known for his adventure stories of the west.

7:45 p.m., Thurs. Oct. 9, 1986 – Andrew Lloyd Weber's *Phantom of the Opera* debuted at Her Majesty's Theatre in London, in the first of more than 5,500 shows where not a single seat has ever gone unsold for any performance.

Phantom met with phenomenal success worldwide, playing in 94 cities in 17 countries to over 58 billion people during its first 14 years. The musical has grossed over $1.3 billion while playing in such venues as New York, Vienna, Toronto, San Franciso, and Tokyo.

Phantom of the Opera has won seven Tony Awards, including Best Musical, seven Drama Desk Awards, and two Olivier awards.

The play centres on a man, his scarred face hidden by a mask, who haunts the Paris Opera House.

For the stage production, the Phantom's make-up takes two hours to apply, and 30 minutes to remove. Each performance has 130 cast, crew, and orchestra members. Over 200 costumes are used, along with 281 candles, 250 kg of dry ice, and 10 fog and smoke machines.

Phantom of the Opera is based on the book by Gaston Leroux.

7:46 p.m., Mon., June 5, 1989 – The first major league baseball game at Toronto's Skydome began. The Milwaukee Brewers opened the $500 million facility by defeating the Toronto Blue Jays 5–3. A record Blue Jay crowd of 48,378 fans saw the opener.

The Skydome missed by seven minutes the honour of becoming the world's first athletic facility with an operating retractable roof. That mark belongs to Montreal's Olympic Stadium which started its matchup between the Expos and St. Louis Cardinals at 7:39 p.m. that same night.

Skydome suffered a rainout during its first month of operation when water falling through the roof caused postponement of a ball game between Toronto and Milwaulkee. Skydome's roof failed to close completely – a victory of sorts for Mother Nature.

Skydome is also home to the Toronto Argonauts of the Canadian Football League. The Toronto Raptors of the National Basketball Association also played there before moving to the Air Canada Centre in February, 1999.

7:49 p.m., Sat., Aug. 19, 1978 – The first transatlantic balloon crossing was completed when the *Double Eagle* carrying Americans Ben Abruzzo, Max Anderson and Larry Newman, landed in a field west of Paris after a flight of 138 hours and six minutes.

7:49 p.m., Mon., June 3, 1963 – Pope John XXIII died after a long struggle with cancer at age 81. Born Angelo Roncalli in 1881, he was elected Pope in 1958. During his five-year reign, he made efforts to modernize the church and was hailed as a champion of peace and religious unity.

7:50 p.m., Mon., June 15, 1896 – A 33-metre (110-foot) wave crashed into the beach at Sanriku, Japan, killing twenty-seven thousand people. The majority of the dead had been attending the annual Shinto festival on Sanriku's beach and were at prayer when the massive wave hit.

7:51 p.m., Wed., Mar. 24, 1999 – Air raid sirens sounded in Belgrade for the first time since the Second World War as NATO launched its attack on the Serbian province of Kosovo – the first assault on a sovereign nation in NATO's 50-year history.

The attack was the beginning of a sustained bombing campaign that lasted until May. Late in 1998, NATO ordered Yugoslavian President Slobodan Milosevic to end his eight-month "ethnic cleansing" campaign against the Albanian Kosovo Liberation Army. NATO renewed its order again in January, 1999. The Serbians ignored it. Kosovo's ethnic Albanians signed a peace agreement in March, but the Serbians held out, and peace talks broke off.

A 33-metre (110-foot) wave crashed into the beach at Sanriku, Japan killing 27,000 people.

The greatest evacuation in American history was completed.

NATO bombing was finally ended on June 20 after a peace agreement was reached under which Serbia withdrew all of its troops – 40,000 of them – from Kosovo 11 hours before the NATO deadline of midnight.

7:52 p.m., Wed., Oct. 30, 1975 – The greatest evacuation in American history was completed as the last U.S. troops were lifted by helicopter from the roof of the American embassy in Saigon. More than 6,000 people, 1,000 of them American citizens, were taken by helicopter from Saigon to ships waiting in the South China Sea.

President Ford ordered the evacuation after the Viet Cong entered the city, forcing surrender of the South Vietnamese.

America's involvement in Vietnam ended in the first ever U.S. retreat from a major armed conflict.

7:55 p.m., Fri., Oct. 16, 1987 – In a dramatic scene carried live on nationwide television, rescuers lifted 18-month-old Jessica McClure to the surface after she had spent 58-1/2 hours in a well in Midland, Texas where she had fallen three days earlier. Rescue teams worked around the clock to dig a parallel shaft and free the little girl. Robert O'Donnell was sent into the narrow shaft to lift her out. Jessica was rushed to hospital where she was found to be in relatively good condition despite her ordeal. O'Donnell, who had been severely affected by the stress of the rescue effort, committed suicide in 1995.

8 p.m. to 8:59 p.m.

- 🕐 *War of the Worlds* broadcast begins
- 🕐 Marilyn Bell swims Lake Ontario
- 🕐 Mark McGwire breaks Maris home run record
- 🕐 Final episode of *M*A*S*H* begins
- 🕐 U.S. hostages in Iran allowed to leave
- 🕐 Sir Francis Chichester sails Atlantic solo

8:00 **p.m., Mon., Mar. 17, 1941** – The doors opened to the National Gallery of Art in Washington, D.C. – often called the "American Louvre." The gallery was built after financier Andrew Mellon donated his entire $19 million art collection to the country, plus the additional $8 to $9 million needed to house the collection. Mellon died in 1937. He never saw the finished building.

Six thousand people were invited to the opening ceremonies, although nearly 8,000 actually attended. President Franklin D. Roosevelt was principal speaker at the event, which was held at the site of the long-demolished Baltimore and Potomac Railroad Station (where President Garfield had been assassinated in 1881).

The National Gallery of Art contains over 100,000 *objets d'art*. Among its holdings is the only painting by Leonardo da Vinci in the Western Hemisphere, *Give Vra Die Benci*.

8:00 **p.m., Sun., Apr. 13, 1955** – Fred Astaire, legend of theatre, Broadway and vaudeville, made his television debut on the *Ed Sullivan Show*. Astaire, who had tap-danced his way into the hearts and memories of millions, finally made it into their living rooms.

Astaire's many films included *Top Hat*, *Funny Face* and *Broadway Melody*, in which he danced with such notables as Ginger Rogers, Judy Garland and Rita Hayworth.

Alaska became an American state.

He and Gene Kelly are generally regarded as Hollywood's finest dancers. In 1980, Astaire, a widower for many years, married 37-year-old Robyn Smith, one of the first successful female jockeys.

Fred Astaire died at 4:25 a.m., Monday, June 22, 1987. He was 88.

8:00 **p.m., Wed., July 13, 1793** – Jean-Paul Marat, radical and bloodthirsty leader of the French Revolution, was murdered in his bathtub in Paris. Marat, who hoped to become absolute dictator of France, was stabbed in the lung and heart by a woman who claimed to be carrying important information about a counter-coup against the revolution. In fact the assassin, Charlotte Corday, wanted to avenge the deaths of friends Marat had ordered executed. Corday was caught as she tried to escape, and was herself executed four days later.

Marat had just turned 50 when he was killed.

8:00 **p.m., Mon., June 30, 1958** – Alaska became an American state by a Senate vote of 64–20. "The Land of the Midnight Sun," state number 49, was the first state not to be contiguous with the lower 48.

Alaska is the largest, coldest, and most northerly state; it is also the only U.S. territory once a Russian possession. The United States purchased Alaska in 1867 for $7.2 million. The move was much criticized at the time; many referred to the new territory as "Seward's Folly," after the U.S. Secretary of State who had negotiated the sale.

8:00 **p.m., Thurs., May 14, 1998** – The NBC smash hit *Seinfeld* aired its final episode. Two hours later, one of television's landmark shows was history, although reruns may keep the series in circulation for many years.

Seinfeld, which revolved around the lives of four self-obsessed New Yorkers, began in 1989, as *The Seinfeld Chronicles* – a summer replacement series. The comedy took some time to catch on but finally reached cult status. Creator Jerry Seinfeld, a standup comedian, liked to think of his series as a "show about nothing," but the program made George Constanza, Cosmo Kramer, Elaine Benes and the "Soup Nazi" household names.

8:00 **p.m., Mon., July 4, 1929** –Boston Pops conductor, Arthur Fiedler, presented the first of some 30 outdoor concerts in Boston, bringing symphony music to the masses. Fiedler's orchestra was made up of 46 musicians, about half of the total members of the Boston Symphony. During that first season, Fielder conducted six free concerts a week, for five weeks in a row at an outdoor location near the Union Boat Club on the Charles River Basin.

The Boston Pops was the realization of a long-time dream for Fiedler, who reasoned that if art masterworks were available for pennies at a museum, classical music should be just as accessible. By the end of the first season, the Boston Pops concerts were drawing 10,000 people a night.

Fiedler would conduct the Boston Pops Orchestra for 50 years, and for the first 25 of those, he never missed a performance. In 1938, he initiated the Wednesday morning Children's Concerts which proved equally popular.

Fiedler delighted audiences with his unconventional choice of music. He was the first conductor to present Beatles songs through a symphony orchestra. The Boston Pops repertoire included light classics, show tunes and Top-10 pop hits. Fiedler was an incredibly energetic man; in 1976 – at the age of 82 – he made 164 appearances outside of Boston.

Next to music, Fiedler's passion was fires. He would cruise Boston streets looking for blazes, helped by his fire department radio. On his 75th birthday, the Brookline, Massachusetts, Fire Department let Fiedler drive a pumper, with its sirens blaring, to his Boston Pops concert at Symphony Hall.

Arthur Fiedler died of cardiac arrest at 7:00 a.m. on Tuesday, June 10, 1979. He was 84.

8:00 **p.m., Thurs., Oct. 5, 1950** – *You Bet Your Life*, hosted by zany and unpredictable Groucho Marx, debuted on NBC television. The humorous quiz show, which had been on radio since 1947, remained part of the NBC prime-time lineup for 11 seasons, capping a great career for Marx, whose wild antics and rapier wit brought laughter to millions.

The Marx Brothers started out as a vaudeville team, but rocketed to fame after making the transition to movies. Their long list of comedy classics includes *A Day at the Races*, *A Night at The Opera*, *Duck Soup* and *Animal Crackers*.

Groucho often refused to follow the scripts of his movies, instead inserting his own ad libs with hilarious results. Unlike his brash, fast-talking personna, Groucho was moody and shy in private life, and his biting wit is

You Bet Your Life, **hosted by zany and unpredictable Groucho Marx, debuted.**

The War of the Worlds broadcast, a Halloween prank that exploded, began on CBS radio.

said to have cost him many a friend. He once claimed he "insulted nearly everyone worth insulting."

Marx died at 7:25 p.m., Friday, August 19, 1977 of a respiratory ailment in Los Angeles. He was 86 and the last survivor of the Marx Brothers comedy troupe that included Chico and Harpo. Younger brother Zeppo, who starred in some early Marx Brothers films, died in 1979.

8:00 **p.m., Tues., Apr. 16, 1889** – Charlie Chaplin, comedic genius and silver screen superstar (before the term was coined), was born in Walworth, England.

Chaplin, who acted in, produced, and wrote such cinema classics as *The Gold Rush*, *City Lights* and *Modern Times*, amazingly never won an Academy Award except the honorary Oscar awarded in 1972.

In 1952, Chaplin left the U.S. for Switzerland, amid accusations he was pro-Communist. He would not set foot again in America until the early 1970s, when he was treated like a conquering hero on his brief visit.

During the height of his fame, Charlie Chaplin received 70,000 letters in two days.

He died on Christmas Day, 1977, in Switzerland at the age of 88.

8:00 **p.m., Thurs., Nov. 4, 1920** – KDKA Pittsburgh began its broadcast of the U.S. presidential returns – the first major news story covered over the airwaves. When the broadcast concluded four hours later, listeners knew that Warren Harding had defeated James Cox to become the 29th American president.

8:00 **p.m., Sun., Oct. 30, 1938** – *The War of the Worlds* broadcast, a Halloween prank that exploded, began on CBS radio. Although the show, purportedly about Martians landing near Princeton, New Jersey, was accompanied by several announcements telling its audience that what they were hearing was a dramatization of the H.G. Wells classic science fiction story, many listeners believed the news was true, and many of those who listened to the broadcast or heard about it panicked. Traffic jams, clogged phone lines (recording a 500 per cent increase in calls), and mass hysteria resulted. New Yorkers rushed outside with handkerchiefs over their mouths to prevent inhalation of Martian gas.

Directing the radio play was Orson Welles, also known as the voice of *The Shadow*. Welles delivered a public apology in the wake of the panic.

8:00 **p.m., Mon., Nov. 15, 1926** – The NBC radio network signed on the air with a gala show that lasted over four hours. The program was carried by 25 affiliates in 21 cities as far west as Kansas City. The show included opera performances, the New York Symphony, four of New York's society orchestras, a vaudeville act and the political humour of Will Rogers. An estimated two million listeners tuned in for the big broadcast.

8:00 **p.m., Mon., Sept. 1, 1975** – *Gunsmoke*, the longest-running series in the history of prime-time television to feature continuing characters, made its final network appearance. The show lasted 20 seasons in CBS's prime-time lineup with James Arness in the title role as Marshall Matt Dillon.

Gunsmoke debuted on CBS radio in 1952, with William Conrad in the title role. John Wayne declined the TV role, saying he did not want to commit to a weekly series. The Duke, however, suggested a friend of his, the relatively unknown Arness, who would lead the show into the top 10 by its second season, and to the number-one spot for four years in a row beginning in 1956–57. *Gunsmoke*, which was one of 30 westerns on network TV at one time, was the last of its genre by 1975.

8:00 **p.m., Sun., Mar. 24, 1935** – The *Original Amateur Hour* with Major Bowes made its first appearance on the NBC radio network. The show became a national craze almost overnight and auditioning for the *Original Amateur Hour* became the thing to do during the desperate Depression times of the mid-1930s.

Contestants by the thousands came from all over the U.S. – hitching rides, taking buses and jumping on trains just for a chance at 15 minutes of fame. Many were on the air for a lot less time than that – being "gonged-off" in mid-act.

The odds of actually appearing on the show were estimated at 70,000 to one, but still the people came – tap dancers, vocalists, instrumentalists – anyone with a talent to showcase. The radio audience voted their favourites.

The Original Amateur Hour made its first appearance on the NBC radio network.

Winners received encore performances plus a possible spot in the year-end championship.

Ringmaster was businessman Major Bowes, manager of New York radio station WHN, where the show had debuted a year before, capturing, by one estimate, 90 per cent of New York's radio audience.

The excitement waned by the mid-40s and the show was cancelled in 1945. Major Bowes died, by all accounts a rich man, in 1946.

8:00 p.m., **Thurs., Nov. 20, 1947** – *Meet the Press*, the longest-running show in network television history, appeared for the first time in primetime. The show was nicknamed "America's Press Conference of the Air."

Meet the Press's format, which features a panel of reporters questioning a leading public figure, has never changed. In 1965, the show moved from prime time to its current Sunday daytime slot.

Meet the Press originated in 1945 as a radio promotion for *American Mercury Magazine*.

8:00 p.m., **Thurs., May 9, 1946** – *Hour Glass*, television's first hour-long entertainment series, debuted on NBC. The show, virtually forgotten today, was the forerunner of all of TV's variety shows.

Hour Glass was the first show to develop its own star (hostess Helen Parrish), and one of the first to lure a well-known radio star to the small screen (when ventriloquist Edgar Bergen appeared with his dummy Charlie McCarthy). During its run, advancements were made in the development of staging and pacing for TV.

Hour Glass lasted only one season, making its final appearance March 6, 1947. Helen Parrish died in 1959 at the age of 35.

8:00 p.m., **Tues., June 8, 1948** – *Texaco Star Theater* with Milton Berle, one of the most popular shows of television's golden age and a TV pioneer in its own right, made its debut on NBC.

Texaco Star Theater was not originally designed with Berle as permanent host. However, he made such an early impression that by September, 1948 he was given the full-time reins. After that, there was no stopping the man known as "Mr. Television." With Berle's zany routines and corny jokes, plus a wide variety of big-name guests, the show landed in the top five in the ratings for each of its first four seasons. In addition to being a TV star, Berle was something of a TV salesman – people bought the box just to see the man everybody was talking about. The show's appeal began to fade in the mid-50s as Westerns, dramas and private eye shows increased in popularity. It was cancelled in 1956.

8:00 p.m., Mon., Oct. 14, 1912 – Theodore Roosevelt, campaigning on the Progressive or Bull Moose ticket for president, was shot as he was about to address a crowd in Milwaukee. John N. Scrank, 36, a German immigrant bartender, fired one shot from a .38 Colt revolver at point-blank range. The bullet passed through a doubled-over, 100-page speech in Roosevelt's breast pocket, through a metal spectacle case and carried on to fracture a rib. Scrank was quickly apprehended.

Roosevelt insisted on making his speech and did so, hardly even referring to the written text which had saved his life. He finally went to hospital where doctors treated the wound but decided not to remove the bullet. The former president recovered completely but carried the bullet with him to his grave. Scrank was found not guilty by reason of insanity and committed to an institution where he died in 1943.

8:00 p.m., Thurs., July 3, 1986 – A fanfare of 120 trumpets led by composer John Williams sounded on Governor's Island in New York to herald the beginning of Liberty Weekend – the 100th anniversary of the Statue of Liberty's arrival on U.S. soil from France.

U.S. President Reagan activated a 1.6 kilometre long laser which transformed the Statue into a beacon of red, white and blue. Three thousand guests paid $1,000 each for their dinner and a front-row seat at the festivities which included performances by Neil Diamond, Andy Williams and Gregory Peck. Another 1.5 billion (estimated) television viewers from around the world also watched America celebrate itself.

Legendary crooner Rudy Vallee died in Hollywood, California, at age 85 while watching the event. In 1962, Vallee boasted he'd be front page news until the day he died. The *Toronto Star* carried his obituary on page 21.

The former president recovered completely but carried the bullet with him to his grave.

Pete Rose of the Cincinnati Reds became base-ball's all-time hit leader.

8:01 **p.m., Wed., Sept. 11, 1985** – Pete Rose of the Cincinnati Reds became baseball's all-time hit leader when he rapped out hit number 4,192 to break Ty Cobb's long-standing record. The milestone safety was a second-inning line single to left centre field off San Diego righthander Eric Show. Rose broke down in tears as more than 47,000 fans at Cincinnati's Riverfront Stadium gave him a seven-minute standing ovation. Coincidentally, Rose's record-breaking hit came 57 years to the day after Cobb played his last major league game.

Rose retired as a player the next year, winding up his career with 4,256 hits. In 1990, he was ruled ineligible for baseball's Hall of Fame after receiving a lifetime ban for gambling.

Baseball historians later discovered that Cobb's actual total was 4,189 career hits – he had been credited with two extra hits by mistake in the 1910 season. So when Rose singled off Show on September 11, 1985, he, in fact, already held the record.

8:04 **p.m., Tues., Apr. 19, 1904** – Fire broke out on the second floor of the E. & S. Currie Neckwear factory near Toronto's lakefront. Whipped by high winds, the "Toronto Fire," spread quickly to other buildings in the area and soon twelve hectares of the city's wholesale area was aflame. Despite the combined and herculean efforts of Toronto, London and Buffalo fire departments, damage totaled $10 million. Incredibly, no one was injured.

8:05 **p.m., Wed, Feb. 20, 1974** – NHL defenceman Tim Horton began his final game. He was named the third star in the game won 3–2 by the Buffalo Sabres over the Toronto Maple Leafs at Maple Leaf Gardens.

Horton died at 4:30 the next morning when his car went out of control on a highway near St. Catharines, Ontario. He was thrown 37.4 metres (123 feet).

Horton entered the NHL during the 1949-50 season. He would help the Leafs to four Stanley Cups before being traded to the New York Rangers in 1970. He was claimed by Pittsburgh during the intra-league draft of 1971, and by Buffalo in the 1972 draft.

On February 20, 1965, Tim Horton opened the first of his donut stores in Hamilton, Ontario. As of June, 2000, the Tim Horton franchise had 1,700 stores in Canada and the U.S.

8:05 **p.m., Thurs., Oct. 23, 1958** – North America's deepest coal mine at Springhill, Nova Scotia, collapsed, resulting in the deaths of 74 men. Eighty-two miners were rescued shortly after the rescue operation began, and 19 remained trapped underground. Six days later, 12 of the men were brought to the surface alive in one of the greatest rescues in the history of mining. The worst injury suffered was a broken leg. Eight days after the original collapse, rescue workers found one more man alive – Barney Martin, who had spent the entire time in a small cavity by himself.

The disaster all but ended the mining industry in Springhill, and one-third of the town's population left within two years.

Toronto's Marilyn Bell became the first person to swim across Lake Ontario.

8:06 **p.m., Thurs., Sept. 9, 1954** – Toronto's Marilyn Bell became the first person to swim across Lake Ontario, completing the grueling journey from Youngstown, New York, to Toronto's CNE breakwater in 21 hours. Although the distance is 33 kilometres (21 miles) as the crow flies, Bell was forced to swim 51 kilometres (32 miles) to achieve the journey. She battled eels, nausea and numbing cold. An estimated crowd of 100,000 watched her complete the historic achievement. Bell was only 16 years old, five foot two and all of 53 kilograms (119 pounds). She was showered with prizes and gifts worth $50,000.

The *Toronto Telegram* had originally arranged to have well-known California swimmer Florence Chadwick tackle the lake on a solo attempt. But she was challenged by Marilyn Bell and another Ontario swimmer, Winnie Roach. Bell was the only one of the three to complete the crossing.

8:06 **p.m., Sat., Apr. 15, 2000** – Ironman Cal Ripkin, Jr. capped an amazing career by becoming the 24th player in major league history to reach 3,000 hits. His milestone hit – a single – was Ripkin's third hit of the game against the Minnesota Twins at the Metrodome in Minneapolis. Ripkin was greeted at first base by former Baltimore Orioles teammate Eddie Murray, who reached the 3,000-hit milestone in 1995, also in Minneapolis. After the game, Ripken typically signed autographs for an hour before going out for a quiet dinner with his family.

Cal Ripkin is best known for his streak of 2,632 consecutive games played – which broke the record of 2,130 set by the New York Yankees' Lou Gehrig from 1925 to 1939. From 1982 to 1998, Ripkin did not miss a game

Charlie "Bird" Parker, regarded as one of the great jazz saxophonists of all time, died.

until he voluntarily took himself out of the Baltimore lineup just before the last game of the season.

8:10 p.m., Mon., Dec. 3, 1894 – Robert Louis Stevenson, whose classic writings included *Treasure Island* and *The Strange Case of Dr. Jekyll and Mr. Hyde*, died of a stroke at his house in Samoa. Stevenson, who had gone to Samoa in hopes of curing his lifelong tuberculosis, was 44.

8:10 p.m., Thurs., Sept. 17, 1908 – Lieutenant Thomas E. Selfridge of the U.S. Signal Corps died three hours after a plane piloted by Orville Wright crashed in a field at Fort Myer, Virginia. Wright was seriously injured but recovered. The aviation pioneer was trying to demonstrate that planes could be used by the War Department. Selfridge's death was the world's first airplane fatality

8:15 p.m., Sat., Mar. 12, 1955 – Charlie "Bird" Parker, regarded as one of the great jazz saxophonists of all time, died of a heart attack in New York. He was 34, although doctors estimated the condition of his body to be that of a 53-year-old.

Parker, who won five prestigious *Down Beat* magazine awards and is credited with starting the "be-bop" movement, struggled with drug and alcohol addiction throughout his adult life. As his fame grew, he was showered with gifts of drugs and alcohol. One jazz club owner noted, "He had the oldest looking face I ever saw."

8:16 p.m., Fri., June 19, 1953 – Ethel Rosenberg, convicted along with her husband of espionage against the United States, was pronounced dead in the electric chair at Sing Sing Prison in Ossining, New York. Her husband, Julius, had been electrocuted just 10 minutes earlier. The Rosenbergs, who proclaimed their innocence to the end, became the first Americans to be executed for espionage and the first husband and wife to pay the death penalty. They had been found guilty of passing details of American atomic bomb development to the Soviet Union.

8:18 p.m., Tues., Sept. 8, 1998 – Mark McGwire broke Roger Maris's 37-year single season home run record, by slamming his 62nd homer of the year for the St. Louis Cardinals. The record blast, off Chicago Cubs starter Steve Traschel, came on the first pitch of the fourth inning and barely cleared the left field wall. The 341-yard shot was McGwire's shortest home run of the season. The ball was recovered by Cardinal groundskeeper Tim Forneris, who returned it to McGwire in a post-game ceremony.

McGwire finished the season with 70 home runs. Chicago Cub, Sammy Sosa, was right on his heels with a year-end total of 66 round-trippers.

8:18 **p.m., Thurs., Aug. 15, 1935** – The Arctic Sky Cruiser carrying world renowned humourist, Will Rogers, and aviator Wiley Post, crashed in Alaska. Both men died instantly. The duo had just taken off on a scheduled 10-minute trip from an isolated Inuit village to Point Barrow when the plane's engine died, plunging it into a riverbank.

8:20 **p.m., Mon., July 1, 1935** – A riot broke out in Regina between police and unemployed relief camp men heading to Ottawa to present their grievances. One policeman died. Dozens of others were injured in the clash, along with several civilians. The men, mostly from British Columbia and Alberta, had arrived in Regina two weeks earlier as part of the "On To Ottawa Trek."

The march began June 3 in Vancouver, when a crowd of protestors climbed atop a CP freight train bound for Ottawa. They were rebelling against conditions in government-sponsored work camps set up in remote areas of Canada during the Depression. Inmates worked a six-and-a-half-day week for 20 cents a day, were crowded into insufficient quarters, poorly fed, and without outside stimulation.

After leaving Vancouver, the trekkers, as they were known, were joined by supporters from railtowns along their route – places like Kamloops, British Columbia, Calgary, Alberta and Moose Jaw, Saskatchewan. The Canadian public supported the Trek, and protesters were greeted with offers of food and shelter at each stop. By the time the "On to Ottawa Trek" arrived in Regina, more than 2,000 unemployed workers had massed together. Thousands more waited to join the march in Winnipeg, Thunder Bay, Ontario, and Toronto. R.B. Bennett's Conservative government was determined to prevent that from happening.

Mark McGwire broke Roger Maris's 37-year single season home run record.

British workers connected two halves of the 49.8 kilometre (31 mile) under–sea rail tunnel between England and France.

Police, acting under orders from Ottawa, moved in with tear gas on a meeting of about 300 people in Regina's Market Square. The trekkers and their supporters responded by walking through the streets swinging clubs and throwing rocks at police. The police fired bullets back at the protesters.

The "On To Ottawa Trek" was smashed in Regina – although, ironically, the Trekkers were ultimately successful. R.B. Bennett's Conservative government was soundly defeated at the polls a few months later. Mackenzie King, the new Liberal Prime Minister, disbanded the camps.

8:25 p.m., Tues., Oct. 30, 1990 – British workers connected two halves of the 49.8 kilometre (31 mile) undersea rail tunnel between England and France, using a five-centimetre (two-inch) probe. Preliminary tests indicated the two segments of the channel tunnel were only 50 centimetres (20 inches) out of alignment.

The linkage realized a dream first envisioned in 1802 by Napoleon, who hoped to defeat England by connecting Britain to Europe with a land passage. Work on an underground tunnel connection was actually begun in 1882 and again in 1974, but was abandoned on both occasions.

The Channel Tunnel, or "Chunnel," built at a cost of $17 billion, opened to traffic in 1994. In its first six years of operation, more than 3.5 million cars and one million trucks travelled through the tunnel. More than eight million passengers went through by train and four million tonnes of goods were delivered.

8:30 p.m., Sun., Oct. 8, 1871 – The Great Chicago Fire, one of the largest urban holocausts in U.S. history, sparked to life. As legend has it, a cow owned by a Mrs. O'Leary kicked over a kerosene lamp setting its barn ablaze. The fire spread quickly. Within 27 hours, over 18,000 buildings in the heart of the city were destroyed, including all the great hotels, theatres, six railway depots, the City Hall, the Opera House, the Water Works and the Chicago historical society with all its records, including Lincoln's original draft of the Emancipation Proclamation. Chicago, constructed largely of wood, and without rain for six weeks, was a tinder box. Some buildings burned to the ground in five minutes.

The fire left 300 dead, 200 missing and another 250,000 homeless. The value of buildings and properties destroyed was nearly $200 million. Ironically, the O'Leary house survived and, supposedly, so did the cow.

8:30 p.m., Mon., Sept. 26, 1960 – The first American debate between two presidential candidates to be nationally televised went on the air from a Chicago studio. Although the exchange produced no major fireworks or gaffes, the contrast between a youthful, relaxed John Kennedy and his haggard, tense Republican opponent, Richard Nixon was startling. Kennedy looked much better on TV, an advantage that proved to be the turning point in an election decided by just over 100,000 votes of some 68 million cast.

Nixon improved his appearance and image during three subsequent debates, but the initial impression remained in voters' minds.

A subsequent survey revealed that two million people voted for Kennedy solely on his appearance during debate number one. In an indication of how style often triumphs over political substance, voters who listened to that first debate over the radio, thought Nixon had won.

8:30 p.m., Thurs., Oct. 16, 1958 – The original quiz show *Twenty–One* aired for the last time on network television.

Twenty–One premiered on Sept. 12, 1956 with a format loosely based on the card game blackjack – two contestants competed against each other to answer questions supplied by emcee Jack Barry. Each player was stationed in an isolation booth, and unable to hear the other's response. The winner was the first person to accumulate 21 points.

The show was plagued with scandal during 1958 when its producers admitted contestants were often given the answers in advance. Former *Twenty–One* winner Herb Stempel told the media how the game had been rigged. Professor Charles Van Doren – a popular champion, who amassed $129,000 on the show – also admitted his part in the fraud, and paid dearly for the admission. Van Doren lost his teaching job, was relieved of his regular spot as commentator on the *Today* show and suffered much personal humiliation.

Ironically, the biggest *Twenty–One* winner, Elfrida Von Nardoff, apparently won her money without subterfuge. She took home $220,500.

Twenty–One was revived in January, 2000 with a completely new format as prime-time game shows enjoyed a new spurt of popularity.

8:30 p.m., Mon., Feb. 28, 1983 – The final episode of *M*A*S*H* – "Goodbye, Farewell and Amen," which lasted for two and a half

The first American debate between two presidential candidates to be nationally televised went on the air.

The final episode of M*A*S*H was broadcast on CBS.

hours, was broadcast on CBS. It was the highest-rated non-sports show in television history of the time.

Based on the eponymous hit movie, M*A*S*H debuted in 1972. The show's black, anti-war comedy propelled it into the top 10 for its second season, where it would remain the rest of its 11-year run.

Only two characters stayed with the show from beginning to end – Alan Alda as the central figure Benjamin Franklin Pierce and Loretta Swit as Major Hoolahan (the only key female role). The loss of major stars McLean Stevenson (as Lieutenant Colonel Blake) and Wayne Rogers (as Trapper John) failed to hurt the show's popularity – they were replaced by Henry Morgan (as Colonel Sherman Potter) and Mike Farrell (as Captain B.J. Hunnicut) and life went on.

M*A*S*H was based on a book by Richard Hooker, a doctor who had actually served in a Korean War MASH unit.

8:30 **p.m., Tues., Feb. 1, 1949** – A Greyhound bus carrying 34 people slammed into a Cadillac driven by golf great Ben Hogan on a dark Texas highway. At the last second, Hogan released the steering wheel to throw himself across his wife's lap, saving her life, and his own.

Hogan suffered a fractured collarbone, a broken pelvis, facial and internal injuries and a crushed left leg. It took 90 minutes for a medic to see him and another two hours before he arrived at an El Paso hospital.

Hogan spent two months in hospital before he was able to begin his own outpatient recovery – to which he dedicated his life until he reached the point where he could golf again. Hogan captained the U.S. Ryder Cup team in 1949, and was back on the golf course within seven months of the accident, hitting shots in scenes for his biographical movie Follow The Sun (in which Glen Ford played the title role).

In January, 1950, Hogan played his first post-accident tournament, the Los Angeles Open. He lost the playoff to Sam Snead. Hogan played in pain much of the time, with his legs heavily bandaged, but won the U.S. Open in 1950.

In 1953, he capped his comeback by becoming the first player to win three professional majors in the same year – the Masters, the U.S. Open and the British Open. They were his last major tournament wins.

Ben Hogan retired from competitive golf in 1971. He died in 1997, aged 84.

8:30 **p.m., Fri., Dec. 15, 1939** – *Gone With The Wind* premiered at the Grand Theater in Atlanta, Georgia. The theatre, decked out to resemble a southern plantation, was roped off two and a half hours before the event so that screen stars attending the movie would not be crushed by the crowd. Among those on hand were Clark Gable, who starred as Rhett Butler, Vivien Leigh, who played Scarlett O'Hara, producer David O. Selznick, and Margaret Mitchell, author of the book on which the film was based.

The film, with its Civil War theme, was an immediate hit and is now considered a classic. *Gone With the Wind* won the Oscar for best picture in 1939, beating out *The Wizard of Oz* and *The Grapes of Wrath*.

Author Margaret Mitchell wrote the book during the 1930s while she was at home, recovering from a broken ankle. Originally entitled "Tomorrow is Another Day," the manuscript was submitted to several publishers before it was finally accepted for publication by Macmillan. The book has been translated into 37 languages, outselling every other single title with the exception of the Holy Bible. *Gone With the Wind* was awarded the 1937 Pulitzer Prize for fiction.

Mitchell died at 11:59 a.m. on Tuesday, August 16, 1949 – five days after being hit by a car while she was crossing an Atlanta street. Earlier, in a letter written to a book reviewer, Mitchell prophesied the manner of her death.

In 1995, the Road to Tara Museum unveiled a second work of fiction by Mitchell. *Lost Laysen*, a novella, is a love story set on the South Pacific. Mitchell wrote it when she was 16.

8:30 **p.m., Mon., Nov. 12, 1951** – The Canadian National Ballet made its debut at the Eaton Auditorium in Toronto. The performance marked the beginning of a three-night run for the company which today is known as the National Ballet. The first-night offerings, presented under the artistic direction of Celia Franca included "Les Sylphides," "The Dance of Salome" and the "Polovetsian Dances" from Prince Igor. Tickets were $1.50, $2.50 and $3.00.

Since that inauspicious beginning, the National Ballet has hosted some of the world's greatest dancers, including Karen Kain, Veronica Tennant, Barysnikov, Nureyev, Dame Margot Fonteyn, Rex Harrington, Victoria Bertram and Jeremy Ransom.

Gone With The Wind premiered at the Grand Theatre in Atlanta, Georgia.

The Beatles hit the stage on the *Ed Sullivan Show*.

8:30 **p.m., Sat., Feb. 1, 1896** – The debut performance of Giacomo Puccini's famed opera, *Le Vie De Boheme*, more popularly known as *La Boheme*, was staged at the Turin Opera House. This was a widely heralded event, and coloured posters were used for the first time to announce the Italian premiere. Many members of the Italian royal family were on hand. The performance lasted seventy-five minutes.

Some reviewers panned the work, but public reception was so enthusiastic that the opera played to 24 sold-out performances – three times the number originally anticipated. Today, *La Boheme* is recognized as one of Puccini's greatest operas.

Puccini, whose works also include *Tosca* and *Madame Butterfly*, died of cancer of the throat at 4:00 a.m., Saturday, November 29, 1924. He was 66 and had been working on *Turandot*, considered by many to be his greatest creation, virtually up to the moment of death. The opera remains unfinished.

8:30 **p.m., Mon., Apr. 8, 1991** – Willie Shoemaker, 59, winningest jockey in thoroughbred racing history, was paralyzed for life after his car slid off a highway near San Dimas, California. Shoemaker, whose blood alcohol level was well above the legal limit, suffered a broken neck and internal injuries.

"The Shoe," who weighed only two and a half pounds at birth, topped out at four foot 11 inches fully grown. The canny veteran won 8,833 races during a career that spanned 41 years. His successes included four Kentucky Derbys, two Preakness Stakes and five Belmont Stakes. He netted $123.4 million in purses. Shoemaker turned to training in 1990 and had a winner two days after his injury. He also became a popular novelist.

8:32 **p.m., Sun., Feb. 9, 1964** – The Beatles hit the stage on the *Ed Sullivan Show* to begin their first live appearance on North American television. The Fab Four played five songs – "All My Loving," "Till There Was You," "She Loves You," "I Saw Her Standing There" and "I Want To Hold Your Hand." Their efforts were virtually drowned out by the screaming of adoring fans. An estimated 73 million television viewers watched the event – in addition to fans already at the theatre, which had received more than 50,000 requests for tickets.

Sullivan discovered the Beatles in August, 1963, while visiting England on a talent search.

8:33 p.m., Tues., Jan. 20, 1981 – Iranian authorities announced the release of American hostages, held for 444 days. Minutes later, the 52 captives were herded at gunpoint aboard a plane supplied by Algerian mediators. The plane took off towards the Turkish border, bound for the U.S. military base in Frankfurt, Germany, and freedom. The Americans had spent 14 nightmarish months in the hands of Iranian "students," who took over the U.S. Embassy in Tehran in November, 1979.

Freedom for the hostages was obtained after the U.S. agreed to return Iranian assets frozen in the U.S. Iranian officials delayed the release until President Jimmy Carter had officially passed on the reins of power to his successor Ronald Reagan.

Carter was on hand to greet the hostages in West Germany by special request of the new U.S. President.

8:35 p.m., Thurs., Oct. 24, 1935 – Dutch Schultz, notorious beer-runner, racketeer and underworld denizen, died of gunshot wounds suffered the night before in a New York tavern. Schultz, whose real name was Arthur Flegenheimer, was shot along with three companions while examining account books and papers. All three of Schultz's aides died in the attack, perpetrated by two gunmen believed to be from a rival gang.

8:35 p.m., Sat., Jan. 29, 1820 – King George III, whose 60-year reign as English monarch ranks second only to that of Queen Victoria (63 years), died of terminal diarrhea at Windsor Castle. He was 81. "Farmer George," as he was nicknamed, was insane, blind and deaf by the end of his reign. His successor was his son who had handled the king's duties as regent since 1811.

8:40 p.m., Mon., Oct., 26, 1992 – The Canadian Press notified its members that, based on early electoral returns, the Charlottetown Accord was dead. Canadian voters had rejected the proposal in a referendum, ending one of Canada's most divisive and controversial electoral campaigns.

Iranian authorities announced the release of American hostages, held for 444 days.

The Accord sought to recognize the province of Quebec as a distinct cultural society.

At stake, was the renewal of Canada's Constitution. The Accord sought to recognize the province of Quebec as a distinct cultural society, and to change the Canadian Senate from an appointed to an elected body.

Despite a well-financed campaign backed by many of Canada's leading politicians and business leaders, the deal went down to defeat – and Canada's Conservative government suffered another setback in its attempt to establish a Constitution approved by all segments of Canadian society. After the vote, Prime Minister Brian Mulroney announced that the federal government would concentrate on the national economy, putting the Constitutional question on the back burner. Many Canadians applauded the decision.

8:45 p.m., Tues., July 28, 1750 – German composer, Johann Sebastian Bach, considered the father of modern music, died following a stroke at age 65.

Bach was known in his lifetime as a skilled organist, as a teacher and as a conductor. He was not recognized for his composing genius until well after his death. His works were not brought to light until the 19th century.

Bach was a prodigious composer. He wrote more than 800 pieces of serious music, including the famed "Brandenburg Concertos." Four of his sons (Bach had 20 offspring by two wives) became well-known composers in their own right.

8:45 p.m., Sat., Feb. 19, 1927 – CFRB Toronto signed on as Canada's first batteryless radio station. Its call letters meant just that – Canada's First Rogers Batteryless. The station was owned by brothers E.S. (Ted) and J. Elsworth Rogers. It originally shared time at 1030 kc with the long-forgotten CKOW. The two brothers had invented an alternating current tube that replaced batteries used in radio transmitters of the era.

Radio was a craze in the 1920s. Newspapers often carried listings from stations far away. The February 19, 1927 issue of the *Toronto Globe* listed program schedules for KFON–Long Beach, California, WBAP–Fort Worth, Texas, and WGN–Chicago. Radio enthusiasts would often practice "Dxing," the popular name for the hobby of pulling in as many stations – distant and otherwise – as possible. (D in "DX" stands for distance, X for the unknown.)

8:49 **p.m., Fri., Mar. 3, 1972** – *Pioneer 10*, the most ambitious space probe of its era, blasted off from Cape Canaveral. The probe took the first close-up pictures of Jupiter in December, 1973, and would later become the first man-made object to leave our solar system in June, 1983.

8:50 **p.m., Wed., Jan. 3, 1990** – General Manuel Noriega, President of Panama, surrendered to U.S. authorities after taking sanctuary in the Vatican Embassy in Panama City for six days. Noriega was sought by the Americans on racketeering and drug charges. He had been on the run since December 20 when U.S. troops invaded Panama to drive him out of office and install the government of Guillermo Endera.

U.S. troops outside the Vatican embassy attempted to flush Noriega from his refuge by blasting non-stop rock music at the embassy. Noriega, an opera buff, finally surrendered and was brought to Miami for trial.

8:56 **p.m., Sun., May 28, 1967** – Francis Chichester became the first man to complete a solo, around-the-world boat voyage. The 65-year-old Englishman wrapped up a 45,865-kilometre (28,500-mile) trip he had begun nine months earlier. Chichester was knighted for his accomplishment.

8:56 **p.m., Fri., Nov. 19, 1999** – IRS agent John Carpenter became the first person to win $1 million in a lump sum in a TV game show. Carpenter, 31, of Hampton, Connecticut, hit the jackpot when he answered 15 questions correctly on ABC's *Who Wants To Be A Millionaire?* Carpenter's 15th question was: "Which U.S. president appeared on the TV show *Laugh–In?* (Richard Nixon).

8:58 **p.m., Sun., Dec. 8, 1963** – Pan Am Clipper Flight 214, en route to Philadelphia from San Juan, Puerto Rico, crashed near Elkton, Maryland after being struck by lightning. Eighty-one people died. Investigators found that lightning had struck the plane's left wing, which in turn ignited the contents of a reserve fuel tank.

Francis Chichester became the first man to complete a solo, around-the-world boat voyage.

9 p.m. to 9:59 p.m.

- ⏱ **Lindbergh baby kidnapped**
- ⏱ **Falklands War ends**
- ⏱ **Richard Nixon resigns**
- ⏱ **Hank Aaron hits 715th home run**
- ⏱ ***All in the Family* debuts**
- ⏱ **Stalin dies**

9:00 **p.m., Wed., Mar. 2, 1932** – The 20-month-old son of aviator Charles Lindbergh was taken from his crib at the family's home near Princeton, New Jersey. The kidnapping sparked the greatest manhunt in U.S. history.

A ransom note left at the scene demanded $50,000, which Lindbergh said he would pay. On May 12, however, the baby's body was discovered in woods just eight kilometres (five miles) from the Lindbergh home. An autopsy concluded the child had been murdered soon after the kidnapping.

More than two years later, illegal German immigrant Bruno Hauptmann was arrested and charged with first-degree murder. Circumstantial evidence linked him to the crime. In March, 1935, Hauptmann was found guilty, and later executed. His wife fought unsuccessfully for more than a half-century to clear his name.

9:00 **p.m., Mon., Feb. 27, 1933** –A police officer on patrol in Berlin's German Reichstag noticed smoke in the building. Before sounding the alarm, he fired shots at several men running from the scene, apprehending one – a Communist identified as Marinus Van der Lubbe. The fire lasted through the night and reduced the legislative building to ashes. The next morning, German Chancellor Hitler blamed the fire on the Communists and ordered all 100 Communist members of the Reichstag arrested one week before the legislative elections. The crackdown removed the Communists as a political force and the Nazis swept to victory in the elections. Many historians believe the Nazis set the Reichstag fire themselves and then framed the Communists to destroy the party.

9:00 p.m., Sun., Oct. 8, 1871 – One of the world's worst fires began when high winds fanned the tiny Wisconsin sawmill community of Peshtigo. The blaze spread with blinding speed through drought-parched communities, fields and forest. One eyewitness called it "a fire tornado." The fire killed an estimated 1,500 people and destroyed nearly 1.3 million acres of forest.

The Peshtigo fire was largely overshadowed by the Great Chicago Fire, which occurred the same night.

9:00 p.m., Sat., July 3, 1976 – Israeli commandos began their raid on Entebbe. Working with split-second precision, the commandos freed 105 mostly Jewish and Israeli hostages being held by pro-Palestinian hijackers in a passenger terminal at Uganda's Entebbe Airport. Two hostages died in the operation, and all of the hijackers were killed. The plane had been hijacked the previous Sunday on a flight from Athens to Paris.

9:00 p.m., Thurs., Dec. 16, 1773 – The Boston Tea Party came to an end as angry colonists threw the last of some 342 chests of tea (Ceylon and Darjeeling) off three British ships. The colonists staged the Tea Party not, as commonly believed, to protest a new British tax on tea. They were trying to prevent the East India Company's duty-free product from reaching the Colonial market and bypassing American merchants.

150 protesters with axes – including Paul Revere – took part in the raid, which lasted less than half an hour. The rebellious action helped fan the flames of dissent which led to the American Revolution.

9:00 p.m., Fri., May 9, 1958 – Ella Fitzgerald appeared on the *Frank Sinatra* television show, one of the few times the two giants of 20th century music ever appeared together on TV.

The fire killed an estimated 1,500 people and destroyed nearly 1.3 million acres of forest.

Riots broke out shortly after four white police officers were acquitted of all but one count in the beating of black motorist, Rodney King.

Fitzgerald, the "First Lady of Song," and the most honoured jazz singer of all time, first gained attention in 1934, when she won the Harlem Amateur Hour. By 1939, she had her first major hit, "A Tisket, A Tasket," which was number one in the U.S. for 10 weeks. She had 53 chart records between 1936 and 1963, winning 12 Grammys along the way. Fitzgerald won the *Down Beat* poll as top female vocalist more than 20 times and in 1967 was honoured with a Lifetime Achievement Grammy.

Fitzgerald died June 15, 1996 at the age of 79 in Beverly Hills, California.

9:00 p.m., Wed., Apr. 29, 1992 – Los Angeles mayor Tom Bradley declared a local state of emergency in the wake of riots which broke out shortly after four white police officers were acquitted of all but one count in the beating of black motorist, Rodney King. The March, 1991 brutalization was captured on videotape and showed King being struck at least 50 times with blows from police batons. King suffered serious injuries in the attack. The jury which voted for acquittal did not include a black person.

The resultant riots caused the death of 52 people. At least 600 buildings were set aflame, with damage estimated as high as $1 billion. The Army, National Guard and Marines were called in to restore order, but it was not until May 4 – five days after the riots – that the dawn-to-dusk curfew was lifted. Los Angeles Police Chief Darryl Gates resigned June 26, to be replaced by Willie Williams, the city's first black police chief.

9:00 p.m., Thurs., Aug. 21, 1986 – An enormous bubble of deadly carbon dioxide broke loose from the depths of Lake Nios in the West African country of Cameroon. Within seconds, 1,700 people were dead along with countless animals and birds. One witness who stumbled upon the scene said it was "as if a neutron bomb had exploded," killing all living things but leaving everything else intact.

Scientists estimate the bubble may have been formed during the 18th century, growing steadily in the waters of Lake Nios over the years. It is believed that an earthquake or landslide might have triggered the deadly gas's release.

9:00 p.m., Mon., June 14, 1982 – The six-week Falkland Islands war between Britain and Argentina ended with the Argentine surrender at Port Stanley. Seven hundred and twelve Argentinians and 255 British soldiers died.

The war began April 2 when Argentine forces invaded the Falklands, a British territory for 149 years. Britain declared war and imposed a blockade of the islands. By the end of May, British forces had established a beachhead and, with the help of strong air and sea support, were able to reclaim their colony.

9:00 **p.m., Mon., Sept. 21, 1970** – It was the debut of *Monday Night Football*, ABC's daring, controversial and ultimately successful bid to bring the pigskin to prime time. The Cleveland Browns beat Joe Namath and the New York Jets 31–21.

The star of the telecasts was a man people loved to hate, Howard Cosell. The tell-it-like-it-is sportscaster offended many fans, and he was often accused of making the broadcast more entertainment than sports. Nevertheless, the troika of Cosell, Don Meredith and Keith Jackson (replaced after the first season by Frank Gifford) got the ratings, and a free rein from ABC.

Meredith left the show after three years, to return in 1977 and leave again in 1985. Cosell left in 1984 and sharply criticized his former partners in his book *I Never Played the Game*. Only Frank Gifford remained into the show's third decade, but he was gone by the end of the 90s. Cosell died in 1995.

9:00 **p.m., Mon., Apr. 9, 1979** – The Academy Awards began with more than the usual buzz of excitement because the legendary John Wayne was on hand to present the award for best picture. The winner was *The Deer Hunter*, and hundreds of millions watched as the Duke, frail but determined, made the Oscar presentation to director Michael Cimino. The audience at the Dorothy Chandler Pavilion in Los Angeles cheered as the Duke made his final major public appearance.

Wayne, who symbolized the red, white and blue for many Americans, died of cancer in a Los Angeles hospital at 5:23 p.m., Monday, June 11, 1979 – just two months later. He was 72. Best known for his starring roles in such western classics as *Stagecoach* and *The Alamo*, John Wayne did not win an Oscar until 1969, and then for a non-Western, *True Grit*. He was listed among Hollywood's top 10 box office draws every year but one from 1949 to 1968.

It was the debut of *Monday Night Football*.

The *Ed Sullivan Show* (then known as *Toast of the Town*) premiered on CBS-TV.

9:00 p.m., Sun., June 20, 1948 – The *Ed Sullivan Show* (then known as *Toast of the Town*) premiered on CBS-TV. It would last 24 seasons – the longest-running variety show in TV history – and become a Sunday night institution.

Sullivan's show had everything – slapstick, ballet, rock music, dancing bears, Broadway, you name it. Behind it all was Sullivan, deadpan, awkward and homely-looking, but with a keen eye for talent. A veritable who's who of the entertainment world appeared on his show, with Elvis Presley's appearance (from the hips up only) in 1956 and the Beatles American debut in 1964 among the best remembered. It was truly "a really big SHEW."

Sullivan, in constant pain from ulcers for much of his adult life, died in 1974 – three years after the show went off the air in June, 1971.

9:00 p.m., Mon., Jan. 19, 1953 – In a case of art imitating life, or perhaps the other way around, "Little Ricky Ricardo" was born on the *I Love Lucy* show. Twice as many people watched that episode as did the Eisenhower inauguration the next day.

When Lucille Ball became pregnant in 1952, CBS worried about what her viewers would think. The network wanted Lucy to disguise the pregnancy. Husband Desi Arnaz wanted it written into the script. And so it was (although CBS insisted the word "expectant" be used instead of "pregnant").

CBS initiated a major promotional campaign about the pregnancy leading up to the "Lucy Goes to the Hospital" episode. The real Lucy gave birth to a baby boy by caesarean section, on the same day the show finale was aired.

9:00 p.m., Mon., Aug. 6, 1956 – The ill-fated Dumont television network broadcast its final show, an entry called *Boxing from St. Nicolas Arena*. Long forgotten now, Dumont was American television's fourth network during the 40s and 50s.

Dumont had hopeful beginnings. The network was involved in experimental television in the early 30s, and had marketed the first large screen (35-centimetre or 14-inch) home TV set in 1938. It was right behind NBC in setting up a network in 1946–47, and, helped by financing from Paramount Pictures, had the most elaborate facilities in the industry. However, when competitor ABC merged with United Paramount Theatres, the writing was on the wall. Dumont struggled and, by 1956, went out of business.

9:00 **p.m., Wed., Jan. 11, 1928** – British writer Thomas Hardy, whose works include *Far from the Madding Crowd* and *Tess of the D'Urbervilles*, died of old age at Max Gate, England. He was 87.

Hardy was originally a draftsman who turned to writing as a sideline. He became disillusioned with fiction after *Tess of the D'Urbervilles* was condemned as immoral. Hardy's ashes are in Poet's Corner at Westminster Abbey.

9:04 **p.m., Thurs., Aug. 8, 1974** –U.S. President Richard Nixon announced his resignation on U.S. national TV, telling the nation that his defense against impeachment would paralyze the country. Nixon, the 37th president, was succeeded by Gerald Ford shortly after noon the next day.

Richard Nixon was a rookie U.S. senator with a reputation as an anti-Communist crusader when Dwight Eisenhower chose him as his Republican presidential running mate in 1952. Almost immediately, Nixon ran into controversy when a newspaper claimed he had used funds from a secret slush fund for out-of-pocket expenses while Senator. Nixon admitted the fund existed but denied using it for personal expenses. Public support for him was strong, and Eisenhower kept him on the ticket.

Nixon served two terms as vice-president under the popular Eisenhower and won the Republican nomination for president himself in 1960. He lost the presidential election to John Kennedy by a narrow margin. In 1962, Nixon was defeated by Pat Brown for California governor. At a post-election news conference, the bitter Nixon told reporters "You won't have Nixon to kick around any more because, gentlemen, this is my last press conference."

In 1964, Nixon campaigned for Republican nominee Barry Goldwater. By 1968, Nixon was again a front-runner for the Republican presidential nomination, which he won on the first ballot.

Nixon went on to edge Democrat Hubert Humphrey in the national election by a margin almost as close as the 1960 defeat. He became the first man since Andrew Jackson in 1828 to win the presidency on his second attempt. Nixon was easily re-elected over George McGovern in 1972.

U.S. President Richard Nixon announced his resignation on U.S. national TV.

Colombia's largest volcano, Nevado del Ruiz, erupted for the first time in nearly 400 years.

Nixon had many accomplishments as president: getting the U.S. out of Vietnam, becoming the first president to visit China, improving relations with that country, and the SALT arms limitation agreement with the Soviet Union, leading to several more such agreements over the next two decades. However, his administration was dogged by, and eventually buried by, the infamous Watergate scandal.

Nixon became the first president to resign, admitting to nothing more than errors of judgement. His successor, Gerald Ford, pardoned him of any crimes he may have committed or taken part in while president.

Nixon was busy in retirement, writing several books and visiting many foreign heads of state. He became the Republican party's eminence grise. Richard M. Nixon died April 22, 1994. He was 81.

9:07 p.m., Mon., Apr. 8, 1974 – Hank Aaron's long quest to become baseball's all-time home run king ended when the Atlanta slugger belted his 715th homer off Al Downing of the Los Angeles Dodgers to surpass Ruth's legendary mark of 714. Ironically, April 8 was one of the few dates on which Aaron had never previously homered.

Aaron's historic blast was caught in the Braves bullpen by reliever Rick House (which became his major claim to fame in the big leagues). Aaron finished up with 755 career homers – the last with Milwaukee at age 42, on July 20, 1976. Henry Aaron covered 82 kilometres (51 miles) just by rounding the bases after his home runs.

The all-time lifetime home run record in professional baseball belongs to Sadahara Oh, who hit 868 in the Japanese league.

9:08 p.m., Tues., Nov. 13, 1984 – Colombia's largest volcano, Nevado del Ruiz, erupted for the first time in nearly 400 years. More than 25,000 people died. It was the most destructive volcanic eruption since Mount Pelee blew her top in 1902.

The eruption was followed by an avalanche of mud that wiped out the town of Armeno and most of its inhabitants. A study released one month before the disaster had concluded that an eruption was imminent and that Armeno was vulnerable. Tragically, this information was never relayed to the town's inhabitants.

9:11 p.m., Thurs., Mar. 17, 1955 –A riot broke out at the Montreal Forum following the first period of a Stanley Cup match between the Canadiens and the Detroit Red Wings.

Montreal fans, infuriated at a decision by NHL President Clarence Campbell, to suspend Canadiens star Maurice "Rocket" Richard for the rest of the playoffs, responded with a violence unprecedented in hockey history. They hurled ice and bottles, pelted and punched Campbell, and set off a tear gas bomb that sent spectators rushing for the exits, coughing and choking. The riot spread outside the Forum as thousands of fans went on a seven hour rampage of destruction and looting. Hundreds of innocent bystanders were accosted. Police arrested more than 100 people, but, miraculously, no one was hurt.

Detroit was awarded the win by forfeit. Richard had been watching the game from the stands after being banned from the playoffs for his part in a stick-swinging brawl in Boston.

Maurice Richard, the Montreal Canadiens all-time leading scorer, died May 27, 2000. He was 78 years old. Tens of thousands of Canadians lined up along Montreal's Rue de Ste. Catherine to pay their respects to the hockey giant.

9:12 p.m., Sat., May 8, 1982 – Canadian Formula One driver Gilles Villeneuve died seven hours after suffering a broken neck and severe head injuries during a practice run for the Grand Prix of Belgium. Villeneuve, one of the most aggressive drivers on the circuit, died after his car catapulted off the rear wheel of another car and somersaulted into a sandbank. The French-Canadian hero, who once admitted he would likely die or be seriously injured because of his go-for-broke style, won six races in four years on the Formula One circuit. Villeneuve was 32.

9:14 p.m., Sun., Nov. 14, 1948 – Prince Charles, the future King of England, was born at Buckingham Palace. Charles, who weighed in at seven pounds, six ounces, was the first baby born at the Palace since 1866.

Charles came into the world just six days before the first anniversary of the wedding of Princess Elizabeth and Prince Philip on November 20, 1947.

A riot broke out at the Montreal Forum following the first period of a Stanley Cup match.

Patricia Hearst, daughter of millionaire publisher Randolph Hearst, was kidnapped.

The princess became Queen Elizabeth II when her father, George VI, died in 1952.

9:15 **p.m., Thurs., Apr. 6, 1893** – The longest recorded boxing match with gloves on began in New Orleans. The bout between Andy Bowen and Jack Burke lasted 110 rounds, ending seven hours and 19 minutes later at 4:34 a.m., when neither man was able to continue. First declared no contest, the result was later changed to a draw.

9:20 **p.m., Mon,. Feb. 4, 1974** – Patricia Hearst, daughter of millionaire publisher Randolph Hearst, was kidnapped from her apartment in Berkeley, California. A previously unknown group calling itself the Symbionese Liberation Army demanded $4 million worth of food be distributed to the poor as ransom for her release.

The story took a major twist in April when Hearst assisted the SLA in the robbing of a San Francisco bank. Earlier, she had sent a message to her parents saying she was joining the SLA cause. In May, police stormed a house and killed five people suspected in the kidnapping – but Hearst was not found until September, 1975, when she was arrested in San Francisco. Convicted of armed robbery in March, 1976, Hearst was sentenced to seven years in prison, but the sentence was commuted in January, 1979 by President Carter. Later that year, Patty Hearst married her bodyguard, Bernard Shaw.

9:23 **p.m., Fri., Aug. 20, 1999** – The T. Eaton Company filed for bankruptcy, giving up an uphill struggle to survive after 130 years. Earlier, major supplier Tommy Hilfiger, Ltd., moved into Eaton's Quebec stores with a court order and began seizing merchandise. The bankruptcy move came after last-ditch efforts to find a buyer for the department store chain failed.

Eaton's began liquidating its stock the week after the bankruptcy announcement. The company that Timothy Eaton started in 1869, which had grown to become a Canadian institution, did not die completely. Sears purchased several Eaton's stores and retained the historic name at some locations.

9:24 **p.m., Thurs., Nov. 4, 1847** – Felix Mendelssohn, German composer and conductor, whose best-known work is the "Wedding March," died of a stroke at age 36. Mendelssohn, a child prodigy, wrote his "Midsummer Night's Dream" at the age of 17 and later composed the masterful "String Quarter in F Minor" among other works. The music world is also indebted to Mendelssohn for his rediscovery of the work of J.S. Bach after years of neglect.

9:24 **p.m., Tues., Nov. 15, 1994** – Martina Navratilova's singles career ended, as she lost to Gabriella Sabatini in a New York tournament.

Navratilova won a record 167 singles championships, 18 of them in Grand Slam tournaments (she won 31 more Grand Slam titles in doubles). During the 1980s she was victorious in an incredible 92 per cent of her singles matches. Navratilova won Wimbledon nine times and won at least one tournament for each of her 21 years on tour.

In 2000, Navratilova made a comeback as a doubles competitor.

9:30 **p.m., Tues., June 1, 1926** – Marilyn Monroe was born in a Los Angeles hospital. Her birth name was Norma Jean Baker. The future sex symbol and screen icon would live to be only 36 years old.

Monroe starred in films such as *The Seven Year Itch* and *Some Like It Hot*. An insecure woman prone to depression, she wed three times, including marriages to baseball star Joe DiMaggio and playwright Arthur Miller. It wasn't until Monroe applied for her first marriage licence at 16 that she discovered she was illegitimate. Her mother, Gladys Baker, had a history of mental disturbances and was confined to an institution for most of Marilyn's childhood.

In 1945, while working in a defense plant, Monroe was asked to pose for some photographs to help boost morale in the military. In 1946, 20th Century Fox signed her to a one-year contract and changed her name to Marilyn Monroe.

9:30 **p.m., Wed., Oct. 28, 1959** – A caller to the Lowe's Midland Theater in Kansas City warned that a bomb would explode – right in the middle of a concert given by opera singer Maria Callas. The bomb was planted somewhere in the orchestra pit, said the caller. Callas was unfazed.

Marilyn Monroe was born in a Los Angeles hospital.

The "No" vote in the Quebec Referendum finally edged ahead of the "Yes" vote.

She insisted on singing the first section of her program before the theatre was evacuated.

"I had to let them see me, otherwise someone would have said, ah, that's Callas for you, always cancelling," she explained.

No bomb was found.

Callas, American-born but of Greek heritage, was one of the 20th century's greatest opera singers. She retired in 1965 after an 18-year career that took her to all the world's great opera houses. Maria Callas died, aged 53, of a heart attack in Paris at 1:30 p.m. on Thursday, September 16, 1977.

9:30 p.m., Mon., Oct. 30, 1995 – The "No" vote in the Quebec Referendum finally edged ahead of the "Yes" vote, after trailing all night. When it was all over, Québécois voting not to separate from Canada eked out a narrow victory over those voting in favour of separation – 50.4 to 49.6 per cent – a margin of 52,000 votes out of 4.6 million cast. Turnout was an incredible 94.5 per cent. Quebec premier Jacques Parizeau resigned the next day in the wake of election night comments wherein he blamed the loss on "money and the ethnic vote."

Some observers credited a massive pro-Canada rally in Montreal on the Friday before the vote as the spark that edged the "No" vote to a win.

Lucien Bouchard, popular leader of the federal separatist Bloc Québécois, succeeded Parizeau as Quebec premier. Bouchard vowed to hold yet another referendum – Quebec's third – when "winning conditions are," as he put it, "right."

9:30 p.m., Fri., Sept. 5, 1997 – Mother Teresa, the petite nun with an enormous heart, died of cardiac arrest.

Mother Teresa, called "the Saint of the Gutters" by many, was awarded the Nobel Peace Prize in 1979. She opened her "Missionaries of Charity" with 12 original followers in Calcutta. Today, Missionaries of Charity has thousands of followers working in 450 centres around the world.

Calcutta was Mother Teresa's adopted home, although she was born in what is now Macedonia. She was plagued with health problems during her later years, and suffered a heart attack while meeting the Pope in 1983.

Mother Teresa's motto was: "Pray together and we stay together, and if we stay together, we'll love each other as God loves you."

9:30 **p.m., Sun., Sept. 8, 1935** – Huey "Kingfish" Long, the powerful Louisiana Senator who made more enemies than friends with his dictatorial tactics, was shot as he walked from the chamber of the Louisiana House of Representatives. He died about 30 hours later, aged 42. Long's assassin was Dr. Carl Weiss, who himself died in a hail of bullets from Long's bodyguards seconds afterwards. Weiss was the leader of an anti-Long faction and son-in-law of Judge P.H. Pavy, another opponent of the Senator.

A month earlier, Long claimed to have overheard a plot to kill him while he was staying in a New Orleans hotel. A bomb was sent to his office earlier that year, but failed to explode.

Long, a vociferous critic of President Roosevelt, was considered a possible third-party presidential candidate for 1936.

All in the Family, one of television's most controversial series and also one of its most popular, debuted.

9:30 **p.m., Tues., Jan. 12, 1971** – *All in the Family*, one of television's most controversial series and also one of its most popular, debuted on CBS.

TV would never be the same again.

The show, based on the British series *Till Death Do Us Part*, featured Archie Bunker, a bigoted, middle-aged working-class man played by Carroll O'Connor. No minority group was safe from the outspoken Archie, who lambasted black people, Puerto Ricans and any ethnic or religious group apart from his own. Archie was really in his glory with son-in-law Mike Stivic (played by Rob Reiner), who was not only Polish but a liberal and an unemployed student. Rounding out the cast were Edith Bunker, Archie's slow-witted but well-meaning wife (played by Jean Stapleton), and daughter Gloria (Sally Struthers), a dizzy blonde.

All in the Family was the number-one ranked show in the Nielsen ratings during each of its first five seasons on the air. The show's successor, *Archie Bunker's Place* made the top 15 for three years.

9:30 **p.m., Sun., Oct. 2, 1955** – *Alfred Hitchcock Presents*, the popular suspense anthology, was shown on CBS-TV for the first time. The program featured dead pan introductions and summations from the pudgy English director. The show became the *Alfred Hitchcock Hour* in 1962. It left the air in 1965, was revived in 1985, cancelled in 1986, and finally revived again in 1987 with Hitchcock's black and white introductions colorized.

Hockey Night in Canada **debuted on the CBC television network.**

Despite his TV success, Hitchcock is best remembered for his work on the silver screen. Hitchcock, who often noted that he " liked to make the audience suffer," directed such classic films as *Vertigo, North by Northwest* and the chilling *Psycho.* His innovative camera techniques and masterful timing kept many an audience on the edge of its seats. Film connoisseurs delighted in one of Hitchcock's more eccentric habits – he would cast himself in a small cameo role, sometimes lasting only a few seconds – in every film he made.

In 1940, Hitchcock's *Rebecca* won the Oscar for best picture, the only time one of his films was so honoured.

Alfred Hitchcock died at 9:17 a.m., Tuesday, April 29, 1980 in Los Angeles at the age of 80.

9:30 **p.m., Mon., June 24, 1957** – CBC-TV televised *Front Page Challenge* for the first time. It would remain on the air for 38 years as the longest-running public affairs show in Canadian history.

The show invited a panel of "experts" to identify the hidden newsmakers of the week through a series of questions to which the responses would be either yes or no – much like the game "Twenty Questions."

Win Barron was the show's first host; the panel consisted of Gordon Sinclair, Scott Young, Toby Robbins and Alex Barris. The hidden newsmakers of the week were Alfred Scadding, survivor of the Moose Bay mining disaster, Madame Alex Legros, the midwife present at the birth of the Dionne quintuplets, and Montreal mayor Jean Drapeau. Future guest newsmakers would include Eleanor Roosevelt, Gordie Howe, Duke Ellington and Pierre Trudeau.

In June, 2000, veteran *Front Page Challenge* panelist, Betty Kennedy, who was with the show from 1962-1995, was appointed to the Canadian Senate.

9:30 **p.m., Sat., Nov. 1, 1952** – *Hockey Night in Canada* debuted on the CBC television network with a matchup between the Toronto Maple Leafs and the Boston Bruins at Maple Leaf Gardens. The game actually began at 8 p.m., but did not go to air until 90 minutes later. Boston won the contest 3–2.

CBC's policy of not televising *Hockey Night in Canada* games from the first drop of the puck continued into the latter half of the 60s, although the broadcast time for an 8:00 p.m. game was moved up to 8:30 p.m. Many fans would listen to the first part of the game on radio before switching to the televised portion.

9:30 **p.m., Thurs., Sept. 2, 1880** – The first night game in baseball history concluded at Nantasket Beach, Massachusetts, as some 300 spectators watched an amateur team representing Jordan, Marsh & Company play to a 16–16 tie with rival department store, R.H. White & Company. The field was illuminated by 36 carbon arc lamps propped on three 30-metre (100-foot) towers.

Apparently the first experiment in night baseball did not go well. Spectators could discern little more than the pitcher's movements; inadequate lighting caused many errors and mishaps on the field.

The first night game involving professional teams was not played until 1927, and the major leagues did not introduce the practice until 1935.

9:34 **p.m., Wed., July 13, 1977** – A blackout hit the Big Apple on the hottest night of the summer. The resultant chaos was accompanied by looting; 3,300 people were arrested and 78 of York York's finest were injured as the city's ugly side turned uglier.

New York's subways were immobilized, as were trains, elevators – anything that relied on electricity for power. And, perhaps worst of all, there was no air-conditioning in the 32-degree Celsius (90-degree Fahrenheit) heat.

Power was restored to most areas the next day. The blackout was caused by lightning from an electrical storm that stung power lines and generating stations.

9:34 **p.m., Thurs., July 8, 1993** – One hundred and fourteen years of boxing ended at New York's Madison Square Garden when Lonnie Bradley floored fellow middleweight "Big Time" Marcel Huffnaker with a left hook to end the last match in the Garden's history.

Boxing had had a long run at the Garden, beginning in 1879. Thousands of bouts followed, among the more famous, Joe Frazier vs. Mohammad Ali in 1971. Garden boxing faded from prominence with the advent of cable, pay-per-view television and the development of other, more glamorous venues, such as Las Vegas.

A blackout hit the Big Apple on the hottest night of the summer.

U. S. President Lyndon Johnson told a stunned nation that he would not stand for re-nomination.

Only 1,706 people watched the last fight card at the Garden. No mention of the fact that it was the last fight card appeared on the marquee.

9:35 **p.m., Sun., Mar. 31, 1968** – U. S. President Lyndon Johnson told a stunned nation that he would not stand for re-nomination by the Democratic Party. His announcement came at the end of a 35-minute televised speech to some 70 million Americans on the war in Vietnam. The subject was fitting, because it was the Vietnam War that led to the demise of the Johnson presidency.

Almost lost in the shock of the announcement, was Johnson's order, earlier in the speech, to halt the bombing of North Vietnam.

Lyndon Baines Johnson became the 36th American president on November 22, 1963 following the assassination of John F. Kennedy. He served as a healing force during the dark days following the assassination, but his administration proved to be controversial. While praised for the Civil Rights Act of 1964 and for his war on poverty – the so-called Great Society – Johnson's millstone proved to be Vietnam.

U.S. involvement in Vietnam, which had its roots in the Kennedy administration, escalated greatly under Johnson, who dispatched the first group of 3,500 Marines to that country in February, 1965. By 1968, the number of U.S. troops in Vietnam was 550,000. The war spawned an anti-war movement that divided the country and undermined the U.S. war effort.

Prior to the presidency, Johnson represented his home state of Texas in the House, and then the Senate. He accepted the number-two spot on the 1960 Democratic ticket reluctantly, but historians believed that Kennedy would have lost the election without the strength of his running mate's presence.

Johnson died at 4:33 p.m., on Monday, January 22, 1973, while en route to a San Antonio, Texas, hospital after suffering a heart attack at the LBJ Ranch. Johnson, the first southerner to occupy the Oval Office since Andrew Johnson a century before, was 74.

9:39 **p.m., Fri., Aug. 6, 1926** – Gertrude Ederle became the first woman to swim the English Channel, and she did it in the fastest time the feat has ever been done. The New York swimmer crossed the channel in exactly 14-1/2 hours, breaking the previous record by more than two hours. Ederle also beat Wall Street odds of 3–1 against the success of her achievement.

9:40 **p.m., Wed., Feb. 16, 1898** – The USS *Maine* blew up in Havana harbour with the loss of 266 lives. The news fueled hysteria in the United States, and led to the Spanish-American War, which U.S. Secretary of State John Hay would call a "splendid little war." Canadians, although generally sympathetic with the Americans, were prevented from entering into the conflict by British neutrality laws. Spain transferred its diplomats to Canada and espionage was rampant.

The war ended in December, 1898. Spain was forced to cede Cuba, Puerto Rico, Guam and the Philippines to the U.S. for a payment of $20 million.

No one knows for sure how the *Maine* was blown up. U.S. researchers at the time suggested a mine; the sensationalist press was relentless in linking that hypothesis to the Spanish government. However, a study conducted 62 years later, by U.S. Admiral Hyman Rickover, concluded that the explosion was caused by an accidental fire aboard ship. And even if the *Maine* was blown up by a mine, some historians believe extremists, and not the Spanish government, may have been involved. Ferdinand Lundberg, a biographer of William Randolf Hearst, has even suggested the newspaper magnate may have been behind the explosion. The mystery of the *Maine* continues.

9:40 **p.m., Sun., Aug. 6, 1978** – Pope Paul VI, who had served for 25 years on the throne of St. Peter, died following a heart attack at his residence at Castel Gandolfo. He was 80. Paul created controversy during his reign when he upheld the Roman Catholic church's ban on artificial methods of birth control, despite the world-wide population explosion. In 1966, another papal ruling permitted Roman Catholics to eat meat on Fridays for the first time in the church's history.

9:40 **p.m., Thurs., Feb. 3, 1966** – The unmanned Soviet module *Luna 9* became the first man-made spacecraft to achieve a soft landing on the moon. Less than three and a half years before *Apollo 11*, the Soviets appeared well on their way toward placing the first man on the moon. However, a series of mishaps and technical problems hit the Soviet space program, and the Americans achieved that distinction.

Soviet module *Luna 9* became the first man-made spacecraft to achieve a soft landing on the moon.

Joseph Stalin died of a stroke at age 73.

9:45 p.m., Thurs., Aug. 11, 1994 —The Seattle Mariners completed an 8–1 victory over the Oakland A's, and all of major league baseball went out on strike. A proposed salary cap, and the free agency system were at the heart of the players' union dispute with the major league baseball owners. The Mariners–A's game turned out to be the last game of the season as players stayed on strike until the following April.

Scattered boos were heard as Mariner Randy Johnson hurled the ball past Oakland's Ernie Young for the final out. Fittingly, the last pitch of the season was a strike.

9:50 p.m., Thurs., Mar. 5, 1953 – Joseph Stalin died of a stroke at age 73. Stalin, who ruled Russia as its undisputed leader for nearly 30 years, had been in a coma for four days prior to his death.

Stalin came to power in 1924 following the death of Vladimir Lenin. Shrewd and ruthless, his name meant "Man of Steel". The Soviet dictator eliminated those who disagreed with his policies and those who posed a threat to his power. He is reported to have sent about 20 million people to their deaths, as well as forcing equally large numbers into labour camps.

Stalin shocked the world when he signed a non-aggression pact with Hitler in 1939. It proved to be a smart move, buying the Soviets time to prepare for a Nazi strike. The Russian defeat of Hitler at Leningrad in 1943 is regarded as the turning point of World War II, as Stalin crushed the German army.

The United States and the Soviet Union, former allies, became enemies after the war, as the Western world feared Communist domination. And the world entered into the Cold War.

After his death, Stalin was replaced as premier by Georgi Malenkov, although Nikita Krushchev rapidly emerged as the true Soviet leader. Soviet leaders of the Cold War sharply downgraded Stalin's reputation in the country.

10 p.m. to 10:59 p.m.

- Chinese quash pro-democracy demonstration
- *Twilight Zone* debuts
- Mt. Etna erupts
- Charles Lindbergh lands in Paris
- John Lennon gunned down
- Neil Armstrong steps on moon

10:00 **p.m., Sun., Oct. 18, 1931** – Many U.S. citizens observed a voluntary "dim-out" in honour of Thomas Alva Edison, who had died earlier that day. Edison, whose inventive genius gave the world the electric light, the phonograph, the movie camera, and over 1,000 other inventions, died at his home in West Orange, New Jersey. Edison was 84 years old and had suffered from uremic poisoning.

A suggestion that all electric power in the U.S. be turned off briefly as a tribute was dismissed as being too dangerous for the nation. So a "dim-out" was observed instead.

Edison, who had only three months of formal education and was partially deaf, created his first invention – an electric vote-recorder – when he was 21. Ironically, it was one of his few inventions that did not sell. Edison was more successful with his dictating machine, his mimeograph machine and his storage battery. He was also the originator of the modern research laboratory, where many creators work together as a team, a common practice in industry today.

10:00 **p.m., Mon., July 27, 1953** – The guns in Korea were stilled by armistice, after three years of battle. The war was not officially over, but there would be no more fighting. The Korean conflict cost the lives of 56,000 Americans, 516 Canadians, more than a million South Koreans

Chinese troops began firing into a crowd of pro-democracy demonstrators gathered in Beijing's Tiananmen Square.

and an equal number of Communists. Millions of South Koreans were left homeless.

The war left a stalemate. Korea was divided between the Communist North and a democratic South. A demilitarized zone separating the two nations would be patrolled by over 1,700,000 troops. Relations between the two countries were virtually non-existent. Finally, in June, 2000, North Korea signed an accord with its southern counterpart, putting an official end to war on the Korean peninsula, and beginning a peace process that may ultimately lead to a union of the Koreas once again.

10:00 p.m., Fri., June 2, 1989 – Chinese troops began firing into a crowd of pro-democracy demonstrators gathered in Beijing's Tiananmen Square. By the time the guns fell silent, more than 2,000 people lay dead.

The Chinese pro-democracy movement began in April when students rallied in support of democratic reform after the death of Hu Yoabang, Chairman of the Communist Party. They were joined by Chinese intellectuals, workers, and civil servants. Tiananmen Square became a focal point for change, in China and around the world. By May, there were over a million people in the Square. The protestors proved to be a disruptive embarrassment to hard-liner Deng Xioping's government during a historic state visit by Soviet leader Mikhail Gorbachev. On May 20, Deng placed the country in a state of martial law. The protestors, aware that the world was watching, demanded the government resign. Deng ordered the pro-democracy movement crushed.

During the massacre, Chinese troops fired wildly into groups of demonstrators and even drove tanks over occupied vehicles. Hundreds of people were arrested and many others were executed all over China as the government successfully quashed the revolution.

The United States halted arms sales to China in response, but refused to cut diplomatic or economic ties.

10:00 p.m., Fri., Dec. 11, 1936 – Edward VIII began his abdication speech, wherein he announced he was giving up the throne "for the woman he loved." The monarch told his British subjects it would be impossible for him to fulfill his duties without the support of the woman he wanted to marry, Mrs. Wallis Simpson, an American twice divorced.

Although Edward, who was also leader of the Church of England, was technically allowed to wed a divorced woman and retain his crown, the royal family believed that the public outcry against such a move would undermine its position. The situation was complicated by Edward's apparent admiration for the early policies of Germany's National Socialist party.

Edward became the Duke of Windsor. He and Mrs. Simpson were wed in 1937. The ceremony was not attended by any member of his immediate family.

Edward's brother, Albert, the Duke of York, succeeded him and reigned as George VI. It would be he, and his wife Elizabeth, who would help steer Britain through the horrors of World War II.

The first Trans-Canada flight from Toronto's Malton Airport departed for Vancouver.

10:00 p.m., Mon., Apr. 3, 1939 – The first Trans-Canada flight from Toronto's Malton Airport departed for Vancouver. It was not a direct flight; the plane stopped in North Bay, Kapuskasing, Winnipeg, Regina, and Lethbridge before finally touching down in Vancouver at 11:10 a.m. PST, more than 10 hours later. The historic flight, on a Lockheed 14 Super Electra, carried 10 passengers and a crew of three. The round-trip cost $225, not cheap considering the value of a dollar in 1939.

Today, Malton airport is known as Pearson International Airport, and a non-stop Toronto-Vancouver flight takes about four hours.

10:00 p.m., Tues., Feb.. 14, 1984 – Nine perfect scores of 6.0 flashed on the scoreboard at Sarajevo's figure skating arena during the 1984 Winter Games in Yugoslavia. Ice dancers Jayne Torvill and Christopher Dean of Britain earned the perfect scores for artistic impression in the free skate finale of the ice dancing competition. It was the first time in the history of competitive figure skating that nine perfect scores had been so awarded.

Torvill, who worked in an insurance office, and Dean, a police constable, entered the 1984 Games as heavy favourites. Following a fifth-place finish in the 1980 Games in Lake Placid, Torvill and Dean won three world ice dancing titles to establish total dominance of their sport.

For the 1984 Games, the British duo skated a breathtaking four-minute interpretation of "Bolero" that elicited a thunderous ovation and a shower of flowers from an appreciative audience.

Rocky Marciano, the only heavy-weight boxing champion to retire with an undefeated record, died in a plane crash.

10:00 p.m., Sun., Aug. 31, 1969 – Former ditch-digger Rocky Marciano, the only heavyweight boxing champion to retire with an undefeated record, died in a plane crash near Newton, Iowa. He was headed to a party the next day marking his 46th birthday. Marciano, who retired after knocking out Archie Moore in 1955 for his 49th straight victory, held the heavyweight crown for three years.

In 1969, Marciano "defeated" Muhammad Ali in a computerized fight to determine the all-time boxing champion. Marciano died before the result was announced.

10:00 p.m., Fri., Nov. 21, 1980 – The famed "Who Shot J.R.?" episode of *Dallas*, aired on CBS. Nearly 80 per cent of the night's television audience tuned in to find out who perpetrated the evil deed which ended the *Dallas* season of the previous spring.

All summer long, *Dallas* fans argued about the possibilities, and betting parlours took in millions of dollars. Finally, late in the first show of the fall season, viewers had the answer. The culprit was Kristen – played by Mary Crosby. J.R (played by Larry Hagman) recovered from his wounds, of course, and, equally predictably, Kristen was never prosecuted.

Dallas ended its 13-year run on CBS on May 3, 1991.

10:00 p.m., Thurs., Jan., 15, 1981 – The gritty police drama *Hill Street Blues*, debuted on NBC. The critically-acclaimed show spent six seasons in NBC's prime-time lineup.

Hill Street Blues focused on the events in and around Hill Street Station, the fictional precinct run by its respected captain Frank Furillo (Daniel J. Travanti). The large ensemble included, among others, Officer Andy Renko (Charles Haid), Detective Mick Belker (Bruce Weitz), Lieutenant Norman Buntz (Dennis Franz), Lieutenant Howard Hunter (James B. Sikking) and Joyce Davenport (Veronica Hamel), Furillo's second wife.

No holds were barred in this realistic series created by Steven Bochco, which mixed drama and comedy, to reveal the underside of police work. Each show opened with a 7 a.m. roll call, establishing the stories to be followed in the episode. Each show ended at night; viewers had effectively lived a day in the life of "The Blues."

In 1982, the creators of *Hill Street* explored another milieu when they introduced television viewers to life at Boston's *St. Elsewhere* hospital. This dramatic series would also remain in prime time for six seasons, despite less-than-blockbuster ratings. It was both an artistic, and a critical success, raising the art of TV drama to new highs. The show's stories mirrored real life; not every ending was a happy one – a fact which served to endear *St. Elsewhere* to its loyal viewers.

10:00 p.m., Tues., Sept. 27, 1938 – *The Pepsodent Show* starring Bob Hope debuted on the NBC radio network. It was the beginning of a 10-year run and the highlight of Hope's 20-year radio career. *The Pepsodent Show* was one of the most popular shows in the history of radio, drawing an audience share as high at 40 per cent in 1942.

Its star, born in England, in 1903, as Leslie Townes Hope, first tried vaudeville with a partner named George Byrne, but soon tired of it. In 1928, Hope discovered the monologue, and never looked back. By the early 30s, he had already appeared in his first major Broadway role in *Ballyhoo* of 1932.

Bob Hope was a comedy machine. Once, during a four-minute monologue, he fired off 24 jokes. The rapid-fire delivery seemed effortless, but in fact was the result of much hard work. At one time, Hope had 12 writers. He would rehearse his material in 60 to 90-minute sessions before a live audience, sometimes spending an hour on a one-word change. Eventually, the script would be pared down to a 37-minute routine of his best material, and that would go on the radio.

Hope's radio years paralleled a successful film career that included the famous "Road" movies with Bing Crosby and Dorothy Lamour. Hope continued to appear on television after finishing with network radio in 1955. And for years, he entertained the troops overseas with his popular U.S.O. tours. Thanks for the memories, Bob.

10:00 p.m., Tues., Apr. 16, 1935 – *Fibber McGee and Molly* debuted on NBC's Blue Network. The show, which ran for 24 years on network radio, featured Jim and Marian Jordan as Fibber and Molly McGee.

Early episodes focused on the couple's travels down U.S. Route 42 in an old jalopy. Later, the show was located around the home. Everything was

The Pepsodent Show Starring Bob Hope debuted on the NBC radio network.

The science fiction anthology, *Twilight Zone*, debuted.

played for laughs. McGee told a traffic court "a red light was a dead light if the light ain't lit." Other characters, family members, friends, and residents of the imaginary town of Wistful Vista, were introduced on a regular basis. There was also music – presented by such talents as the Ted Weems Orchestra, or Perry Como. And all of it was live.

Fibber McGee and Molly was the top-rated show of 1943 and for many other years after that. The down-to-earth, non-pretentious approach meant that everyone could relate to it.

10:00 **p.m., Fri., Oct. 2, 1959** – The science fiction anthology, *Twilight Zone*, debuted on CBS-TV.

Twilight Zone was the brainchild of Rod Serling, Emmy-Award-winning writer whose work included *Requiem For a Heavyweight*, the first 90-minute drama written especially for the TV screen.

Serling was born on Christmas Day in 1924. He would enlist in the U.S. Army 11th Airborne Division and see combat in the Philippines before turning to the crafting of words. By 1955, Serling was able to support himself and his family through his writing.

He wrote 92 episodes for *Twilight Zone*, and the show rapidly achieved cult status for its eerie explorations of mysteriously haunting personalities and ironic themes. Serling was angered by network censorship of creative drama, and believed that by giving his program an outer space setting, some of the constraints other writers faced might not be applied to his work.

CBS aired a total of 152 *Twilight Zone* episodes during the five years the show was on the air. Each was introduced by Serling personally. One of the introductions used was: "You unlock this door with the key of imagination. Beyond it is another dimension – a dimension of sound, a dimension of sight, a dimension of mind. You're moving into a land of both shadow and substance, of things and ideas. You've just crossed over into the Twilight Zone."

Many top actors appeared on *Twilight Zone*, including Burt Reynolds, Robert Redford, Dennis Hopper, Burgess Meredith, Peter Falk, William Shatner and Buster Keaton.

The original show went off the air in 1964 but has been shown in reruns ever since. Rod Serling returned to his alma mater, Antioch College in Ohio to lecture and teach. He continued to write screenplays – *Seven Days in May* (1964) and *Planet of the Apes* (1968) were only two of his many lasting creations. He also came back to TV as creator and host of the mystery anthology series *Night Gallery*, which ran on NBC from 1970 to 1973.

Rod Serling died on June 28, 1975 in Rochester, New York, from the results of a coronary bypass operation. He was 50.

10:00 **p.m., Thurs., July 8, 1954** – NBC broadcast the first regularly scheduled network show to appear in colour. It was a little-known live comedy series called *The Marriage*, starring future Oscar-winner Jessica Tandy and veteran character actor Hume Cronyn, both of whom brought their roles to TV from radio. *The Marriage* lasted for only seven episodes.

10:00 **p.m., Fri., Mar. 8, 1669** – Sicily's Mount Etna erupted. 20,000 people were killed as lava buried more than 14 cities and towns. The city of Palermo was covered with lava at depths of up to 12 metres (40 feet).

10:00 **p.m., Sun., July 21, 1935** – Louis "Satchmo" (short for Satchelmouth) Armstrong, a man who never forgot his roots, opened the first in a series of six concerts for underprivileged black people in New Orleans. Admission for the first three shows was $1.00 apiece. Admission for the last three performances was free. All of the concerts were staged at the Golden Dragon.

Claiming to be born on July 4, 1900, Louis Armstrong learned to play the cornet as an inmate in a New Orleans reformatory. He rose from his humble beginnings to become one of the world's best-known and loved entertainers. Armstrong's popularity spanned three generations, from his first hit, "Muskrat Ramble" in 1926, to the posthumous hit "Wonderful World" in 1988. Perhaps his best-known song came near the twilight of his career, when "Hello Dolly" burst from Broadway to the top of the *Billboard* charts in 1964, 32 years after Armstrong's only other number-one song, "All of Me," in 1932.

When asked the secret of his success, Armstrong explained, "I set myself to be a happy man, and I made it."

Louis Armstrong was 71 years old when he died in New York of a heart attack on July 6, 1971.

20,000 people were killed as lava buried more than 14 cities and towns.

The last Beatles concert wrapped up at San Francisco's Candlestick Park.

10:01 p.m., Mon., Sept. 29, 1966 – An unforgettable era in music ended as the last Beatles concert wrapped up at San Francisco's Candlestick Park. The Beatles' 34-minute set began with "Roll Over Beethoven" and concluded with "Long Tall Sally." Preceding the Fab Four on stage were the Ronettes, the Cyrkle and the Remains. More than 25,000 screaming Beatlemaniacs watched the show.

The Beatles did not know that Candlestick would be their last live gig. The final three and a half years of the group's assocation was spent in the studio, turning out such classic albums as *Sgt. Pepper's Lonely Hearts Club Band*, the *White Album* and *Abbey Road*.

10:02 p.m., Thurs., Nov. 12, 1981 – The first manned balloon crossing of the Pacific was completed when *Double Eagle V*, carrying Americans Ben Abruzzo, Larry Newman and Ron Clark along with Rocky Aoki of Japan, crash-landed in a remote area near Covelo, California. They had crossed the California coastline about an hour earlier – four days after leaving Nagashima, Japan.

The Pacific crossing was a constant battle because of ice. The craft lost so much altitude at one point, that cameras, tape recorders, video tapes and clothes were thrown overboard to keep it aloft.

10:04 p.m., Thurs., Mar. 16, 1978 – British oil tanker *Amoco Cadiz* ran aground off France's Britanny coast. The ship broke in two, spewing 44 million gallons of oil onto nearby beaches and fishing grounds.

The accident took place almost 12 hours after the ship's steering system failed, leaving the craft helpless in bad seas and high winds. All 43 crewmen on board were rescued by helicopter.

10:04 p.m., Wed., May 1, 1991 – Nolan Ryan amazed the baseball world when he fired the seventh no-hitter of his career – at age 44. The Texas right-hander tied a Ranger team record for strikeouts by fanning 16, as the Rangers blanked the visiting Toronto Blue Jays 3–0. Going into the game, the Jays had the highest batting average in major league baseball.

Ryan tossed his first no-hitter in 1973 while with the California Angels. He has three more no-hitters than the number-two man on the all-time list, Sandy Koufax.

10:08 **p.m., Mon., Apr. 13, 1970** – *Apollo 13* astronaut Jack Swigert radioed "OK, Houston, we've had a problem here."

Just moments before – and only nine minutes after completing a television broadcast from the command module – Swigert and fellow astronauts James Lovell and Fred Haise were startled by a loud bang. Unknown to them, an oxygen tank had exploded aboard the command module. The astronauts were stranded 205,000 km from earth in a spacecraft carrying insufficient oxygen. Mission control quickly assembled a rescue plan which would see the spacecraft loop around the moon before heading back to earth, and splashdown. With an unreliable engine in the command module, all course corrections would have to be made by the lunar module – an unprecedented situation. The astronauts were forced to transfer from the relatively spacious command module to the cramped and cold lunar module, where they would spend the next three and a half days.

Just prior to re-entry, the exhausted travellers transferred back to the command module and a waiting world held its breath.

Apollo 13 splashed down within sight of its recovery vessel – aircraft carrier *Iwo Jima*. Ironically, it was the most accurate splashdown in history and the fastest recovery. The three astronauts were tired and more than a little stressed, but all of them passed medical muster upon their return.

None of the astronauts flew into space again. Swigert died of cancer in 1982 – the first U.S. astronaut to die of natural causes.

The story of the *Apollo 13* mission was immortalized in the film *Apollo 13*, directed by Ron Howard, and starring Tom Hanks – who won an Oscar for his performance.

10:10 **p.m., Tues., July 1, 1941** – WNBT in New York City broadcast the world's first television commercial, a 20-second ad for Bulova watches that ended with the announcer reading the time. The spot cost $9.

10:13 **p.m., Fri., Apr. 14, 1865** – President Lincoln was shot in the back of the head by actor John Wilkes Booth as he watched the play *Our American Cousin* at Ford's Theater in Washington, D.C. Lincoln died just over nine hours later.

President Lincoln was shot in the back of the head by actor John Wilkes Booth.

The MD-11 jumbo jet crashed into the Atlantic Ocean off Peggy's Cove, Nova Scotia.

10:14 **p.m., Wed., Sept. 2, 1998** – Swissair Flight 111 captain Urs Zimmerman radioed, "Pan! Pan! Pan! We have fire in the cockpit" to the control tower in Moncton, New Brunswick. Seventeen minutes later, his MD-11 jumbo jet crashed into the Atlantic Ocean off Peggy's Cove, Nova Scotia. The pilot had dumped fuel just prior to the crash as he prepared for an emergency landing in Halifax. All 229 aboard the aircraft died. The time of the crash – 10:31 p.m. – is marked annually by a moment of silence at a memorial near the crash site.

Stories of good luck and bad emerged after the accident. Swiss tennis player Marc Rosset, 27, and his coach cancelled plans to fly on Flight 111 in order to practise. UN official Pierce Gerety, 56, wasn't so lucky. He was bumped from one flight to another, then to a third flight – Flight 111.

Cockpit voice recordings later suggested that the Swissair pilots disagreed on emergency procedures shortly before the crash. The co-pilot wanted to ignore rules about dumping fuel and land the plane immediately. The pilot rejected that proposal, preferring to follow emergency procedures by the book. As the pilots debated what to do, the cockpit filled with smoke, and the plane plummeted.

10:15 **p.m., Sat., Nov. 28, 1942** – Busboy Stanley Tomaszewski tried to replace a light bulb in the Melody Lounge at Boston's Cocoanut Grove Club. Instead, he ignited an artificial palm tree.

The flames spread with lightning speed, dancing across the cloth ceiling, showering sparks on the crowd. Within seconds, the Melody Lounge was a cauldron of smoke and fire, jammed with screaming patrons. The flames spread to the main dining room upstairs. Diners attempting to escape found the main entrance blocked by the crowd fleeing the Melody Lounge. Ten of the nightclub's twelve exits were blocked or permanently locked.

Four hundred and ninety-one people died, most of them from smoke inhalation. Among the victims was western movie star Buck Jones, who was on hand to promote war bonds. The death toll might have been higher. A victory party scheduled that night for supporters of the Boston College football team was cancelled when the team was upset 55–12 by Holy Cross. The Cocoanut Grove fire led to major efforts in fire prevention and control for nightclubs and other related places of assembly.

10:15 **p.m., Tues., Feb. 13, 1945** – British bombers unleashed their first air raid over Dresden, the city nicknamed "The Florence of Germany." Bombs rained on the historic city for two days, killing 135,000 people. Countless works of priceless art were destroyed as were rare architectural structures from the 17th and 18th centuries.

The raid aroused much controversy because Dresden, with very few defenses, did not pose a military threat, and the Allies had the war well in hand.

Dresden has been rebuilt and its cultural status restored. Much of the older city has been recreated, albeit with modern building materials.

10:15 **p.m., Sat., June 6, 1891** – Sir John A. Macdonald, Canada's first prime minister, died following a stroke in Ottawa. The man known as the Father of Canada was 76.

Macdonald led the effort to bind the loosely associated collection of British colonies in North America into the Dominion of Canada. A native of Glasgow, Macdonald arrived in Canada at age five. He won his first elective office – as a Kingston alderman – at age 28, and quickly moved up the political ladder. Soon, the young politician began advocating his vision of an independent Canada. His efforts came to fruition the morning of March 11, 1867 when Ontario and Quebec voted to unite with Nova Scotia, New Brunswick and Prince Edward Island. By royal proclamation, the new country of Canada came into being July 1, 1867. John A. Macdonald received a knighthood for his work.

Macdonald, whose battles with the bottle were as legendary as his skill as a legislator, was forced from office by scandal in 1873 but returned in 1878. As Prime Minister, he pushed hard for a national railway that would link the western provinces with those in the east, spanning the continent from sea to sea. The completion of the Canadian Pacific Railway in 1885 was testament to Macdonald's ability to get things done against enormous odds. In 1884, Canadian soldiers were called upon to put down a Métis rebellion led by Louis Riel. Riel was taken prisoner, found guilty of treason and hanged.

Sir John A. Macdonald, Canada's first prime minister, died following a stroke.

Jacqueline Kennedy Onassis, often called America's eternal First Lady, died.

10:15 **p.m., Thurs, May 19, 1994** – Jacqueline Kennedy Onassis, often called America's eternal First Lady, died of cancer in her New York apartment. The widow of President John F. Kennedy and Greek tycoon Aristotle Onassis was 64.

Jackie was perhaps the closest the United States will ever come to having a queen. She helped set American fashion, was responsible for restoring and preserving the White House, was a popular figure on the world stage (the President once introduced himself as "the husband of Jacqueline Kennedy"), and even became an accomplished book editor. The moment of her life most people remember was when she cradled the head of the dying president in her hands after he was assassinated in Dallas in November, 1963.

Jackie was working as a photographer when she met John Fitzgerald Kennedy in 1951. They married in 1953. She would spend the rest of her life in the public eye despite every effort to live a private life. At one time, Jackie went 25 years without granting an interview. She did, however, tape 18 hours of her thoughts and reflections during the late 1960s. These will not be released until 2067, or after the death of her surviving child, Caroline.

10:20 **p.m., Tues., May 21, 1991** – Rajiv Gandhi, former prime minister of India, was killed when a bomb went off as he stepped out of his car to address an election meeting in southern India. Gandhi, whose grandfather and mother were both former prime ministers, was decapitated by the bomb that also took the lives of 13 others. The assassination took place in the middle of India's weeklong elections, which were postponed after the killings.

Just prior to his death, Gandhi had placed a garland on the statue of his mother, Indira, who was assassinated by her Sikh bodyguards in 1984.

The prime suspect in the assassination, a Tamil named Sivarasan, committed suicide three months later as police closed in on his hideout.

10:20 **p.m., Fri., May 29, 1942** – John Barrymore, "the Great Profile," considered one of America's greatest actors, died of myocarditis at age 60. Barrymore, who became the talk of the theatre world with his performances in *Hamlet* and *Richard III* during the 20s, also appeared in several movies. He performed *Hamlet* 101 times, a record unequalled by future thespians.

10:21 **p.m., Fri., May 20, 1927** – Charles Lindbergh made aviation history and became an instant international hero as he completed the first solo non-stop flight from New York to Paris. Lindbergh's *Spirit of St. Louis* landed at Le Bourget Airport after a 33-hour journey. He had flown 5,793 kilometres (3,600 miles).

Lindbergh, 25, took off from New York's Roosevelt Field. His plane was overloaded with gasoline, and almost crashed into trees at the end of the runway. Flying by dead reckoning, Lindbergh dropped to within a few metres of the Atlantic waves at one point. Upon arriving in Paris, he was mobbed by nearly 100,000 admirers. He was awarded the French Legion of Honour and received a ticker-tape parade in New York upon his arrival home. Not bad for a man who as a child had a severe fear of heights.

Lindbergh's charmed life was shattered on March 1, 1932 when his first child, Charles Augustus III, was kidnapped from the Lindbergh home in Hopewell, New Jersey.

Many people felt that Lindbergh's star waned when he began speaking out against American involvement in World War II and joined America First, an anti-war group. He was publicly insulted in April, 1941 when President Roosevelt called him defeatist. The America First movement collapsed after Pearl Harbor and Lindbergh supported the war effort, although he was barred from serving in the armed forces.

Lindbergh was a key figure in the establishment of Pan American Airlines. His wife, Anne Morrow Lindbergh, was a best-selling diarist, with a world-wide audience.

Charles Lindbergh embraced the cause of conservation during his later years, and worked hard for the Save the Whales cause. He died in 1974 at the age of 72.

10:30 **p.m., Thurs., Sept. 28, 1972** – Canadian right winger Paul Henderson scored a goal with just 34 seconds left in the game to give Canada a 6–5 win over the Soviet Union and triumph in the much-heralded Summit Series. Henderson's goal capped a Canadian comeback from a 5–3 deficit in the game, which was played in Moscow.

Foster Hewitt's famous call of "He scores! Henderson!" is firmly rooted in the minds of those who watched the game from half a world away. Canadians stood still, from St. John's to Victoria.

Charles Lindbergh made aviation history and became an instant international hero.

Leonardo da Vinci, a genius in both the worlds of art and science, was born.

Henderson scored the winning goal in each of the last three games as the Canadians won four, lost three and tied one in the tightly-contested series.

The series began at 8:29 p.m. on Saturday, September 2, 1972 when American referee Gordon Lee dropped the puck between Canadian Phil Esposito and Soviet Vladimir Petrov at centre ice at the Montreal Forum. Many fans predicted an 8–0 sweep for Team Canada, which was made up entirely of National Hockey League stars (superstar Bobby Hull had been deemed ineligible after defecting to the World Hockey Association). The underdog Soviet Union stunned the Canadians 7–3 in game one – alerting many Canadians to just how far Soviet hockey had come.

10:30 p.m., Sat., Apr. 15, 1452 – Leonardo da Vinci, a genius of both the worlds of art and science, was born in Vinci, Italy. Leonardo created some of the world's great artistic masterpieces, including the *Mona Lisa*, *The Virgin on the Rocks* and *The Last Supper*. But his scientific studies were equally, if not more amazing. Leonardo had notebooks crammed with projects and plans for future work. His detailed drawings of the human anatomy are nothing short of astounding. And more than four centuries before it flew, da Vinci drew diagrams of a helicopter. This man of many talents even taught himself to write left to right because as a left-hander he felt it was more natural.

Leonardo was somewhat hard on himself. Just before his death in 1519, he mused, "I have not laboured at my art as I should have done."

10:30 p.m., Wed., Oct. 29, 1969 – The first message was sent over ARPAnet, forerunner of the Internet, eight weeks after the first "node" of the Internet was connected late on the morning of September 2, 1969 at UCLA (University of California at Los Angeles). Three more nodes were connected before the year was out: Stanford Research Institute (SRI), University of California at Berkeley and the University of Utah.

Internet pioneer Leonard Kleinrock described the event as follows: "The transmission itself was simply to 'login' to SRI from UCLA. We succeeded in transmitting the 'l' and the 'o' and then the system crashed! Hence, the first message on the Internet was 'Lo!' We were able to do the full login about an hour later."

10:30 **p.m., Fri., Feb. 8, 1861** – Seven American states formally approved the Constitution of the Confederacy. North Carolina, Georgia, Florida, Alabama, Mississippi and Tennessee officially joined South Carolina in seceding from the United States to form the Confederate States of America. The Civil War between the North and the South would begin just over two months later.

10:30 **p.m., Sun., Oct. 31, 1926** – Harry Houdini, master conjurer and escape artist, died of peritonitis. He was 52.

Houdini's end was hastened when a man reputed to be an amateur boxer visited the star's dressing room and asked whether Houdini could, as claimed, withstand a heavy blow to the stomach. Houdini agreed to be punched but failed to brace himself in time for the three violent blows that followed. The resultant internal injuries led to his death the following day.

Houdini's ability as an escape artist was legendary. He freed himself from locks, sealed chests and prisons in a career that gained him worldwide fame, and some fortune. Houdini also dabbled in the occult. He promised to communicate with his widow after death, but several efforts by psychics to speak with him "from the other side" proved fruitless. His wife gave up trying in 1936. Ten years was long enough to wait for any man, she said.

10:30 **p.m., Sun., Mar. 28, 1920** – "America's Sweetheart," silent film star Mary Pickford married cinematic swashbuckler, Douglas Fairbanks, Sr., in Glendale, California. Both had recently been divorced from former mates, and their romance had long been rumoured.

Mary Pickford was born in Toronto as Gladys Marie Smith in 1893. She made her stage debut at age five and her first film at 16. By the time she was 23, Pickford was making $675,000 a year. When she joined First National, her salary rose to between one and two million dollars per picture, depending on the film's profits. Pickford was the first international screen idol, and the first to have her name emblazoned on a movie marquee. In 1919, she founded United Artists with Charles Chaplin, D.W. Griffith, and Douglas Fairbanks. Pickford would produce, direct, and star in her own work – unheard of for a woman at the time. She retired from filmmaking after winning the Oscar for best actress in 1929 for her role in *Coquette*.

Houdini's ability as an escape artist was legendary.

Benny Goodman's music was down-right shocking to audiences in the mid-1930s.

Pickford and Fairbanks were divorced in 1936. That same year she married bandleader Buddy Rogers. They were together for 41 years. Mary Pickford died of a stroke at 2:00 p.m., Tuesday, May 29, 1979 in a Hollywood, California, hospital. She was 86. At the time of her death, Pickford's fortune was estimated at $50 million.

10:30 **p.m., Sat., Oct. 14, 1939** – *Grand Ole Opry* debuted on the NBC radio network after 14 years as a fixture on WSM Nashville, Tennessee. NBC carried a 30-minute segment of the four-hour show, which ran from 8 p.m. to midnight on WSM. *Grand Ole Opry* remained on NBC until December 28, 1957, and is still heard on WSM in an estimated 30 states. *Grand Ole Opry* is a country music institution and has featured almost every top country music star.

Grand Ole Opry began in November, 1925 as a one-hour show on WSM. Its first guest was an old fiddler named "Uncle" Jimmy Thompson, 83, who had fought in the Civil War. He was accompanied on the piano by his niece.

According to the legend, the name *Grand Ole Opry* was born when host and founder George Hay finished the show with the words: "You've been in the clouds with grand opera; now get down to earth with us in a shindig of grand ole opry."

10:30 **p.m., Tues., Apr. 3, 1990** – Sarah Vaughn, legendary jazz singer whose nickname "The Divine One" summed up her appeal and popularity, died of cancer eight days after her 66th birthday. Vaughn's hits included "Broken Hearted Melody," "It's Magic," "Make Yourself Comfortable" and "Whatever Lola Wants."

10:30 **p.m., Sat., Dec. 1, 1934** – *Let's Dance*, the program that introduced Benny Goodman to national radio audiences, debuted on NBC.

Goodman's music does not seem revolutionary today, but it was down-right shocking to audiences in the mid-1930s. On *Let's Dance*, Goodman's swing tunes came between the Latin beat of Xavier Cugat and the easy-listening sounds of Kel Murray and, despite featuring the talents of drummer Gene Krupa and singer Helen Ward, did not catch on over the radio. NBC cancelled the show, which had been sponsored by the National Biscuit Company. The last program was heard on March 25, 1935.

Tastes change, however, and by 1939, when *Benny Goodman's Swing School* hit the CBS airwaves, swing was the hottest sound in music.

Chicago-born Goodman provided unforgettable jazz for nearly half a century, playing clarinet with his orchestra. One hundred and sixty-four of his songs made the charts between 1931 and 1953. His best known works include "Moon Glow," "Sing, Sing, Sing" and "Jersey Bounce."

Goodman switched to a classical style when the big band era faded in the late 40s but continued playing jazz. In 1962, he became the first jazz artist to tour the Soviet Union. Goodman, whose opening theme "Let's Dance" is one of his most remembered tunes, always ended his concerts with "Goodbye."

Benny Goodman was found dead of a heart attack on Friday, June 13, 1986.

10:30 p.m., Thurs., Apr. 3, 1930 – *The Academy Awards* was broadcast for the first time on KNX radio in Los Angeles. *All Quiet on the Western Front* was named best picture.

The first Academy Awards presentation in 1928 was without radio coverage. The silent film *Wings* took best picture that year. Network television began showing the Oscars in 1953 with host Bob Hope.

10:35 p.m., Mon., Sept. 19, 1881 – James Garfield, America's 20th president and the last to be born in a log cabin, died at Elberon, N.J. He was 49.

Garfield died from his wounds two and a half months after being shot twice from behind by Charles Guiteau at the Baltimore and Potomac railway station in Washington, D.C. Guiteau, originally a Garfield supporter, turned against the president after being rejected in a bid for a diplomatic post.

Garfield's doctors were partly to blame for his death. They probed the president's internal injuries with bare fingers and unsterilized instruments – a practice common at the time – that resulted in blood poisoning.

Garfield had been a compromise choice for the Republican nomination of 1880, and he narrowly defeated Democrat Winfield Hancock in the general election of that year. The margin of victory was less than 10,000 votes out

The Academy Awards was broadcast for the first time on KNX radio.

During his career, Gretzky set or tied 61 NHL records.

of some nine million cast. Prior to his presidency, Garfield had been a U.S. representative from Ohio for 17 years. He remains the only president elected while still a member of the House. Garfield also has the obscure distinction of being the first lefthander to ascend to the presidency – later presidential southpaws were Truman, Ford and Bush.

10:35 p.m., Sun., Nov. 1, 1987 – René Lévèsque, leader of Canada's separatist "Parti Quebecois," died of a heart attack at age 65. Lévèsque's party swept to power in 1976. A 1980 referendum that would have given the PQ the power to negotiate for an independent Quebec was defeated. Lévèsque was voted out of office in 1981.

10:36 p.m., Mon., Nov. 22, 1999 – Hockey's greatest record-holder, Wayne Gretzky, received a standing ovation after acknowledging his induction into the Hockey Hall of Fame in Toronto. During his career, Gretzky set or tied 61 NHL records. These include career goals (894), career assists (1,963) career points (2,857), goals in one season (92) and points in one season (212). Gretzky, who at five was skating circles around players twice his age, retired in 1999 after 20 years in professional hockey.

The NHL decreed that his number 99 sweater will never be worn again. Gretzky took the number after joining the junior Sault Ste. Marie Greyhounds when his first choice, 9, was already taken. He kept the number after turning pro and is the only NHL player who has – or ever will – wear number 99 on his jersey.

10:40 p.m., Thurs., Feb. 7, 1828 – The longest speech in the history of the English House of Commons ended, as Henry Peter Brougham concluded a six-hour talk on Law Reform. The text of his speech occupied 12 columns in the *London Times* the next day. A man of many words, Brougham also holds the record for longest House of Lords speech. There he spoke for six hours on the second reading of the Reform Bill.

10:40 p.m., Sun., July 22, 1934 – John Dillinger, America's Public Enemy number one, died in a hail of police bullets as he left a

Chicago movie theatre. Dillinger, one of the most feared criminals of his day, entered and exited the theatre in the company of a woman, the so-called "Lady in Red." Officials later discovered that Dillinger had had a facelift, had his fingerprints altered and grew a mustache in hopes of avoiding detection. But as Chicago's Police Chief Mel Purvis noted: "you couldn't miss if you'd studied that face for as long as I have."

Dillinger's crime career, first as a petty thief and later a nationally known bank robber, spanned 14 years. However, only one murder was actually pinned on him, that of a patrolman in a 1934 bank heist.

10:45 p.m., Tues., May 4, 1971 – A devastating landslide eliminated the village of Saint–Jean Vianney, Quebec. Thirty-one people died and 38 houses disappeared when a river of clay loosened by heavy rains inundated the village. Many were watching a televised Stanley Cup playoff game between Montreal and Chicago at the time.

The Canadian government later declared the area unfit for habitation. Survivors were relocated to nearby Arvida, Quebec.

10:45 p.m., Tues., Mar. 31, 1931 – Knute Rockne, one of American college football's greatest coaches, died in a plane crash with seven others near Bazaar, Kansas. He was found with a rosary in his hand. Rockne, who led Notre Dame to five undefeated seasons and helped pioneer the forward pass, had been flying to Los Angeles to appear in a movie. More than 100,000 people lined his funeral route.

10:45 p.m., Sun., July 25, 1886 – Franz Liszt, Hungarian pianist and composer best known for his "Hungarian Rhapsodies," died of pneumonia at age 74. A superb showman, Liszt would throw his gloves to the floor and toss back his hair in a theatrical gesture before attacking the keyboard. His recitals were legendary. One of Europe's greatest musical pioneers, Liszt also helped promote the careers of other composers such as Wagner, Schumann and Berlioz.

10:45 p.m., Thurs., Sept. 20, 1973 – Pop star Jim Croce was killed when his chartered Beechcraft D-18 crashed on takeoff at Natchitoches Municipal Airport in Louisiana. Croce's lead guitarist and four

A devastating landslide eliminated the village of Saint–Jean Vianney, Quebec.

John Lennon was gunned down outside his Manhattan residence.

others also died when the plane clipped a pecan tree before crashing. Croce had played a concert earlier that night at Northwestern State University. He was 30 years old.

The Philadelphia-born Croce scored two top-10 hits before his death, "You Don't Mess Around With Jim," and the number-one smash "Bad, Bad Leroy Brown." He had three more top ten songs after his death, including "Time In A Bottle," number one in November, 1973.

10:47 p.m., Tues., Oct. 15, 1946 – Herman Goering, the most powerful Nazi in Germany after Hitler, died shortly before he was to be executed at Nuremburg Prison for war crimes. The Nazi leader took a cyanide capsule. Goering, who was 47, created the Luftwaffe and laid the basis for Germany's police force later controlled by Heinrich Himmler. He amassed a large art collection, mostly stolen, during his term as president of the Reichstag.

10:50 p.m., Mon., Dec. 8, 1980 – John Lennon was gunned down outside his Manhattan residence. He died in hospital a short time later. Mark David Chapman, who had stalked Lennon for days, was arrested on the spot. He later pleaded guilty to the crime and was given 20 years to life in prison. Ironically, Lennon had recently donated money to the New York Police Department to purchase bulletproof vests.

Lennon, who was working on a comeback album the day he was shot, had recently released the single "(Just Like) Starting Over." After his death, the song rocketed to number one on the *Billboard* singles chart where it stayed for five weeks. It was the first number-one song in five years for the former Beatles lead guitarist, vocalist and songwriter. Lennon is perhaps best known for his 1971 hit "Imagine," a peace anthem that belied his violent end.

10:50 p.m., Wed., Nov. 16, 1960 – Clark Gable, the "King" of Hollywood actors for more than a quarter century, died of heart failure. He was 59. Gable was so popular at one time that theatre marquees advertised: "This week, Clark Gable," rather than name the movie.

Gable was a modest man who said he never considered himself a great actor. Nevertheless, he captured the hearts of millions with his roles in *It Happened One Night*, *Mutiny on the Bounty* and about 60 other films. In

1939, he co-starred with Vivien Leigh in one of Hollywood's most memorable films, *Gone With the Wind*. His final line in that movie was his most famous: "Frankly, Scarlett, I don't give a damn."

Gable costarred with Marilyn Monroe in his last movie *The Misfits*. Some believe his heart ailment was aggravated by stunts he insisted on performing in the film.

10:50 **p.m., Sat., Dec. 14, 1861** – Albert of Saxe-Coburg-Gotha, husband of Queen Victoria, died of typhoid fever at Windsor Castle. Albert, whose condition was aggravated by his constant worrying, was 43. Queen Victoria mourned his death for 40 years until she herself died in 1901 *(see 6:30 p.m.)*.

10:51 **p.m., Tues., Oct. 18, 1977** – Capping what Dodger manager Tommy Lasorda called "the greatest single performance I've ever seen," Reggie Jackson smashed his third home run on as many pitches to lead the New York Yankees to an 8–4 victory over Los Angeles. The dazzling effort helped the Yanks post a four-games-to-two victory in the World Series – their first world title since 1964. Jackson was named the World Series MVP for hitting five homers, scoring 10 runs and accumulating 25 total bases.

10:55 **p.m., Sat., Feb. 17, 1877** – Journalism and communications history were made as the first news dispatch was sent by telephone. The story – a lecture and demonstration by Alexander Graham Bell of his new invention the telephone – appeared in the *Boston Globe* February 18, 1877. The historic story was not bylined, even though the author's initials – H.M.B – appear at the bottom.

10:56 **:15 p.m., Sun., July 20, 1969** – American astronaut Neil Armstrong became the first human to walk on the moon, achieving a dream man had strived toward for centuries. His first words, "That's one small step for a man, one giant leap for mankind," were apparently thought up by Armstrong after the space module the *Eagle* landed that afternoon (at 4:17:43 p.m.). The astronaut claimed he hadn't prepared the statement in advance.

American astronaut Neil Armstrong became the first human to walk on the moon.

The United States launched its first satellite into space to orbit the earth.

Armstrong was joined 19 minutes later by second-in-command Buzz Aldrin and the two explored the moon's surface for about two hours in front of a TV audience estimated at 600 million – or one-fifth the earth's population. While on the moon, the two collected soil and rock samples, set up scientific instruments, planted the American flag and even took a call from President Nixon.

Aldrin re-entered the capsule ahead of Armstrong, earning the obscure distinction of being the first man to leave the moon.

Apollo 11 had blasted off from Cape Kennedy at 9:32 p.m. on July 16. It spashed down in the Pacific July 24.

10:58 **p.m., Fri., Jan. 31, 1958** – The United States launched its first satellite into space to orbit the earth. The 13.9 kilogram (30.8 pound) *Explorer* was equipped to measure cosmic radiation and transmit data back to Earth – but it was clearly a propaganda victory as the Americans successfully entered the space race. The Russians had stunned the world by launching their first satellite nearly four months before. *(see 7:30 p.m.)*

11 p.m. to 11:59 p.m.

- 🕚 Soviet troops enter Czechoslovakia
- 🕚 Johnny Carson opens *Tonight Show* for first time
- 🕚 Invasion of D–Day begins
- 🕚 First artificial heart implant operation begins
- 🕚 *Titanic* hits iceberg and sinks
- 🕚 Adolf Eichmann executed

11:00 **p.m., Tues., Aug. 20, 1968** – Several hundred thousand Soviet troops crossed the border into Czechoslovakia to quell a liberal movement in the Soviet satellite. Within hours, Red Army troops were patrolling Prague as Soviet aircraft flew overhead. Thirty Czechs were killed and more than 300 injured when the Soviets stormed the national radio station.

Czech leader Alexander Dubcek, who had initiated many of the reforms that led to the Soviet invasion, reluctantly agreed to toe the Soviet line and abandon his democratic changes. In April, 1969, Dubcek was replaced as secretary of the Czech Party by hard-liner Gustav Husak.

11:00 **p.m., Wed., Nov. 24, 1971** – A man calling himself D.B. Cooper commandeered a Northwest Airlines plane shortly after takeoff from Los Angeles. "Cooper" ordered the plane to land in Seattle where he let the passengers go in exchange for $200,000 in $20 bills and four parachutes. The man parachuted near Woodland, Washington, and was never seen or heard from again.

When Cooper parachuted, a thunderstorm was raging, winds were blowing at 320 kilometres (200 miles) an hour and the temperature was − 21° Celsius (−7° Fahrenheit). He was wearing only a light business suit.

Poisonous cyanide gas began to leak from a Union Carbide pesticide plant near Bhopal, India.

Years later, bills were discovered near where Cooper parachuted but there was no sign of his body. His fate, and true identity, remain a mystery and the subject of much speculation.

11:00 **p.m., Tues., Jan. 17, 1893** – Rutherford B. Hayes died in Fremont, Ohio after suffering a heart attack at a train station. Hayes had been elected 19th president in the closest and most controversial election in U.S. presidential history. He was 70.

Hayes is better known for how he was elected president than for anything he did in office. The 1876 Republican nominee for president trailed Democrat Samuel Tilden in both the popular vote and the electoral college. When voting ended, Tilden led the electoral college 184–166, one short of a majority, but the 19 remaining electoral votes were in dispute. Every one of the 19 votes was awarded to Hayes, eight votes to seven, by a Republican-leaning panel, and Hayes emerged the winner, 185–184. Tilden is said to have taken it well and discouraged his followers from violent rebellion. Hayes acquired the nickname "Old Eight and Seven" after his victory.

Before entering the White House, Hayes was U.S. representative and later U.S. governor for Ohio. As president, he presided over the final withdrawal of Union troops from the South. He was also the first president to visit the west coast. He did not run for a second term.

Hayes is one of three presidents elected despite winning fewer popular votes than his nearest opponent. The others were John Quincy Adams in 1824 and Benjamin Harrison in 1888. Five others – Woodrow Wilson in 1912, Harry Truman in 1948, John Kennedy in 1960, Richard Nixon in 1968 and Bill Clinton in 1992 – won with less than 50 per cent of the votes cast.

11:00 **p.m., Sun., Dec. 2, 1984** – More than 2,000 died and 50,000 were blinded or otherwise injured when poisonous cyanide gas began to leak from a Union Carbide pesticide plant near Bhopal, India.

In a horrific scene, the streets of Bhopal were filled with hundreds of people gasping for breath or stumbling blindly among the corpses of fellow victims and animals killed by the gas. An estimated 200,000 people fled for their lives in the middle of the night as the gas continued to spread.

Union Carbide blamed a malfunctioning tank valve for the leak and immediately closed the plant. Numerous lawsuits were filed against the company, including a $15 billion class action suit brought by the Indian government.

11:00 **p.m., Tues., Feb. 13, 1968** – At the Westminster Kennel's Dog Show, the last champion was crowned at the old Madison Square Garden in New York City. "Ch. Stingray," a Lakeland Terrier belonging to Mr. and Mrs. James A. Farrell of Darien, Connecticut, was named best dog.

The "old" Madison Square Garden was actually the third in a line of Manhattan arenas dating back to 1879. But this MSG may have had the most colourful history. From its opening in 1925 to its closing in 1968, about 250 million people attended 144 different kinds of events, ranging from sports, such as basketball, boxing, hockey, and track and field, to circus events, political rallies and concerts.

The old Madison Square Garden was replaced by a new facility with the same name.

11:00 **p.m., Fri., Feb. 23, 1821** – English poet John Keats died of tuberculosis in Rome. He was only 26. Keats, convinced his work would be forgotten, asked that his grave be nameless and contain the epitaph "Here lies one whose name was writ in water."

11:01 **p.m., Sun., Oct. 27, 1991** – Pinch-hitter Gene Larkin drilled a one-out bases-loaded single in the bottom of the 10th inning to give the Minnesota Twins a 1–0 victory over the Atlanta Braves, ending one of the most exciting World Series ever. The seventh-game triumph capped a fall classic that featured three extra-inning games and five games decided by a one-run margin. Twins pitcher Jack Morris was named the Series Most Valuable Player after tossing a seven-hitter to become the first pitcher to go 10 innings in a World Series in 23 years. The Twins, who, like the Braves, finished in last place in their division the previous year, became the first team to go from the cellar to the World Series championship in one year.

11:05 **p.m., Mon., June 25, 1906** – Millionaire Harry K. Thaw allegedly shot famed architect Stanford White in a crime of passion during a musical show on the roof of Madison Square Garden. It became one of the most talked-about crimes of the early 20th century.

English poet John Keats died of tuberculosis.

Hurricane Hazel slammed into the north shore of Lake Ontario at Toronto.

Thaw's wife Evelyn had become White's mistress and Thaw was determined to get even. After a mistrial in 1907, Thaw was found not guilty by reason of insanity in 1909 and sent to an asylum. He escaped, was recaptured, and at a third trial in 1915, Thaw was found both sane and innocent of the charges against him. He was released and Evelyn divorced him soon after. Thaw died of a coronary in 1947, aged 75.

11:05 p.m., Thurs., Oct. 15, 1964 – Cole Porter, one of America's greatest songwriters and composers, died at age 72 of heart failure. Porter's classics tunes include "Begin the Beguine," "I've Got You Under My Skin" and "Night and Day."

Porter endured more than 30 leg operations after a 1937 riding accident. He suffered from chronic pain during the last 27 years of his life but still flourished, writing numerous Broadway musicals.

11:08 p.m., Wed., Jan. 30, 1945 – The German troop ship *Wilhelm Gustloff* was torpedoed by a Russian submarine off Danzig (now Gdansk), Poland. Between 4,000 and 7,000 died in the maritime disaster. The ship was carrying refugees and soldiers back to Germany from the Russian front. Only a handful of the thousands aboard were rescued from the icy Baltic Sea.

11:10 p.m., Fri., Oct. 15, 1954 – Hurricane Hazel, downgraded to a tropical storm but still deadly, slammed into the north shore of Lake Ontario at Toronto. By Saturday morning, when the rain finally stopped, 18.2 centimetres (7.2 inches) had fallen on the unprepared city killing 83 people. The heavy rain carried by winds gusting to 115 kilometres (72 miles) turned normally placid local rivers into torrents, overflowing their banks and wiping out anything in their path. Houses were carried into Lake Ontario and some bodies showed up months later on the New York side of the lake.

Thirty-six of the dead lived on one street in Toronto's west end. Among those who died were five volunteer firemen. It remains Canada's only major hurricane-related disaster, technically considered a tropical storm by the time it reached Toronto.

In addition to those killed in Ontario by Hurricane Hazel, an estimated

500 others perished as the storm ripped its way through Haiti and the east coast of the United States.

11:15 **p.m., Tues., Oct. 2, 1962** – Johnny Carson made his first appearance on NBC's *Tonight Show* beginning a television tradition that would last three decades. His first guest was Groucho Marx, who had turned down a chance at the host's chair (as had Jackie Gleason and Bob Newhart). Also on the first show were Joan Crawford, Tony Bennett, Rudy Vallee and Mel Brooks. Carson replaced Jack Paar, who had quit the show in a huff six months earlier after NBC deleted one of his jokes.

Carson was relatively unknown to late-night TV audiences when he began the *Tonight Show*, most of his previous experience being in game shows. But his quick wit and unflappable nature soon made him a major star and eventually a TV legend. His numerous run-ins with the network also became famous as he attempted to increase his salary and cut back his on-air time. He succeeded in both and by 1978 was making $3 million a year for working three nights a week. By 1991, his gross from the *Tonight Show* and other ventures was $55 million a year.

Carson hosted the *Tonight Show* for the final time on May 22, 1992, 30 years, 22,000 guests and an estimated 700,000 jokes later. The man called "the biggest star television has ever produced" was replaced by Jay Leno.

11:15 **p.m., Fri., July 18, 1969** – Massachusetts Senator Edward Kennedy made a wrong turn on Chappaquiddick Island, Massachusetts, and went off the side of a bridge connecting the island to the mainland, according to a statement he gave police. The body of his companion, Mary Jo Kopechne, was pulled from the water at 8:55 the next morning. Kennedy claimed he tried and failed to rescue Kopechne and in a state of shock returned to his hotel, not reporting the accident to police until the next day. Kennedy was later charged with leaving the scene of an accident, given a two-month suspended sentence and placed on probation for a year.

The Chappaqiddick incident dogged Kennedy's political career and crippled his chances at the White House. Questions are still being raised as to his conduct that night and whether he deserved a more severe punishment.

Johnny Carson made his first appearance on NBC's *Tonight Show*.

Pablo Picasso, arguably the greatest artist of the 20th century and certainly the most prolific, was born in Malaga, Spain.

11:15 **p.m., Sat., Oct. 25, 1881** – Pablo Picasso, arguably the greatest artist of the 20th century and certainly the most prolific, was born in Malaga, Spain.

Picasso produced an estimated 20,000 works of art (an average of five a week) and was also an accomplished sculptor, potter and lithographer. He is best known for his painting. His most famous works include *Les Demoiselles* and *Guernica*. He painted in numerous styles in his career and was at the forefront of new developments in art. Picasso left behind works valued at $750 million. Even thieves like his work – more Picasso paintings are reported stolen than those of any other artist.

Picasso died at his estate in southern France on Sunday, April 8, 1973 at 11:45 a.m. He was 92.

11:15 **p.m., Fri., Nov. 13, 1868** – Gioacchino Rossini, Italian composer of the operas *The Barber of Seville* and *William Tell*, died of cancer. He was 76. Rossini wrote 38 operas by his 37th birthday, but only two full-scale works in his last 39 years. He claimed he preferred to compose rather than perform so he could stay in bed all day.

11:15 **p.m., Fri., Dec. 4, 1868** – The mail boats *America* and the *United States*, which usually passed each other on the Ohio River without incident, collided, killing 72. The accident, near Bryant's Creek, Indiana, ignited a fire that engulfed the entire stretch of river in flames. Both ships were reduced to smoldering wrecks in less than five minutes. Cause of the disaster was an inexplicable navigational error by the *America* pilot, who proceeded along the Indiana shore instead of the Kentucky side as usual, putting his ship on a collision course with the *United States*. The ships collided head on.

11:15 **p.m., Sun., Aug. 3, 1958** – The atomic submarine *Nautilus* became the first vessel to reach the North Pole. At the time of arrival, 116 men were aboard the sub – the greatest number of men assembled at the pole at one time. The *Nautilus* took 96 hours to cover the 2,945 kilometres (1,830 miles) in history's first trans-polar underseas voyage.

11:16 p.m., Mon., June 5, 1944 – The invasion of D-Day began. The first of more than 185,000 troops landed on the north coast of France in history's greatest sea-land invasion. Also involved were 1,213 warships, 4,126 landing craft, 1,087 aircraft and 20,000 vehicles.

The invasion was led by paratroopers, many of whom served as Allied infantrymen behind enemy lines, others as saboteurs. They were followed by assault troops who waded the final few yards to the beaches. In the Allies' favour was the fact that the Germans believed the landing would take place much further north. Despite the surprise in timing and location, more than 9,000 Allied casualties were recorded.

Within three weeks, the major French port of Cherbourg had been freed and the German retreat had begun.

11:20 p.m., Fri., Feb. 28, 1986 – Swedish Prime Minister Olaf Palme was shot and killed while walking home from a movie with his wife in Stockholm. Palme was not accompanied by bodyguards, believing he would never be the target of an assassin. A man was arrested in the shooting but later released. Despite a multitude of theories, Palme's killer has not been found.

11:20 p.m., Mon., May 30, 1960 – Russian novelist and poet Boris Pasternak died of lung cancer at 70. Pasternak won the 1958 Nobel Prize for literature for his novel *Dr. Zhivago*, but was forced by the Soviet government to decline it.

Dr. Zhivago was banned in the U.S.S.R. because it condemned Marxism. Anticipating problems with the authorities, Pasternak had the manuscript smuggled out of Russia and published in Milan. The book and a subsequent film adaptation met with worldwide acclaim and Soviet wrath. After Pasternak died, the woman on whose story he had based the book – Olga Ivanskaya – was sentenced to eight years hard labour.

11:20 p.m., Mon., July 17, 1944 – An explosion ripped through the Port Chicago, California, weapons shipping depot. The explosion on the pier ignited munitions on the SS *E.A. Bryan*, and the contents went off like an enormous bomb. A second ship, the SS *Quinault Victory*, was spun in the air and torn in two. Three hundred and twenty

The invasion of D-Day began.

Italian ocean liner *Andrea Doria* and Swedish liner *Stockholm*, collided.

men died and 390 were injured in the worst U.S. homefront disaster of the Second World War.

Three weeks after the explosion, 258 black sailors refused a Navy order to return to work at the shipyards. Fifty of the men were convicted of mutiny and given prison sentences of up to 15 years. All were released after 16 months and given discharges "under honourable circumstances" – less than an honourable discharge. The other 208 received summary court martials resulting in short jail sentences, fines and discharges.

11:22 p.m., Wed., July 25, 1956 – Italian ocean liner *Andrea Doria* and Swedish liner *Stockholm*, collided in the busy waters south of Nantucket, Massachusetts, known as the Times Square of the Atlantic.

The *Andrea Doria* suffered the worst damage. Fifty-one of her passengers died and the ship listed so badly the portside lifeboats could not be lowered. By contrast, the *Stockholm*'s bow was smashed but she remained afloat. Within two hours of the first distress call, French liner *Ile de France* arrived and began taking on *Andrea Doria* passengers. The *Ile de France*, *Stockholm* and several other ships rescued 1,650 survivors from the doomed ship. The *Andrea Doria* sank at 10:09 a.m. the following morning, 11 hours after the collision.

11:23 p.m., Wed., Nov. 25, 1964 – The final run began of the Staten Island–Brooklyn ferry, the last of New York's ferries. The ferries, which debuted in 1712, had been put out of business by bridges and tunnels which allowed for easier car travel. Aboard the final run of the *Tide* were several hundred college students drinking beer and champagne, several steamboat enthusiasts and regular commuters.

11:27 p.m., Wed., Dec. 1, 1982 – Doctors at the University of Utah's Medical Centre began operating on Barney Clark, a 61-year-old Seattle dentist near death from heart disease. Seven and a half hours later, the surgical team led by Dr. William DeVries had completed the world's first implant of an artificial heart into a human being. Clark, who had only hours to live when the operation began, survived for three and a half months on the mechanical heart, known as the Jarvik-7. He died March 23, 1983 of what doctors called "secondary complications."

11:30 p.m., Sat., Sept. 4, 1965 – One of history's greatest humanitarians, Albert Schweitzer, the "Grand Docteur," died at age 90 in Lambarene, Gabon.

Schweitzer, born in Upper Alsace, near Switzerland, spent 60 years fighting disease in Africa. A highly regarded organ player and authority on J.S. Bach, Schweitzer, a medical doctor, established a hospital in Lambarene offering free treatment to the natives.

Schweitzer won the Nobel Peace Prize in 1952.

11:30 p.m., Thurs., Nov. 14, 1889 – Jawaharlal Nehru was born. Nehru would be the first prime minister of the newly independent India for 27 years (1947–1964). He was internationally regarded as a great statesman who advocated diplomacy over force. A disciple of Gandhi, Nehru helped lead India into the industrial age. He died in 1964, aged 75.

11:30 p.m., Tues., Aug. 4, 1964 – In a major escalation of the Vietnam War, President Johnson announced he had ordered retaliatory strikes against North Vietnam after renewed attacks against American destroyers in the Gulf of Tonkin. The move was overwhelmingly supported in the House and Senate, but many of those who voted in favour expressed misgivings about increasing U.S. involvement in Vietnam.

11:30 p.m., Sat., Oct. 11, 1975 – *Saturday Night Live*, the television show that launched the careers of John Belushi, Chevy Chase, Dan Aykroyd, Bill Murray and many others, debuted on NBC. The first show was hosted by comedian George Carlin. The 90-minute show quickly achieved cult status with Saturday evening viewers. By the 1977–78 season, it had surpassed the *Tonight Show* as the most popular program on late-night television.

Often outrageous and always live, the show featured topical skits, bogus newscasts and performances by musical stars, all done in an off-beat fashion suitable for the late-night time slot. The show's success became its undoing, however, as all of its major stars eventually left to pursue other interests. Despite numerous changes in cast, it has remained a late-night fixture on NBC.

Saturday Night Live **debuted on NBC.**

**The ocean liner
Titanic struck an
iceberg.**

11:30 **p.m., Wed., July 7, 1967** – Vivien Leigh, best remembered for her Academy Award winning portrayal of Scarlett O'Hara in *Gone With the Wind*, died after a choking spasm in her London apartment. Leigh, who battled tuberculosis for over 20 years, was 53.

Leigh also won the best actress Oscar in 1951 for *A Streetcar Named Desire*, pushing herself through a demanding schedule despite her ever-worsening illness. She was prone to coughing fits and mental breakdowns, problems that led to the end of her 20-year marriage to Laurence Olivier in 1960. Despite her troubles, she was rehearsing yet another play – Edward Albee's *A Delicate Balance* – at the time of her death.

11:35 **p.m., Mon., Dec. 6, 1982** – Lethal injection was used for the first time to execute a criminal. Charles Brooks, convicted of killing an auto mechanic in 1976, died after being injected with a mixture of drugs at the Department of Corrections in Huntsville, Texas. Brooks was 40.

In lethal injection, drugs are administered which render the victim unconscious, cause him to stop breathing and induce cardiac arrest. It is estimated lethal injection victims die within 10 to 30 seconds of the drugs entering their bodies.

11:39 **p.m., Sat., Oct. 23, 1993** – Left-fielder Joe Carter slammed a three-run homer to give the Toronto Blue Jays their second consecutive World Series title. On a pitch from Philadelphia reliever Mitch Williams, Carter's homer gave the Jays an 8–6 victory and wrapped up the best-of-seven series in six games. It was the second time the World Series had ended on a home run. *(see 10:31 a.m.; 3:36 p.m.)*

11:40 **p.m., Sun., Apr. 14, 1912** – The ocean liner *Titanic* struck an iceberg and sank to the bottom of the North Atlantic in less than three hours. *(see 2:20 a.m.)*

11:40 **p.m., Thurs., Mar. 2, 1944** – An Italian freight train stopped in a tunnel near Balvano, Italy, leading to a disaster that would kill an estimated 500 people.

The train wasn't supposed to be carrying passengers but about 650 were aboard when it stopped in the tunnel because a locomotive ahead of it was having engine trouble. The train sat in the tunnel for 38 minutes while deadly carbon monoxide fumes seeped into the lungs of the sleeping passengers. Not knowing that many of his passengers were dead, the engineer moved the train further down the track and stopped in another tunnel. Lethal carbon monoxide gas then filled the lungs of many passengers not poisoned during the first layover. Shortly after 5:00 a.m., the brakeman awakened to discover what had happened. He ran to the Balvano station, pointed up the track and whispered, "They're all dead," before collapsing.

Because of military censorship, details of the disaster were not published until years later. The 500 victims were buried in a common grave.

11:45 p.m., Wed., June 15, 1938 – Cincinnati's Johnny Vander Meer became the first and only pitcher in major league history to throw two consecutive no-hitters. The "Dutch Master" knocked out Leo Durocher who hit a fly to centre-fielder Harry Craft, completing a 6–0 no-hit game against the Brooklyn Dodgers. It was the first night game ever played at Brooklyn's Ebbets Field.

Just four days earlier, Vander Meer tossed a 3–0 no-hitter against the Boston Bees, the first by a Cincinnati pitcher in 19 years. Vander Meer's streak of hitless innings ended in his next game when Boston's Debs Garms singled in the fourth inning of a 14–1 Cincinnati victory.

11:45 p.m., Sat., Sept. 9, 1972 – The U.S.–Soviet basketball final at the 1972 Olympics, one of the most controversial sports matches ever, began in Munich. Two hours later, the Soviets had defeated the Americans 51–50 in a finish that is still disputed.

The controversy started with three seconds remaining after Doug Collins sank a couple of free throws to give the Americans a 50–49 lead. The Soviets inbounded the ball but the referee called a time-out after noticing a disturbance at the scoring table. That left one second on the clock, but officials set the clock back to three seconds after the Soviets protested the time-out. On the next play, Ivan Yedeshko threw a long pass to Sasha Belov, who stuffed it for the winning basket. A U.S. appeal to disallow the basket failed.

The American team voted unanimously not to accept their silver medals which remain in the custody of the International Olympic Committee. It was

362

Johnny Vander Meer became the first and only pitcher in major league history to throw two consecutive no-hitters.

the first loss for the Americans at the Olympic basketball tournament after 62 straight wins dating back to 1936.

11:49 p.m., Wed, July 10, 1985 – An explosion rocked the Greenpeace ship *Rainbow Warrior* as it sat docked in the Auckland, New Zealand, harbour. The crew scrambled for the safety of the shore but one man, Fernando Pereira, went to his cabin to retrieve his cameras. A second explosion went off two minutes after the first. Pereira's body was found four hours later.

Police determined that the explosion was a deliberate act of sabotage by French agents hoping to halt an expected anti-nuclear protest by the *Rainbow Warrior* in the South Pacific. Two French secret service agents, Alain Mafart and Dominique Prieux, were charged with manslaughter and sentenced to 10 years in jail. France initially denied involvement in the bombing but after an international outcry, Prime Minister Fabius admitted French secret service agents had bombed the *Rainbow Warrior* under orders. New Zealand Prime Minister David Lange called it "a sordid act of international state-backed terrorism."

In June, 1986, in a deal worked out with the assistance of UN Secretary-General Javier Perez de Cuellar, France agreed to apologize and pay compensation of US $6.5 million to New Zealand. In return, the two agents would be detained at the French military base on Hao atoll for three years. They were freed less than two years later.

11:50 p.m., Thurs., Nov. 16, 1933 – The United States announced that it was finally recognizing the Soviet Union – 16 years and nine days after the Communist government took over.

11:55 p.m., Mon., Nov. 4, 1605 – Guy Fawkes was arrested in the cellars underneath the Lords Chamber for attempting to blow up the English Houses of Parliament. Fawkes and his fellow conspirators had hidden 36 barrels of gunpowder in the cellars in anticipation of the opening of Parliament November 5. However, one of the conspirators tipped off a member of the House of Lords, and Fawkes was caught red-handed. After being tortured on the rack, Fawkes was executed in January, 1606.

The anniversary of Fawkes's capture is celebrated annually in England as Guy Fawkes Day.

11:55 **p.m., Sat., Nov. 10, 1979** – A freight train carrying deadly chlorine gas derailed in Mississauga, Ontario. Within 24 hours, amid fears of chlorine poisoning, 223,000 residents were told to leave the city in one of history's largest peacetime evacuations. A week later, when the danger of chlorine poisoning had passed, people were allowed to return to their homes.

11:55 **p.m., Mon., Jan. 20, 1936** – King George V of England died at the age of 70 after ruling Britain for over a quarter century. More than three million mourners lined the funeral route of the popular monarch.

George V was the first English monarch of that name to die on a weekday. King Georges I through IV all died on a Saturday.

11:58 **p.m., Thurs., May 31, 1962** – Adolf Eichmann, the "Merchant of Death," on whose orders millions of Jews died during World War II, was hanged at an Israeli prison. His death came two years after he was kidnapped by Israeli agents in Argentina and flown to Israel for trial. Eichmann, who was 56, claimed he was only following orders. He showed no remorse for his crimes.

11:58 **Two minutes to midnight, 1953** – This was the closest to midnight the Doomsday Clock ever came.

The Doomsday Clock first appeared on the front cover of the June, 1947 edition of *The Bulletin of Atomic Scientists*. It symbolically represents, in the opinion of the magazine's editors, how close the world is to nuclear Armageddon. It came closest in 1953 after the U.S. tested the hydrogen bomb. It was furthest from midnight – 17 minutes – in 1991 after the end of the Cold War.

The clock continues to appear on the *Bulletin*'s cover. A panel of scientists debates the international climate to decide if the hands of the clock should move. The clock itself hangs on a wall in the editorial offices of the magazine at the University of Chicago, near where the first controlled nuclear chain reaction occurred in 1942.

King George V of England died at the age of 70 after ruling Britain for over a quarter century.

Bibliography

Barnaby, K.C.   *Some Ship Disasters And Their Causes*. Hutchinson © 1976

Ballard, Robert.   *The Discovery Of The Titanic*. Warner © 1987

Beadle, Jeremy.   *Today's The Day*. Signet © 1981

Bishop, Chris & Drury, Ian C.   *Battles Of The 20th Century*. Temple-Aerospace © 1989

Bond, Peter.   *Heroes In Space*. Blackwell ©

Boughton, Simon.   *Great Lives*. Doubleday © 1988

Brooks, Tim & Marsh, Earl.   *The Complete Directory To Prime-Time Television*. Ballantine © 1981

Bugliosi, Vincent.   *Helter Skelter*. Bantam © 1974

Campbell, Robert.   *The Golden Years Of Broadcasting*. Rutledge-Scribners © 1976

Canning, John.   *Great Disasters*. Longmeadow Press © 1976

Chandler, David.   *The Dictionary Of Battles*. Ebury © 1987

Cleary, Margot Keam.   *Great Disasters Of The 20th Century*. Bison Group © 1990

Cray, Ed, & Kotler, Jonathan.   *American Datelines*. Facts On File © 1990

Cornell, James.   *The Great International Disaster Book*. Scribners © 1982

Daniel, Clifton (Editor-In-Chief).   *Chronicle Of The World*. Chronicle Publications © 1989

    Chronicle Of The 20th Century. © 1987

Degregorio, William A.   *The Complete Book Of U.S. Presidents*. Dembner © 1989

Donaldson, Norman & Betty.   *How Did They Die*. St. Martin's Press © 1980

    How Did They Die 2. St. Martin's Press © 1980

Falconi, Carlos.   *Popes In The 20th Century*. Weidenfeld & Nicolson © 1967

Falls, Joe.   *The Boston Marathon*. Macmillan © 1971

Furniss, Tim.   *Manned Space Log*. Jane's © 1983

Forbes, Malcolm.   *They Went That A-Way*. Ballantine © 1988

Garrison, Webb.   *A Treasury Of White House Tales*. Rutledge Hill © 1989

Gipe, George.   *The Last Time When*. World Almanac Publications © 1981

Goldstein, Norm.   *Front Page*. Gallery © 1985

Haines, Max.   *Crime Flashback*. Toronto Sun © 1981

Hart, Michael H.   *The 100*. Hart © 1978

Hellicar, Eileen.	*Prime Ministers Of Britain,* David & Charles © 1978
Herman, Gary.	*Rock 'N' Roll Babylon.* Perigee © 1982
Hirsch, Jr., E.D., Kett,Joseph E., & Trefil, James.	*The Dictionary Of Cultural Literacy.* Houghton, Mifflin © 1988
Hoffman, Mark (Editor).	*The World Almanac And Book Of Facts.* Pharos © 1986
Kane, Joseph Nathan.	*Famous First Facts.* H.W. Wilson © 1981
Keylin, Arlene.	*The Depression Years.* Arno Press © 1976
	The Forties. Arno Press
	The Fabulous Fifties. Arno Press
	Great Lives. Arno Press
	Hollywood Album. Arno Press
Keylin, Arlene & Demirjian, Arto.	*Crime.* Arno Press © 1976
Keylin, Arlene & Brown, Gene.	*Disasters.* Arno Press © 1976
Kingston, Jeremy & Lambers, David.	*Catastrophe & Crisis.* Facts On File © 1979
Lewis, Tom.	*Empire Of The Air.* Harper Collins © 1991
Lewisohn, Mark.	*The Beatles Recording Sessions.* Harmony © 1988
Lord, Walter.	*A Night To Remember.* Bantam © 1955
Manchester, William.	*The Death Of A President.* Harper & Row © 1967
Mcfarlan, Donald (Editor).	*1991 Guinness Book Of World Records.* © 1990
Neal, Harry Edward.	*Mystery Of Time.* J. Messner © 1966
New York Times.	*The New York Times Book Of Baseball History.* Nytb © 1975
Panati, Charles.	*Panati's Extraordinary Endings Of Practically Everything And Everybody.* Harper & Row © 1989
Postman, Andrew & Stone, Larry.	*The Ultimate Book Of Sports Lists.* Bantam © 1990
Rasky, Frank.	*Great Canadian Disasters.* Longman's Green & Co. © 1961
Reidenbach, Lowell.	*Baseball's Greatest Games.* The Sporting News
Roskolenko, Harold.	*Solo.* Playboy Press © 1973
Robertson, Patrick.	*Shell Book Of Firsts.* Ebury Press © 1974
Readers Digest.	*Great Disasters.* © 1989
Schultheiss, Tom.	*A Day In The Life.* Quick Fox © 1981
Trager, James.	*The Peoples Chronology.* Holt, Rinehart & Wilson © 1979-1994

Wallace, Irving & Amy.   *The Two.* Bantam © 1978

Wallenchinsky, David.   *The Complete Book Of The Olympics.* Penguin © 1988

Wallenchinsky, David,   *The Book Of Lists.* William Morrow & Co. © 1977
Wallace, Irving & Amy.

Wallenchinsky, David,   *The Book Of Lists 2.* William Morrow & Co. © 1980
Wallace, Irving, Amy & Sylvia.

The Book Of Lists 3. William Morrow & Co. © 1983

The Peoples Almanac. William Morrow & Co. © 1975

The Peoples Almanac 2. William Morrow & Co. © 1978

The Peoples Almanac 3. William Morrow & Co. © 1981

Ward, Geoffrey C.   *The Civil War.* Knopf © 1990

Whitburn, Joel.   *Pop Memories 1890-1954.* Record Research © 1986

Whittingham, Richard.   *Rand Mcnally Book Of Adventure.* Rand Mcnally © 1982

Worth, Fred L.   *The Complete Unabridged Super Trivia Encyclopedia.* Warner

Rock Facts. Facts On File © 1985

Index